Southern Illinois University Press
Carbondale and Edwardsville

Lafayette and the Liberal Ideal 1814–1824

Politics and Conspiracy in an Age of Reaction

Sylvia Neely

For Mark

Copyright © 1991 by the Board of Trustees,
      Southern Illinois University
All rights reserved
Printed in the United States of America
Designed by Jason Schellenberg
Production supervised by Natalia Nadraga
94   93   92   91   4   3   2   1

Library of Congress Cataloging-in-Publication Data

Neely, Sylvia.
    Lafayette and the liberal ideal, 1814–1824: politics and
conspiracy in an age of reaction/Sylvia Neely.
        p. cm.
    Includes bibliographical references and index.
    1. Lafayette, Marie Joseph Paul Yves Roch Gilbert Du Motier,
marquis de, 1757–1834—Influence. 2. France—Politics and
government—1814–1830. 3. Statesmen—France—Biography. I. Title
DC146.L2N44 1991
944.04'0920—dc20   90-25649
ISBN 0-8093-1733-8   CIP

The paper used in this publication meets the minimum requirements of
American National Standard for Information Sciences—Permanence of
Paper for Printed Library Materials, ANSI Z39.48-1984. ⊗

Contents

Illustrations

Acknowledgments

I would like to thank Stanley Idzerda, Linda Pike, and others at the Lafayette Papers Project who unselfishly shared their accumulation of materials with me and offered encouragement at an early stage of my research. Alan B. Spitzer told me about the valuable collection of Voyer d'Argenson materials at the Université de Poitiers. I especially wish to thank Mme Dominique Parcollet, who generously gave me access to her copies of the Charles Goyet correspondence. Closer to home, the staff of the University of Notre Dame Library was always helpful and understanding, especially Sue Dietl and Pam Paidle. I could not have done my work without the support of the interlibrary loan department of the Helmke Library at Indiana University–Purdue University at Fort Wayne. The late Ruth Harrod, Cheryl Truesdell, and their staffs searched diligently for the items I needed. I wish to thank the history department of the University of Notre Dame and the Summer Grants Program at IPFW for financial support for my research. Stanley Idzerda and Linda Pike read the manuscript and offered helpful suggestions for improvement.

Many people on the staffs of the libraries and institutions listed in the works cited provided assistance to my research. I would especially like to thank the staffs at Special Collections of the University of Chicago, the Lilly Library, the Benjamin Franklin Papers at Yale University, Cornell University Library, and Duke University Library. Jennie Rathbun of the Houghton Library at Harvard University and Martha Hodges of the Labor Management Documentation Center at Cornell University sent me copies of materials which I otherwise would have been unable to examine. Mme Chantal de Tourtier-Bonazzi of the Archives Nationales in Paris gave me helpful advice. Baron Jacques Daru gave his permission for me to use the materials in the Archives Daru at the Archives Nationales. René de Chambrun allowed me to consult his card catalogue of materials at La Grange and gave me a tour of the château.

ACKNOWLEDGMENTS

Three people deserve special recognition. The first was a man whom I unfortunately never met. Louis Gottschalk greatly facilitated further research on Lafayette by donating his materials to the University of Chicago and allowing their immediate consultation by the public. His meticulous scholarship and service to the historical profession will be remembered. The second, Professor Leon L. Bernard of the University of Notre Dame, encouraged my research on this subject from the beginning. As director of my dissertation, he allowed me to follow my interests and provided invaluable assistance in my later historical career. I am sorry that he did not live to see this book's publication. The third, the person who contributed the most to the appearance of this book, is Mark Neely. Although it may be trite to say that without him it would not have been written, the statement is literally true. His support, both moral and material, was indispensable. He kept me going during times of discouragement, forced me to face difficult stylistic problems, and sometimes even managed to make the headaches seem enjoyable and worthwhile. To him this book is dedicated.

Lafayette and the Liberal Ideal 1814–1824

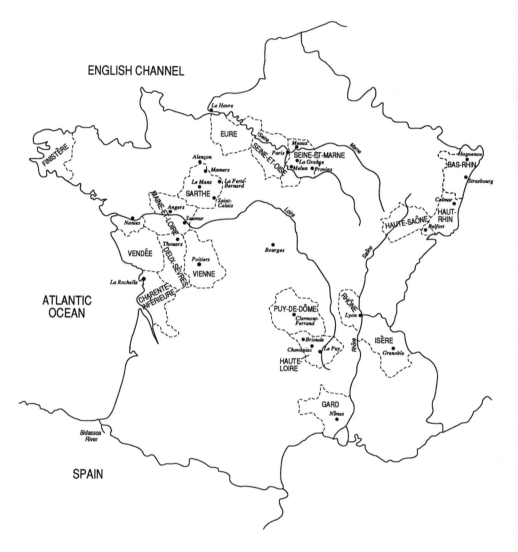

ENGLISH CHANNEL

ATLANTIC
OCEAN

SPAIN

Le Havre

FINISTÈRE

EURE

Alençon

Mamers

Le Mans *La Ferté-Bernard*

SARTHE

Saint-Calais

MAINE-ET-LOIRE

Angers

Nantes

Saumur

VENDÉE

Thouars

DEUX-SÈVRES

Poitiers

VIENNE

La Rochelle

CHARENTE-INFÉRIEURE

Paris

Isère

SEINE-ET-OISE

Meaux

La Grange

Melun

SEINE-ET-MARNE

Provins

Marne

Haguenau

BAS-RHIN

Strasbourg

Colmar

HAUT-RHIN

HAUTE-SAÔNE

Belfort

Saône

Loire

Bourges

Bidassoa River

PUY-DE-DÔME

Clermont-Ferrand

Brioude

Chavaniac

Le Puy

HAUTE-LOIRE

RHÔNE

Lyon

Rhône

ISÈRE

Grenoble

GARD

Nîmes

Restoration France:
Places mentioned in the book

Introduction

During the Bourbon Restoration period in France, Lafayette personified liberalism for many of his contemporaries, yet modern historical literature has completely ignored his later life and has not bothered to ask what the symbol of liberalism actually stood for. Chantal de Tourtier-Bonazzi, conservator at the Archives Nationales and author of a guide to Lafayette documents in France, states that only two works on Lafayette can be trusted: Etienne Charavay's one-volume biography written in 1898 and Louis Gottschalk's six-volume work, which deals with Lafayette's early years. For a knowledge of Lafayette's later years, then, one must turn to Charavay, who devotes only nineteen pages to the period from 1815 to 1824.[1]

These eventful years cannot be adequately covered in such a short space. Lafayette was twice elected to the Chamber of Deputies, sought election unsuccessfully twice, and actively promoted other liberal candidates. He helped journalists and authors in France to publish books, newspapers, and pamphlets that articulated an opposition political philosophy. He maintained friendships with foreign authors, such as Jeremy Bentham and Frances Wright, and saw to translations of works he admired. He encouraged revolts in Spain, Italy, and Greece; promoted the cause of the new South American republics; and carried on an influential correspondence with politicians in the United States, including Thomas Jefferson and James Monroe. As a leader of the Carbonarist conspiracies in France, his activities were constantly monitored by the French police and taken seriously by foreign governments fearful of international revolution. Admired and venerated by supporters of liberalism, young and old, as an incorruptible, tireless, and responsible fighter for their cause, he was vilified by royalists and reactionaries as the embodiment of the dangerous and subversive forces let loose by the French Revolution.

Modern one-volume biographies of Lafayette are inadequate for assessing his activities and are marred by numerous errors.[2] Nor do histories of liberalism accord Lafayette the place his busy career surely merits. A recent four-hundred-page survey of liberalism from the Revolution to 1875 makes no attempt to assess Lafayette's contributions. Instead, he is dismissed in a couple of sentences as a slow-witted and cowardly skirt chaser.[3] This lack of serious attention to Lafayette's career has resulted in a great deal of misinformation and confusion about him and about liberalism during the Restoration. Lafayette's political position in this period has been described by various authors as radical, republican, Bonapartist, *doctrinaire*, and constitutional monarchist.[4] Because biographies of his political associates are also difficult to find, it is not possible to infer what his positions were from reading about them. Only Benjamin Constant has been treated in some depth.[5] Fortunately, Alan B. Spitzer's carefully researched study of the Carbonarist revolts provides insight into Lafayette's conspiratorial activities. But, of course, it offers little about his career in politics.[6]

Because so few reliable works have been produced about his life, even serious and careful scholars make errors when dealing with Lafayette. One recent biographical sketch in a reputable dictionary has Lafayette taking "no part in French affairs until 1814, when he was welcomed back to France by Louis XVIII." In fact, Lafayette had been in France since 1800. In a symptomatic error, the dictionary overlooks his political career in the early Restoration, noting only that, after his tour of the United States in 1824–1825, "he resumed an active role in politics."[7] Another work, a large survey of the revolutionary tradition in the nineteenth and twentieth centuries, presents several errors in a brief section on Lafayette, because the author was forced to rely on the only work that deals exclusively with Lafayette's later life, a sketchy and inadequate book published in 1893.[8]

The reasons for this lack of serious attention to Lafayette's career are readily apparent. When Louis Gottschalk began his monumental biography of Lafayette by publishing the first volume in 1935, scholars in the United States naturally deferred to his acknowledged mastery of the subject and abandoned the field entirely. Unfortunately, Gottschalk and his collaborator, Margaret Maddox, managed to take Lafayette's story only up to 1790. The result has been to leave "virgin 44 years of the life of the hero of two worlds," as Tourtier-Bonazzi puts it.[9] Scholars in France have not filled the gap because, despite the popular title by which he is known, Lafayette has been more an American hero than a French hero. His brand of progressive constitutional monarchism did not long survive him. Revolutionaries became more revolutionary than he, and monarchists could not forgive him for having once been a revolutionary. He left no school of "Fayettists" to burnish his image through the years. By the late nineteenth century, international revolution increasingly meant Communist revolution, and Lafayette could not be put forward convincingly as a forefather of socialism. Yet his views were too liberal and internationalist to appeal to conservative nationalists of the late nineteenth century.

The liberalism that Lafayette incarnated in the early nineteenth century was a self-consciously international ideology locked in combat with an opposing international ideology of conservative legitimacy. This book is meant to contribute to an understanding of the way opposition politics worked in France, as well as of the way the international network of liberal activists operated. The early years of the Restoration saw the emergence of an electoral system in France which set many precedents for the future. Lafayette played an important role in shaping an electoral opposition. Carefully tracing Lafayette's friends and associates reveals some surprising ties and illuminates the beliefs and goals of many groups.

Focusing on Lafayette is especially useful because he cultivated acquaintances with liberal reformers in many countries. His wide-ranging connections, moreover, are revealing because politics is usually described within a national context. But decisions made by politicians and conspirators during the Restoration were shaped by a concern for their possible impact in other countries. Lafayette routinely considered the effect that developments in France would have on the progress of liberalism elsewhere. And liberals throughout the world looked to him as a source of support and encouragement.

Lafayette's cosmopolitan concern for political change throughout the world marked him as an heir of the eighteenth century. Charles de Rémusat remarked that "He frankly espoused the opinions of his century." Rémusat also remarked, "No man has had more enemies, nor more desperate and more diverse ones. No man has been so shamefully attacked in his talents, his intentions, his opinions, his conduct, his intelligence, his character. Something will remain from that concurrence of all hatreds and prejudices. He will be misunderstood."[10] And the misunderstanding has continued to the present.

Lafayette has been misunderstood in part because his political thought is not easily accessible. He was not a political philosopher and did not leave behind a coherent explanation of his actions. The six-volume *Mémoires, correspondance et manuscrits du général Lafayette*, published after his death by his family, contains only a few genuine memoirs. It is primarily a selective and sanitized edition of his letters and speeches. But even bravely wading into the remaining voluminous manuscripts of his correspondence will not necessarily bring easy rewards. Lafayette seemed to write letters with an eye to the future. He was guarded and formal. The great merit of his letters is that, though he was often reticent, he did not routinely seek to mislead.[11]

He has been called a simpleton. He was not, though his ideas were simple and his way of expressing them ineloquent. They were simple in the same way that the self-evident truths of the Declaration of Independence were simple. Lafayette and Thomas Jefferson shared a conviction that the enormous progress made in the eighteenth century in understanding the laws of political organization had born fruit in America and that the rest of the world would eventually follow the American example. To the end of his life Lafayette remained, as much as he was a child of the American Revolution, a product of the cosmopolitan spirit of the French Enlightenment. The progress of one country was linked to the progress of others. It is this cosmopolitan faith that, surviving in an increasingly nationalistic Europe, as much as anything makes him seem an anomaly, like a specter from another, more virtuous and heroic age. He was cosmopolitan in another sense as well: he constantly tried to look beyond his narrow class interests. Such disinterestedness was highly praised in his own day yet regarded with cynicism in the twentieth century. Though not insincere, it occasionally made him blind to the power of group loyalties and eccentricities. He frequently misread the motives of those around him (and sometimes his own). In pursuit of his goals he willingly worked with anybody from whatever nation or social class. He was neither condescending toward those who were socially inferior nor patronizing toward women. But his

6

trusting nature could also lead to errors in judging the worth and reliability of associates.

As a young man Lafayette became intoxicated with the notion that political improvement could bring happiness to people. He embraced the ideals of the Enlightenment, liberty, sovereignty of the people, and individual rights, which he believed were opposed by obscurantism, oppression, despotism, and privilege. His faith in these ideals never wavered. He became famous at the age of nineteen, when he left a favored position in French society and a pregnant wife (Adrienne de Noailles) to join the American colonists in their fight against the British. During the American Revolution he learned the value of public opinion and became aware of the power of politics.[12] George Washington became his friend and idol. Back in France Lafayette agitated for change. He promoted emancipation of slaves, equal rights for Protestants, free trade, constitutionalism, and representative institutions. As a member of the Assembly of Notables in 1787, Lafayette called for the convening of a national assembly. In 1789 he was elected to the Estates General by the nobility of Riom in Auvergne. When the Estates General became the National Assembly, he submitted to it a draft for the "First European Declaration of the Rights of Man and of Citizens." Three days later the fall of the Bastille transformed the Revolution and his political role. He became commandant of the newly created Paris National Guard, and for the next two years his popularity gave him enormous authority in France.

The way Lafayette used that power during the French Revolution was inevitably controversial, and it continued to be the source of polemics during the Restoration. To the royalists he was the deserter of his class and the destroyer of the monarchy. They faulted him for failing to prevent the march of the crowds to Versailles in October of 1789 and accused him of sleeping instead of protecting the king, after he reluctantly accompanied the National Guard troops to the palace.[13] Royalist writers of the Restoration pictured him as the inveterate enemy of the Bourbon dynasty.

On the other hand, later writers, sympathetic to the more radical phases of the Revolution, have faulted him for supporting the king after the flight to Varennes and have even accused him of connivance in the king's departure. In the atmosphere of heightened radical suspicion after the flight to Varennes, Lafayette's popularity waned, especially after the National Guard put down with severity the republican demonstration at the Champ de Mars. After the promulgation of the Constitution of 1791, Lafayette went into temporary retirement but emerged to take a military command in the war. His attempts to rally support for the king in the summer of 1792 and to undermine the growing power of the Jacobins brought demands for his arrest and impeachment. He urged the preservation of the Constitution of 1791, but after the arrest of Louis XVI and the passage of a decree of impeachment against him, Lafayette left the country, an action interpreted by most modern historians of the French Revolution as treason. The Prussians and Austrians did not regard him as an ally, however, and kept him in prison for the next five years.

Finally released in 1797, he lived in exile in Germany and Holland with his family for two years. Though still officially barred from France, Lafayette risked returning after Napoleon Bonaparte's coup d'état and, thanks to Adrienne's skillful negotiating, received permission to take up residence at La Grange. Neither a supporter of the Jacobins nor an ally of the enemies of the French Revolution, Lafayette returned to France with his faith in the early ideals of the French Revolution still intact. The Napoleonic regime did not live up to those ideals, and Lafayette distanced himself from politics. As he devoted himself to scientific agriculture, he watched the progress of Napoleon's career and hoped that the empire would soon be replaced by a government more to his liking. In the spring of 1814, repeated military setbacks signaled that Napoleon's reign would finally come to an end.

1

The Hundred Days

The Lafayette family lived thirty miles from Paris on an estate called La Grange. Lafayette's wife, Adrienne de Noailles, had managed to salvage this part of her inheritance from the wreckage of the French Revolution. A tree-lined avenue led over a moat to the imposing château which dated from the Middle Ages. The walls were covered with ivy planted by Charles James Fox, the English politician, during a visit at La Grange. The wide gardens, redesigned by Hubert Robert, were scenes of childish play and of gentle meanderings for the numerous guests of the always-hospitable General Lafayette. From his circular library in one of the towers of the château, Lafayette could look over the grounds and call down instructions to the laborers below.[1] Like his friend Thomas Jefferson, he took his agricultural pursuits seriously, introducing a flock of merino sheep onto his estate and always striving to return home in time to oversee the wheat and wine harvests.

Vigorous and healthy despite his eventful fifty-six years, Lafayette stood tall and erect with a florid complexion set off by a short brown wig.[2] He walked with a slight limp, the result of his willingness to endorse new scientific advances. In 1803, he had undergone an experimental procedure for setting his broken hip which had proved both painful and unsuccessful.

Lafayette doted on his family and maintained that he was happiest when he was at La Grange with them. Unhappily, Adrienne had enjoyed the restful existence at La Grange for only eight years before dying in 1807. She had never fully recovered from the insalubrious conditions of the imprisonment she had unselfishly chosen to share with her husband at the Austrian prison of Olmütz. Their son, George Washington Lafayette, took up his mother's role as Lafayette's devoted assistant. Thirty-four years old in 1814, George was married to Emilie de Tracy, daughter of the philosopher Antoine Destutt de Tracy, and they had three children.

Lafayette's daughter Anastasie was two years older than George. While the family was in exile at Lemkühlen (near Hamburg) in 1798, she had fallen in love with Charles de Latour-Maubourg, the younger brother of an aide who had been imprisoned with Lafayette at Olmütz.[3] The impediment of their lack of fortune was overcome by love and by Adrienne's support, and they were married. Anastasie and Charles were the parents of three children by 1814. Lafayette's younger daughter, Virginie (named for George Washington's native state), had married Louis de Lasteyrie in 1803, and they had four surviving children.

Lafayette's family shared his interest in politics and social reform. In their letters they usually discussed political news as well as private matters. Visitors at La Grange joined their discussions of current affairs and listened to Lafayette reminisce about historical events in which he had played a role. All members of the family had felt the consequences of openly expressing their antipathy to Napoleon. George had gone along with his father in voting against Napoleon's life consulate in the plebiscite of 1802. In a letter to Napoleon, Lafayette had explained that it was not the life consulate itself to which he objected but the constitution's failure to guarantee liberty. "It is appropriate to the principles, to the commitments, to the actions of my entire life, to wait to give it my vote until it is founded on bases worthy of the nation and of you."[4] This well-known family position had stymied the military careers of George and Louis de Lasteyrie. George had saved General Emmanuel de Grouchy's life at the Battle of Eylau, yet Napoleon still blocked his promotion to captain. He left the army in 1807.[5]

In the next year Lafayette joined other liberals, including George's father-in-law, Destutt de Tracy, in a shadowy conspiracy to plan a government that would take charge should Napoleon suffer a major defeat on the battlefield.[6] After the exposure of this so-called Malet conspiracy, Lafayette escaped Napoleon's vengeance only because Joseph Fouché, the minister of police, intervened and because one of the conspirators, Venceslas Jacquemont, under interrogation, steadfastly denied Lafayette's involvement.[7]

Despite the obvious risk, Lafayette still refused to distance himself from anti-Bonapartist conspirators who sought his support. As he told a friend, "I could not allow myself to discourage, for the sake of my personal safety, any project in favor of liberty."[8] He was probably more often suspected than actually involved in plotting, since his notorious opposition to Napoleon encouraged others to use his name in their schemes—without his knowledge.

Though Lafayette looked forward to the replacement of Napoleon's empire by a more liberal regime, his patriotism recoiled at the defeat of his country's armies and at the foreign invasion of the country in 1814. In the spring of that year he came to Paris to be by the side of two mortally ill relatives, and he stayed on, as the allies approached the capital, to do whatever he could to hold back the enemy. His offer to lead a regiment of the National Guard came to nothing, but George, Lasteyrie, and Latour-Maubourg enlisted. Lafayette then tried to interest one of Napoleon's marshals in a scheme to compel the emperor to abdicate.[9] Eager to be rid of the "modern Attila," he wanted to bring about "a National insurrection against domestic despotism the Succès of which would lead to a treaty with or a Spirited attack Upon the foreigners." Either eventuality would make the French masters of their own government. His schemes proved fruitless. He broke into tears as the enemy entered Paris.[10]

Tired of the endless wars and exactions of the empire, the French generally accepted with equanimity the restoration of the Bourbon dynasty in the person of Louis XVIII, brother of the guillotined Louis XVI. Lafayette shared in this optimism. Later, after the divisive Hundred Days, he would maintain that he knew from the beginning that "this restoration would be nothing but a more or less gradual or disguised counterrevolution."[11] But his letters written in the spring of 1814 show that he was in fact guardedly hopeful that the Bourbons would reestablish the constitutional monarchy that he had worked for in the early years of the French Revolution. He was pleased that the allies and especially Czar Alexander I had

> liberal opinions and dispositions; it was shown that
> not only the best, but the only means of salvation was
> returning to the first principles of the Revolution and to
> the constitutional throne of the Bourbons. This evi-

11

dence rallied all the friends of liberty. Each one pruned his doctrines or his secondary objections in order to unite on several essential points. We have been assured that the king and his family have decided to go in the same direction, and in general, their conduct and speeches have been in keeping with this assertion. The arrival of the king will decide the acceptance, the formation, and the evolution of this constitutional order. I have great hopes then, and I yield to them with all my heart.[12]

Other liberals were hopeful too. Benjamin Constant even had kind words for the king's brother, the comte d'Artois, leader of the most intransigent royalists, when he wrote, "It is impossible to be more moderate than Monsieur."[13] Old revolutionaries like Lazare Carnot hoped that their opposition to Napoleon would help them find a place under the new regime.[14] Lafayette waited anxiously for the arrival of the king in France, disappointed that he had not been made a member of the provisional government but pleased that George was named aide-de-camp of the new war minister.[15] He believed that the monarchy could succeed, but only under certain circumstances. "If the dynasty, called back to a legal throne, adopts, as it has announced and as I hope it will, principles essential to public liberty and the institutions that will guarantee them, its name will be a further pledge to internal peace. If not, things will be stable neither for them nor for us.[16]

Lafayette's hopes for the new regime seem to have been fueled more by hatred of the Napoleonic system than by realistic assessments of what the Bourbons were likely to do. He wrote flatteringly to his childhood friend the comte d'Artois that the prince's return was "a guarantee of public happiness and liberty."[17] However, strained relations between Lafayette and Louis XVIII went back a long time, back to the lost world of Versailles before the French Revolution when Louis XVIII was still the comte de Provence. Lafayette's in-laws, the powerful Noailles family, had thought of securing a post for their young relative in the count's retinue. Lafayette thwarted their plans by deliberately insulting Provence at a masked ball; he then made sure that the prince understood that he had recognized him behind the mask.[18]

Lafayette's refusal to be connected with Provence suggests that his ambition already craved wider fields than those available to a courtier of the king's brother. He soon became fascinated by the American struggle for independence and the opportunities for glory and distinction that it provided. A political motive might also have lain behind his rejection of Provence. In 1775, the count advocated increased royal power to combat the Parlements. Lafayette disagreed, sharing the prevailing attitude of informed public opinion that the Parlements were guardians of liberty against the absolute power of the Bourbon monarchy. Moreover, this anti-Parlement policy did not triumph, and for some time Provence was excluded from the center of power.[19] Lafayette had no reason to attach himself to a prince whose influence was in decline.

His differences with Provence continued into the French Revolution. The count jealously guarded the power of the king and wanted no changes in what he called the "old constitution." Lafayette, of course, disagreed, as did other liberal nobles (like the Noailles) who favored a constitutional monarchy. He always blamed the intransigence of conservatives like Provence for the failure of his moderate goals in the early Revolution. If, instead of fleeing the country at the first opportunity, they had remained to defend their king, the violence of the late stages of the Revolution would have been avoided and the new constitutional order would have succeeded. Lafayette's contempt for the émigrés resulted in his using the term *Coblentz* (for the German town where émigrés gathered) as his most damning insult for the rest of his life.

From Coblentz the two royal brothers called for a foreign invasion of France, sealing the king's fate by claiming to represent his wishes. After the arrest of Louis XVI in 1792, Lafayette was forced to flee the country to escape from his Jacobin enemies. During Lafayette's years of Austrian imprisonment, Provence continued to pursue policies distasteful to Lafayette. With the successive deaths of Louis XVI and his young son, the comte de Provence inherited the Bourbon crown, truculently called for a return to the old powers of the monarchy, and declared that *biens nationaux* (lands confiscated and sold during the Revolution) should be restored to their original owners. He also dismissed from his service two members of the Noailles family because of their moderate views. In 1814 Lafayette still remembered this episode with bitterness. "It would have been better . . . to have forgiven the royalists, who, instead of going to Coblentz, had, on 10 August, stayed by the side of the king, such as MM. de Noailles d'Ayen and de Poix."[20] Surely those royalists who had been loyal to the martyred king and had not rallied to Napoleon deserved more gratitude.

By 1814 Louis XVIII had moderated, but he was still unwilling to go as far as Lafayette would have liked in accepting the changes wrought by the Revolution. When the Napoleonic Senate hastily wrote a constitution in April 1814, which they wished Louis XVIII to accept before they would endorse his assumption of the throne, he rejected it. He knew that successful rule would require some kind of constitutional system with legislative bodies, but he meant to rule not at the invitation of a legislative body but by right of birth and legitimate succession. He appointed his own commission to write a charter for the new government.

Louis XVIII rejected the Senate's constitution because it limited his power. But Lafayette thought it did not go far enough in defining the rights of the nation. Though he had only rumors of its contents to go on, Lafayette wrote an extended critique in a letter to a friend, pointing out dangerous omissions and vague provisions, which might leave open the way to despotism or the renewal of aristocratic power. Under the Napoleonic system, district assemblies, made up of all citizens, chose arrondissement and departmental electoral colleges whose members served for life. These colleges chose candidates from among whom the Senate chose the members of the *Corps Législatif*.[21] The statement in the proposed Senate constitution, that the *Corps Législatif* "would be elected as at present except that elections will be direct," seemed insufficient to Lafayette. Surely the Senators did not mean to continue the aristocratic practice of life terms for members of the electoral colleges.

He did not like the proposed senate either. Lafayette was opposed to hereditary bodies on principle, but if the document's framers were determined to make the senate hereditary, they ought at least to stipulate a maximum size for that body. The document also failed to provide for popular election of municipal officials and justices of the peace, something Lafayette thought necessary to keep the old aristocratic lords from dominating the towns. The king's war-making powers seemed too broad, the budgetary review process not clear. "Since they want to follow the

English model they must not neglect the principal safeguards of that constitution," Lafayette observed, such as a mutiny bill, a habeas corpus law, and a definition of national as opposed to royal property. Though he preferred the American to the British system, he recognized the mechanisms of freedom developed in the British constitution.[22]

The king's new charter had not yet appeared, but Lafayette thought the new regime seemed already to be headed in the wrong direction by rejecting the tricolor emblem, which Lafayette had created immediately after the fall of the Bastille and to which the French people had become attached over the last twenty-five years.[23] Nevertheless, Lafayette swallowed his disappointment, dressed in his old military uniform, and presented himself at court, where, he reported, he was "very well received" by the king and his brother. Yet he never went again.[24] Though polite, the king made it clear that there was no place for Lafayette in his government. Without an office, Lafayette would be denied access to the two inner rooms at court and could enter only the outer Salle des Maréchaux, along with anyone else properly attired.[25]

Lafayette's meeting with another member of the Bourbon family, the duc d'Orléans, pleased him more. Though Lafayette had fought bitterly with the elder duc d'Orléans during the Revolution, he approved of the son, who had spent some time in exile in the United States. Orléans told Lafayette how much he admired him, and the two men found themselves in agreement on many questions. Reminiscing about this visit later, Lafayette would conclude that Orléans was "the only Bourbon compatible with a free constitution."[26] But in May 1814 he still held out hope for Louis XVIII's regime. He assured his American friend Albert Gallatin that the heavily censored newspapers of France could not adequately express the widespread "spirit of liberty" that existed.

> *Commissioners of the king are now debating Constitutional articles with a Committee of senators and members of the legislative corps equally named by him. But the last resort is to those two bodies and . . . public opinion. . . . I am so taken up with this great concern that it does in great measure divert my thoughts from the preliminaries [of the peace treaty] which deprive France of those natural, proper, well earned frontiers*

which under the tricolor cockade, had been secured I thought for ever.[27]

On the same day that he wrote that letter, Lafayette met one of the authors of the preliminary peace treaty, Czar Alexander I of Russia, who at the time was playing the role of a liberal emperor, a magnanimous victor in his bitter struggle with Napoleon. He maintained that he would not deal with Napoleon, that he would respect the old boundaries of France, and that he would honor a constitution written by the Senate for the French people. Though uncommitted at first, Alexander was soon persuaded by Charles-Maurice de Talleyrand and the British to back Louis XVIII's accession to the throne. However, when Louis rejected the Senate constitution and treated the czar with great haughtiness, Alexander began to regret his decision.[28]

When he first met Lafayette at the Paris home of Mme de Staël, another of Napoleon's adversaries now back from exile, Alexander told him that there was little hope of the Bourbons ever promoting liberal policies. The duc d'Orléans, he believed, was the only Bourbon with liberal ideas. Then why, Lafayette asked the czar, had he reinstated the Bourbons? Alexander responded that he had had no choice. Although he urged Louis to make concessions to the nation, the representatives in the *Corps Légis-latif* had confounded his intentions. They had not insisted that Louis accept the Senate constitution and were ready to recognize the king without conditions. This exchange confirmed Lafayette's view that a provisional government intent on wresting constitutional guarantees from Louis XVIII would have gained Alexander's backing and succeeded.[29]

The Russian leader made an enormously favorable impression on Lafayette, who was especially pleased by Alexander's willingness to help the United States settle its war with England. At the request of the American commissioners in Europe, Lafayette was trying to secure the mediation of one of the powers. He first approached Baron Wilhelm von Humboldt, the Prussian minister and brother of his good friend the scientist Alexander von Humboldt.[30] Failing with the Prussians, Lafayette next contacted Frédéric de La Harpe, Alexander's old Swiss tutor (who was acting as the czar's agent in Paris). La Harpe placed before the czar a memorandum on the question of mediation written by

William H. Crawford, the American minister in Paris. Alexander told Lafayette that he had read Crawford's paper with interest, but he had his doubts about the United States because of their divisive political system. Lafayette assured him "that they were the happiest and freest people upon earth" and explained that political parties were necessary "in a commonwealth." Alexander then agreed to be a mediator, but the British rejected his offer.[31] "He really is a great, good, sensible, noble-minded man," Lafayette told Crawford, "and a sincere friend of the cause of liberty."[32]

Alexander insisted that the charter promised by Louis XVIII be completed before the allied monarchs left France.[33] The hastily written document that resulted reassured former revolutionaries that no inquiries into past political opinions would be made and promised owners of national lands that their property would not be disturbed. It established a legislature of two houses: an upper Chamber of Peers named by the king and a lower Chamber of Deputies elected by departments. Because time ran out, the commission left the composition and workings of the electoral colleges to be determined by statute. The king's considerable prerogatives included the exclusive right to originate legislation and to appoint and dismiss ministers, as well as extensive authority over questions of war and peace. The Charter nevertheless guaranteed some of the important gains of the Revolution: freedom of the press, equality before the law, careers open to talent, and freedom from arbitrary arrest.

Lafayette's greatest objection to the Charter of 1814 was that it rested exclusively on the authority of the king. He still clung to the maxim of the eighteenth-century revolutionaries, reinforced by his American experience, that a written constitution provided the most solid foundation for government. Attempting to apply these principles in France, Lafayette had been the first to introduce a draft of a declaration of rights in 1789 and had tried in vain to preserve the Constitution of 1791 despite its flaws. The Charter of 1814 would never comport with his theoretical understanding of what a constitution should be. He complained to Jefferson about "the illegality of a charter where the Sovereignty of the people is flatly denied."[34] Lafayette thought that the nation as sovereign had made a constitution in 1791 and again in 1795, both documents deriving from "the legal source." He admitted that "*the granting of the charter* is a completely different principle," yet he felt that, as a practical matter, France must accept the flawed document because "it has recognized several of the rights proclaimed by the legitimate national power, and many excellent institutions" could develop along with the Charter.[35]

In the end, Lafayette acquiesced to the Charter because he believed that the only choice lay between "Bonaparte or the Bourbons . . . in A Country where the Idea of a Republican Executive Has Become Synonimous With the Excesses Committed" by the republican government of the Revolution. To have prevented the restoration of the Bourbons would have required working with the despised Bonapartists, "Unpatriotic in their Source, Ruinous in their effects." Instead, he and his friends hoped that, by accepting the Bourbons, they could "direct this turn of the Revolution towards the original principles Upon which it Had Been Begun—How far We May Succeed is Yet Uncertain." The new government had already made some "Egregious Blunders." Nonetheless, "two evident facts Must Be aknowledged. There Has Been a More proper Sense, and positive Care of public liberty Under this Restoration than at the time of Charles the Second, and there are Now More Symptoms and chances of freedom than Could Have Been expected Under the Masterly despotism and iron Hand of Bonaparte."[36]

Lafayette's initial rapprochement with the Bourbons was roughly consistent with his aspirations during the French Revolution: to establish a constitutional monarchy in which a weak king would preside over a government answerable to the legislature. As in the Revolution, he now also feared that the experiment might be destroyed by the pretensions of "the Aristocratical party." The Bourbons should have secured "a More National title to their throne, and [thus] a shield Against the Extravagancies of their own party."[37] As time went on, Lafayette grew more discouraged about the possibilities of founding a "Stout Constitutional System" under this regime. A bill passed in August limiting freedom of the press was an early blow to his hopes. The precise development of his disillusionment, though, is difficult to trace. His reminiscences about this period, written after the Second Restoration, emphasized his hostility toward the Bourbon government and minimized his suspicions of Bonapartists, many of the latter having since become his political allies. His reactions at the time were surprisingly mild, as he waited to see how the new institutions would develop.

By the spring of 1815, Lafayette had become discouraged, and he was not alone. He began to hear of plots to overthrow the increasingly unpopular royal government. Though not a participant himself, he knew about a conspiracy organized by Fouché and some Napoleonic generals who intended to replace the king with the duc d'Orléans.[38] In one of his frequent trips to Paris, Lafayette discussed with Benjamin Constant the growing hostility toward the Bourbons. Constant then confided to his diary, "The future is very uncertain. Only one thing is sure: the hard-liners want nothing to do with us. They will destroy themselves and us as well."[39] The hard-liners ("*purs*") were extreme royalists. Constant believed that they endangered the regime by refusing to cooperate with constitutional royalists like Lafayette and himself. Frustrated, Constant later wrote angrily in his diary, "Well, since I'm rejected, I'll take the hint, and since they want me in the opposition, I'll join it."[40]

The opposition Lafayette and Constant intended to mount at this time was not an armed insurrection but a vigorous political challenge at the polls. The Napoleonic legislative chambers, provisionally maintained by Louis XVIII, had ended their sessions in December. The Charter called for a Chamber of Peers and a Chamber of Deputies. Lafayette intended to work for the election of constitutional deputies to this new chamber in hopes that sufficient numbers would be chosen to bring about a change in the direction of the government.[41] The king would then be forced to accept more liberal institutions. But, Lafayette explained later, "if the resistance of the Bourbons and of their party had made necessary another 14 July, it could have been carried out once again under the auspices of the civil authority and the best-intentioned men of the revolution."[42] He envisioned, then, not a mere army revolt, but an insurrection made legitimate by the representatives of the people, and that revolt, only if the king ignored the election results. In any case, he thought a rising against the Bourbon government could succeed only after the Allies had completed their meetings at Vienna and their armies had been dispersed.[43]

Napoleon's unexpected return to France in March 1815 upset the plans of all sides.[44] Lafayette was appalled to see the former emperor greeted warmly as he made his way up from the south and concluded that only the blunders of the royal government could explain this dramatic reversal. Their rejection of the tricolor had left it as a rallying emblem for Napoleon. They had insulted the army by creating elite corps staffed by émigrés. Clergymen and émigrés had criticized owners of *biens nationaux* with impunity. Reimposition of the hated *droits réunis* (certain taxes, which the comte d'Artois had pledged to abolish), censorship, and persecution of regicides had made people suspect that the government's promises would not be kept. One of the king's ministers even declared that only the émigrés had followed "la *ligne droite*," thus arousing fears of further reprisals and of the loss of national lands.[45]

Despite his considerable disenchantment with the royal government, Lafayette still preferred it to Bonaparte and therefore hastened to Paris to try to save the king.[46] Perhaps now Louis would be forced to enter into the "national pact" Lafayette had wanted ten months earlier, turning his back on the Allies and cultivating the loyalty of the French people. Several eleventh-hour meetings between royalists and liberals to try to shore up the popularity of the government came to nothing. Discussions at the home of Joseph-Louis-Joachim Lainé, the president of the Chamber, included royal officials, prominent political figures (François-René Chateaubriand, the duc de Broglie, Marc-René-Marie Voyer d'Argenson, Trophime-Gérard de Lally-Tolendal, and Benjamin Constant), and a representative of the king's close advisor, the duc de Blacas. Lainé and the abbé de Montesquiou, the minister of the interior, suggested replacing some ministers with more liberal men. There was talk of substituting Lafayette for the comte d'Artois as head of the National Guard. Lafayette himself attended one of the sessions and rather impractically proposed calling members of "all the national assemblies since 89" as a moral force to counter the military. His recommendation to give the duc d'Orléans more prominence than the other royal princes was not likely to please the suspicious royalists.[47]

Such measures might have worked to increase the king's popularity several months earlier, but it was too late now with Napoleon rapidly nearing Paris. Furthermore, many royalists still recoiled from compromising with liberals, preferring to rely on old Napoleonic ministers, like Fouché, whose ability and wiliness they hoped would match Napoleon's. Blacas's representative apparently objected to Lafayette's heading the National Guard because "it would be impossible to do such violence to the king's personal feelings."[48]

The rapid changes of the Hundred Days caught almost everybody off guard. Plagued by uncertainty, doubt, or fear, people made choices that in retrospect sometimes seemed foolish or cowardly, illogical or inconsistent. Historians are hard-pressed to sort out and make sense of the actions of the participants in this eventful period. Lafayette's decisions are as difficult to understand as anyone's. Up to the last minute, he was still trying to find a way to salvage the Bourbon regime. With the departure of the king, three main choices were available to him: follow the king to Ghent, retire to La Grange, or participate in the Napoleonic regime of the Hundred Days. It is hardly surprising that he did not join the Bourbons at Ghent. Lafayette had consistently condemned those who emigrated to seek the help of foreigners. The second choice seemed more logical. During the Napoleonic Empire, Lafayette had lived quietly at La Grange, refusing office and ostentatiously rejecting the legitimacy of the emperor. But this time, Lafayette did not retire to his rural retreat. Instead, he chose the third option: to participate in the political system of the Hundred Days.

Why did he make this startling decision? How could he lend his support to the man he had always hated, "the cleverest and most inflexible enemy of liberty?"[49] The answer is that he intended to use his political participation to undermine the Napoleonic regime. He became a representative because he did not expect Napoleon to stay in power long. Indeed, he intended to do everything he could to hasten his demise. His hatred of Napoleon had not diminished, but the uncertainties of the period now dictated a different course. During the Empire, Napoleon's power had seemed secure. Now anything was possible. Lafayette preferred to be at the center of action in Paris rather than isolated at La Grange.

The real story of what Lafayette was doing during the Hundred Days has remained obscure, in part because Lafayette himself obscured it. In memoirs written after the Hundred Days, he tried to clear himself of charges of vacillation or betrayal by formulating a rather abstract patriotic rationale for his actions.

21

But his explanation is not completely convincing. He argued that, once the Bourbons left the country, he felt it his patriotic duty to protect France from a foreign invasion and to work to establish the kind of government that the country wanted. Lafayette maintained that such actions were consistent with a higher form of patriotism, which put principles and the integrity of the country above devotion to a particular dynasty. "This is what men who see the entire state in one dynasty do not understand, and what seems very simple when patriotic doctrine, founded solely on the interests of liberty and of the nation, has frankly put all secondary interests in their places."[50]

Lafayette's explanation at least conformed to one of his deeply held beliefs: that too much emphasis was normally put on the person of the head of the government. Much more important, he believed, were the principles behind the institutions of the nation. "My real disagreement with exclusive republicans, actually, is that in their eyes the rights and the will of the nation and the principles of justice are less important than the managerial form of their executive power."[51]

However, his explanation left out a great deal and purposely played down two aspects of his behavior. Lafayette minimized his active opposition to Napoleon, which his new political associates of the Restoration, many of them former Bonapartists, would not have appreciated. And he obscured the disagreements among those who participated in the short-lived government of the Hundred Days because they were all on the same side after 1815: they were now the *indépendants* in opposition to the Bourbons.

He especially played down his differences with one of his closest political associates during the Restoration, Benjamin Constant. Like Lafayette, Constant negotiated with royal officials at the approach of Napoleon in 1815. There was talk of making him a peer, and he went so far as to publish a strongly worded article in the *Journal des débats*, calling Napoleon a tyrant, lauding the representative government of Louis XVIII, and promising not to crawl from one ruler to another. The article appeared on 19 March. That night Louis XVIII left Paris for exile in Belgium, and Constant soon came to regret that he had ever published it.[52] With the help of Lafayette, who introduced him to William H. Crawford, Constant fled Paris but returned a few days later to find the Bonapartists assiduously courting him.[53]

22

He succumbed more easily to the emperor's blandishments than did Lafayette. Napoleon had returned to France spouting liberal sentiments, calculating that he would need the support of the liberals in establishing his new government. Lafayette remained suspicious, noticing that Napoleon's public pronouncements became less and less liberal as he traveled northward: "republican in Provence, half-republican in Lyon, absolute emperor in Paris."[54] Despite the advice of both Lafayette and Mme de Staël that he not cooperate with Napoleon, Constant was quickly persuaded to write the constitution, the Acte Additionel, for the new "liberal" empire. He too had some doubts about Napoleon's devotion to liberty, but he entered into his new role with the intention of making it last.[55]

Lafayette continued to warn Constant against trusting Napoleon. "I have been reproached all my life . . . for giving in too much to my sanguine nature; I will respond that it is the only way to do something out of the ordinary. One would, indeed, never try anything extraordinary if one despaired of success. Why is it that today, when my most skeptical friends have become trusting, I seem to have also, in the opposite direction, changed my character?" He was convinced that rule by Napoleon, "with his talents and his passions, is the one which offers the fewest chances for the establishment of true liberty." A free people could have only two types of ruler, Lafayette believed: the head of a republic, whose actions were constantly reviewed by the people, or a constitutional monarch, irremovable but acting only through ministers who could be removed. He asked Constant whether Napoleon— "impetuous, . . . enterprising, and . . . impatient of contradiction"—would submit to either of these arrangements for very long. Would the emperor yield authority to a freely elected legislative system, with open debates reported by a free press? Would he guarantee personal freedom? "Up to the present, I do not see that he would be willing."[56]

Guarding his own independence fiercely, Lafayette refused any post under the revived empire, but he did agree to meet with Joseph Bonaparte in Paris on the morning of 21 April.[57] Lafayette considered Joseph a decent man, but he told him frankly that he distrusted his brother. Fearing that "the return of the Bourbons would make us suffer the fate of Poland and the destruction of the advantages of the revolution," Lafayette explained that he now supported the imperial government "as the lesser of two evils." But he revealed that he did so "with the desire that this government endure for as short a time as possible."[58] Joseph offered to make him a peer, but he refused, saying he was "a man of the people, [and] it is by the choice of the people that I will emerge from my retirement."[59]

The Acte Additionel was published on 23 April along with an ordinance calling for a plebiscite to approve it.[60] Still suspicious of Napoleon's intentions, Lafayette met on 25 April with Constant and with Generals Mathieu Dumas, Horace Sébastiani, and Antoine Lavalette to discuss ways of holding Napoleon to the new constitutional system. Lafayette advocated calling elections for the Chamber of Representatives before the plebiscite, even if it meant using the old Napoleonic electoral colleges.[61]

Napoleon agreed to immediate elections, and when Lafayette heard the news he consented to be a candidate at the departmental college of Seine-et-Marne, which opened at Melun on 8 May.[62] Lafayette was elected president of the college and then received the largest number of votes for deputy.[63] He had agreed to be a candidate in this admittedly irregular election held before the plebiscite. But when he came to vote for the Acte Additionel, constitutional scruples still dictated that he express reservations about some of its features and about the lack of discussion in its preparation. "However, since the rights of popular sovereignty have been recognized, and since they cannot be alienated in any particular, any more than can the rights which are essential to each of us, I vote *yes* despite the illegalities and with the above reservations, because I wish to hasten with all my power the meeting of a representative assembly, that primary means of salvation, defense, and amendment."[64]

Lafayette was in Paris during the weeks before the opening of the Chamber of Representatives, and he immediately launched into anti-Napoleonic schemes. He did not expect the emperor to last beyond the national emergency. If Napoleon lost the war against the allied powers, Lafayette reasoned, it was important to have an independent opposition ready to negotiate for France. If Napoleon won, his renewed strength would encourage him to reimpose a dictatorship unless there were those prepared to prevent it. In either case, Lafayette wanted to be ready to act.[65]

24

He appears to have been already contemplating a coup d'état to be staged at the time of the Champ de Mai ceremony of 1 June, held to announce the results of the plebiscite on the constitution and to begin the new system officially. Lafayette approached Fouché, who had resumed his post as minister of police, and Lazare Carnot, who had joined a Napoleonic government for the first time. Carnot rejected Lafayette's proposal because he was convinced of the sincerity of the emperor's conversion to liberalism. Fouché, who agreed with Lafayette that Napoleon could not last and who was carefully cultivating his ties to all groups to cover any eventuality, nevertheless rejected the scheme, arguing against getting rid of Napoleon since he enjoyed the backing of the army. Lafayette reminded them that "revolutionary France had defeated Europe a long time before the name of Bonaparte became famous."[66] At the end of May he apparently told Constant of his plans to topple Napoleon. Constant disapproved. "Lafayette will not make it and will very quickly become unpopular."[67] By 8 June Lafayette reported progress in his arrangements. "George [Washington Lafayette] already has a little circle of young men who could become very useful; but nothing is organized yet."[68] Since a revolutionary uprising had to be delayed, Lafayette fought Napoleon in the Chamber, backing his plans for defense, while opposing him on all other issues.

At the same time, Lafayette may have been maintaining ties to the royalist camp through correspondence with his old friend, Mme d'Hénin. She had gone to Ghent with her longtime companion, Lally-Tolendal, a liberal royalist and friend of Lafayette's, who edited the royal newspaper in exile.[69] Lafayette elaborately explained to her his participation in the Napoleonic system. "The current crisis, more extraordinary than any other, is so violent that it cannot last long," he predicted. He and his friends feared that the court at Ghent was "farther removed from our principles now than it was at the Tuileries." Hinting broadly at his intentions to bring Napoleon down, he said that the foreign powers made a mistake by invading France. The crisis made Napoleon "a necessary defender, whereas if they did not invade the frontier and left him to grapple with public opinion and his own character, he would find himself in a much more awkward position." He added significantly that he could speak to her more freely than he could write to her of these matters.

Lafayette wished Louis had been willing to "devise the Charter in consultation with the representatives of the nation, offer it to the French people, replace by election deputies whose powers had expired, grant freedom of the press, have good ministers, reassure the purchasers [of national lands] . . . and form the National Guard six months earlier." If these things had been done, Lafayette assured her, he would have been willing now to work for the king's return.[70] Though he obviously thought the chance remote, he may still have been leaving open the possibility of backing the return of Louis XVIII should he prove willing to abide by the conditions Lafayette thought indispensable for constitutional monarchy.

Soon after opening on 3 June, the Chamber of Representatives declared its opposition to Napoleon by its first item of business: the choice of a president. Lafayette did not want to be elected because it "would make me perhaps the spokesman for many things which would not suit me."[71] He joined his son George, who was deputy for the Haute-Loire, and other political associates in working for the election of Jean-Denis Lanjuinais, a critic of Napoleon who had voted against the life consulate and the empire and had been one of the authors of the Senate resolution calling for Napoleon's resignation in 1814.[72]

Lanjuinais won, but the representatives feared that Napoleon might neutralize their unwelcome choice by naming him to the Chamber of Peers. If that happened, the next two highest vote getters, Lafayette and a man named Flaugergues, were prepared to announce their refusal to serve.[73] But Napoleon accepted the election. Though he claimed not to desire it, Lafayette was then chosen to be one of the four vice presidents.[74]

The Chamber and Napoleon also clashed over the oath of allegiance to the constitution and to the emperor, an oath required of the deputies at the official opening. Lafayette opposed the oath, in part because he and his friends considered themselves the equivalent of a constituent body with a mandate to revise the constitution and in part because they did not intend to remain loyal to Napoleon for long. However, knowing that he did not have enough votes to change the oath, Lafayette reported proudly that he had "so skillfully used this small opposition that Joseph Bonaparte sent his aide-de-camp to my house in the evening, after I had retired, and the next morning, as soon as I awoke to ask me insistently to see him." They reached an agreement to administer the oath en masse, thus permitting each person to do as he wished.

This compromise did not last, Lafayette explained, "because "Gᵃˡ Sébastiani, delighted at having dined with the emperor, [Michel] Regnault de Saint-Jean-d'Angely, Benjamin Constant, etc., organized a maneuver, according to which at the opening of the session [of 7 June], a simpleton of our party [Dupin aîné] made a motion not to swear the oath."[75] As Lafayette had foreseen, the proposal to postpone the oath was soundly defeated. After Lanjuinais promised that in the following day's session an explanation would be made that swearing the oath in no way precluded "changes or improvements to the constitutions of the empire," he agreed to do it.[76]

Lafayette and Napoleon finally came face-to-face on 7 June, when the emperor arrived at the Chamber for the official inauguration speech. They met stiffly and warily. Napoleon greeted him by observing, "It has been 12 years since I've had the pleasure of seeing you." Lafayette responded "rather dryly: 'Yes, Sire, it has been that long.'" Later, as Napoleon was preparing to leave, he again spoke to Lafayette, who remembered the scene this way: "'I find you rejuvenated,' he said to me; 'country air has done you good.'—'It has done me a lot of good'; I answered. And since neither one of us wanted to lower his eyes, we read there what each was thinking, but I found the muscles of his face contracted and even moved in a quite extraordinary way." Despite a rather good speech, Napoleon looked bad, Lafayette thought, like "an old tyrant, mad at the role which his position forced him to play."[77]

As a member of the committee to draft the response to the emperor's speech, Lafayette insisted that they should prove they were *"la représentation nationale"* rather than *"le club Napoléon."*[78] He suggested asking in their message what more could be done to bring about peace. This proposal was voted down after Regnault declared "that the only way to peace . . . at present is for the emperor to leave again for the island of Elba."[79] That point was, of course, precisely the one Lafayette wanted to make.

Only Napoleon, he believed, stood in the way of peace. The war was aimed at

> *a single man at the expense of a large country. . . . One feels a great distress in thinking that with him gone one*

*could avoid the war, and that with him here one cannot
refuse to help him without bringing on the dismemberment, or at least the enslavement of France, which he
would enslave himself, as soon as he had the means.*

*Our position is false and sad; it is however the
only one we can take with any glimmer of a hope of
saving our country. The assembly, rather independent
on many points, sustains nonetheless zealously the
Bonapartist interest which it believes linked to the defense of the country and to the preservation of the benefits of the revolution.*

If they were to have any hope of avoiding an imposed settlement
on the country they had to support strenuous defense efforts. It
seemed essential to negotiate from a position of strength. For this
reason and because of simple patriotism, Lafayette supported
Napoleon's military preparations, while at the same time wanting
to be rid of him as soon as possible. As late as the middle of June,
Lafayette still hoped that the Allies' declarations, that they were
fighting Napoleon and not France, offered an avenue to peace. The
difficulty lay in persuading his fellow representatives to force
Napoleon to abdicate. "Everybody maintains that without Bonaparte we would have peace; but up till now the assembly would feel
lost and the army would be furious if abdication were proposed,
even if he could take up the reins of the empire again immediately
if the Allies did not keep their word."[80]

The situation changed dramatically on the evening of 20
June when news of Waterloo reached Paris. The emperor himself
arrived during the night, and Lafayette heard rumors the next
morning that Napoleon planned to dissolve the Chambers and
declare a dictatorship. He verified the truth of the rumor with
Joseph Fouché and Michel Regnault de Saint-Jean d'Angély, then,
without consulting others, he decided to strike before the emper-
or did.[81] As soon as the meeting opened on 21 June, Lafayette
climbed to the podium to make his first speech to the assembly, a
speech intended to rouse the old French revolutionary fervor and
to create a national movement to save the country.

*When, for the first time in many years, I raise a voice that
the old friends of liberty will still recognize, I feel called*

*to speak to you, Sirs, of the dangers to our nation which
you alone at the present time have the power of saving.*

*Sinister rumors have spread, they are unfor-
tunately confirmed. Now is the time to rally around our
old tricolor flag, the one of 89, the one of liberty, of
equality, of public order; it is that one alone which we
must defend against foreign pretensions and against
internal threats. Permit, Sirs, a veteran of that sacred
cause, who was always an outsider to the spirit of faction, to submit to you, several preliminary resolutions,
whose necessity, I hope, you will appreciate.*

The Chamber listened with rapt attention to this figure from the
revolutionary past and greeted his proposals warmly. Even Bonapartists seemed ready to abandon their defeated leader, who could
no longer defend the country and whose presence meant a continuation of the war. The representatives endorsed Lafayette's proposals, declaring that the nation's independence was in danger,
that the Chamber would meet in permanent session, and that any
efforts to dissolve it would be considered treason. They praised
the army and requested reports from the ministers of war, foreign
affairs, interior, and police.

Another of Lafayette's proposals called for arming the Paris
National Guard, "whose patriotism and proven zeal for the last
twenty-six years offer a sure guarantee to liberty, to property, to
the tranquillity of the capital, and to the inviolability of the
representatives of the nation." In Lafayette's scheme, the National
Guard was a key to keeping the foreigners at bay, maintaining
order, and saving the honor of the nation. But others had no wish
to see a force of this kind let loose, nor to see the first head of the
Paris National Guard preparing to play a large role in coming
events. At the suggestion of Philippe-Antoine Merlin de Douai, a
Napoleonic stalwart, the vote on this part of the resolution was
postponed. Fouché, who knew that Napoleon was doomed, favored the proposal to keep the Chamber in session, but he
intended to use that body for his own ends. He did not want the
revival of an independent National Guard under Lafayette's influence to complicate his schemes.[82]

Napoleon sent his brother Lucien, along with the ministers
called for in the resolution, to plead his cause. Antoine Jay

(presumably speaking for Fouché) challenged them: Was not Napoleon himself an obstacle to peace? he asked. Lucien answered that the allies were in fact fighting France and not merely the emperor; that Napoleon would safeguard the country from partition; and that, if the Chamber abandoned Napoleon, public opinion would find it guilty of "inconstancy" and "fickleness."[83] Lafayette responded heatedly. "By what right does the previous speaker dare to accuse the nation of having been fickle, of having lacked perseverance towards Emperor Napoleon? It followed him in the sands of Egypt and in the deserts of Russia, onto fifty battlefields, in defeat as well as victory . . . and it is for having thus followed him that we must mourn the blood of three million Frenchmen!"[84]

The Chamber came to no decision, except to continue negotiations between its leaders and the ministers that night. Their meeting lasted till 3:00 A.M. Lafayette raised the question of abdication, but no decision on it was made.[85] It was not until the next day that Napoleon's inevitable abdication took place. In accepting it, the Chamber studiously avoided any mention of the succession, though Napoleon had resigned in favor of his son. Instead of a council of regency for Napoleon II, they opted for a provisional government of five men. Lafayette wanted to be one of the five, but a parliamentary maneuver orchestrated by Fouché kept him out. The original wording of the resolution called for three men to be chosen *from* the Chamber of Representatives and two *from* the Chamber of Peers. But the resolution voted upon was changed to read that they would be chosen *by* each Chamber. The Representatives, voting first, chose two peers, Carnot and Fouché. There was then a runoff election between the next-highest vote getters, General Paul Grenier and Lafayette. Lafayette lost. The Chamber of Peers then chose two of their own members to complete the government.[86]

Lafayette blamed his defeat on the change of wording and on his lack of backing by any particular group. Bonapartists thought he was an Orléanist; Orléanists resented his refusal to commit himself to their man; and former republicans, turned Napoleonic noblemen, distrusted his opposition to hereditary nobility. Fouché, on the other hand, had the support of all parties.[87] Benjamin Constant confided in his diary, "They have excluded Lafayette."[88]

In reminiscences of these events, Lafayette did not mention the possibility that he lost votes because he seemed too sympathetic to the Bourbons, but this perception might have influenced some delegates as well. The government consisted of three regicides (Carnot, Fouché, and Nicolas-Marie Quinette), who could be expected to protect the interests of extreme revolutionaries.[89] Lafayette was no regicide and had done nothing publicly during the Hundred Days to proclaim his opposition to the Bourbons. His resolution declaring the Chamber to be in permanent session mentioned national independence, but national independence was perfectly compatible with negotiations to bring Louis XVIII back under a more rigorous constitutional system. The tricolor flag of 1789 was, after all, the standard of the constitutional monarchy under Louis XVI. He might prefer the duc d'Orléans, but he had done nothing yet to show that he would be unwilling to settle for Louis XVIII under proper conditions.

Another possible explanation for his electoral defeat was that many expected him to be named head of the National Guard. After Napoleon's abdication, a proposal had been made to give him that post, but Fouché thwarted this, too, arranging for the Chamber to delegate its power of appointment to the provisional government (the presidency of which he had assumed), and then naming André Masséna to head the National Guard.[90] He completed Lafayette's isolation by sending him to negotiate with the allied powers, along with others he wished to get rid of. Benjamin Constant would serve as the delegation's secretary. They departed for the front on 24 June.[91]

Lafayette would have preferred to stay in Paris, but he told Mme d'Hénin that he had decided "to accept everything and not to compromise at all on the commitment I had made to devote myself to spare my country the miseries of war and the fate of Poland as well as the internal and external political disasters which I saw were threatening her. My personal existence and even my reputation are to me in comparison but very secondary interests."[92]

His fears that a Bourbon restoration imposed by the Allies would mean the loss of national independence were increased by Crawford's report from England. "Your idea that foreign troops will garrison all the strong places of France if the King is placed again upon the throne are perfectly correct."[93] It was this humiliating foreign occupation and possible dismemberment of France that the delegation to the allied powers hoped to prevent. Yet the delegation's desire to negotiate for a different monarch would likely lead to more humiliating impositions than if Louis XVIII were replaced on the throne. The delegates intended to consider any arrangement. Fouché's instructions were to negotiate in favor of Napoleon II, but this was a mere formality designed to appease the army.[94] The delegates' only hope was that the Allies were sincere in declaring that they were fighting Napoleon, not France, and would therefore be willing now to engage in fruitful negotiations.[95]

Lafayette had no doubt heard rumors that the Allies disagreed about the future of France. The Austrians allegedly favored giving the throne to Napoleon's son, while Alexander I of Russia championed the duc d'Orléans. For reasons of domestic politics, the British had proclaimed that their goal was to defeat Napoleon, not to restore the unpopular Bourbons. In truth, as early as April, Viscount Castlereagh had told the duke of Wellington that their policy should be the restoration of Louis XVIII.[96] The Battle of Waterloo not only defeated Napoleon but, by making the British the victors, also ensured the king's restoration.

The commissioners from Paris first made contact with General Blücher's army at Laon. They rejected an armistice offer requiring France to surrender several forts but advised the government in Paris to send special commissioners to continue negotiations for an armistice. Although they did not see Blücher himself, they reported optimistically that he had sent word through an aide that "France would not be hampered in any way in its choice of government."[97] This assertion was almost certainly overstated. If, as seems likely, the delegates intended to spur the Representatives in Paris to resist the unconditional restoration of Louis XVIII, they succeeded. Fouché had almost persuaded key people in the Chambers to declare for Louis XVIII on the grounds that his becoming king was inevitable. The report put an end to that maneuver.[98]

Lafayette's hopes lay with Czar Alexander, and as soon as the commissioners caught up with the allied headquarters at Haguenau, Lafayette wrote him a flattering note, recalling their conversation of the previous year, which had greatly influenced Lafayette's actions.

> *Sire, you were on the verge of ensuring France's liberty and happiness. I saw you distressed by the circum-*

stances outside your majesty's control which disrupted your noble and generous views. Permit me to add that you deigned to indicate to me your regret at not having spoken to me sooner. Liberty and country, sire, have my first affections, but I am too attached to your person and to your glory not to feel a particular happiness in foreseeing the immense obligations that the cause of humanity and of France will owe you.[99]

But now the czar refused to see him. In this second invasion of France, he was no longer the conqueror. Moreover, while still priding himself on his liberal reformist views, Alexander was becoming fearful of revolutionary agitation, disappointed in democracy, and increasingly attracted to the mystical advice of Mme de Krüdener. The commissioners managed to meet with representatives of the four powers, but the negotiations were brought to an end by Sir Charles Stewart, who declared peevishly that he had no authority to negotiate for Britain. The British were almost as fearful of a strong, revolutionary France as they were of Napoleon.[100]

Alexander refused to meet with Lafayette because his position had changed in the preceding year. Displeasure at the French people's welcome of his enemy Napoleon also lay behind Alexander's acceptance of the restoration of Louis XVIII and his sponsorship of the Holy Alliance, by which the sovereigns of Prussia, Austria, and Russia pledged themselves to an "indissoluble fraternity" to protect "religion, peace, and justice" throughout Europe.[101]

Alexander's old mentor, Frédéric de La Harpe, regretted the czar's about-face and his rejection of Lafayette. Even though Alexander increasingly ignored it, La Harpe continued to send his former pupil advice. In 1818 La Harpe told Alexander that he should have met the delegates, who were all "highly estimable. . . . General Lafayette, friend and comrade-in-arms of Washington, a man as distinguished by the heroic actions of his youth as he is commendable by his moral qualities, was surely worthy to be spokesperson for his nation." But the czar had closed his door to him, and "the results have been quite deplorable, and will be felt for a long time."[102] Lafayette recalled later that by 1814 he had already suspected that *most courts in Europe invoked constitutions only to tranquilize people over the most essential rights of liberty; but I would not have guessed that one year later the same Emperor Alexander, having the most beautiful opportunity to repair the misfortunes of his liberality, would return with such an infatuation for legitimacy, such a need of using, after the fall of Bonaparte, a million and a half bayonets to reestablish Louis XVIII without conditions, or on conditions about which he had so bitterly complained to me, and would not be willing even to listen for an instant, either as ambassador or as an individual, to one of the last confidants of his philanthropic laments.*[103]

He complained that although he and his colleagues had repeatedly told the Allies that anything compatible "with French independence and liberty" could be negotiated, the Allies had "wanted to come to Paris and subjugate France by giving it a king without conditions."[104]

Unlike the European monarchs, Lafayette took constitutions seriously, and he was disappointed to be absent while the Chamber in Paris drafted one to be imposed on the new regime. He reminded his son George of the importance of various principles: elected local officials, a large representative body meeting yearly, a nonhereditary upper chamber, an independent judiciary, and a national guard. The committee writing the constitution should consult with Destutt de Tracy, Jean-Antoine Gauvain Gallois, Pierre-Claude-François Daunou, Charles-Joseph de Lambrechts, and Venceslas Jacquemont. He wanted "a strict constitution. If we succeed, it will be necessary to take what we give them; if we are overturned, the people must know what it has lost and what it must regain."[105] A similar motive had inspired Lafayette to introduce a declaration of rights in the early stages of the French Revolution, even before the fall of the Bastille. Thomas Paine recalled that Lafayette had hoped its principles might survive, even if the National Assembly itself were destroyed.[106]

While Lafayette concentrated on constitutions and negotiations, Fouché was intriguing with royalist agents to ensure the return of Louis XVIII. He later boasted that it had been accomplished with a minimum of bloodshed.[107] Lafayette, on the other hand, was willing to risk bloodshed to establish the principle that the king should not return to power until he acknowledged the right of the people to choose their own government. If "instead of sending me to charge the allied powers to keep their word," Lafayette told an old friend, "I had been placed in the government, I would have pronounced in favor of a battle before capitulation, and I would have followed our brave army to the banks of the Loire."[108] Fouché further defended his maneuvers by arguing that the office he received in compensation allowed him to mitigate the vengeance of the royalists.[109] Lafayette doubted that an individual could do much along these lines in the absence of a contract between the king and the people guaranteeing rights. On this score the Chamber of Representatives agreed, declaring in a resolution on 5 July that "a monarch cannot offer real guarantees, if he does not swear to maintain a constitution enacted by national representation and accepted by the people."[110]

On the following day, Lafayette, as spokesman for the returning commissioners, reported that they had received assurances that "the foreign courts did not claim the right to interfere in the form of our government."[111] The Allies may have professed their intention to allow the French nation to decide, but they obviously were not keeping their word. By this time Lafayette and the other commissioners knew that was the case. The deliberate distortion in Lafayette's speech can only be explained as the first shot in the political battles of the Second Restoration. The diplomatic maneuvering was over for all intents and purposes, and his reiteration of the Allies' declaration served only to throw light on their hypocrisy and to underline the Chamber's distaste for a government imposed by foreigners. As if to emphasize the illegitimacy of Louis XVIII's reigning without their approval, for the next two days the Chamber continued useless debate on a constitution that would certainly never be accepted.

Arriving at the hall on 8 July, the members found it locked and posted with guards to keep them out. Lafayette boldly invited the Representatives to meet in his "Small Rooms, as many as could Be crowded in them, from whence We proceeded to our president's [Lanjuinais] and subscribed the evidence of our Being excluded by force of arms."[112] Since Louis XVIII had returned to French soil and had already adjourned the Chambers, royalists pronounced this final act of resistance an egregious example of the Chamber's treason. Their die-hard gesture of defiance took courage since they could anticipate severe retaliation from the triumphant royalists.

Lafayette's attempt to find what he termed a *national* solution for France had failed, but his goals were clear. Some Americans understood them, even if many Frenchmen did not. Albert Gallatin, one of the American commissioners at Ghent, sent an able summary of events to Thomas Jefferson.

> *Our opinion of Bonaparte is precisely the same. In that La Fayette's and every friend of rational liberty in France did coincide. The return of that man was generally considered by them as a curse. Notwithstanding the blunders and rooted prejudices of the Bourbons, the alienation of the army and the absolute want of physical force had made them, upon the whole, harmless, and as soon as the termination of the congress at Vienna and the dissolution of the coalition would have left France independent of foreign interference, they must in the course of things either have been overset or have governed according to public opinion. After Bonaparte's restoration, it was hoped by some that his weakness would compel him to pursue a similar course; others, placing confidence in the declarations of the allies, hoped to get rid both of him and of the Bourbons. All saw the necessity of defending the country against foreign invasion, but the fatal catastrophe was not, to its full extent, anticipated by any.* [113]

The Hundred Days marked Lafayette's reemergence into politics after a long period of retirement. When they were over, he had moved unambiguously into opposition to the Bourbon governments of the Restoration. Napoleon's return ruined the possibilities for accommodation and compromise that Lafayette had glimpsed during the First Restoration. When the royalists gained control again, they lashed out against those who had participated in the Hundred Days, whom they now saw unmistakably as enemies. This was a wrenching change for Lafayette, who had always supported constitutional monarchy, believing that the

French people preferred the traditional Bourbon crown and that a limited monarchy was compatible with his notions of rights and liberties. New alignments now forced him to reconsider some of his assumptions.

Before the Hundred Days, Lafayette had been suspicious of Bonapartists and unwilling to cooperate with them. But at the end of the Hundred Days, Bonapartists had joined with liberals in rejecting Napoleon and in trying to impose a constitutional monarchy. Now Lafayette believed, "Bonapartism, and Jacobinism Have dissolved themselves into the great mass of the patriotic, national, and inwardly tricolored party with whom the elements of our demolished army are Heartily United."[114] The enmity of the Bourbons threw these heterogeneous groups together. Lafayette was willing now to work with his former enemies because he had come to trust them more during the Hundred Days. They called themselves *indépendants,* meaning that their primary loyalty was neither to Napoleon nor to the king, but to the nation.

The Hundred Days gave birth to the myth of the "liberal" Napoleon, who wanted to give the French people a genuine constitution and more freedoms. The myth endured because of something else that occurred in this period. By combining liberals and Bonapartists into one party, the Hundred Days ensured that liberal criticism of Napoleon would thereafter be muted. Lafayette loathed Napoleon and continued to criticize him privately, but in public he, and even more so other liberals, restrained the vehemence of their denunciations. Benjamin Constant, for example, who wrote the Napoleonic constitution, was hardly in a position to denounce his old enemy unambiguously.[115]

These political realignments disrupted Lafayette's private life as well. Mme de Staël, whose criticism of Napoleon continued unabated, was troubled by Lafayette's participation in the Hundred Days. Even more important for him, the Hundred Days brought a serious falling out with his mistress and friend, Mme de Simiane. Their relationship, begun shortly after Lafayette returned from the American Revolution, had survived the French Revolution despite their differing political views. But after the Hundred Days, Lafayette never again visited her country home, and she was no longer a part of the intimate family circle at La Grange.[116] He alluded to these relationships in an 1830 letter to Mme de Staël's daughter.

*I passed the first years of the Revolution in the inti-
mate society of female friends, and especially of one
friend who was very dear to me. There was continual
difference of opinion without disturbing our mutual affections. I was less fortunate at the period of the Hundred Days. The distress of this friend, the rebuke of her
whose memory is so dear to us did not prevent me from
following the instinct of my duty.*[117]

Mme de Simiane demanded from Lafayette an explanation
of his actions. What was she to tell her friends? Lafayette's long
response turned into an attempt to come to terms with his past,
to sum up what he stood for. He was at pains to show that he had
been consistent, honest, and principled throughout. He hoped
that "if you do not approve of me, you will at least agree that I have
never departed from a line of opinions and sentiments where I
have been loved or hated, but where I could not have been misunderstood." Before the Revolution, though he had cooperated with
the nobility, "no member of the nobility, the clergy or the Parle-
ment, can accuse me of having disguised my popular sentiments
and wishes: I always told them and wrote to them that I would not
resist the court for the sake of caste or corporate privileges, but for
the sake of the rights of the nation."[118]

Despite his republican principles, Lafayette was proud of
his support for Louis XVI, whose reign he had thought essential
for France at the time.[119] He had served him faithfully, especially
after the October Days, when the king's welfare had become his
responsibility.

*If I have been wrong in theory, or if I have sometimes
yielded to the surrounding impulses (for one must realize today that, in times of trouble, men in power do not
do all that they want to), at least one will agree that in
periods of power, as in those of misfortune or retirement, my sentiments, my opinions, and my conduct
have been unchanging. My principles on the essential
rights of the nation and its citizens, my zeal to claim
and maintain them have always gone before other political considerations.*

Even after the public lost confidence in the king following his attempted flight, things might have worked out if the "fury of the emigration had not revived the suspicion of the public, the power of the Jacobins, and a crusade of kings against us."[120]

Lafayette tried to make decisions based on principle and the best interests of the country. He went so far as to say, "personal considerations have never influenced my political conduct."[121] Such statements inevitably ring false today, and one cannot help suspecting that he was deceiving himself. Yet they must be taken seriously if his motives are to be understood. In his day, the statement was not thought vain. Like many of his basic beliefs, this one arose in the era of the American Revolution, when the young soldier was praised for turning his back on the luxuries of the French court to help the foreign rebels. To Americans, his participation in a cause in which he had no personal interest (he even refused a salary) seemed more commendable than the participation of the Americans themselves, who had something to gain from the outcome. The republican ideology of the eighteenth century stressed the value of putting public good over personal interest. Lafayette surely agreed with Thomas Paine's statement that "the word *republic* . . . means the *public good*, or the good of the whole, in contradistinction to the despotic form, which makes the good of the sovereign, or of one man, the only object of the government."[122]

Naturally, what Lafayette saw as the public interest often coincided with his own interest. But if one is to make sense of Lafayette's actions (some of which baffle those seeking more practical explanations), one must recognize how much this goal of acting in a disinterested fashion mattered to him and to those who admired him. He did not always choose the side that was advantageous to himself—not out of a simpleminded inability to distinguish it but out of a conscious desire to live up to an ideal of disinterested statesmanship. Only a despot would put his own interest first, and despotism was what he hated most in the world.

With the fall of the emperor, he told Mme de Simiane, he had given in "for a moment to old memories, trying to persuade myself that these princes might well have learned and forgotten something." But he quickly saw that they intended to promise without delivering on those promises. He came out of retirement at Napoleon's return only because he was called by "a national interest superior, in my opinion, to all the dynasties of the world."[123] He wondered how she could reproach him for not working for Louis XVIII's return when the disastrous results were now so apparent. Despite the hatred the court felt toward him, Lafayette assured Mme de Simiane that he would still prefer the Bourbons if he could be convinced that "they will yield finally to the evidence of their interest, of their security," by protecting the rights of the nation.[124]

Lafayette had not won in the Hundred Days, but he saw no reason to apologize either. He hoped to keep alive the ideas of constitutional government, national self-determination, popular sovereignty, property rights, and freedom of speech and of the press. These ideas had been defeated during the Hundred Days, but he never wavered in his conviction that they would triumph eventually.

2

Liberalism in Retreat

With the restoration of the Bourbons, those who had taken part in the Hundred Days scrambled to protect themselves from the vengeance of the returning royalists. Lafayette did all he could to help his acquaintances escape the disruptions of the enemy occupation and the change of governments. For example, citizens of Meaux, a town in Seine-et-Marne, asked him to intercede on behalf of fellow townsmen held hostage by the Prussians. Lafayette requested Alexander von Humboldt to speak to Blücher.[1] Bonapartists escaping to the United States, like Michel Regnault de Saint-Jean d'Angély, General Emmanuel de Grouchy, Joseph Lakanal, and General Simon Bernard, secured letters of introduction to Lafayette's old American friends, and he offered to write them for Joseph Bonaparte.[2] Lafayette, who could always separate personal feeling from public policy, even expressed his willingness to help Napoleon escape to the United States. After the emperor "Had Been overthrown He found in me the private feelings to which He was entitled," Lafayette told Crawford.[3] He also asked the Russians about the welfare of another member of Napoleon's family, Hortense Beauharnais, whose mother, Josephine, had helped him during his captivity and whose kindness he could not forget "even if I be today called Bonapartist by the powerful enemies of Napoleon."[4]

Because invading Russian troops had taken up residence at La Grange, Lafayette spent the summer in Paris. In August he traveled to Melun for the elections for a new legislative chamber, but with little hope of being elected himself. Because no permanent election law had yet been passed, the government had authorized the convening of the old Napoleonic electoral colleges. The departmental prefects had been given the authority, which once resided with the emperor, to appoint twenty members in addition to those chosen by the citizens. This power, together with the presence of foreign troops in the department and fear of reprisals against those who had participated in the Hundred Days, assured government success. Fouché, now Louis XVIII's minister of police, was chosen one of the four Seine-et-Marne deputies. Lafayette was not.[5]

When occupying troops finally abandoned La Grange in September, Lafayette returned home. He was eager to be reunited with his large family, now including eleven grandchildren since the birth of a son to Emilie in August.[6] None of them was on the lists of political opponents banished by the government, but various duties kept them away most of the fall. In November, Virginie was the only one of his children with him. George was overseeing the family estates in Auvergne.[7]

Most of Lafayette's political colleagues were not on the list of proscription either, but they nonetheless thought it prudent to lie low. Benjamin Constant, for example, who managed to have his name removed from the lists, decided to go to England for a while.[8] Deprived of the company of his French political friends, Lafayette found consolation in writing to old American acquaintances as he tried to understand the lessons of recent events.

Lafayette frequently enclosed in these letters a copy of the declaration passed by the Chamber of the Hundred Days on 5 July, which had repeated the basic principles of constitutional monarchy as elaborated during the French Revolution: a king had to agree to abide by a constitution written by representatives of the people and approved by the nation. It was, he told Jefferson, "Very Similar to what Had Been declared in July 1789."[9] The government of Louis XVIII, according to Lafayette, failed to live up to these principles. The king had been imposed by the Allies, instead of being the free choice of the French people. He had promulgated the Charter of 1814 and could presumably revoke it or parts of it at will. Lafayette watched in dismay as the *Chambre Introuvable* (the popular name for the Chamber elected in 1815 after Louis's restoration) passed laws limiting freedom of the press, permitting the arrest of those who invoked Napoleon's name or incited disrespect for the king, and reinstituting exceptional courts with jurisdiction over political offenses. These courts (*cours prévotales*) were revivals of Old Regime courts, which

Lafayette had persuaded the National Assembly to eliminate at the beginning of the Revolution.[10]

Recent events had taught Lafayette that the Allies, while professing to be fighting Napoleon, were in fact assaulting the principles of the French Revolution. The government of Louis XVIII was nothing more than "an Instrument in the Hands of the Allies to disarm first, then to Oppress the Country." Lafayette's only consolation lay in his confidence that the "Mass of the people" understood what was happening and would emerge even more devoted to liberty.[11] France, now reduced to its frontiers of 1789, would be occupied by 150,000 foreign troops on the northern and eastern borders for five years and forced to pay an indemnity of 700 million francs.[12]

Lafayette found a few rays of hope amid the dismal developments. One of his associates of the Hundred Days, Jean-Denis Lanjuinais, who had kept his seat in Louis XVIII's Chamber of Peers, antagonized the royalists in October 1815 by comparing the law on arbitrary imprisonment to the infamous Law of Suspects of 1793 and having his remarks printed and circulated. When Lafayette expressed support, Lanjuinais responded that all the accusations against him were false except for his having had the speech printed, and he insisted that his printers had obeyed all of the provisions of the new press law.[13]

Another of Lafayette's friends also caused a stir over this bill, this time in the Chamber of Deputies. Marc-René Voyer d'Argenson had been Lafayette's aide-de-camp when he had commanded the Army of the Center in 1792 and had spent the later years of the Revolution on his lands near Poitiers. Although Voyer d'Argenson accepted employment under Napoleon as prefect at Antwerp in the department of Deux-Nethes in 1809, he crossed his difficult master by refusing to confiscate the property of the town's mayor, accused of embezzling funds. His struggle with Napoleon led to his resignation in 1813 and earned him a reputation for honesty. Voyer d'Argenson turned down a post from the Bourbons, saying he would refuse any such offer until they ruled under "a free constitution . . . approved by the nation and with ministers answerable to the representatives of the people."[14] Lafayette and d'Argenson renewed their friendship during the First Restoration and served together in the Chamber of Representatives of the Hundred Days and on the mission to Haguenau.

D'Argenson, one of a handful of liberals elected to the *Chambre Introuvable*, represented a department whose population was not typical of the Restoration electorate. The Haut-Rhin in Alsace was German speaking, largely Protestant, industrial, and devoted to the principles of the Revolution. D'Argenson owned and managed iron foundries at Oberbrück. In the debate over the law to arrest people for shouting Napoleonic slogans ("seditious cries") d'Argenson mentioned the persecution of Protestants in the south of France. "Some held that seditious cries, that incitements to revolt have been heard; others have broken my heart by announcing that Protestants have been massacred in the Midi." His speech was interrupted by shouts, and, though he insisted he was not asserting the truth of these rumors, the Chamber passed a motion calling him to order.[15]

Lafayette clutched eagerly at expressions of liberal sentiment in this reactionary period. He was so struck by the promise shown in a speech by the young peer, the duc de Broglie, that he sent copies of it to Jefferson and James Madison.[16] Broglie, d'Argenson's stepson, was beginning his political career and his friendship with Lafayette. In 1816, he stopped at La Grange on his way to Italy to join his fiancée, Albertine, the daughter of Mme de Staël. Albertine, a striking and intelligent redhead, was almost certainly offspring of the notorious liaison between Benjamin Constant and Mme de Staël.[17] These people were among Lafayette's closest friends (outside of his own family), as well as being his closest political associates. Their connections illustrate an important characteristic of politics during the Restoration: it was organized around and maintained by social contacts and networks of dependents.

In 1816, though, chances for genuine political life seemed remote, and Lafayette continued his exile at La Grange, reading the papers and asking his friends for news but refusing to go to Paris.[18] His ties to America remained important. Americans abroad came to see him, as did Europeans requesting his help in settling in America. Winfield Scott visited La Grange in December 1815 and invited Lafayette to a celebration in Paris to commemorate the first anniversary of the Battle of New Orleans.[19] George Flower and Morris Birkbeck picked up letters of introduction to Lafayette's American friends as they set out to carve a community out of the Illinois wilderness.[20]

In the summer, Lafayette greeted eagerly the news of the arrival of the new American minister, Albert Gallatin. Lafayette invariably made friends with the American representatives in France, and his ties to Gallatin would be especially close. Still refusing to go to Paris, Lafayette explained to Gallatin, "I have taken it as a line of conduct to keep myself in absolute retirement, not only to obviate the objections too often made to unfortunate patriots of their connections with me, but also to mark in a negative way, the only one that is now possible, my perfect disapprobation of the actual order of things."[21] They met at the country estate of an expatriate American, Daniel Parker, at Draveïl, about two hours' drive from Paris. Originally from Massachusetts, Parker had prospered by selling supplies to American revolutionaries and by trade with the Orient and had made a fortune in France during the French Revolution by purchasing national lands.[22] After their meeting at Draveïl, Lafayette urged Gallatin to come to La Grange, but negotiations with the French government over American indemnities kept the minister in Paris.[23]

Gallatin brought letters for Lafayette from America, including one from President Madison reporting a lack of progress on settling the conflicting claims to Lafayette's Louisiana lands. In 1803, Congress had awarded Lafayette a grant of lands in the Northwest Territory due him as a veteran of the Revolution. Jefferson managed to have this award changed to an equivalent amount of land in recently purchased Louisiana. Lafayette's plans for disposing of part of the property to pay his debts were confounded by numerous conflicting claims. He sold some to Baring Brothers; then in 1812, two Englishmen, Sir John Coghill and a Mr. Seymour, acquired the bulk of the lands. This transaction cleared Lafayette's debts, but the legal complications were not yet over. Lafayette entered into another agreement with Coghill by which the Englishman would share in the ownership of the remaining tract near New Orleans in return for paying Lafayette eighty-five thousand francs. However, it was so difficult to identify and take possession of the remaining lands because of legal problems and uncertain title that the disputes continued until after Lafayette's death. Perennially struggling with these real estate matters, Lafayette had to abandon his early sanguine hopes about the disposition of his potentially valuable property.[24]

Another letter brought by Gallatin, this one from Thomas Jefferson, carried an apology to Lafayette for a delay in translating into English Destutt de Tracy's work on political economy. Jefferson had at first entrusted the task to a translator whose work was so inadequate that Jefferson himself undertook the translation. He spent "five hours a day on it, for between two and three months." The book would finally appear only in 1818. Jefferson was satisfied with the results, believing that this work and Tracy's commentary on Montesquieu would "render more service to our country than all the writings of all saints & holy fathers of the church have rendered."[25]

Jefferson, like Lafayette, thought France was much better off without Napoleon.

> *Had Bonaparte obtained the victory, his talents, his egoism, and destitution of all moral principle, would have rivetted a military despotism on your necks. In your present situation, however afflicting and humiliating I think it certain you will effect a constitution in which the will of the nation shall have an organised controul over the actions of it's government, and it's citizens a regular protection against it's oppressions.[26]*

It pleased Lafayette that his friend approved of the stand he had taken because not everybody did. Should Napoleon have been forced to abdicate? Would the country have been better off with him in power? These questions agitated people at the time and continued to cause debate.[27] William H. Crawford, for example, reflected glumly on France's situation in a letter to Lafayette. "I believe things cannot grow worse, & I fear there is no reason, to expect they will become better." "Even after the Battle of Waterloo," he asserted, "the independence of the country was indissolubly connected with the fate of Buonaparte." He would have been preferable to the traitor Fouché and might have led a nationalist rising, which would have had an effect "upon the ultimate issue of . . . the war." Lafayette obviously believed that things would have been worse with Napoleon and quoted Jefferson's assessment in response (though without identifying the author). Lafayette confessed that patriotism made him wish ardently for a French victory at Waterloo, whatever the political consequences.

The real disaster had been Napoleon's return from Elba: "Matters were, of themselves, coming round to a better order." The expected elections would have forced the government to compromise or to face patriotic revolts once the Allies had dispersed. Napoleon, Lafayette countered, could not have been the leader of a genuinely popular rising and furthermore was the leader most likely to cause the allied powers to reunite in opposition to France.[28]

Despite his disappointments, Lafayette told Jefferson he was generally hopeful. "The true doctrines Have Made Great progress. there are Axioms at which we Have Seen You and I, Not thirty Years Ago philosophers and patriots Stare, and which are Now Common place Sayings."[29] The two old revolutionaries were still waiting for the fulfillment of their dreams, consoled by the faith that their political doctrines would prevail as progress and enlightenment gained ground.

In the meantime, Lafayette stayed resolutely away from Paris and the reactionary regime. He welcomed visitors to La Grange, though, and in the summer of 1816 these included two who would become friends and significant disseminators of his political image. Lady Sydney Morgan, the Irish nationalist novelist, and her husband were touring France. She persuaded one of the prominent society people she met in Paris, the princesse de Beauvau, a distant relative of Lafayette's, to secure an invitation to La Grange to see the man "who has been for so long an object of respect and admiration for all those who love virtue and esteem talent." Meeting him "was among *the aims* of our desires and of our trip."[30]

Alexander von Humboldt warned Lafayette that Lady Morgan's visit was not entirely disinterested, that she was writing a book.[31] The resulting work introduced the English to the new society in France, now open to them after the isolation of the war years. Lady Morgan's vivacity and enjoyment shone through as she described in detail whom she met and what she saw, all of her comments informed by her contempt for *ancien régime* pretensions, her dislike of the Catholic revival, and her sympathy for the liberal cause. She approached La Grange "with the same pleasure, as the pilgrim begins his first unwearied steps to the shrine of sainted excellence." Lafayette appeared more youthful than she had expected. "On the person of La Fayette, time has left no impression; not a wrinkle furrows the ample brow; and his un-bent, and noble figure, is still as upright, bold, and vigorous, as the mind that informs it." He regaled them with anecdotes of Napoleon and displayed the improvements he had made on the farm, "his sheep-folds, his cow-stalls, his dairies, (of which he was justly proud, and occasionally asking me, whether it was not something in the English style)."[32] Lady Morgan was impressed as well by the devotion of the peasants to their master and by the entertainments provided by the young people of La Grange for the servants and the peasants of the neighborhood. She assured her English readers that Lafayette was well acquainted with English literature, which he pursued along with other studies in his well-stocked library.

Lady Morgan's book (entitled simply, *France*) appeared in both French and English in 1817. By that time her enthusiastic praise of Lafayette could exert an influence on politics because the French political climate had changed considerably since her visit in the summer of 1816. The government headed by the duc de Richelieu had been trying to chart a moderate course, to satisfy returning royalists without antagonizing those groups who had benefited from the revolutionary and Napoleonic eras. The foreign powers, especially Russia and its influential ambassador in Paris, Pozzo di Borgo, thought such moderation was essential if Louis XVIII's reign was to endure. However, their efforts were being frustrated by the reactionary *Chambre Introuvable*, which dur-ing the 1815–1816 session had prevented passage of the govern-ment's electoral bill by proposing amendments designed to keep themselves in office. These amendments would also have altered portions of the Charter, and these threats to the inviolability of the Charter caused nervousness in some quarters, especially among owners of national lands purchased during the Revolu-tion. Signs of unrest in the country, symbolized by the Didier conspiracy, which broke out in Grenoble shortly after the end of the parliamentary session, convinced Richelieu to dissolve the Chamber and call new elections. The ordinance to that effect, issued on 5 September 1816, was presented as a return to strict adherence to the Charter. Its appearance immediately altered the activities of the *indépendants*.

Lafayette had not foreseen this change. As late as 3 Septem-ber 1816, he was predicting that the extreme royalists (called ultra-royalists or ultras) would destroy the ministerial party, just as the Jacobins had destroyed the Girondins in the Revolution. Instead, the Richelieu government had acted to cripple the far right. When the ordinance of 5 September was published, Lafayette welcomed it as a step in the right direction, but he feared that the government, by not going far enough to provide for "a system of patriotic elections," would still be defeated by the ultras.[33]

The new state of affairs prompted him nonetheless to seek out old political allies, like Guillaume-Louis Ternaux, an industrialist and politician who, unlike most of Lafayette's political associates, had accompanied Louis XVIII to Ghent during the Hundred Days.[34] In September 1816, Lafayette praised Ternaux's proposal to revive the National Guard by recruiting Napoleonic soldiers who had been retired at half pay. The National Guard was a subject dear to Lafayette's heart, and he advised Ternaux that, in order to maintain proper constitutional guarantees, the head of the guard should be a minister answerable to the Chamber. If such an institution had existed the year before, Lafayette believed, Napoleon could not have returned to power. He was, naturally, already thinking of the coming elections and praised Ternaux's willingness to run. The Chamber needed courageous men, Lafayette wrote. "Feeble and colorless men who form what is called the belly [le ventre] of assemblies have always ended by strengthening the violent party: they will submit to the white Jacobins just as before they submitted to the red Jacobins."[35]

Lafayette tried to consult Lanjuinais, too, but could not see him because Lanjuinais was planning a trip to Paris. In his letter postponing the meeting, Lanjuinais said that Lafayette's chances for election in Seine-et-Marne were not good. "You are apparently not considered a sufficiently *moderate* Charter constitutionalist." Indeed, Lanjuinais expressed scant hope for *indépendant* success in any department because the government held so much power to mold the electoral colleges and to muzzle the press.[36]

Lafayette sent similarly gloomy news to d'Argenson, though he hoped his friend would have better luck. He predicted the election of a few more deputies "of our shade of opinion"—Etienne-Louis-Hector Joly in Franche Comté, Jean-François-Marie Delaitre, Ternaux, and Lafayette's brother-in-law, Théodule de Grammont—than in the last Chamber, but he felt certain that the majority would still be composed of those favoring the views of

Royer-Collard and of the comte de Villèle. Pierre-Paul Royer-Collard, the most prominent member of the small *doctrinaire* group, was a moderate royalist, supporting representative institutions but willing to see more royal power than Lafayette favored. Joseph de Villèle, on the other hand, advocated old-fashioned royal authority and seemed uncomfortable with the institutions established by the Charter. Those who shared his views (the ultra-royalists or ultras) were often described as more royalist than the king.[37]

Under the voting system devised for the election of 1816, each arrondissement electoral college nominated candidates, but the final selection was left to the departmental college. Lafayette was not nominated in any Seine-et-Marne arrondissement. Nevertheless, on 4 October he traveled to Melun to vote in the departmental electoral college.[38] The three deputies selected were staunch ministerial supporters and thus typical of the winners in a majority of the elections. The government had defeated the bothersome ultras, who retained only about ninety seats. The group on the far left (ten or so out of 238 deputies) included Lafayette's friends Voyer d'Argenson and Grammont.[39] As soon as the new session began, Voyer d'Argenson repeated his condemnation of persecutions of Protestants and called for measures to halt the depreciation of *biens nationaux*.[40] Lafayette sent the printed speech to friends throughout Seine-et-Marne.[41]

Prospects for the liberals now seemed a little brighter. Mme de Staël returned to Paris and reopened her salon. Benjamin Constant came back from his self-imposed exile in England. But Lafayette still hesitated to end his rural retirement to visit his old friends. A trip to Paris might give the impression that he wanted to be involved in the affairs of the Chamber, "to which no election has carried me." His visit might cause "some inconvenience for Mme de Staël, given the degree of hatred" that the royalists felt toward him.[42]

By the end of November, Lafayette's scruples about going to Paris had been overcome. He had business to attend to there, involving in part an inheritance owed to him by the comte de Suffren.[43] There were political considerations, too, especially after the new electoral bill, sent to the Chambers on 28 November, made a more open and stable political system seem likely.

On his trip to Paris in December 1816, Lafayette tried to arrange a meeting for his political friends at the home of the

Parisian deputy Jacques Laffitte. Laffitte, more famous at this time as a banker than as a politician, would soon lend his name to the group of deputies of the far left who met at his home, the *réunion Laffitte*. A more moderate group on the left would be known as the *réunion Ternaux*. These affiliations were not yet formed, but in December 1816, Lafayette was already working to bring the deputies who shared his point of view together. The meeting was to include Voyer d'Argenson, other deputies whom d'Argenson recommended (Jacques-Charles Dupont de l'Eure, Charles Beslay from Côtes-du-Nord, Alexandre Martin de Gray, and Louis-Joseph- Hyacinthe Ponsard from Morbihan), as well as Lafayette, his son George, and Jacques-Antoine Manuel. Laffitte had promised that they would spend the entire evening in deep conversation. For some reason, the meeting never took place, but the outlines of a political opposition preparing to promote candidates and cooperate in the Chamber could already be discerned.[44]

Lafayette's friends naturally favored the electoral bill, and the docile Chamber passed the government's bill with ease. Since dissolution of the *Chambre Introuvable* had been justified on the grounds of returning to a strict interpretation of the Charter, the basic guidelines for election set out there had to be observed: electors must be thirty years old and pay three hundred francs a year in direct taxes; deputies must be forty years old and pay one thousand francs in direct taxes. Yearly elections would choose one-fifth of the deputies, each serving a five-year term.

The bill provided a surprise in another respect. Previously, elections had occurred in stages, with a primary assembly choosing the members of a second assembly, which actually did the electing. The authors of the Charter had assumed that elections would occur in stages and that their eligibility requirements would apply only to the small number chosen to the electoral college, which actually did the electing. But since the Charter had not stipulated the details of the electoral system, the government now presented a genuinely ground-breaking proposal: direct election. The electoral college, instead of being a small group chosen from among those who met the minimum requirements, would now consist of *all* men in the department who met the qualifications. The meetings would be held at the *chef-lieu* (local seat of government) of each department or at another town designated by the authorities. The government hoped that the location of the meeting and the influence of the president of the college, a government appointee, would ensure election of their supporters and undermine the ultras' success. The government designed the electoral system to defeat the ultras and apparently did not fear a revival of serious revolutionary or Napoleonic sentiment in the small and prosperous electorate.

The principle of direct election was welcomed by Lafayette's friends in the Chambers, though Lafayette thought that the electorate should be larger than the one hundred thousand qualified to vote under the law. He hoped that lower tax qualifications, greater numbers of deputies, and more locations for voting "would one day generalize much more this right of representation."[45] Liberals are often depicted as advocates of a limited electorate. In Lafayette's case, this view is inaccurate. The need to defend the inviolability of the Charter made the liberals of the Restoration defend equally staunchly the electoral provisions in it, but Lafayette's private correspondence shows his personal desire to extend the suffrage.[46]

The liberals supported the government's electoral bill, but on the issue of personal liberty they consciously sought to carve out a position separate from that of the government. Lafayette was pleased that Voyer d'Argenson planned to speak in the debate on the law to renew the government's powers of arbitrary arrest and imprisonment. He did not want the ultras to monopolize this issue. The ultras, Lafayette told one correspondent, "have adopted the tactic of showing themselves in several respects more liberal than [the] Government."[47]

When d'Argenson requested some ideas for a speech on the subject, Lafayette proposed arguing against the law on the grounds that it originated in Napoleonic oppression. If the law must be retained, Lafayette thought, it should at least include provisions to limit imprisonment to three months, to inform the detainee of the charges against him, and to give him the right to counsel. In truth, he thought such a law completely unnecessary. The example of English law permitting similar arrests (cited by supporters of the bill) was misleading because in that country freedom of the press served as an effective counterweight. Lafayette used the example of the United States. Only once, he related, had such a law been proposed in that country, during the presidency of John Adams, but the Senate's proposal was rejected by the House of

Representatives and "public tranquillity" returned.[48] Here Lafayette's pro-American views had misled him into believing that the infamous Alien and Sedition Acts were never passed or enforced.

Lafayette felt certain that the ultras' concern for liberty was an insincere "tactic of circumstance." Nonetheless, their presenting these ideas as "axioms that no one contests any longer" was certainly helpful. The ministers, on the other hand, still saw danger to the crown from personal and press freedom, but they had at least allowed the right to vote to "the hundred thousand citizens" who qualified under the Charter and had "moderated the counterrevolutionary movement and the measures of reaction. Some independent deputies, some peers vote with one or the other party according to whether they approach our opinions."[49] Lafayette here expressed the quintessential position of an *indépendant* politician. Tied to no particular regime, he supported whichever side seemed to be promoting his principles. Neither ministerial nor ultra-royalist, neither Napoleonic nor Jacobin, the *indépendant* boasted that his devotion was to the nation.[50]

Although Lafayette and his friends were politicians, it is important to realize that they were not politicians in the modern sense. Their first moves toward political organization were quite hesitant, even after the passage of the electoral law of 1817. Active and open political debate had not existed in France for about twenty years. The very notion of a "party" conjured up images of the parties of the Revolution, which no one wanted to emulate or revive. Hatred of political parties was one of the assumptions of the age, reflected in the arguments over the electoral bill of 1817. For example, François Guizot, who helped to draft the bill, hoped its effect would be to dissolve all party distinctions and bring all to unite behind the king.[51] A party was assumed to be a group disloyal to the sovereign.[52]

Similarly hostile attitudes toward political parties were still much in evidence even in the United States, where, twenty years before, Lafayette's mentor, George Washington, had warned against the baneful effects of parties in his farewell address. Lafayette's American correspondents continued to assume that parties were selfish, narrow, and inimical to the good of the whole.[53] It is not surprising, then, to find that political organization and interest were at a low level in France, where the frequent changes of regime made any opposition seem not only selfish but disloyal. Lafayette, though greatly influenced by his American experience, developed a more tolerant attitude toward political groups than did many Americans. When Czar Alexander had castigated the United States for instability because of the agitations of political parties, Lafayette had answered that parties were necessary in a commonwealth.[54]

To Lafayette, public opinion expressed within a constitutional framework was the essential legitimizing force in a nation. For public opinion to be expressed, there had to be guarantees of liberty for citizens. He had no illusion that disagreements would disappear when opinion was allowed free rein. But he had faith that public opinion, if given opportunity for expression, would come around to his point of view eventually. He was sure that the kind of nation he wanted was what most citizens, once enlightened and free to choose, would also wish. The contrast between the American and the French Revolutions taught him the dangers of getting too far ahead of public opinion. Thomas Jefferson reminded Lafayette of this important truth shortly after the fall of Napoleon.

> *A full measure of liberty is not now perhaps to be expected by your nation, nor am I confident they are prepared to preserve it. More than a generation will be requisite, under the administration of reasonable laws favoring the progress of knowledge in the general mass of the people, and their habituation to an independent security of person and property, before they will be capable of estimating the value of freedom. . . . Possibly you may remember at the date of the jeu de paume, how earnestly I urged yourself and the patriots of my acquaintance, to enter then into a compact with the king, securing freedom of religion, freedom of the press, trial by jury, habeas corpus, and a national legislature, all of which it was known he would then yield, to go home, and let these work on the amelioration of the condition of the people, until they should have rendered them capable of more. This was as much as I then thought them able to bear, soberly and usefully to themselves. You thought otherwise, and that the dose might be still larger. And I found you*

were right; for subsequent events proved they were
equal to the Constitution of 1791. Unfortunately, some
of the most honest and enlightened of our patriotic
friends, (but closet politicians merely, unpractised in
the knowledge of man) thought more could still be ob-
tained and borne. . . . You differed from them. You were
for stopping there, and for securing the Constitution
which the National Assembly has obtained. Here, too,
you were right; and from this fatal error of the republi-
cans, from their separation from yourself and the con-
stitutionalists, in their councils, flowed all the
subsequent sufferings and crimes of the French na-
tion.[55]

Lafayette continued to be more optimistic about the French nation than his American friend, but he had learned essentially the
same lessons from the two Revolutions. He knew that he had to
moderate his optimism and give the French people a chance to
learn the importance of proper political institutions and how to
protect them.

This realization, though, did not dictate passivity. On the
contrary, he believed liberal principles needed to be vigorously
promoted and defended against the powerful forces trying to
oppress the people and keep them ignorant. On the international
level, the Holy Alliance had been created to prevent the spread of
revolutionary ideals. The Church also fought against these principles. On the national level, the remnants of the Napoleonic
police, now in the service of the Bourbons, continued their work
of oppression. Royal officials were appointed and therefore not
beholden to public opinion. Local officials should be chosen by
the people, not appointed by central authorities, Lafayette thought.
He and his friends worked tirelessly to build accountability into
the system, as his frequent remarks on a citizen militia demonstrate. And his belief in the importance of public opinion explains
why elections to the Chamber of Deputies were so important to
him: they were the only elections in the country at any level, the
only expression of the will of the people.

He envisioned a time when the ministers of the king would
be responsible to the Chambers and removable by them. Thus, as
deputies of the left were elected, he hoped that they would some-

day be able to shape new governments. A constitutional monarch should reign but not rule directly. This conception was strikingly different from even the moderate royalism of Royer-Collard, who in the debate on the electoral bill argued, "In France the entire government is in the hands of the king. . . . The day when the government will be determined by the majority of the Chamber, the day when it will be established in fact that the Chamber can dismiss the ministers of the king, that day, there will be an end, not only to the Charter, but to our royalty; that day, we will become a republic."[56] If that was a republican sentiment, then Lafayette certainly did not exaggerate when he called himself a republican.

These views did not automatically make Lafayette an enemy of the Bourbons.[57] To the extent that the Bourbons disagreed with these principles, Lafayette opposed the Bourbons, but, as his actions in the Hundred Days show, his objection was not to the dynasty but to their rejection of the principle of popular sovereignty. It was assumed that Louis XVIII would be more likely to accept limitations on his sovereignty than would his brother and heir. After the Second Restoration, Lafayette did not conspire to remove the Bourbons from power, for he was not convinced that the people of France wished them to go or that it would be possible. He hoped that, while working within the institutions provided by the admittedly deficient Charter, changes essential for liberty could be achieved. With liberty would come almost-unlimited benefits to society, Lafayette believed. Prosperity would naturally flow from liberty, but so would much else. He even suggested that the superiority of the speeches made by American statesmen must be due to the perfection of their institutions.[58]

In 1817, on the eve of the first test of the untried political system, Lafayette concentrated on obtaining the freedoms that would make public expression possible. He encouraged his friends in the Chamber who were fighting the law allowing arbitrary arrests. And he promoted education to produce enlightened citizens who could appreciate representative government. Lafayette became an active supporter of a new educational technique called *enseignement mutuel*. Secondary education in France was administered by the centralized system inherited from Napoleon, but primary education was still in the hands of the Catholic teaching orders. Schools were too few and too likely to inculcate the wrong values, according to the liberal opposition; *enseignement mutuel* seemed to offer a practical alternative.

Originating in England (where it was called *monitorial instruction* or the *Lancastrian system*), the technique made the instruction of large numbers of students possible because the students themselves did most of the teaching. A master would train a few students, who would in turn pass on their knowledge to others, who would do the same. Mutual education could thus reach many more students than could the simultaneous system used in the Catholic schools. For economic reasons, the ministries of the early Restoration also championed the technique. But the primary motive of the left was obviously political: to put education into the hands of lay teachers rather than the conservative Catholic teaching orders. The Church fought back, but without much success at first, since *enseignement mutuel*, had the backing of the government and an organized pressure group: the *Société pour l'encouragement de l'instruction élémentaire*.[59] An 1817 ordinance requiring religious instruction in the schools failed to calm Catholics' fears about the irreligious tendencies of the schools and their sponsors. Liberals, in their turn, accused the Church of fighting these *écoles mutuelles* because they wished to keep people in ignorance.

Lafayette helped to found an *école mutuelle* in Courpalay, a town near La Grange, and provided financial support for it. In March 1817, seventy students were receiving free education there. *Enseignement mutuel* was especially strong in the department of Seine-et-Marne, thanks mostly to the prefect, Comte de Germain. Despite opposition from priests, Germain could report in 1819 that three thousand students were following this educational method in twenty-four communes of Seine-et-Marne.[60] The Lafayette family also promoted *enseignement mutuel* in the department of Haute-Loire, site of the ancestral château. George Washington Lafayette sponsored a school in Brioude and also contributed to one for the *chef-lieu*, Le Puy.[61]

Even more essential for spreading the liberal message was a free press. The agitation in favor of press freedom and the trials of journalists and writers who ran afoul of the censorship laws became important political issues during the Restoration. Journalists also served as catalysts for organizing networks of like-minded political sympathizers, especially important in an era that frowned on political parties and thought campaigning for office unseemly. Lafayette certainly recognized the value of the press; and during 1817, as his interest in active politics grew, he renewed contact with, or met for the first time, several writers who worked for the success of the left.

One of these was Marc-Antoine Jullien, who, though more radical than Lafayette during the French Revolution, had by the Restoration come to hold similar views on many issues.[62] Jullien had been associated with Lanjuinais on the newspaper the *Indépendant* during the Hundred Days. When government censorship forced it to cease publication, this important organ of liberal opinion reemerged as the *Constitutionnel*, a name it retained until the middle of 1817, when it ran into trouble with the government again. Shortly after the passage of the electoral law in February 1817, Jullien wrote the *Manuel électoral à l'usage de MM. les electeurs des départements de la France* to acquaint voters with the new electoral system, to persuade them that political activity was respectable, and to argue that candidates on the left who had supported now-discredited regimes could be trusted. Labels, he warned, could be misleading. Someone accused of republicanism who was honest, who had supported the republic when it existed and still favored liberty by defending the constitutional throne, was a republican in the same mold as Michel de L'Hospital, the duc de Sully, and Henry IV, "that is to say, *friend of the public good*, of the '*patrie*,' which forms henceforth with the *monarchy* an indivisible whole." Lafayette hoped that Jullien would publish a revised edition before the elections in the fall. To this end, he lent the author a book on the history of the boroughs of Great Britain and introduced him to Albert Gallatin, who could supply information about American voting practices.[63]

Lafayette was intimately involved at the same time with another liberal publication and its writers. The *Censeur européen*, edited by Charles Comte and Charles Dunoyer, began publication in the spring of 1817, and from the very beginning it was in Lafayette's camp. The contributors were friends and associates of Lafayette and Voyer d'Argenson, and the articles usually reflected their views. The first volume contained articles by Comte, Dunoyer, and Arnold Scheffer, as well as book reviews of a work on armies and militias and of Jean-Baptiste Say's *Traité d'économie politique*. Their report of the debate on the law on individual freedom quoted generously from speeches by Broglie and d'Argenson, which, according to the author, best treated the issues involved.[64] The second volume, which appeared in April 1817, contained a review by Augustin Thierry of Jullien's *Manuel électoral*. Citing the constitutions of the various states of the United States that excluded government functionaries from elective office, Thierry advocated the same restrictions for France: "We will be a representative nation only when we have as representatives men practicing an independent industry, and offering at the same time moral guarantees of their steadfastness in that industry, and their intention of seeking their fortunes only through it."[65] As an example of the kind of person to be elected, he pointed to Lafayette, whose disinterested independence and virtuous life he then praised for six pages. Lafayette's name headed the list of "industrious men" who merited election.

Lafayette and Voyer d'Argenson must have sponsored the publication.[66] The political theory advanced by Comte and Dunoyer was one Lafayette would certainly have endorsed. The economic ideas of Jean-Baptiste Say were featured prominently. Say, a longtime friend of Lafayette's, had learned English during a commercial apprenticeship in Great Britain and was converted to laissez-faire principles by reading Adam Smith. The first edition of *Traité d'économie politique* appeared in 1803. Although a member of the Tribunate, Say opposed Napoleonic economic policies and refused the emperor's offer to name him director of *droits réunis*. At the end of the wars, Say revisited England, where he met David Ricardo and Jeremy Bentham.[67]

Say's ideas, and therefore those of Comte and Dunoyer, were strongly influenced by the notion of utility. Society ought to promote useful endeavors and not waste its resources on useless extravagances or destructive warfare. Because of his understanding of the way in which products acquire their value, Say fought mercantilist assumptions that one nation or one individual could get rich only at the expense of another. As a person prospered in useful enterprises, he could provide markets and opportunities to others who would prosper in their turn. His arguments were decidedly antiaristocratic. Luxuries did not promote general prosperity, investments did. Spending, he argued, was good if it was reproductive rather than unproductive. An aristocrat who spent money on retainers was spending unproductively. A farmer who gave his wealth to workers who improved the farm and increased his wealth was an example of reproductive spending. Good consumption satisfied genuine needs. A nation was on the right path if its citizens enjoyed objects that were "convenient rather than splendid, a lot of linen and not much lace; . . . good clothes and no embroidery. In such a nation public institutions will have scant splendor and a lot of utility."[68]

Say's vision resembled what Americans called *republican simplicity.* Indeed, the United States provided the example frequently cited in the *Censeur européen* of a successful society that promoted useful endeavor, enjoyed freedom, and survived with minimal government. Idleness and idle classes (aristocrats and priests) constituted the real enemies to progress, and the *Censeur* promoted their opposites as virtues: industry and productive workers. The editors had an almost-Jeffersonian suspicion of large, wasteful government expenditures and a fear of intrusive government power.

Lafayette sympathized with these political and social principles, extensions of the notions of progress and liberty that he had advocated ever since his involvement in the American Revolution. In his day, Lafayette came to stand for these virtues. Admirers frequently praised the simplicity of his manners. He was a man of liberty and order, the two virtues inextricably linked in this vision of society. Calling the aristocratic Lafayette a man of simple tastes sounds odd to modern ears. What commentators apparently meant by that term was that Lafayette had forsaken the idle pretensions of his class for the solid achievements of agriculture and the self-sufficient habits of the independent yeoman. Thierry praised Lafayette for not grasping after power and position during the Napoleonic era. Instead, Lafayette remained a citizen. "Faithful to the habits of liberty, he cultivated his fields like Washington, and practiced in silence the genuine civic virtues, simplicity and industry."[69]

As its name indicated, the *Censeur européen* was cosmopolitan and favored dropping the barriers to trade within Europe. Lafayette's views, too, were decidedly cosmopolitan. He never forgot that progress should be promoted beyond the borders of France, and he had confidence that similar institutions would be applicable to all Western cultures. Lafayette and the authors of the *Censeur* were in the tradition of the eighteenth century. They were inspired more by political economy than by literature. Utility appealed to them more than the arts and beauty. They had a fundamental, almost-visceral hatred of aristocratic pretensions and hoped to promote by their new ideas the welfare of all parts of society. They believed that self-interest, rightly understood, not narrow greed, would result in progress, democracy, freedom, and happiness. Though Lafayette attended plays and read the latest novels, his interest in the arts was purposefully utilitarian. In our postromantic age, his attitude seems shallow and unfeeling. To his admirers in his own time, Lafayette's no-nonsense approach to social issues seemed forward-looking and liberating. In our post-Marxist age, Lafayette's interest in political economy of the Smith, Say, and Bentham varieties seems narrowly bourgeois. In his age, the ideas seemed to be rigorously scientific and to be the source for spreading prosperity and harmony through all classes of society and all nations of the world. They were more an attack on aristocratic luxury than a defense of bourgeois wealth. Say emphasized the interconnectedness of all members of society. Thierry echoed the idea of connectedness, this time on the national level, in his 1817 work, *Des nations et de leurs rapports mutuels*. From 1817 on, the contributors to the *Censeur* would be close friends of Lafayette's.[70]

One of the young journalists who cooperated with Lafayette was Augustin Thierry, who would become a famous historian. Thierry's work first appeared in the *Censeur*'s second volume. He had collaborated previously with Henri de Saint-Simon, who developed a political philosophy similar to that of Comte and Dunoyer at about the same time. The reasons for Thierry's leaving Saint-Simon and joining the *Censeur* have been debated by historians.[71] The ties between the journal and prominent political leaders must have weighed heavily in his decision. Comte and Dunoyer would make it possible for him to associate with the politicians and writers he admired and not merely write about them. In June Thierry went for his first visit to La Grange. Years later, he would recall Lafayette as "the man whom I loved so much and whose character I admired so much. It is at La Grange that I received my education in civic morality and until my last breath, I will be faithful to the principles of that great and noble school which will not perish."[72]

Thierry was probably still at La Grange when the government stopped the sale of the third volume of the *Censeur euro-*

péen and arrested Comte and Dunoyer for inciting disobedience to the king by printing the notorious *Manuscrit venu de Sainte-Hélène*, supposed to be the memoirs of Napoleon. The motive of the editors was surely not to promote the fortunes of Napoleon, for Comte and Dunoyer had consistently opposed him, even during the Hundred Days. Indeed their article was a strident condemnation of the emperor for destroying the gains of the Revolution and for acting consistently against the best interests of the French nation and in favor of his own selfish aggrandizement. But this very condemnation could be read as a strong defense of the heritage of the Revolution and of the rights of the French nation. While accusing Bonaparte of tyranny, the editors passed over without comment the harsh criticism of the Bourbons contained in the manuscript. Under the laws of the Restoration, printing such a work was almost certainly illegal, whatever their motives.[73]

Lafayette went immediately to Paris to join others in trying to gain the release of the editors, but to no avail. With Comte and Dunoyer away at their well-publicized trial, which (with appeals) lasted six months, much of the responsibility for their newspaper fell into the hands of Augustin Thierry. Lafayette's influence on Thierry became apparent in the next volume of the newspaper, in which Thierry reviewed the recently published correspondence of Benjamin Franklin, a book lent to him by Lafayette.[74] Later Thierry praised the productive quality of American life in a review of Destutt de Tracy's commentary on Montesquieu.[75]

American productivity and abundance must have seemed especially enviable in France in the summer of 1817. Unusually wet and cold weather had caused the failure of the 1816 harvest, and famine was sweeping Europe. Once the meager supplies of the winter had been exhausted, scarcities led to grain riots and widespread begging. At La Grange on one June day, 860 pieces of bread were distributed, but still more beggars appeared. Soup kitchens were set up in the nearby village of Rozay. Relief was slow in coming because bad weather also delayed the harvest in 1817.[76] After a brief visit with Ternaux at Saint-Ouen and a stop in Paris for the Fourth of July dinner in celebration of American independence (an occasion he rarely missed), Lafayette set out for the Auvergne. The rest of his family had already gathered at the château at Chavaniac, and their departure from La Grange helped to ease the demands on the scarce resources. The famine was less serious in Auvergne.[77]

Mme de Staël's declining health also troubled Lafayette. While in Paris in June, he had inadvertently distressed Albertine, now the duchesse de Broglie, by his inquiries about her mother, who was too ill to come down to dinner.[78] Lafayette left Paris with regret, worrying that her condition was getting worse. He had seen little of her for fear of tiring or annoying her. "She knew I was there, and twice had me called." Two days after he wrote these words to d'Argenson, Mme de Staël died.[79]

His friendship with her had lasted a long time. It dated, Lafayette recalled, "almost from my childhood, for on my first return from America, welcomed with great goodness into her father's house, I found in this astonishing young person, the most amiable kindness. From that time on and in all the vicissitudes of my life I have received from her only the most flattering, the most constant, the most generous marks of friendship." His affection for her had never weakened, "neither by absence nor even in the midst of the whirlwind which surrounded her; her true friends were always sure to find her again, and her loss is for me a great calamity." Lafayette worried about Albertine's health and wanted to be with her and the rest of her family as soon as possible. He suggested that they all visit La Grange after the elections in mid-September, or perhaps it could serve as a refuge for "poor Rocca," the young man whom Mme de Staël had married the year before and who was himself also quite ill.[80] Albertine, who had gone to Coppet for her mother's burial, accepted Lafayette's kind invitation, but she decided to go right away.

Leaving his family behind at Chavaniac, Lafayette departed on the five-day return trip to La Grange, arriving on 17 August. He made a quick, two-day visit to Paris but was soon back at La Grange to greet the duchesse de Broglie and to console her. Some of her mother's friends did not approve of Albertine's decision to seek asylum at La Grange. Prosper de Barante, for example, complained about her "joining that society, that party." He predicted that such associations would cause talk and that the spitefulness of "the Paris salons . . . will embitter her, and eventually all of that will ruin her life."[81] Lafayette's society was obviously considered too radical for most of those in fashionable social circles. On the second of September, Albertine's husband

and her brother Auguste joined her at La Grange, bringing with them from Paris the young American George Ticknor, who stopped briefly on his way to Italy.[82] Two other members of Mme de Staël's entourage completed the group: August Wilhelm Schlegel and Fanny Randall.[83]

Lafayette's personal problems and extensive travel during the summer of 1817 left him little time to prepare for the elections under the new law, which were held on 20 September. When he left Paris in July, rumor had it that elections would be held on 1 September, and he intended to be back in the Paris area before that date. But a return so near the time of the elections would not allow for organizing an electoral committee or for choosing candidates. Lafayette had been making frequent trips to Paris ever since the passage of the electoral law in February 1817, and he undoubtedly met with political colleagues and sympathetic journalists.[84] His attempt in December 1816 to organize a meeting at Laffitte's home was certainly not the last. But organization had still not progressed very far. The traditional picture of Lafayette participating in an increasingly active electoral committee during the summer of 1817 must be dismissed as fanciful.[85]

He certainly cooperated with his friends in urging liberals to run for office, and he kept in touch with political associates; but politics in this era did not require the kind of rigidly established party committee that the authors of some accounts seem to expect. With a small electorate of wealthy individuals, political ties could be maintained through the normal course of social life. Thus, Lafayette's trip to Auvergne was primarily a family event, but it had political overtones as well. As he passed through the department of Puy-de-Dôme, he took time to meet with political acquaintances.[86] At Chavaniac the Lafayette family received visitors every day, including the artist Horace Vernet and a former senator and former member of the Chamber of Peers, Louis-Gustave Doulcet de Pontécoulant. Lafayette made plans to see an old friend named Jean Girot-Pouzol while in Auvergne and saw a great deal of Antoine Bonne Chevant, a political leader from the nearby town of Brioude with whom George maintained a detailed and friendly correspondence.[87] Lafayette was pleased that his son was well liked in the area and obviously hoped that George would represent the Haute-Loire in future assemblies. All prominent politicians maintained ties with local leaders in the regions with which they were most closely identified. But the connections were still rather intimate and personal. They communicated in their own names, not in behalf of an impersonal political committee.

The lack of clear direction in the liberal cause is evident in the Paris election, the focus of most of the attention. Lafayette was only one of many men who coveted one of the eight seats Paris had to fill. The lack of a residency requirement for election allowed him and many others to aspire to it. The only restriction was that half of the delegation for a department reside in that department. The government was determined to secure the reelection of Etienne Pasquier, the president of the Chamber of Deputies, and was willing to compromise with some liberals, if necessary, to achieve that end. The ministry decided to negotiate with the popular Jacques Laffitte, whom Pozzo di Borgo (a close friend of the prime minister's) described as "a vain man, unruly and surrounded by what is most suspicious in Paris, but whom it would be difficult to exlude, even if the court and the government exerted themselves to try."[88] They offered him the vice presidency of one of the Paris electoral college's twenty sections if he would drop his support for Benjamin Constant, Lafayette, and Jacques-Antoine Manuel. He refused. The government next tried to negotiate with Benjamin Delessert, the rich industrialist and candidate of the center left. But, Richelieu told Minister of Police Elie Decazes, he too had refused to support Pasquier.

> *If he is not elected it will be the greatest misfortune that could happen to France, and to us, for it will result in demonstrating that our influence is nonexistent, that all idea of stability will vanish, it will be even worse if Manuel and La Fayette are chosen, all our dreams of liberation, of evacuation of the foreigners will go up in smoke. We must not neglect anything, then, to try to prevent all of these evils, especially since rightly or wrongly we will get the blame, since it will be the first test of our election law which we went to so much trouble to have passed. So put all your know-how into it, sirs, and try to preserve us from this misfortune.*[89]

The government's efforts paid off. On the first round liberal candidates held the top four places, though only Laffitte received the requisite majority to be elected. Pasquier came in a dismal ninth, not far ahead of Lafayette. But on the following rounds, as minor candidates were dropped, the government's position improved. With seven men to elect on the second round, Delessert (center left) and Antoine Roy (ministerial) won election. In the third round (called *ballottage*), voting was limited to the top ten candidates to fill the remaining five seats. Lafayette came in last, with only 2,673 votes. The government had managed to bring Pasquier to victory and with him four other government supporters. The *indépendant* group had won only three seats: Laffitte, Delessert, and Casimir Périer.[90]

Lafayette was furious at the government's maneuvers to "deflect this manifestation of attachment to the principles of 89." Ultras and ministerials had united to prevent his election, he charged. They had maintained that the king's health would suffer if Lafayette were elected. Newspapers were forced to publish articles attacking the *indépendant* candidates. "All government departments were busy, all the police were in movement, all the commissioners, all the *gendarmes* were rushing through the city and the villages night and day." Even the diplomats joined in this effort.

> *They said, without doubt to make me unpopular, that I was the tricolor flag itself. But they added that my nomination would cause the failure of the negotiations for the removal of foreign troops, and they dared say that if the liberal electors succeeded the allied army would march on Paris, and these exaggerated remarks, so flattering to me, were being repeated not only in the salons and the cafés but even out loud in the electoral meetings.*[91]

Lafayette was proud of the support he had received despite the extraordinary efforts of the government and despite the fact that "even in the front ranks of our like-minded colleagues there were persons who thought it necessary to give in to circumstances. All of that only bestows greater merit on the constantly increasing minority by which I was honored." He was sorry to lose, believing he could have been "useful in that Chamber."[92]

Ultras and ministerials had indeed combined against Lafayette. Pozzo di Borgo reported that "the danger of seeing M. de

Lafayette and his collaborators, more clever and more depraved than he, presented to the Chamber of Deputies, where they would have sat for five years, struck Monsieur and his courtiers. . . . During the battle, everybody spoke of harmony, it is now the theme of the day."[93] Monsieur (the king's brother) as leader of the ultras had joined more moderate royalists in preventing disaster in Paris.

Despite Lafayette's personal disappointment, *indépendants* had done well throughout the country, gaining about twelve seats to give them some twenty-five deputies. He was heartened by this demonstration of improved public opinion. The example of Paris would have a salutary effect on the following year's elections in the provinces, he thought, where the results would be still better if the voting qualifications were lowered to two hundred francs.[94] The royalists controlled the Chamber, but it was not at all certain that their shaky coalition could continue to defeat the liberals.

3

Politics at Home

Despite his loss, Lafayette returned to La Grange optimistic after the Paris election of 1817. He wrote to Thomas Jefferson that things were "not so desperate as one Might Mourn them." In spite of the "Bed of lies" created by the Holy Alliance, the principles of government based on national self-determination were making headway in Europe. "France, vainquished, fettered, and watched as it is, does still Hold the Intellectual and patriotic lead." The country might be suffering under foreign domination, but most of the population were sound.

> The whole peasantry of the Nation, the inferior classes
> of the towns, excepting a few departments, are Unani-
> mous in their attachment to the Revolution, in their
> Hatred of foreign influence . . . But the excesses of the
> Revolution Have Been so abominable that altho the
> Energies of the people are not inferior to those of 1789,
> and their Sense of Their Rights much more distinct, the
> existing abuses and designs of privileged tribes find a
> great auxiliary in the general fear of an other Revolu-
> tionary tempest.

Despite being "an Immense Majority" in the nation, people with his views were poorly represented as yet in the Chambers. Still, there were enough to "put Questions, Reveal facts, and publish truths."

Deputies enjoyed the valuable privilege of being able to express their opinions with impunity and have their remarks reported in the press. Others were less fortunate. Journalists resorted to publishing in irregular installments or in pamphlets to escape the censorship of periodicals. But they could still be arrested for opinions expressed in their publications. "Some [pamphlets] are seized; authors are fined or Emprisoned. friends Rise Up in their Support. . . . So are we obliged to work Again to Rebuild what, Had it Not Been for the Jacobiners, Bonaparte, the foreign powers, and the Nobles and princes of this land, would Have Been Honestly and firmly Established five and twenty Years ago. But, this time, it is not only a french, it Has Become an European Business."[1] Liberal journalists willingly courted prosecution. Lafayette told Lady Morgan that "patriotism . . . compels them to risk frequent punishment and many truths are spread every day in the capital and in the departments, despite the precautions taken to prevent this type of communication."[2]

Lafayette encouraged journalists who promoted his point of view and gave them access to his extensive library. Arnold Scheffer was one of the writers who worked closely with Lafayette. Born in Holland in 1796 while it was part of France, Scheffer and his brothers (the artists Ary and Henry) chose French citizenship when the territory was divided again. Like his friend Augustin Thierry, Arnold wrote for the *Censeur européen*. By 1817 the young writer's antigovernment pamphlets had already brought criticism from François Guizot.[3] When Scheffer published *De l'état de la liberté en France* in December 1817, the reaction was more serious. The authorities seized the pamphlet and arrested the author.

Lafayette was delighted with the pamphlet, which, he told d'Argenson, was the first to deal with the delicate questions of the Revolution. Naturally, the government found irritating "a work which spares neither Bonapartism, nor the 10th of August, nor the 18th of Fructidor, nor Coblentz, nor foreigners, nor reactions, nor the civil list."[4] Lafayette sent warm praise to the author: "It breathes that patriotic purity which spares no violation of liberty, and which forgives no pretension of power."[5]

Lafayette had obviously been the inspiration for the pamphlet, and his was one of the few names mentioned in it. "I was going to add," Lafayette wrote coyly, "that the author deals only with things and not at all with individuals, but gratitude warned me that there is no rule without an exception. It is not only because of pride that I am sorry your book was seized."[6] Scheffer's work described Lafayette as "steadfast in his attachment to constitutional liberty." Furthermore, the first chapter seemed designed to fit the circumstances of Lafayette's own life. Scheffer argued that representation, though essential, could be harmful if it were not "truly national," and could become "the most powerful instrument" of despotism instead of "the guarantee of public liberty." He concluded that in recent French history only two representative bodies had been "constantly independent and faithful to the cause of liberty": the National Assembly of 1789 and the Chamber of Representatives of the Hundred Days. These were the only assemblies in which Lafayette had served. The immediate purpose of Scheffer's pamphlet was revealed in his direct appeal to voters to choose "an *indépendante* majority" in the next Chamber to ensure tranquillity, to raise France's standing in the world, and to revive industry.[7]

Lafayette went to Paris in late December to help the incriminated journalist and returned there in January for his trial. Joseph Mérilhou, who had previously defended Comte and Dunoyer, took on the delicate task of defending not only Scheffer but also liberal leaders whose actions during the Hundred Days were equally under attack in the trial. The government charged Scheffer with inciting disobedience to the king by praising the Chamber of the Hundred Days and its protest of 8 July 1815 against being dissolved. The prosecutor noted that there may have been justifiable motives for serving in this Chamber, but those who protested the orders of the returning monarch were "an illicit, arbitrary, unconstitutional and shadowy gathering, and the writer who makes himself the apologist of this seditious resistance, is himself guilty of sedition."[8] Lafayette wanted the defense attorney to declare in the name of the protesters that they were proud of "this last circumstance of our duties as representatives."[9] Such a response would surely not have helped Scheffer, who was found guilty anyway on 24 January 1818.

While he was awaiting appeal, Scheffer continued to write political articles with the encouragement of Lafayette, who, in a rare moment of political caution, advised the young author to adopt a more "moderate tone," which would suit his "political situation" without damaging his "energy." Scheffer asked Lafayette for information about the "Pilnitz coalition," the agreement between Austria and Prussia threatening intervention in France in 1791. Lafayette, who saw the coalition as a forerunner of the Holy Alliance, recommended histories and memoirs on the subject and invited him to La Grange to read them.[10] Instead, Scheffer was forced to flee to Belgium to escape the sentence of the appeals court. It proved more severe than the original sentence: one year in prison, a fine of five thousand francs, five years of "surveillance," and a surety bond of two thousand francs.[11] D'Argenson lent him money and gave him letters of introduction to people in Belgium.[12]

Lafayette also abetted the pamphleteering of Scheffer's friend Thierry by lending him copies of the *Moniteur* for a work criticizing the press laws. In mid-December, Thierry sent Lafayette what he had written so far. Lafayette praised it but recommended that the young author seek the advice of d'Argenson as well.[13] The finished work, which Thierry wisely published anonymously, appeared in January 1818.[14]

Lafayette, while working closely with the writers of the *Censeur*, had fewer contacts with other liberal writers. For example, he apparently had no prior knowledge of the most famous liberal pamphlet of the year, Benjamin Constant's work on freedom of the press.[15] Indeed, he seems to have had little correspondence with Constant during this period. Though they ran in the same social circles and shared similar political views, Lafayette was not as intimate with Benjamin Constant as he was with Voyer d'Argenson. Their personalities were markedly different, and doubtless the rather earnest and straightforward Lafayette sometimes found the mercurial and tortured Benjamin Constant an uncongenial acquaintance. Constant was brilliant and witty, a literary as well as a political figure. He had prodigious energy, which he often squandered in a turbulent personal life and on gambling. Such immoderate behavior led one of his political associates, Charles Goyet of the Sarthe, to advise Constant to spend more time at home. No one needed to give Lafayette such advice. He loved to be surrounded by his family and to play the role of the congenial host at La Grange.[16] Though only ten years older than Constant, Lafayette seemed to have retained more of the rational contentment of the eighteenth century. Conversely, Constant appeared more in tune with the romantic nineteenth century.

Lafayette was considerably older than Voyer d'Argenson, too, yet their friendship was closer, perhaps because of the similarities of their background. Both sprang from pre-Revolution nobility and had fought as soldiers during the Revolution. Lafayette and d'Argenson, who already enjoyed considerable status in society, devoted themselves single-mindedly to their cause, unconcerned that others often perceived their goals as utopian.[17]

By contrast, Constant was Swiss-born, an intellectual, an outsider. More intelligent than the other two, he was correspondingly dissatisfied with his lot and impatient to make a name for himself. He felt that he had done nothing to guarantee lasting fame, nothing to match his genius. Constant's contribution to the liberal cause was more immediate and more obvious than that of his two friends. In early 1818 he helped to found the *Minerve*, the liberal organ with the greatest impact on electoral politics, and his writing contributed enormously to its success.[18] Neither Lafayette nor Voyer d'Argenson was apparently involved with its founding or publication, perhaps because they already had their own organ, the *Censeur*.

Unlike Constant, Lafayette was sure of lasting fame. From an early age his exploits had been celebrated, and he was a well-known figure throughout the New World as well as the Old. He proudly cultivated his foreign connections. Early in 1818, for example, he attended as usual the annual dinner in Paris celebrating George Washington's birthday, received a visit from the British parliamentary reformer the duke of Bedford, and helped an agent of the government of Buenos Aires gain acquaintance with Albert Gallatin.[19] Throughout the period, too, he watched the progress of republicanism in Haiti.

Haiti had first claimed Lafayette's attention before the Revolution, when he had searched for a means of promoting emancipation in the French colonies. In the 1780s, he bought a plantation in Cayenne and created a model program intended to provide a profitable means of gradually giving slaves their freedom.[20] He promoted the French *Société des amis des noirs*, of which he was an early member, and pushed unsuccessfully for emancipation in the early years of the French Revolution.[21] Though the reactionary climate of the early Restoration was hardly conducive to a revival of an abolitionist organization, especially one based on principles of natural rights, Lafayette resumed his aquaintance with antislavery activists like the abbé Henri-Baptiste Grégoire.[22] He corresponded with British abolitionists and met with Thomas

Clarkson when he came to France in September 1814 to try to enlist Louis XVIII's support to end the slave trade.[23] In 1818 he helped Dunoyer prepare an article on the slave trade for the *Censeur*. Lafayette asked Gallatin for notes on the history of the subject. Dunoyer's article, in addition to describing the slave trade in America, also commented on the development of the *Société des amis des noirs* in France and mentioned that Lafayette's experiment at Cayenne was "the first attempt at gradual emancipation made outside the United States."[24]

Independent Haiti had become divided into a republic in the south led by Alexandre Pétion and a monarchy in the north under King Henri Christophe. Lafayette naturally preferred the former and in May 1818 willingly wrote a letter of introduction to President Pétion for a French doctor planning to start a medical school in Haiti. Doctor Antoine-François Jenin de Montègre boasted fine medical credentials and, importantly, liberal sympathies. He was friendly with Sir Charles Morgan, also a doctor, who shared his interest in medical research.[25]

Shortly after Montègre's departure, Lafayette began to doubt the wisdom of his introduction for he feared that Montègre was an agent of the French government. Former colonial landholders had been pressuring Louis XVIII to reassert French sovereignty over Haiti, and in 1818 there were rumors that Pétion was willing to negotiate for French protection in return for giving up some measure of sovereignty. Lafayette did not wish to be involved in any enterprise of this sort. He wrote worriedly to the abbé Grégoire that he had no reason to suspect a man who was a friend of the Morgans and who had, besides, given him the impression that Grégoire backed his mission.[26] Lafayette's fears over Montègre's real purpose did not last long since news soon came from Haiti that Dr. Montègre had died shortly after his arrival.[27]

While Lafayette longed to play a role on the international scene, pressing concerns, both personal and political, forced him to focus his attention on matters close to home. First in importance were the elections anticipated for the fall of 1818. By the spring, a confusing series of conspiracies and secret memoranda had given the liberals an issue to use against the government. The catalyst for the controversy was a pamphlet about a Lyon uprising written by one of Lafayette's friends, Charles Fabvier.

During the height of the famine in June 1817, several towns around Lyon had risen in rebellion. Arrested rebels were severely punished. A civilian police official in Lyon, named Sainneville, complained about the severity, accusing the prefect, Christophe de Chabrol de Crouzol, and the military commander, General Simon de Canuel, of exaggerating the dangers to enhance their own reputations. These two men and their supporters responded that their quick action had saved the city from a dangerous revolution. The government attempted to smooth over the controversy by assigning Chabrol and Canuel to other posts and by sending Marshal Auguste de Marmont, the duc de Raguse, to investigate.[28]

The attempt to hush up the affair failed because Colonel Fabvier, a member of Marmont's staff, became convinced that the authorities had manufactured the rebellion to make themselves look like heroes. In a pamphlet published in January 1818, Fabvier charged them with using agents provocateurs to incite gullible peasants to revolt. Lafayette hoped that the pamphlet would provoke the authorities to reply, so that Fabvier could publish the rest of his evidence against them.[29] Soon, indeed, the entire matter became the subject of intense debate in the press, and all of the principals traded charges and countercharges.

In June, Canuel sued Fabvier and Sainneville for libel, but soon after he had to go into hiding because he had been implicated in another conspiracy. The conspiration du bord de l'eau (so called because the conspirators met in the Tuileries Gardens overlooking the Seine) was an alleged ultra plot to kidnap the king and force him to abandon his moderate ministry for a more conservative one. This case soon became confused in the public's mind with another ultra effort to change the direction of the government, the so-called Note Secrète. An ultra-royalist politician, Baron de Vitrolles, had written a secret memorandum to Czar Alexander warning him that France was headed toward revolution and asking him to use his influence to change the ministry.[30] The various cases dragged on in the courts for months. Richelieu came to regret that the bord de l'eau conspirators had ever been charged, telling Elie Decazes, "This prosecution has given the indépendant party a strength which has not been useless to them."[31]

Lafayette understood the advantages for his side in these

events. The ultras looked underhanded and unpatriotic, and the government was caught in a politically uncomfortable position. If the ultras defended themselves by saying that the alleged conspiracy had been invented by the government, then the liberals could argue that the same was true for the supposed Lyon conspiracy. Liberals could charge that the government's lethargic prosecution of the ultra conspiracy was motivated by fear that the investigations would reach too close to the throne or was proof of the spurious nature of the accusations. Lafayette recognized that the government was bound to look bad. "If the government does not get the credit for clearing this up, they will be convicted of powerlessness and accused of deception, a situation which, even unmerited, must deprive them of a little of their prestige."[32]

In answer to the ultras' charge that the country was about to succumb to Jacobinism, the government defended itself by stressing that their policies had been so successful at ensuring the stability of the country that the foreign troops could soon be safely removed. This argument had unfortunate consequences for the government's attempt to defeat the liberals in the coming elections because it prevented their using the most telling issue against the left: that they were the party of dangerous revolution.[33]

Naturally, the liberals' hopes rose for the 1818 fall elections. Lafayette's best chance lay in his home department of Seine-et-Marne, one of the group scheduled for that year. But another opportunity was provided by the death of a Paris deputy named Goupy, whose vacant seat was to be filled in a by-election at the same time as the general election. As early as the spring, the *indépendants* in Paris tried to generate interest in this race by holding a dinner to honor the deputies of the Chamber. Held on 5 May at a restaurant called l'Arc-en-ciel, the dinner attracted four hundred guests who honored about twenty deputies, including Bernard-François Chauvelin, d'Argenson, Edouard Bignon, and Dupont de l'Eure.[34] The popular and influential Jacques Laffitte did not appear, neither did Lafayette.

Lafayette learned of the meeting only the day before it was held, when Mme Bignon, the wife of the deputy of the Eure, urged him to attend. He hesitated, fearing that, unless other candidates were to be present, he would be suspected of having "left my retreat at the news of M. Goupy's death, whereas I am far . . . from wanting to put myself in opposition to them." On the other hand, he did not want to spurn a banquet celebrating *indépendant* deputies and their cause. He begged d'Argenson for advice and chided him for not keeping him "informed of what is going on in the patriotic world." In the end, he decided not to go. He had never received an invitation from the sponsoring committee, and Lafayette worried that the sponsors might consider that his "arrival from afar, this trip of thirty leagues would give the dinner a too-tricolored complexion."[35] He wanted to be sure, though, that the guests and deputies understood that he had not refused an invitation and that he shared their purposes, so he enclosed a letter for d'Argenson to read at the dinner (at his discretion).

Lafayette's hesitant behavior about the dinner is surely proof that he was not a member of some tightly knit committee that carefully planned liberal strategy. Many different individuals promoted *indépendant* politics, and they did so in their own ways. Lafayette apparently did not even know who was in charge of the banquet, and d'Argenson could tell him the names of only two members of the committee, Joseph Mérilhou and Paul-Antoine Fayolle, but not the name of the third.[36] The liberals did not all agree on the policies to follow, as Laffitte's refusal to participate demonstrates. Attributing all opposition activities to some well-organized committee under a stable leadership is therefore misleading.[37]

Lafayette spent the summer of 1818 almost entirely at La Grange, though he did make a quick trip to attend the traditional American Fourth of July dinner in Paris. He was annoyed that the newspapers neglected to print his toast, which, characteristically, tied together the liberal cause throughout the world: "to the Holy Alliance of nations in the cause of equality of rights and universal liberty."[38] One of the obligations keeping Lafayette close to home was the indisposition of his daughter-in-law, Emilie, who was having a difficult pregnancy. On 11 July, she gave birth to a son, Edmond, Lafayette's twelfth grandchild.[39]

Another obligation keeping Lafayette at home was the use of La Grange in 1818 as a refuge for several of his associates. Victor Jacquemont, the eighteen-year-old son of the man whose courage had saved Lafayette and Destutt de Tracy at the time of the Malet conspiracy, had been wounded in a chemistry laboratory experiment and decided to recuperate at La Grange. Later, as he began to make his name as a scientist, he credited his stay at La Grange for awakening in him an interest in botany. In 1825 he was contemplating a visit there, hoping to rediscover

> *the sweet and peaceful memories of the first emotions*
> *of my life. I was weak and listless; I walked on those*
> *grassy lawns, under those magnificent shade trees,*
> *which surround the château, the hopeful daydreams of*
> *convalescence and first youth. It is there also where I*
> *began the study of plants. . . . Later, when I found on*
> *the shores of the Mediterranean myrtles and all the*
> *plants of our "orangeries," when I first trampled in the*
> *Lozere those perfumed prairies of the mountains and*
> *in your Alps those flowered lawns of saxifrages, I cer-*
> *tainly felt intense pleasure; but it was no longer the*
> *wild delight of my most ordinary first discoveries in*
> *the woods of La Grange.*[40]

Charles Comte also sought refuge at La Grange in 1818, not to discover nature but to escape from the police. Volume six of the *Censeur européen* included a brief report about an attempted murder and accused the prosecutor of political bias for neglecting to prosecute the attacker. The prosecutor sued the editors for libel in Rennes on the grounds that the damage to his reputation was done in that city because copies of the journal were sold there. Such a procedure was immediately recognized as a serious threat to press freedom. Hauled before distant courts, far from their editorial offices, writers would have difficulty continuing their publications. Both editors tried to escape, but Dunoyer was arrested and taken to Rennes. Comte, meanwhile, hid at La Grange. The next few issues of the *Censeur européen* were edited there and seem especially marked by Lafayette's influence. Dunoyer's trial in Rennes became a cause célèbre, with enthusiastic demonstrations of support and with much press attention. The editors were found guilty in June, but the verdict was overturned by the Supreme Court in September.[41]

Lafayette also stayed close to La Grange because of the approaching elections in Seine-et-Marne. A candidate could not actively campaign, but it obviously served his interests to be hospitable and accessible before the elections. Lafayette did not know what his chances of winning were, but he intended to present

77

himself, he told d'Argenson confidentially, "with candor and perseverance to the goodwill of the patriotic electors."[42] Other political figures were also renewing their ties with their local electors. Voyer d'Argenson, for example, visited the department of the Vienne, where the liberal voters honored him with dinners.[43]

As the elections drew near, the already-considerable number of visitors at La Grange increased. In October, George wrote, "For about two months we have been leading at La Grange the life of Paris, as to the quantity of people whom we have received, with the difference that we begin to be together from the morning on." The quality of the company was high, George reported, and included Colonel Fabvier, René-Théophile Châtelain, Thierry, Dunoyer, Ary Scheffer, Lady Morgan, and her husband. Other visitors included Auguste de Staël, Voyer d'Argenson, and the British Whig politician Lord Holland and his sociable wife. Scheffer painted portraits of Lady Morgan, Mme de Tracy, and Lafayette. Colonel Antoine-François Carbonel, an army colleague of George's who had become a trusted part of the family circle, entertained them in the evening with his musical versions of the poems of the liberal poet Béranger. During their stay, Lady Morgan reported that there were "seldom less than twenty or thirty guests."[44]

Though the hosts were hospitable and the guests enjoyed themselves, politics was mixed in with the entertainment. Thierry was using Lafayette's library to prepare a series of articles for the *Censeur européen* entitled "Vue des révolutions d'Angleterre," which would include the American Revolution. Lafayette recognized the interesting parallels that could be drawn between it and the French Revolution. He told Thierry that he would find "in the proclamations of the English government, in the parliamentary assertions, in the newspaper paragraphs the same reproaches, the same lies and the same predictions as those of which the French Revolution was the object in its first years."[45]

Lafayette invited Lady Morgan to spend part of her return trip to France at his country estate since, after the appearance of her book, she was no longer received warmly in the conservative social circles in Paris that she had criticized.[46] Recognizing the political value of Lady Morgan's book, Lafayette urged her to bring out a corrected second edition and lent copies of it to friends who were considering translating it.[47]

Even more closely connected to the coming elections was

the publication of a campaign biography of Lafayette. The slim pamphlet of eleven pages, entitled *Notice biographique sur le Général La Fayette*, appeared anonymously in October 1818, in time to be distributed at the meeting of the electoral colleges. The motto on the title page read, "You will never persuade a people who love liberty that they should fear the citizen to whom Washington bequeathed his sword."[48]

The author was Augustin Thierry, who told Lafayette early in the month of the pamphlet's appearance that he had read the materials the general had provided and hoped to present him to the public "as the model of modern patriots." Lafayette's example was a powerful influence on the younger generation of liberals who looked with disgust at the compromises made by their elders during the revolutionary era. Thierry praised him extravagantly.

> *Yes, you are truly the man who has best understood and best served liberty. In my meditations on reason and virtue in politics I have never been able to equal in conception what your conduct has been. I cried upon reading your recollections of the beautiful days of 89, and of the ruin of the Year 8; how great you are in the midst of that crowd of old republicans changed into parvenus and weighted down with the plunder of that people that they pretended to save. . . . In the midst of this reading I repeated several times a verse which I applied to you as soon as I saw you: heroes salvete deûm genus!*

Thierry promised to come to Melun before the elections to "lend my literary industry to your friends, if there is need for arguments against the arguments with which the ministry will no doubt assail you." He concluded by referring to Lafayette's own model of republican virtue. "I embrace you with the same feeling with which you embraced Washington during your first campaigns for liberty; I embrace you as my father in virtue and in steady patriotism. I tremble in picking up my pen to write of you that I will be unable to equal what I feel."[49]

Another talented young man enlisted in the cause was Thierry's friend, Ary Scheffer. Although Lafayette knew Arnold

Scheffer well, he was not so well acquainted with his brother, whom he called "Auguste" in urging him to honor an earlier promise to visit La Grange.[50] Lafayette was impatient for him to arrive because he was to execute a portrait of Lafayette to be used in the coming elections. When it was finished, Cornelia Scheffer, the artist's mother, immediately set to work on a lithograph of the painting. Lafayette explained to Arnold Scheffer that it would be "published at the same time that the original is put forward as a candidate in Seine-et-Marne." He added that "the success of the drawing is more certain than that of the candidate, although the spitefulness with which the latter is honored has been extended in a rather ridiculous manner to the engravings which represent him."[51]

Pictures were especially useful in a political system in which parties and more active campaigning were considered in bad taste. Lady Morgan reported that "every shop is crowded with the pictures of La Fayette and other patriots."[52] Scheffer had portrayed Lafayette dressed in a plain, sober suit and overcoat, holding a top hat and a cane. This widely copied pose communicated an image of the candidate as a civilian and a man of simple tastes, "republican" virtues, and steady habits. These solid virtues contrasted with what was seen as the empty pomp and frivolous decorations of the royalist ceremonies and pictures. The pose also contrasted with Lafayette's earlier image: the fiery revolutionary and man on horseback were nowhere in evidence.[53]

The outdoor scene was perhaps meant to remind the viewer of Lafayette's virtuous retirement from the bustle of public affairs. He had become identified with his rural retreat. La Grange, according to Charles de Rémusat (who married one of Lafayette's granddaughters), was "for him what Versailles was for Louis XIV, his attitude of master of the house, of father of the family, of head of a farm, was a part of his role as politician."[54] Rémusat argued that Lafayette's personality and ideas dominated the society of La Grange as those of Louis XIV had dominated Versailles and that anyone who wanted to be welcome there had to share Lafayette's views and attitudes. An even more apt comparison might be to George Washington and Mount Vernon, for La Grange had another meaning, too. It had become a symbol of republican simplicity, despite its feudal origins. Lafayette was there engaged in the useful, productive, and virtuous profession of agriculture, like

Cincinnatus: ready at any moment to answer his country's call for sacrifice. He was an independent farmer, ready to serve if needed but not lusting after power by fawning on emperors or kings.

This image was more than a political pose. It had become deeply ingrained in Lafayette's personality. His ambition to achieve lasting fame and glory by living out such a republican model, by molding his actions constantly according to a classical ideal, was a peculiarly eighteenth-century attitude, learned perhaps from his mentor, George Washington.[55] A more romantic generation sometimes found the ideal stultifying. Rémusat, for example, criticized the lack of spontaneity at La Grange and pitied Lafayette for always having to be so affable. Yet he recognized, as well, what was good and even appealing in the place: "all that gathering of different minds, ages, sexes, and characters, dominated by honest sentiments, lofty ideas, genuine affections, under the paternal law of an old man beloved by his family, involved tenderly with them, and ready to sacrifice everything, himself and his family, to his glory and his country."[56] Stendhal, who knew Lafayette in the 1820s, recognized the connection between his hospitality and his political purposes. He was primarily a "party leader," Stendhal concluded, who had to be careful not to "displease anybody and to remember everybody's name, at which he is admirable."[57]

While Lafayette played host to his numerous visitors in the summer of 1818, the government became increasingly fearful that he might actually be elected in the fall. As early as June, Louis XVIII wrote wonderingly to Decazes, "do you know that those fellows talk of the possibility of the election of that animal La Fayette with an assurance which would almost rattle my own."[58] Lafayette noticed that the ministry began preparing early for the elections, even before the official convocation of the electoral colleges or the publication of the electoral lists.[59]

The government was waiting to hold elections until after the Congress of Aix-la-Chapelle, so that they could take credit for the announcement of the evacuation of foreign troops from France.[60] Not all elections were to be held on the same day. Though most colleges, including Seine-et-Marne, met beginning on 20 October, six colleges were scheduled for 26 October. The government gave no explanation for the delay, but liberals believed it was to prevent embarrassing elections, especially the election of

81

Camille Jordan by the department of the Rhône. A native of Lyon, Jordan had criticized the action of the authorities in the Lyon controversy, and his election in his hometown would be interpreted as an endorsement of those views by the voters. Since Jordan otherwise generally supported the ministry, the government hoped that he would be reelected in the Ain and that the voters in Lyon (meeting a week later) would not waste their votes on him.[61] Another of the delays can be explained by the desire to prevent the election of Jacques-Antoine Manuel. There was talk of Manuel's election in the Finistère, but if he did not succeed there, he could run in the Paris by-election a week later. To make this impossible, Finistère's election was also postponed.[62]

The government instructed prefects to draw up preliminary lists and post them by the first of August, giving voters plenty of time to make corrections before the elections. On 4 August, Lafayette complained that the lists had not yet appeared in Seine-et-Marne. Later he complained that corrections he had pointed out were being ignored. On 2 October, he wrote crossly to the mayor of the commune of Courpalay (in which La Grange was located) reminding him of these corrections and requesting him to forward them to the proper authorities. Suspicious that the mayor would not do so, Lafayette asked for a copy of the mayor's letter. He also reminded him that the only title he used was "general."[63] Lafayette insisted on that title instead of his old title of "marquis" to emphasize his commitment to the abolition of nobility. Conversely, royalists ostentatiously used his noble title to annoy him. Settling on a title had real as well as symbolic significance at election time, for occasionally votes were disqualified because a candidate's title was omitted on the ballot. The bureau of the electoral college would maintain that it could not decide which of several persons with the same name was actually meant.

In its efforts to defeat Lafayette in Seine-et-Marne, the government enjoyed two special advantages. This department was close to Paris, allowing the ministers to oversee the campaign more easily, to watch government functionaries closely, and to dazzle voters by solicitous attentions during their trips to Paris. An even greater advantage was the able prefect, Comte de Germain. A former chamberlain and aide-de-camp to Napoleon, he had been rewarded with a prefecture for his support of the Bourbon cause in 1814. He was a political moderate and member of the *doctrinaire* group, which included such people as Royer-Collard, François Guizot, and Prosper de Barante, his brother-in-law.[64]

Germain skillfully enlisted government functionaries in the electoral struggle. George Washington Lafayette grumbled that the government employees worked "with all their power, and they use every means, threats, promises, politenesses, etc. in favor of the ministerial candidates." Vast amounts of money were spent and votes were won by promises of appointment to government office. George reported that one tax collector in his neighborhood complained about how little he had been paid: "the *one hundred forty-three francs* that he was given barely cover the expenses that he was forced to make, in distributions of brandy alone."[65] Germain reminded the mayor of Melun (the *chef-lieu* of the department, where the electoral college would meet) that the public inns could not accommodate all the voters and that his employees should open their homes to them. He knew that he could count on them, but "it is best that they be informed in advance of what we expect of them."[66] Germain also used public funds to print a thousand copies of a sixteen-page pamphlet to be distributed at the elections.[67]

Germain employed different tactics with different groups of voters. He asked farmers why they would vote for Lafayette since "he has not one inch of national lands." He reminded former Napoleonic officers that Lafayette was not "one of us." Yet Germain found to his amusement that one old Napoleonic officer explained his vote for Lafayette as reward for his having made possible the Declaration of the Rights of Man.[68]

If Lafayette and his friends can be believed, the tactics of the government went much further: terrorizing voters with warnings that his election would begin the Revolution all over again.[69] To label him an inveterate enemy of the Bourbons, stories were circulated about Lafayette's actions on the night of 5–6 October 1789 and during the Hundred Days. Mme d'Angoulême, Louis XVI's daughter and wife of the son of the comte d'Artois, was reputedly ready to leave the country if Lafayette won.[70] Voters were told that his election would be more frightening to the European powers meeting at the Congress of Aix-la-Chapelle than would the news of the insurrection of one-third of France. Though Lafayette dismissed the idea that the Holy Alliance was worried about him, he was in fact being modest.[71] The powers were watching closely to see whether France's revolutionary enthusiasms were dying down, and the election of a man identified for over thirty years with revolution was bound to be noticed.

The liberal press responded to the government campaign. The *Minerve* mentioned the Lafayette candidacy several times, further proof of the importance of this election. One article questioned how devoted his ultra opponent was to maintaining the sales of national lands. Another came to Lafayette's defense in a review of a book that had criticized his actions during the Revolution.[72] The liberals also had to try to overcome the disadvantages of the date that the government had chosen for the elections. Lafayette feared that farmers would stay away from the polls because elections coincided with wheat-planting time. He suggested that, during the upcoming markets, "Parisians who do business with the farmers of Brie" explain this government ploy to them and try to persuade them to vote anyway.[73]

When the voters came to Melun on 20 October to elect the three deputies of Seine-et-Marne, the electoral college divided into three groups determined alphabetically. Lafayette was in the second, which held its meetings at the prefecture. Each group was presided over by a government appointee, who happened also to be the government's candidate. The first order of business was to elect permanent bureaus to oversee the affairs of the college, count ballots, and adjudicate controversies. The opposition always warned its followers not to neglect this part of the business because it was important to vote out the provisional bureaus selected by the prefect. The vote also gave an early indication of the strength of the parties. Lafayette must have been disappointed to see the easy reelection of the provisional bureaus.[74]

More voters arrived on the following day, when the task of electing the three deputies began. Each voter approached the head table (where members of the bureau were seated), swore an oath to the king and the Charter, and wrote three names on his ballot. The polls closed at 3:00 P.M., and the votes of the three sections then were tallied together. Only Mesnager de Germigny, one of the incumbents, had the requisite majority to win on the first day of voting (598 out of 878 voters, or 68 percent). His victory was not surprising; he was supported by both ministerials and some liberals who found him acceptable because he did not hold government office and was the owner of large quantities of national lands.[75] The next highest totals went to the other two government candidates. Lafayette was fourth with 281 votes. Over sixty individuals received at least one vote.

The second round of voting took place on yet another day. This time the voters wrote two names on their ballots. The government candidates Pierre-Laurent de Saint-Cricq and Pierre-Etienne Despatys de Courteilles emerged victorious with 55 percent and 60 percent of the votes cast, respectively. Lafayette maintained his 32 percent of the vote (273 votes), but that was far short of the majority required for election. On this round, the ultras voted with the ministerials to prevent Lafayette's election. The ultra journal the *Conservateur* commented that "the royalists had a striking opportunity to avenge themselves on the ministers; they did not do it. France will be grateful to them one day for having remained steadfastly moored . . . to their principles of loyalty and attachment to the legitimate monarchy."[76]

The distribution of votes in the election makes it appear unlikely that Lafayette could have won, even had the ultras voted for him. The liberal chances in Seine-et-Marne were perhaps hurt by low attendance, as Lafayette had feared. Only 64 percent of the voters turned out, putting it thirteenth among the twenty departments voting in 1818. But also important was a lack of coordination. Eight major candidates of the left made an appearance on the first ballot, indicating considerable disagreement among liberal voters. The government officials at Melun were in control of the election and ran it the way it was intended to work.[77] George explained his father's defeat succinctly: "This department is too near Paris for people to be able to vote freely."[78] This letter, written on the final day of voting, was addressed to Charles Goyet, the man who would organize Lafayette's victory in a more distant department and turn the government's celebration into mourning.

Though Goyet had been promoting Lafayette as one of the four *indépendant* candidates in the Sarthe since at least July, he did so without the express permission or knowledge of Lafayette, who had no personal or financial ties to that department.[79] The first reference to the Sarthe in Lafayette's correspondence came only in October 1818, when he thanked Charles-Philippe Marchand for his work for the elections. "Your friend in the Sarthe is very valuable; our confidence in him should be complete, just as my gratitude is great that he did me the honor of choosing me as the object of his patriotic zeal."[80] Marchand, a journalist who worked closely with Voyer d'Argenson, was apparently Goyet's tie to national political circles. In April 1818, Goyet had sent Voyer d'Argenson, whose home department of the Vienne was near the Sarthe, a copy of the newspaper he was publishing. D'Argenson encouraged his work of "propagating principles of liberty" and urged him to let people in Paris know whom the liberals in the Sarthe planned to run, so that they could back up their efforts.[81] Goyet also maintained a correspondence in Paris with Martial Sauquaire-Souligné, a native of the Sarthe who was a contributor to the *Mercure*.[82] However, though they had contacts in Paris, Goyet and the liberals in the Sarthe were working independently, choosing their own candidates, and stressing local issues and interests in their effort to defeat the ultra incumbents.

The Sarthe was located in the western part of France, an area noted for royalism and the scene of bitter conflicts stemming from the Revolution. Goyet had been in the thick of those struggles. He had abandoned an early religious career to become an ardent Jacobin during the Revolution and the Directory. As he grew older, his radicalism waned, but his hatred of the Church and the nobility did not. In 1814 Goyet was a lawyer in the *tribunal de commerce*.[83] Jules Pasquier, who would become his bitter opponent, was serving as Napoleonic sub-prefect of La Flèche. When the royalists returned, he was appointed prefect of the Sarthe, partly to compensate his powerful brother, Etienne Pasquier, a minister in the new government.[84]

Goyet supported the regime of the Hundred Days, while Jules Pasquier retreated to the family château to organize ultraroyalists to resist Napoleon. When the Hundred Days were over and Pasquier resumed his prefecture, he looked upon Goyet as one of the most dangerous enemies of the Bourbon government. Goyet was confined to his hometown and not allowed to travel; his home was searched; and he was arrested, though never brought to trial. The reaction of the early Restoration fell especially hard on Goyet's friend and mentor, Rigomer Bazin, a writer who had earlier been imprisoned by Napoleonic authorities as well. When Bazin was killed in a duel with a young royalist, Goyet took his place as the premier liberal writer of the Sarthe, vowing vengeance on ultras and on Jules Pasquier, whom he believed guilty of complicity in the death of his friend.

The instrument of Goyet's campaign against Pasquier was a newspaper entitled *Propagateur d'anecdotes curieuses et intéressantes*.[85] Written to "electrify the peasants of the Sarthe," the *Propagateur* was irreverent and combative.[86] Goyet recognized the importance of national papers like the *Minerve* but believed that reaching the ordinary people in the Sarthe required a less intellectual journal. He and his friends organized a department-wide committee to distribute the paper and to coordinate local liberal activities. Representatives from all over the department met at Goyet's house on Fridays, when they arrived in Le Mans for market day.[87]

So effective was the campaign in the *Propagateur* that Jules Pasquier was removed from office in the summer of 1818. Yet the government had no alternative to the unpopular Pasquier to put forward as a candidate. And the new prefect, François-de-Sales-M.-J.-Louis d'Estourmel, found it impossible to organize a successful election in the Sarthe. Unlike Seine-et-Marne, many of the officials in the Sarthe were ultras unwilling to work for the ministerial candidates. The shakiness of the government's position was perhaps the main reason the elections there were scheduled for the later date. By the time the electoral college opened on 26 October, Goyet and his friends were well prepared. The *Propagateur* had publicized their slate of candidates: two veteran politicians, a respected businessman, and Lafayette.

Although Goyet had been promoting Lafayette's candidacy, the voters in the Sarthe would not want to waste their votes on him if he had already been chosen by his home department. Lafayette assured Marchand that, "as soon as the election in Melun is finished, a man on horseback will leave to announce the news to my son and to you. We must also inform M. Goyet that in any case, success or not, you will send a reliable man carrying the news. We must not leave the good voters of the Sarthe in uncertainty."[88] As soon as he heard the results, George wrote to Goyet that, although he did not know him, he wanted to express his gratitude for Goyet's interest in his father. "It is not my place to praise his love for the cause of liberty, but nevertheless more than any other I know his devotion to that sacred cause." George and Marchand left immediately for the Sarthe.[89]

Goyet had carefully prepared for the election because he realized that, unlike the case in some departments, most of the liberal voters came from the countryside, not from the main city.[90] They had to be encouraged to make the trip to the *chef-lieu* and to remain in town for the duration of the elections. On Sunday night, 25 October, the liberal voters met to decide which men to back for the permanent bureau of the electoral college. Their choices were all elected the next day. On Tuesday, the voting for deputies took place. Goyet's four candidates were the top vote getters. Pierre Thoré-Cohendet, Julien-Pierre-Jean Hardouin, and Jean-Pierre-Guillaume Delahaye de Launay received majorities; Lafayette was next with 48 percent of the votes cast. The next-highest vote getters were the four ultra incumbents. Pasquier had only 21 percent of the votes.[91]

Then came a surprising development: Thoré-Cohendet refused election. He made the announcement hoping that the electoral college would choose his replacement while they were still meeting. But Pasquier, the president of the college, wanting to consult authorities in Paris about how to handle this unexpected situation, adjourned the electoral college for two days. He was hoping, no doubt, that Lafayette's support would evaporate into the countryside before the next session. Goyet acted swiftly to keep his voters in Le Mans. Having engaged a printer to be on call during the elections, he immediately circulated a notice to the liberal voters. "Citizen voter, stay, in order to take part in the elections, until Friday morning. If essential business calls you home, come back on Friday: until three o'clock, you will still be able to deposit your ballot. Voters! don't let yourselves be defeated by intrigue."[92] Pasquier's maneuver failed. The authorities in Paris (no doubt hoping that the next time the voters met they would be more malleable) ruled that only the Chamber of Deputies could accept a resignation and that the electoral college should proceed to the election of only the final deputy. On Friday, Lafayette received 54 percent of the votes (596 out of 1,055 votes).

Lafayette's victory in the Sarthe came through the efforts of a well-organized group of liberals, led by a journalist willing to brave the criticism that opposition politics would inevitably bring down on him. Royalist critics labeled Goyet "the terrible M. Goyet" and the "great elector of the Sarthe."[93] No similar figure existed in Lafayette's home department. The Sarthe's long history of political struggle and innovative political techniques made it easy for its voters to adjust to and take advantage of the new political system of the Restoration. Goyet knew how to mobilize the voters in the countryside who feared losing their national lands and who resented the pretensions of the Church. He was helped to victory by an incompetent and high-handed prefect, who was incapable of using the resources of the government effectively, and by the unwillingness of ultra and moderate royalists to unite to stop liberal victories, as they had done in Seine-et-Marne.

Lafayette had headed for Paris as soon as the elections ended in Melun. On 26 October, news of the surprising election of Jacques-Antoine Manuel in the department of the Vendée reached Paris. The Vendée was synonymous with royalist counterrevolution, and this news was so surprising that, at first, the liberals in Paris suspected it was a trick to keep them from voting for Manuel in the capital. However surprising, it was no trick. The subsequent euphoria healed a rift in the liberal camp. On the day the electoral college opened, three liberal candidates still vied for the vacancy in Paris (Manuel, Benjamin Constant, and Pierre-Paul-Alexandre Gilbert-Desvoisins). That evening, three hundred liberal voters met at Laffitte's house to patch up their differences and agree to back Benjamin Constant. He subsequently lost to Guillaume-Louis Ternaux, a rather liberal industrialist supported by the government in an effort to prevent the election of a candidate even further to the left.[94]

Lafayette would have preferred to represent Paris instead of the Sarthe, an area about which he knew nothing. When he received the news of his election at the end of the week, he confided to his family at La Grange that there had also been a movement to nominate him in Paris and that "the contrary arguments were founded only on the lack of time remaining. Some of my best friends thought that it would have required two days more."[95] In truth, with an overabundance of liberal candidates vying for the Paris seat and with a good chance that Lafayette would win in Le Mans, the liberals were hardly likely to focus their attention on him.

Lafayette and his friends gathered at Lady Morgan's to wait for the news from the Sarthe. She called Lafayette's election "the greatest triumph of public opinion known for years" and boasted that her book "was the best canvasser La Fayette had."[96] The government thought the election a disaster. When the news of the elections of Lafayette and Manuel reached him, Richelieu was at Aix-la-Chapelle negotiating with the Allies. He feared that the Allies might reconsider their decision to evacuate the occupying troops because of fear of a renewal of a "1789 style revolution." Richelieu wrote to Decazes, "I was rather expecting B. Constant . . . but as for La Fayette, it's too much. The effect is dreadful here, and more than one of these gentlemen will show his regret at having signed the evacuation." The king had watched the returns carefully and had been delighted at Lafayette's defeat at Melun.[97] The news from Le Mans therefore proved doubly disturbing. Mme de Broglie recorded in her journal that the king was less upset at the sensational election of the abbé Grégoire in 1819 than he had been at Lafayette's victory in 1818, which had "shaken all of France and virtually Europe."[98]

His election confirmed Lafayette's belief that public opinion was on the liberal side, that he represented a truly national point of view. The liberals were confident that they could continue to make gains under the current electoral system. Of the fifty-five seats up for election in 1818, twenty-six went to *indépendants,* twenty-nine to government supporters, and none to ultras. Though still a minority, the left had doubled its representation in the Chamber.[99] If that pace could be continued, Lafayette and his friends could hope to have a majority soon. In the new session, their fifty deputies would use the podium to spread their message and wield their influence to help their supporters.

On 3 November 1818, Lafayette returned to La Grange, accompanied by the Broglies, Dunoyer, and the Italian revolutionary Federico Confalonieri.[100] At home, Lafayette greeted other visitors (including Voyer d'Argenson and Marchand) and answered messages of congratulations on his election.[101] In a letter to one correspondent, he revealed how much he considered participation in the Hundred Days a determinant of political affiliation in the early Restoration. "My colleagues of 1815 will have no doubt observed that out of seven deputies of the Vendée and the Sarthe, there are six from the Chamber of Representatives; two vice presidents, General Grenier and I, will be joining Dupont de l'Eure in waiting for our colleague Flaugergues."[102] Dupont de l'Eure wrote him delightedly, "Thanks be given to the electors of the Sarthe and to the spirit of liberty which inspired them! I am longing to clasp you in my arms and to see among the deputies of France one of her most illustrious citizens."[103] In November 1818, the future looked bright indeed.

4

The Deputy of the Sarthe

After a peaceful month at La Grange, tending to agriculture and reading the new books written by his friends, Lafayette returned to Paris for the opening of the Chambers on 10 December.[1] Excitement ran high as people vied for tickets to see Lafayette pledge his loyalty to the king and the Charter. "Our Parisians still have a childish side," Mme de Rémusat commented, "this sight strikes everyone as tantalizing. I'll go myself, like the others, if I can get hold of a ticket."[2] Lady Morgan, who viewed the ceremony in the Chamber as Lafayette's guest, said that, when he entered, "every tongue pronounced his name as admiration, fear, or hope dictated."[3]

In a clever article in the *Minerve*, Benjamin Constant pretended that the public's curiosity stemmed from admiration for Lafayette's achievements alone. He reminded his readers of Lafayette's defense of Louis XVI against the Jacobins and maintained that the excitement of the audience was explained by many "memories, different but all honorable." People wanted to see

> *one of the boldest defenders of all national liberties, in the Old and in the New World, the friend of Washington, the enemy of despotism. . . . the man who had sacrificed his popularity, defied death, and undergone captivity in foreign dungeons for defending the constitution to which he had sworn allegiance and the monarch whose inviolability was guaranteed by this constitution. Many of those in service to the royal family were in the galleries. Full of those memories, it is not surprising that they contemplated M. de La Fayette with interest and gratitude.*[4]

By contrast, the ultra journal the *Conservateur* in a satirical article pictured Lafayette as negligent, submissive to vulgar opinion, and childish. The "faithful veterans of the revolution," wrote the author, will be pleased to learn that

a famous white horse, a horse which shared with its master the idolatrous love of the good people of Paris, has not finished its valiant career: he is still alive. With what pleasure will this heroic animal be seen again by its old comrades at arms who fought the campaign of the 5th and 6th October, concluded by the triumphal march from Versailles to Paris. Despite his venerable age, this liberal horse, this independent quadruped, has lost none of his generous vigor. We have been assured that he paws the ground, neighs, and prances joyfully when a little groom, formerly a fifer in the National Guard, plays for him in the stable the beloved tune: Ah! ça ira, ça ira. . . . The incredulous, or those who wish to appear so, will be sure to say that it is not the same horse, that it is his son or somebody else who looks like him. [But] those who knew him well will be convinced that the master of this horse is still riding the same hobbyhorse.[5]

The bitterness of the ultras at the reemergence of Lafayette was surely exacerbated by their disappointment at their declining fortunes. In the center of the new Chamber sat the ministerials, the largest group. Their enemies called them *le ventre* (the belly) and assumed that they were motivated by greed and self-interest rather than by principle. Without a majority, the ministerials had to decide whether to seek allies to the left of center or to the right. The cabinet crisis caused by this question ended with a victory for the king's favorite, Decazes. The new ministry which he dominated came into office at the end of December, committed to courting the left center. On this side sat the curious group called the *doctrinaires*, small in number but containing talented members, like Royer-Collard, who wielded disproportionate influence in the Chamber. Although they are often called liberals and though they shared Lafayette's interests in education and freedom of speech, their differences from Lafayette were great, as the struggles of the next two years would demonstrate.

Lafayette sat on the left side of the Chamber, but there were divisions here as well.[6] He belonged to the far-left group of deputies called the *réunion Laffitte* (because of their regular gathering place in the banker's home). Another group on the left, the *réunion Ternaux*, was slightly more conservative and willing to compromise with the ministry. These *réunions* were the closest equivalents to political parties within the Chamber, though membership in one group or another put an individual under no particular obligations, and these loose associations could do nothing to discipline their members.

The deputies on the left disagreed about the advisable degree of cooperation with the new ministers. In his dispatches to the American authorities, Albert Gallatin noted that this government, having rejected the ultras, would need the support of a sufficient number of deputies on the left. "Much will depend on the wisdom" of the liberal party, he wrote. "The victory is entirely theirs; they need only patience; the ensuing renewals of the three-fifths will give them and the friends of constitutional monarchy united, a decided superiority."[7]

Lafayette, of course, was neither patient nor trusting. The revolutionary ideology of the eighteenth century taught suspicion of power and the importance of vigilance on the part of independent and virtuous men to keep those in power from becoming despotic. Lafayette planned to be vigilant in the Chamber. He acknowledged that the new government had expressed good intentions, and he promised to support the ministers "as long as they follow a patriotic line. . . . We are grateful to them for having succeeded despite the foreigners, and for having broken with the ultras; their only recourse is in national opinion; we will know soon whether they have the confidence to commit themselves to it unreservedly." He thought his side must maintain its "freedom of movement" and goad a timid government by drawing it in the right direction: "for it to remain patriotic, we must be doubly so."[8]

Political considerations accorded with his fundamental philosophy. If the left cooperated openly or enthusiastically with the government, it would be difficult to present themselves at election time as a necessary or useful alternative. Benjamin Constant saw the danger of making possible the election of men he

94

considered unprincipled: "If we make the ministry popular, elections will give us *ventrus* [men of the "belly"]."[9]

The opening of the session of the Chambers coincided with the cabinet crisis and the change of ministers. The deputies therefore found that their work was at a standstill. Lafayette took advantage of the relative leisure to agitate on behalf of the Latin American revolutions, which he interpreted hopefully as continuations of the American Revolution. Historical antecedents might prevent the Old World from following wholeheartedly the example of the United States, but such obstacles did not exist in the New World. He had watched with pleasure in 1817 as Chile adopted "the doctrines of the United States," helped by French soldiers who went to fight in America after the Restoration government cut back the French army.[10] In the spring of 1818, Lafayette had met an agent for the Argentine independence movement, Bernardino Rivadavia, who had convinced him that "His Commonwealth is More Advanced in political knowledge and practice than we are aware of."[11] An article in the *Censeur européen* extolled the progress made in Argentina and predicted that the United States would soon recognize the new South American republics.[12] Hoping to aid their cause, Lafayette introduced Rivadavia to Albert Gallatin, but neither the government of the United States nor that of France could be induced to help.[13]

With his new eminence as a deputy and with a more liberal ministry in power, Lafayette decided to make another effort at getting aid for the Argentines by arranging a meeting for Rivadavia with the new president of the council of ministers, General Jean-Joseph Dessolle. Lafayette hoped that France, freed from "Bonaparte's despotic instinct" (which had precluded "generous diplomacy") and now no longer subject to foreign domination, would pursue a "national" diplomacy, seeking alliances with other liberal nations. His main argument for intervention was economic. The new Latin American nations offered marvelous opportunities for French commerce, but France risked losing out to Britain, which allowed Latin American revolutionaries to use its ports and to recruit soldiers within its borders. The only Frenchmen making a name for themselves in South America had been banished from France. England had an accredited consul at Buenos Aires; the French merchants had only an agent. To reap the rewards of independence, the French should commit themselves without reservation to the South American revolutionaries, as they had to the North Americans in 1778. Besides, he added, a government that upheld the liberty of other nations would be popular with the French people. Despite Lafayette's efforts, Rivadavia returned to Argentina without the support of the French government.[14]

Although Lafayette's interests were wide and he longed to become involved in national and international events, he soon learned that the daily routine of a deputy and the demands of his constituents would absorb most of his attention. He had thought very little about the duties required of the representative of a particular department. On 1 November, Lafayette had written to thank Charles Goyet for his election, but he did not write again. Goyet let it be known through friends that he expected frequent communications from Lafayette. On 17 January, the deputy wrote Goyet a somewhat apologetic letter and henceforth complied with this demand. By the end of March Lafayette had sent twenty-two more letters; however, he took a rather businesslike attitude to this correspondence with Goyet: for the most part he dictated them to a secretary rather than writing them in his own hand as he did for his letters to friends.[15]

Goyet instructed the Sarthe delegation to work for the replacement of ultra office holders and to settle a legal dispute over public lands in his hometown. But his first priority was the delayed election to replace Thoré-Cohendet, whose seat still remained vacant. Goyet had already picked a candidate: Benjamin Constant. Once again acting independently from the leaders in Paris, Goyet told Constant that if he would "promise to accept for the Sarthe, we can promise you success. It is merely a question of telling us clearly that arrangements made or to be made in Paris will not thwart our plans."[16] Constant accepted this proposal and, in marked contrast to Lafayette, began a conscientious correspondence with Goyet. Constant's tone was warmer than Lafayette's. He addressed Goyet as "my excellent friend" and closed with such expressions as "Farewell, my friend. Yours for life." Lafayette was more formal, calling Goyet "my dear Constituent" and closing with "Greetings and sincere affection."[17] Goyet became so fond of Constant that he described him glowingly as having "replaced Bazin in my heart."[18] He respected and admired Lafayette, but Constant was more a friend.

To run the special election in the Sarthe, the government had appointed a new prefect in January 1819, the old one, d'Estourmel, having been removed for his inability to prevent the disastrous electoral results of 1818. Lafayette was pleased with the selection: Louis Pépin de Bellisle, a friend of the duc de Broglie's and previously a well-liked prefect of Côtes-du-Nord. Broglie invited the Sarthe delegation to meet the new prefect at his home on 28 January.[19] Goyet was very suspicious of this fence-mending and immediately instructed the delegation in what subjects to discuss with the new prefect.[20]

Of the Sarthe delegation, only Lafayette and Hardouin attended because Delahaye was ill. They spoke to Pépin de Bellisle of "the interests of the Department and of part of what" Goyet's letter contained, and they planned further discussions.[21] Goyet was not at all pleased with the performance of the delegation. On 14 February, Lafayette wrote him a conciliatory letter, promising that he and Hardouin would copy the important parts of his letter and read them to the prefect "article by article." He apologized for not having written more frequently, citing the inevitable distractions of life in Paris. "Although we are not doing anything very important, our time is taken up by the Chamber, committees, meetings, correspondence, and always a little as well by my connections from various epochs of the Revolution which residence in Paris has renewed."[22]

Meanwhile, Goyet feared that Pépin de Bellisle's continued stay in Paris was a sign that the government had no intention of calling a special election to fill vacancies. He asked Constant why no liberal in the Chamber had demanded the convocation of the colleges. "I will not offend some *indépendants* by believing certain remarks: *they are there, they don't think any longer of the others*. But why don't they protest?"[23] Constant tried to mollify Goyet by assuring him that the liberals in Paris had not lost their zeal. "They wanted to give the ministry time to act: and this inaction on their part has disorganized them a little bit, but certainly neither the independent deputies nor the writers have abandoned their principles."[24]

Goyet's complaints finally moved Lafayette to action. On 8 February, he deposited a motion asking the Chamber to petition the king to call the electoral colleges. After the mandatory waiting period, he read it to the Chamber in the closed session of 12 February. Minister of Justice Pierre de Serre responded that, as soon as they had learned which seats were vacant, they had ordered the prefects to prepare voter lists. Though this explanation was obviously weak (Constant called it "rather awkward"), Lafayette withdrew his resolution, assuming that the point had been made and that the government would now proceed to convoke the colleges.[25]

The government still procrastinated but did at least order Pépin de Bellisle to Le Mans. The Sarthe delegation conferred with him again before he left, repeating Goyet's warning not to fall into the same errors as his predecessor and not to fight the liberal candidates. Lafayette believed that Pépin de Bellisle had no desire to make himself unpopular, "especially when it's a question of a candidate who is a friend of messieurs de Broglie and de Staël," but his instructions might force him to act differently.[26]

The government hoped to develop a ministerial party by attracting some supporters of the left into their ranks. The precarious coalition of liberal revolutionaries and former Bonapartists, forged in the last part of the Hundred Days, was vulnerable, as their disagreements over helping exiles demonstrate. In 1819 the *Minerve* was raising money for former Napoleonic officers who had established the Champ d'Asile colony in Texas. Lafayette had little patience for such an enterprise. He urged Voyer d'Argenson to contribute instead to a collection organized by a man named Ramel in Brussels for the relief of indigent exiles, a "more useful" enterprise than "gifts to Texas where surely no one is hungry."[27] This man was probably Dominique-Vincent Ramel-Nogaret, a regicide and minister of finance under the Directory, who had not been employed by the Napoleonic regime. But, having accepted a prefectural post during the Hundred Days, he was included in the banishment of all regicides who had supported the Hundred Days.[28] Lafayette's sympathies lay with such former revolutionaries, rather than with those who had fled to avoid arrest for complicity in the return of Bonaparte.[29] Electoral politics dictated that the liberals minimize these divisions, but the government, naturally, sought to turn them to its own account by allowing selected exiles to return and by handing out offices.[30]

Benjamin Constant complained in the *Minerve* that the government was trying to

> *make unfaithful to the national cause all men who appear susceptible of abandoning that cause. This minis-*

*try gives reparations, partial favors, which it cites as
proof of a liberal system which, in fact, it does not follow. When one asks about repealing or enacting laws,
it responds by a list of individuals whom it has placed
in office. . . . It tries in this fashion to accomplish in favor of the ministerial system the much vaunted fusion
which the imperial government accomplished ten
years ago, a fusion whose aim was the combination of
all parties upon the remains of all principles.*[31]

Forwarding a copy of this article to Goyet, Constant summed up
the main point. The government's strategy was to "rally the
Bonapartists by offices, and to detach them from principles, there
is the entire secret, and it was right to say so."[32] The image of
Lafayette was a useful tool in this ideological struggle. For example, when the *Courier*, a *doctrinaire* newspaper, attempted to
denigrate the left as the custodians of liberalism by asking whether a study of the lives of those on the left would reveal periods of
service to despotism, Benjamin Constant responded primarily by
invoking Lafayette's life. His commitment to liberty was frequently advanced by publicists of the left to prove the devotion of their
side to the right principles.[33]

The left tried to unite both sides of its coalition by reminding them of their revolutionary origins, of the arbitrary actions of
the *Chambre Introuvable*, and of the principles of constitutionality, which were their guarantee against the vengeance of the
royalists. On 12 February, the *réunion Laffitte* decided that during the legislative session they would stress two main issues:
reorganization of the National Guard along the lines of 1791 and
an end to the exile lists. Lafayette took special interest in the
National Guard. Even before the meeting, George Washington
Lafayette had told a correspondent that the left intended to push
for its reform and asked for petitions to back them up. But George
did not mention the exile question.[34] This issue was raised for
political purposes. By insisting that all exiles had the right to
return, the left encouraged the Bonapartists to make common
cause with the revolutionaries, forced them to think about the
principles involved, and precluded individual accommodation
with the government. Furthermore, it would be a useful issue in
the coming by-elections. Though temporarily set aside by a threat

to the election law which forced the left and the ministry to cooperate, the exile issue would not be entirely forgotten.

On 20 February (the same day that Benjamin Constant sent his article to Goyet), an ultra member of the Chamber of Peers, Marquis François de Barthélemy, asked the Chambers to petition the king to modify the organization of the electoral colleges.[35] Lafayette reacted with horror to this threat from the far right, which by its very vagueness could be interpreted as an attack on the Charter itself. Typically, he saw Barthélemy's proposal as more than a legislative gambit or political ploy. It was part of the international effort to reverse the gains of the Revolution. He explained to Goyet:

> We are in a state of crisis. . . . Ultraism was playing dead. The center of the Chamber was drifting. The new ministerials were not in agreement on the degree of liberality that they should adopt. . . . The indépendants themselves were languishing, not knowing to what point they should sustain the government or fight its delays and its faults. Suddenly a flag of attack was raised in the Chamber of Peers . . . and this first step, if it succeeds, will be followed by many others.

A more urgent petition was now called for than those previously requested on the National Guard and the exiles, and the Sarthe deputies sent a model petition for Goyet to use.[36] The members of the réunion Laffitte decided to work with the réunion Ternaux and the ministry in answering this attack.[37]

The official position of the liberals was that the electoral law must be preserved because it was "the first guarantee of public peace and the most solid basis of the constitutional monarchy."[38] Lafayette went along with this policy, despite reservations about the electoral law. He hoped that the day would come when, "as in the United States, all French citizens will learn to elect their deputies directly." But political circumstances dictated defense of the law: "we mustn't give up one line even if it were an improvement, because the signal was counterrevolutionary and it must be completely defeated."[39] This political crisis marked an important step in the transformation of the Charter into an icon of the left.

Lafayette faithfully attended the debate on the electoral law, even though he was ill at the time. On 22 March 1819, he gave his first speech as a deputy. His remarks show how tenuous the coalition between the ministry and the left was. Seemingly impatient with discussion of the faults of the electoral system, Lafayette focused instead on the lack of progress the Chambers had made while fighting off threats to the election law during their three months in session. It was time, he declared, to give the French people what they had wanted for thirty years: institutions that would guarantee "liberty and order." A bill on press freedom had already been introduced, the budget had to be settled, the present system of municipal government (merely "disguised feudalism") needed to be improved, and the National Guard, juries, and exiles all needed attention. He warned, though, that "behind us are chasms into which a single retrograde step could plunge us again." Adopting the Barthélemy proposal would be, he concluded, "that first retrograde step."[40]

The ministry felt compelled to defeat the Barthélemy proposal, generally interpreted as an attack on the ministry pure and simple. After the Chamber of Peers passed the proposal and then rejected a money bill (already passed in the Chamber of Deputies), Decazes fought back by asking the king to create fifty-nine new peers. Included on the list were moderates loyal to the government (such as the comte de Germain, the prefect of Seine-et-Marne) and some peers excluded from the Chamber after the Hundred Days (such as Lafayette's old friend Louis-Philippe Ségur).[41] The liberals hoped that this increase in the number of peers would be followed by a corresponding increase in the number of deputies. Many even speculated that the Chamber would be dissolved and that elections for an enlarged Chamber would take place that spring. But the ministry had no intention of taking such a risk. Though forced to cooperate with the liberals in the Chamber of Deputies to stop the ultras' attack on the election law, the ministry, far from encouraging the growth of the far left, wanted to win over as many liberals as possible by their moderation and by demonstrating clearly that they rejected the reactionary proposals of the ultras.

The ministry's unwillingness to countenance further liberal electoral victories was illustrated dramatically in the Sarthe. The government still delayed calling the election there, and Lafayette speculated that they delayed because they had been considering calling a general election. Lafayette and Hardouin discussed the scheduling with Decazes, and they finally settled on 25 March.[42] Goyet discovered the true cause of the delay when the electoral lists for the Sarthe were posted on 8 March. The time had been spent eliminating 340 voters from the rolls, "among them, 127 *farmers* from the arrondissement of *Mamers*, the one out of the four where the patriotism and the independence of the electors had the greatest influence in the last elections."[43] Lafayette learned of the exclusions from Benjamin Constant at their usual Friday meeting at Laffitte's. They talked to Decazes about it the next morning.[44] Perhaps because of the need to cooperate during the electoral-law debate, Decazes reversed himself and Goyet was able to get all of the excluded voters back on the rolls.[45]

Lafayette otherwise had little influence in this election. He had initially hoped that Pierre-Claude-François Daunou would be chosen in the Sarthe because he believed Constant's greater fame would have won him a seat elsewhere, such as at Lyon or in the Finistère. But the decision to run Constant had been made early, even before Lafayette arrived in Paris in December, and another place was found for Daunou in the Finistère.[46] Lafayette's involvement was crucial, however, in the election of Claude Tircuy de Corcelle at Lyon. Lafayette naturally took an interest in Corcelle, "commander of the National Guard of Lyon during the Hundred Days, and recently returned from proscription, a very distinguished man in every respect." But the candidate had not visited Lyon, and the liberals there began to worry that Corcelle's absence would permit the ministerial candidate to win. Lafayette was asked to persuade Corcelle to put in an appearance at Lyon and thus guarantee his victory.[47] In the Sarthe, Goyet's careful planning paid off once again. When Delahaye's continuing illness forced him to resign, Goyet put off naming a candidate for his seat for fear of offending a part of their coalition. The liberals in the Sarthe eventually settled on Marie-Jean-Charles Picot Desormeaux, and both liberal candidates received a majority on the first ballot.[48]

Benjamin Constant entered the Chamber of Deputies in time to take a leading role in the debate over the law establishing freedom of the press, part of the government's attempts to satisfy the moderates. The left had long agitated for such a law. In 1818 several of Lafayette's associates, most notably Auguste de Staël and the duc de Broglie, had founded the *Société des amis de la liberté de la presse* to promote their cause. From the beginning Lafayette supported this organization, and he had hosted its meetings several times.[49] Broglie became, along with Barante and Guizot, one of the principal authors of the press bill, which they modeled on British practices.

Lafayette was pleased with the draft of the bill but was disappointed to discover that the version presented to the Chamber on 22 March differed somewhat from the one he had seen.[50] The essential points were the same: press crimes would not be treated any differently from other categories of crimes; there would be trial by jury in press cases; and newspapers would no longer be subject to prior censorship.[51] But, he discovered, police courts rather than juries would decide libel cases, and the amounts required as security money were much larger than he had anticipated. Fearing that departmental papers would be forced out of business by this requirement, he promised Goyet that they would wage a "war of amendments." Requiring a surety bond for a newspaper seemed as unreasonable as asking "a man who is going for a walk to deposit a guarantee of his good conduct in the street," but he wanted to know what a small paper could reasonably manage. "How much could the friends of the *Propagateur* put up in Le Mans for this type of security?"[52] As finally passed, the bill provided for lower bonds in the provinces than in Paris.

Though Lafayette took no significant role in the debate over the press bill, an exchange with the *procureur général* Nicolas-François Bellart publicized his devotion to freedom of the press.[53] When the *Ami de la royauté*, a conservative newspaper, accused Lafayette of crimes during the Revolution, the authorities instituted proceedings against the authors. Lafayette protested the proceedings in a letter reprinted in many newspapers.

> *During the forty-two years that my life has been sub-*
> *ject to public judgment, I have asked no writer to*
> *speak well of me, nor bothered anybody for speaking*
> *ill of me, and furthermore, although very sensitive to*
> *kindness, I have never answered calumny. M. Bellart*
> *will permit me then to refuse his protection, and, with-*
> *out knowing what the offense is, to declare that not*

> *considering myself offended, I disavow all proceedings
> in that regard, and oppose them with all my might.*[54]

Bellart's reply appeared in the newspapers the next day. Calumny had become so common, he explained, that it was impossible to prosecute all the cases, and he was forced to select only especially obnoxious ones. He carried out his duties "with impartiality, without distinction of persons, and with the sole aim of stifling . . . all attempts at quarrels to rekindle civil strife." The personal feelings of "M. le marquis de la Fayette" were not at issue, according to Bellart. Although this exchange allowed Lafayette to associate himself with press freedom and to declare himself above petty accusations, Bellart, too, had made some telling points. He had labeled the press irresponsible and had ostentatiously used the noble title which Lafayette disdained, thus annoying Lafayette and pleasing his enemies.[55] By cleverly presenting their policy as disinterested, the government hoped to elicit support for censorship, but Lafayette's refusal to countenance any limits on freedom of the press foiled the attempt.

The left did well in the by-elections (four of the five deputies elected were *indépendants*) and hoped that the new press law would help them make further gains at the polls. Ironically, though, press freedom, which they desired, would reveal more clearly the divisions within their own ranks and show how unprepared they were to respond to the government's power to manipulate events and attract followers.

Even before the press bill passed, liberals began to make plans to create daily newspapers. Every nuance of opinion seemed destined to have its own paper. Lafayette and d'Argenson helped to transform the *Censeur européen* into a daily to be written by Comte, Dunoyer, Thierry, Marchand, Victor Cousin, and Arnold Scheffer, with occasional articles by Daunou and Say. Lafayette expected Laffitte to help with the surety bond. Benjamin Constant, on the other hand, was putting his energies into the *Renommée*, to be written by Martial Sauquaire-Souligné, Etienne de Jouy, Etienne Aignan, and a man named Hervey, under the editorship of Jean-Pierre Pagès de l'Ariège. The deputies Dupont de l'Eure and Bignon, and Lanjuinais from the Chamber of Peers, were also involved with Constant's paper. The *Constitutionnel*, written by Charles-Guillaume Etienne, Antoine Jay, Evariste Dumoulin, and Pierre Tissot, and the *Indépendant*, written by Jean-François Cugnet de Montarlot and others, completed the quartet of liberal papers.[56] Benjamin Constant explained the differences among them:

> *The journal général or the Indépendant, military, that is to say devoted to the generals who have full right to our esteem for having vanquished Europe and to our interest for being persecuted, but more in opposition than liberal in the sense of that word taken from the point of view of principles. The Journal du Commerce, or Constitutionnel, liberal but attached to the ministry by some of its writers, and trying, even in its opposition, to promote especially one minister [Decazes] at the expense of the others. Perhaps the Censeur, . . . which will be very faithful to principles, but abstract, metaphysical and often untimely. Finally the Renommée for which I will answer, as long as Bignon, Dupont and I will permit our names to be there, and which will surely be constitutional, in the full extent of that word.[57]*

Constant did not include among the papers he called liberal the *Courier*, the organ of the *doctrinaires* such as Royer-Collard, Guizot, and Rémusat.

Goyet objected to Benjamin Constant's plan to be an editor of the *Renommée* because he thought it was incompatible with being a deputy. A journalist, he argued, should excite his readers, but a deputy should be "wise, moderate and firm" and ready to rein in public opinion if it should go too far.[58] But his major worry was that these newspapers would not agree on candidates for the fall elections, a fear that turned out to be warranted. Sauquaire-Souligné had asked Lafayette and Voyer d'Argenson to make the same sort of commitment to the *Renommée* as Benjamin Constant had made, to "use his paper exclusively for what we wanted to insert and to allow him to say so."[59] But Lafayette declined, appearing to agree with Goyet that a deputy should not be publicly identified with a particular paper. Though the one he influenced and supported was the *Censeur*, his ties to it were not proclaimed publicly.

In the spring of 1819, Lafayette tried to keep alive a struggling newspaper by encouraging his friends to subscribe to it. The *Politique* was a short-lived precursor to the more famous *Organisateur*, both written by Henri de Saint-Simon. While Lafayette was pleased with the articles appearing in it, he did not agree completely with Saint-Simon's ideas. He hoped that Saint-Simon would remain under the "friendly censorship" of Hervey. Saint-Simon had plans for expansion, and though Lafayette did not think he and Voyer d'Argenson should support all of the editor's desires, he did think that there were "great advantages to be gained from his ideas, his diligence, and his young collaborators, provided he remains in the American route he is following at present."[60] Lafayette had probably come to know Saint-Simon through the authors of the *Censeur*, who stressed the same antiaristocratic themes.[61]

The left and the ministry had cooperated to save the electoral law and to pass the press bill, but the basic hostility between the two sides had not really diminished. It surfaced again over the issue of the exiles, which the left had put forward provocatively as a party measure. At the instigation of liberal deputies, petitions had poured into the Chamber asking that the exiles be allowed to return. Attempts to arrange a compromise on dealing with these petitions almost succeeded. The committee on petitions had agreed to recommend that they be sent to the government for its attention, if the left would promise not to engage in debate on the issue. However, the ministry intervened, insisting that some of the petitions had to be rejected out of hand. With this, the compromise broke down, and the committee was forced to recommend the defeat of the motion to consider these petitions.[62]

The debate opened on 17 May and the minister of justice, de Serre, declared that those temporarily in exile might be pardoned in the future but "as regards regicides, *never*."[63] The deputies of the left were so taken aback by his unexpected intransigence that they were unable to gain the floor before the session was hastily adjourned amid indignant cries.[64]

De Serre's "never" presented a dramatic demonstration of the differences separating the two sides. The left knew that this ministry was the one most likely to look favorably on its program. If these men fell, worse would take their places. But politics required them to make a distinction between themselves and the ministry, and principle enjoined them to avoid too many compromises. They thought the timid ministry had to be forced constantly further to the left. But the ministry, while wishing to show its moderation and gain the allegiance of opponents by judicious use of appointments and favors, could not appear to have abandoned itself to the left.

The ambiguous relationship between the two sides was quite frustrating for Lafayette, who was not by nature a compromiser and who found negotiating for appointments and favors especially unrewarding. He seemed unprepared for the many duties that faced him as deputy of the Sarthe. Most pressing was Goyet's request to settle a case concerning the common lands of Pont de Gennes and of Montfort (his hometown), which had been ceded to the heir of the former lord. Though Constant and Lafayette met repeatedly with various officials, Goyet complained that they were not devoting enough attention to the matter.[65]

Solution of that matter was complicated by royalist local officials; and the deputies, at Goyet's insistence, continued to urge the government to remove incumbent ultras, especially those in military posts. Hearing rumors that rightist military groups were organizing, Lafayette worked to replace the ultra military commander in Le Mans, preferably with "an old army general who fought at Waterloo and who would have the confidence of the patriots." He tried to persuade his friend General Antoine-Simon Durrieu to accept the post, but he declined.[66]

And the deputies of the Sarthe were swamped with office seekers. Constant said he would be forced to see "two hundred strangers a day" unless he closed his door to them. They had to be wary of tricks in dealing with these strangers. A story circulated that Lafayette had visited an ultra sympathizer from the Sarthe, a Mme de Savare, though Lafayette denied any knowledge of her. To avoid such dangers, they asked Goyet to send along a note with the supplicants from the Sarthe; otherwise, they would be turned away.[67] The deputies encountered endless delays in trying to place their supporters in office. For example, a Mme Bonvoust asked Lafayette to help her husband obtain the post of tax collector at Fresnay. A month passed before the government even began to consider whom to name, and then Bonvoust did not get the job. In March, there was talk of naming him *receveur de l'hospice*, but in May he was still looking for a job.[68]

Lafayette had long championed instituting local elections as a solution to unacceptable government appointments, and he hoped legislation to that end would be introduced during the session.[69] The government proved unwilling to give up its considerable power of appointment, but it did name as director general of town and departmental administration a man with a genuine interest in improving local government, François Guizot. He listened to suggestions for change, in part because he believed that unpopular local officials caused the poor government showing in the elections. When the four deputies of the Sarthe met with him in April, he agreed, according to Lafayette, that "all the administrative personnel of the departments constituted above the population an administrative crust that should be broken, at least at several points." Lafayette passed on Guizot's request for names of honest people "with spotless reputations as far as politics is concerned, in short, names respected by all parties" from which the government could choose replacements.[70]

Constant complained that Lafayette's instructions were impossible. Nobody would satisfy all sides. Instead, he wanted Goyet to suggest people against whom no incriminating evidence existed and to indicate when unfounded rumors against someone could be successfully refuted. In an obvious criticism of Lafayette's industry, Constant asked for a copy of the list, as well, because he would work harder than anybody else. Constant said he had "no personal interest to take care of, I want only to be a deputy for the rest of my life, nor pleasures to distract me nor fine society to pay attention to, so that out of the 18 hours when I am not sleeping, six are sufficient for general questions and 12 belong to the Sarthe."[71]

Constant was not merely jealous of Lafayette's social position. Indeed, Constant did seem more willing to take on the unrewarding tasks of a deputy than did Lafayette, who became impatient at the lack of results. In the middle of May, Lafayette complained to Goyet that nothing seemed to be going right. "The roadblocks to progress that we experience are distressing. I am no more ministerial than anybody else, I believe in the faults of the Prefects and other agents; nonetheless often things occur which are due only to their powerlessness." He knew that the prefect had urged Decazes and others to remove the sub-prefect of Saint-Calais. But Etienne Pasquier opposed the removal, so "nothing has been done." The compromise on the exiles had fallen apart. He mentioned these cases, Lafayette said, "to show the predicaments of this mixed and vague situation which makes the role of the public figure so unpleasant."[72]

The ambiguities of public life sometimes forced Lafayette into unexpected and uncomfortable positions, as his speech on the military budget illustrates. A noted ultra, the comte de la Bourdonnay, proposed reducing the size of the army because, he argued, this reduction would paradoxically increase French security. As France was considered the center of dangerous revolutionary sentiment, other countries would be reassured to see that the government felt its position was so stable that it no longer needed to maintain large armies; and they, in turn, would reduce their own forces. Critical of the army's loyalty, he argued besides that a strong army merely encouraged usurpation.[73]

Lafayette certainly had to oppose an amendment introduced by an ultra who was motivated by suspicion of the army. Yet, he had always preached economy in government and the dangers of a large army. Naturally, his speech in opposition to this proposal proved to be ineffectual and confusing. In a revealing moment, Lafayette said that his rejection of the budget-cutting amendment did not spring from his belief that the ministry's budget was moderate. "It is even less because I am moderate myself; for true moderation consists, not as many people seem to think, in always finding the middle between any two points which vary from time to time, but in trying to recognize the point of truth and holding to it."

His speech emphasized a truth he had learned in the revolutions of the eighteenth century, that the people had the power to combat entrenched interests and to protect themselves from foreigners without and despots within. As usual, he believed that the energies of free people could bring peace and prosperity to the world if properly constructed political institutions existed. But a free political system could not survive with an oppressive military establishment.

Lafayette felt so strongly that the National Guard provided the key to security and freedom that he brought up the subject, even though it was irrelevant to the debate. The section of the budget under discussion was that dealing with military appropriations. The National Guard fell under the jurisdiction of the minister of the interior. It should be discussed anyhow, Lafayette insisted, "because this institution is, in my opinion, the principal defensive force of free countries, and, given the well-established truth that nations, when they want to be, are stronger than armies, I see the guarantee of human independence as well as every national independence, ours especially." The National Guard should be reorganized according to the three essential principles of the law of 1791: "arming of the nation, subordination of armed forces to civilian authority, and election of officers by citizens." Murmurs of disapproval greeted these suggestions, but, undaunted, Lafayette continued with a call for the French army to be composed exclusively of Frenchmen, "and Frenchmen, as many as remain, who fought under the banners of the *patrie.*"

He warned conservatives of the danger of blocking useful improvements. When the reforms of Turgot, Malesherbes, Necker, and Calonne were rejected, "more insurrectionary oppositions" arose. The changes made in the Revolution, though not perfect, had been "beneficial," as the progress in agriculture, industry, education, independence, and public morals amply testified. On the other hand, he repudiated the precedents of the empire, the "enemy of liberty, and therefore of national prosperity."[74] Proud of his effort, Lafayette sent three hundred copies of the speech to Goyet for distribution in the Sarthe.[75]

Later in the budget debate, Lafayette again emphasized his commitment to progress. While discussing appropriations for education, an ultra criticized the educational system bequeathed by the Revolution for not teaching religion and morals. The government spokesman responded that lack of virtue among young people was the fault not of the educational system but of their families and of the corruption of public morals caused by years of disorder. At this, Lafayette rose to defend the new generation. "It is not true that in my youth the moral condition of French society was better than today. . . . I assert, on the contrary, that public morals, marital union, love of fathers for their children, of children for their parents, far from having deteriorated in the last thirty years, have all undergone a very appreciable improvement."[76] Lafayette's belief in progress dictated his vision of an improved younger generation, but he was also influenced by his own current experience. He was surrounded by young people eager to promote the causes dear to him, most notably his loving and selfless son. Writers of talent and discernment, such as Thierry, and journalists willing to risk persecution for the liberal cause, such as Scheffer, were further proof of the virtue of the new generation.

The politics of youth was a matter of controversy in the summer of 1819. A professor at the Paris law faculty, François-Nicholas Bavoux, had been suspended from teaching because his criticism of the criminal law, for being too closely derived from that of the empire, had resulted in noisy student reactions. Those who had applauded his audacious lectures now took to the streets to protest his suspension and petitioned the Chamber of Deputies to have him reinstated. When the student petition came up for debate in the Chamber, Lafayette was one of only nine members who voted against dismissing it.[77] To the government, the Bavoux incident appeared to be part of a conspiracy to spread disorder in the universities since disturbances had occurred in other parts of the country as well. Indeed, student unrest seemed to be sweeping across Europe. The most serious incident occurred in the spring of 1819, when a German student killed a playwright, August von Kotzebue, who was suspected of being a Russian spy and who had criticized the lawlessness of German university students.[78]

Lafayette seemed increasingly attracted to the optimism of youth as he became discouraged by the lack of progress made in the Chamber. He left Paris before the session was over and from La Grange wrote a final report to Goyet. He had not written in a month, another sign of his lack of enthusiasm for his public duties. "I have no intentional fault to blame myself for, I even think that my colleagues and I did what we could to be of service to the department in both private and public matters; but we had little success." Improvements could come only if the next elections brought in "genuine and decided patriots. Then proposals would improve even before and especially during debate, and then, if the citizens will just profit from the advice given from the podium and in the newspapers and other liberal writings, local and departmental administrations can be regenerated." Knowing that Goyet feared that a lack of unity on the left would weaken the chances of electing staunch liberals, Lafayette tried to reassure him. "The needling among the *indépendant* newspapers is not, I hope, disturbing. They will always agree on the important occasions. Each has, nonetheless, its particular nuance."[79]

Lafayette avoided facing the difficulties caused by disunity on the left. He had a vague optimism that men of goodwill should agree on republican principles. Besides, he did not find quiet satisfaction in working behind the scenes to solve knotty practical problems. Impatient with maneuver and delay, he had little desire to find a middle ground on which all could agree. Though his speeches in the Chamber had commanded attention, they had been infrequent. Benjamin Constant, Chauvelin, and Manuel had all been more active in debate. Since voting in the Chamber was secret (each deputy deposited a colored ball into an urn: white for yes, black for no), his legislative record cannot be systematically analyzed. However, when measures were put to a voice or standing vote, he frequently joined a small group of seven to ten members of the left, who remained in opposition to the bitter end. He served as the conscience of the left, the uncompromising model and guide, a role that was incompatible with being an effective parliamentary leader.

His chosen role as the man of principle occasionally got him into quandaries. In June, for example, Decazes founded a society for the improvement of prisons and published a list of members, which included Lafayette's name. Like some others on the list, Lafayette had no knowledge of this organization. Suspicious of the principles that this society might espouse, unhappy at the prospect of meetings presided over by the duc d'Angoulême, and miffed at appearing on the list as "M. le marquis de Lafayette," he nonetheless hesitated to disavow it publicly for fear of offending some who supported it. His friends advised him to ignore the prank "because public opinion will not distinguish between this society and the one on *enseignement mutuel*, encouragement of industry, etc. where I am also in rather bad company although there are, as there are here, commendable men who would be hurt by a resounding refusal on my part." After much soul-searching, he decided to do nothing. He confessed to d'Argenson that he had always shrunk from unpleasant confrontations with his friends. "In the same way when I was seventeen years old, in order not to offend my Noailles relatives, who had arranged for me to receive the hereditary post of the marquises of Noailles as first gentleman of Monsieur, I did not know how to get out of it except by insulting, for no reason, Monsieur himself, who was disgusted with me, twenty years before the beginning of his reign."[80]

Discouraged by the lack of progress in France, Lafayette almost instinctively turned his attention to the United States in the summer of 1819. At Voyer d'Argenson's suggestion, Lafayette was arranging to have translated into French a work on American statistics written by Congressman Adam Seybert of Philadelphia. This useful work would gather into a single volume information otherwise difficult to find and would spread instructive examples of the value of a republican government and a free economy. Lafayette sought Gallatin's help, and the American minister was more than willing to lend assistance by marking errors and providing "additional clarifications or notes." Meanwhile, Lafayette himself began a translation of the Constitution of the United States, to be placed at the head of the volume.[81]

Gallatin's suggestions for revision were gratefully (if anonymously) acknowledged by the translator, who said that the omissions had been approved "by one of the most enlightened citizens of the United States."[82] The translator was Arnold Scheffer, now hiding in Paris. Scheffer wrote two articles in the *Censeur* summing up the lessons Lafayette hoped the French people could learn from Seybert's book. The insistent theme that underlay many of Lafayette's beliefs was here repeated: that liberal political institutions were a necessary prerequisite to happiness and prosperity. A history of a people was more than its battles or diplomatic maneuvers, Scheffer argued. Political economy had to be examined, too, and for that study, statistics were indispensable. Though hard to come by in Europe, statistics were readily available in America. While European nations were torn by dissensions and civil wars,

> *with what pleasure do we now turn our eyes toward that happy people that does not have conspiracies; where no power has the right to pass laws of exception, nor to touch liberty of thought, of speech, and of the press; that sees its prosperity constantly increasing along with its population, unburdened by exorbitant taxes and large permanent armies, where each man can secure for himself by his own work an independent existence.*[83]

The prosperity of this republic was not

*the result of a happy accident, nor of a favorable situa-
tion. It is due to a constitution which guarantees all
freedoms, to an administrative system that places no
obstacles in the way of anything useful, and to the
wisdom of the citizens who, without allowing themselves to be dazzled by the spectacle offered by Europe, remain faithful to the politics which suits
modern nations, nations where the general interest, far
from requiring the sacrifice of individual interests, consists of the bringing together of those interests.*

Scheffer's article stressed the expense and danger of bloated
military establishments, points Lafayette had also tried to make
in his recent speech on military spending.[84]

Shortly after these articles appeared, Lafayette finally succeeded in having Scheffer's sentence set aside. In June 1819, he
had introduced a resolution in the Chamber of Deputies to negate
the penalties on writers condemned under the old press laws.
Before leaving Paris in July, Lafayette had met with the minister
of justice, who told him that a general declaration of amnesty for
those sentenced for press offenses would be impossible but that
he would be willing to review individual cases. In October, Lafayette's good offices resulted in settling the cases of Scheffer and of
another condemned writer, Amédée Féret, who had published the
Homme gris, though the latter had to spend two weeks in jail.[85]

For the elections of 1819, Lafayette and his friends on the
Censeur believed that it was essential to emphasize liberal principles and to choose candidates committed to them. Lafayette had
told Goyet that better laws would come only by choosing "genuine
and decided patriots."[86] To counter the ministry's attempt to win
deputies away from the left by favors and appointments, the left in
1819 insisted that a candidate not hold a government office and
promise not to accept one.[87] The emphasis on principle might
have been caused as well by concern over the precarious health of
Louis XVIII in 1819. If he should die, a strongly liberal Chamber
might be able to prevent his brother and heir from undoing much
of what had recently been accomplished.

For all these reasons, the left was looking for candidates
with proper liberal credentials, with reputations for firmness and
incorruptibility, who had not been seduced by Napoleon. They

increasingly used the term *liberals,* rather than the less precise *indépendants.*[88] It was only logical that they look among their friends and relations for candidates whom they could trust.

Lafayette was especially active in promoting the candidacies of the comte de Lambrechts and General Jean-Joseph Tarayre. Lambrechts, a friend of Grégoire's and Lanjuinais's, had served as minister of justice under the Directory. Consistently anti-Napoleonic, he had voted against the life consulate and the empire, was the first to demand the abdication of the emperor in April 1814, and voted against the Acte Additionel. Lafayette described him to Voyer d'Argenson as "an admirable patriot, as devoted as he is disinterested, free from petty calculations and petty passions, in a word, just what we like."[89] Lambrechts was elected in two departments, Bas-Rhin and Seine-Inférieur, and he opted for the Bas-Rhin.[90]

General Jean-Joseph Tarayre had a distinguished military career and served under King Louis Bonaparte in Holland. During the First Restoration, Louis XVIII had appointed him an inspector of National Guards; and during the Hundred Days, Napoleon had also charged him with reorganizing National Guard units. He was put on the nonactive lists at the Second Restoration. His recent article in the *Censeur* on army reform and a work critical of England showed similarities to Lafayette's thinking. To promote Tarayre's election in the Charente-Inférieure, Lafayette wrote a letter endorsing his candidacy, which he hoped to place in a local rather than a Parisian publication. He favored either a paper in the Charente-Inférieure itself or the *Propagateur de la Vienne,* the paper sponsored by Voyer d'Argenson in nearby Poitiers in imitation of Goyet's *Propagateur.* In a further effort to find regional influences to help Tarayre, Lafayette and Manuel asked one of the latter's fellow deputies of the Vendée to attend the elections in the neighboring department of the Charente-Inférieure.[91]

Lafayette's political efforts in the summer of 1819 were taken in conjunction with a close circle of allies, not a broad-based committee. His closest tie was to Voyer d'Argenson, who was in the Vienne working for the election of General Jean Demarçay. He kept d'Argenson informed of all that was being done in Paris to promote elections in these western departments and proved his confidence in his friend by giving d'Argenson permission to use his name "to be cited, printed, welcomed or held in contempt, wherever yours will be." Lafayette thought this move was probably unnecessary, though, because people would surely assume they agreed since "our fraternity is well known."[92]

Lafayette's name was linked as well to the most notorious election of 1819, that of the abbé Henri-Baptiste Grégoire. The choice of the radical Grégoire seems consistent with the desire of the extreme liberals to find incorruptible men. Grégoire had early supported the Revolution and had became the bishop of Blois in the constitutional church, established during the Revolution. A member of the Convention, he had been absent at the trial of the king, but he had later approved the king's condemnation. To those who charged that he was the equivalent of a regicide, Grégoire responded that he opposed capital punishment. Although he had approved the guilty verdict for the king, he had not expressed approval of the death penalty. He never denied that he was a convinced republican and critic of monarchy.[93] He became a senator under the empire but was consistently hostile to Napoleon. As a member of the liberal circle of intellectuals who congregated in the Parisian suburb of Auteuil, which also included Lafayette's close friend Destutt de Tracy, Grégoire was noted for his advocacy of the revolutionary church and of full rights for Jews and blacks.[94]

During the Restoration, Grégoire continued to publish books and pamphlets and to socialize with prominent liberals both French and foreign. Lady Morgan visited him frequently during her trips to France. The American George Ticknor recorded that during his visit to Paris in 1817 he went often to see Grégoire, who continued to support "with no common firmness the cause of religion."[95] Grégoire met weekly to discuss politics and religion with a fellow Napoleonic senator, Lanjuinais, another advocate of liberal Christianity.[96] Lafayette's ties with Grégoire were based on their commitments to the abolition of slavery and their mutual interest in Haiti. He deferred to him on religious questions.[97]

The election of Grégoire, a well-known man in liberal circles in Paris, would focus attention on two issues that the liberals wanted to emphasize. The first was the arbitrary treatment of exiles. Regicides who took part in the government of the Hundred Days had been exiled, yet here was a man popularly labeled a regicide who was not in exile. A second issue was the status of the Church. Grégoire, a noted advocate of a Gallican church, had written a pamphlet condemning the concordat negotiated with the Pope in 1817. Liberals looked upon ultramontanism as another aspect of international reaction and increasingly championed Gallicanism during the Restoration.[98] Thus Goyet reported that liberals in the Sarthe considered Grégoire's election important "because of the ultramontane influence."[99]

In early July, Lafayette had urged Grégoire to allow his nomination in the Isère. Grégoire seemed to hesitate, saying that there were many fine local candidates and that the voters did not need to search outside the department.[100] Yet modest disclaimers of this sort from candidates were standard, and two days later the *Censeur* published Grégoire's name as one of the four liberal candidates in the Isère.[101]

Publication of Grégoire's name in a national newspaper did not automatically ensure election. Like Lafayette's election in the Sarthe, Grégoire's, too, depended upon the efforts of local activists. Lafayette knew the men in the Isère who devised the Grégoire candidacy.[102] Among them was Joseph Rey, familiar to Lafayette because of his friendship with Destutt de Tracy, whom Rey had sought out after reading his book on ideology. Rey studied law and became a magistrate, but he was dismissed at the Second Restoration for criticizing the Bourbons. Back in Grenoble, he founded in 1816 an organization called the Union, inspired by secret German anti-Napoleonic groups. Though his aim was to spread liberalism by legal means only, he explained that the violence of governments compelled them to secrecy. He made contacts with liberals in Germany, as well as in other French cities in the east, especially Lyon. Rey's group of confederates in the Isère was doubtless valuable for coordinating the effort in favor of Grégoire in 1819.[103]

Lafayette recognized the value of local organization, and he and his friends in Paris were always eager to establish ties with such groups. However, Joseph Rey would later claim for the Union a much more influential role than it deserved. Rey recalled that he had visited Lafayette in Paris to propose that they found a Paris chapter of the Union. Lafayette entered into Rey's schemes, promising to speak to fellow deputies about the group. Limited to thirty or so members, the Paris Union, according to Rey, eventually included the deputies Voyer d'Argenson, Dupont de l'Eure, Claude Tircuy de Corcelle, Tarayre, Demarçay, Guillaume-Xavier Labbey de Pompières, and Antoine Bourreau de Beauséjour; the journalists Comte,

Dunoyer, Châtelain of the *Courrier français*, and Marcelin Desloges of the *Journal du commerce*; the lawyers Mérilhou, Odilon Barrot, François Mauguin, and Saint-Albin Berville; as well as Victor Cousin, Augustin de Schonen, and Louis-Gaspard-Amédée Girod de l'Ain. Since Lafayette already worked closely with these men in promoting liberal politics, it is not clear what additional function the Union served. But the age thrived on secret societies, so such a group (even if somewhat redundant) is not improbable.[104]

Other societies promoting liberal causes included the *Société des amis de la liberté de la presse*, which in the spring of 1819 was being transformed by far-left activists from a group to promote freedom of the press (no longer of use after the passage of the press law) into a kind of political party.[105] Its meetings were attracting more people, and the discussions ranged widely to cover all political and electoral issues. The organization came to be dominated by a different group of people. Constant and Staël quit going.[106] Lafayette, on the other hand, maintained his ties to the society. Though he had hosted some meetings in 1818, he hosted none in 1819, perhaps because the group had grown too large.[107] He was not an active member of the directing board of the society, at least not at the end of 1819.[108] But during the spring, while the Chamber was in session, he attended its meetings, and the *Censeur* regularly carried a description of the meetings after it began daily publication in the middle of June. Other liberal newspapers in Paris and other important liberal leaders distanced themselves from the *Société*. And they disagreed about the *Société's* endorsement of Grégoire and the tactics the group advocated for the coming elections.

Such disagreements within liberal ranks illustrate how misleading it is to imagine a single *comité directeur* in Paris sending instructions to the liberals in the provinces. The election of the abbé Grégoire was made possible by the *absence* of such a group. Had a caucus of parliamentary leaders met in Paris to choose nominees, Constant and others might have been able to head off the candidacy. In the absence of disciplined political parties or of an atmosphere that encouraged such close cooperation, the parliamentary leaders, while wielding considerable influence, had to depend ultimately on journalists and local political leaders to take the initiative. And these people were often more radical than the leaders themselves.

The liberals in the Isère in concert with their friends on the *Censeur* promoted Grégoire's election. The *Indépendant* also endorsed him, but the *Minerve* and the *Renommée* did not.[109] Rey recalled that most politicians on the left reacted to the choice "with anxiety, either because all were not capable of appreciating such a candidate, or because the most timid already had a premonition of the treacherous use to which the ultra-royalists could put such a result of the electoral law. Only one periodical, the *Censeur*, declared openly for that candidacy, and the others barely mentioned it."[110]

Dissent was heard almost immediately. Charles Goyet complained that the Sarthe deputy, Hardouin, did not favor Grégoire's candidacy. Benjamin Constant, in responding to Goyet, was revealingly silent on the question.[111] He, too, feared the consequences of this election. The baron de Barante, a *doctrinaire*, described the dilemma of the liberal leaders this way:

> *M. Constant and the leaders of the left, M. de La Fayette himself, understood the faults of their party; but the need for popularity, the fear of the newspapers, intimacy with journalists, their condescension to young people and zealous partisans, precluded any resistance. They condemned in a whisper what they had not the courage to disavow out loud. As much and more than us, they dreaded the nomination of Grégoire and did not know how to prevent it.*[112]

This judgment seems more accurate for Constant than for Lafayette, who had encouraged Grégoire to run, even if he did not actively promote his election afterward. Yet, Barante's comment contains an important insight: the success of the left depended on what others did to organize and mold opinion.

On 20 July, journalists and activists of the *Société des amis de la liberté de la presse* committed the left to a radical course. The meeting, held three days after the Chambers closed and therefore probably attended by few deputies, narrowly approved a controversial decision to vote for an ultra candidate over a ministerial one if those were the only choices in the final round of voting.[113] Charles Comte defended this tactic in a succinct expression of the attitude that had also prompted Grégoire's nomination.

> *The friends of liberty agree easily on the goal to-
> ward which they are going; but it often happens that
> they are not in agreement on the means that can lead
> them there. They unanimously desire the development
> and consolidation of representative government. . . .
> Some imagine that in order to strengthen it, it is suffi-
> cient to repeat frequently that the Charter is inviolable,
> and to push away without distinction every act by
> which modifications are attempted. Others, and we
> are of that number, think that the best means would be
> to give to national representation such a strength that
> in the future no one would dare to conceive the idea of
> striking at it.*[114]

No security could be found in voting for wishy-washy government supporters, who could not be trusted to maintain the Charter. It was less dangerous to vote for a few ultras, Comte believed, because they were so unpopular that their chances of dominating were negligible.

Lafayette had already left Paris before the night of the meeting, but he probably endorsed the views of his close ally, Charles Comte. Benjamin Constant had not attended the meeting either, but he immediately saw the danger in such a policy. He expressed his disapproval, and thus revealed the split in liberal ranks, the next morning in an article in the *Renommée* warning against voting for ultras. Many ministerial supporters, he pointed out, joined that camp only because it was the strongest. If the ultras became stronger, these weak-willed types would gravitate just as readily in the direction of the ultras, thus giving them the majority.[115]

The ultras, too, decided that their best interests dictated supporting the other extreme rather than the government. Their tactics were crucial in Grégoire's election. On the first round, three moderate liberals received a majority. Grégoire was a distant fourth, followed by a ministerial candidate and then by an ultra. Had the ministerial and ultra voters combined on the second round, Grégoire would have been defeated. Instead, the ultras threw their support to Grégoire.[116] His election, combined with other liberal triumphs (the left won about twenty-five seats), forced the ministry to consider what the ultras had been clamoring for all along: an amendment of the electoral law to try to end liberal victories.

By 1819, Lafayette had become a leader of the most radical wing of the liberals, unwilling to compromise, eager to elect the most intransigent former revolutionaries to the Chamber. He belonged to the *Société des amis de la liberté de la presse*, which was trying to coordinate liberal political activity throughout the country. Such activities made many people at the time (and many since) suspect that Lafayette was conspiring to overthrow the Bourbon government. That he was conspiring seems doubtful. He was working to change the ministry by electing deputies who shared his views on government. The king's ministers, Lafayette believed, should be answerable to the Chambers, and he expected that when liberals controlled the Chamber, they would determine the composition of the ministry. Though Louis XVIII was not amenable to this sort of constitutional monarchy, Lafayette thought that such change must come, that Louis XVIII would be forced to accept it, just as he had accepted other features of government not originally to his liking. It seems unlikely that Lafayette would conspire to overthrow the government when he and his political allies were gaining more and more power within it by legal means.

The liberals agreed on the goal: a constitutional monarchy with a ministry answerable to the Chamber. But they disagreed about how quickly their goal could be achieved. Lafayette wanted to force the issue as soon as possible. Benjamin Constant was more cautious. He feared that antagonizing the moderate royalists would force them into the arms of the ultras and halt progress. From his perspective, Lafayette seemed hasty and his attacks on the ministry unwise, but Constant surely did not consider them seditious.

And there were reasons for impatience. Many feared that Louis XVIII might die at any minute. It had long been expected that a struggle would break out in France following the death of the king. For example, Albert Gallatin wrote in 1817 that there would "be no danger of commotion whilst the King lives." By 1819 he reported improvements in the country, but much still depended on the survival of the king. "There is in this country a rapid progress in favor of liberty and liberal institutions. The present ministry is entirely disposed that way, and if the king lives a few years longer, there is a well-founded hope that those institutions will be so far consolidated as to be beyond the influence of the personal character and opinions of the Sovereign."[117] Rumors circulated that ultras were arming in anticipation of the accession of Charles X. In the middle of May, Goyet told Constant that he was depending on him and on Lafayette to let him know of any developments. "You will not forget that my position would be critical in a city which contains only a small number of thoroughgoing patriots and many partisans of the *chouannerie*."[118]

Developments in Germany increased the fear among French liberals that foreign powers might intervene to help consolidate a reaction. Metternich and Frederick William III of Prussia decided to combat agitation among nationalist student groups by enacting a series of measures to crush conspiracies, censor publications, suspend suspected professors, and suppress student groups. These Carlsbad Decrees were imposed throughout Germany after they were passed by the Diet in September 1819.

Lafayette and his friends wanted to gain as much power as they could while they had the opportunity and were probably preparing as well for the expected armed confrontations. This kind of planning was consistent with the scheming that took place in the Malet conspiracy during the Empire. Furthermore, he was worried that the Chamber, by not restructuring the National Guard, had left them at the mercy of the right.

> It is obvious that we are going to disperse without the nation being armed, without the administration being organized or rather its organization is worse than nothing. A ministerial crisis, a still greater event would find only the adversaries of liberty ready, a circumstance still more unfortunate for them than for us, because liberty would eventually triumph. However the rumors circulating about the condition of the king, are, I think, at least much exaggerated by the party which openly wants his death.[119]

Two letters that Lafayette wrote in August and September 1819 to General Durrieu of the general staff are possible evidence of military preparations.[120] The language of these letters was so impenetrable as to suggest a kind of code. Lafayette said he understood why Durrieu had not written but that he was sorry for the "misunderstanding which deprived me of the pleasure of seeing you at the home of our excellent friend." He hoped Durrieu would join them at La Grange, whose inhabitants all admired the friend in question. "We will speak of this angelic friend and of everything that interests her until we have the happiness of seeing her again in this countryside where eight days had sufficed to perceptibly improve her health; it is hard to conceive of this paternal obsession which while rejecting the attentions and affection of such a daughter has fastened on the idea of La Grange in order to torment us all." Their friend was being deprived of liberty by her father. Several weeks later, Lafayette continued his discussion of this "angelic friend whose situation absorbs all my thoughts as it does yours."[121] Lafayette could, of course, have been describing a real person whose father was tyrannical, but another interpretation is more plausible. The "father" could easily be the king, La Grange could refer to some organization to which Lafayette and Durrieu belonged, and the "angélique amie" might be republican government.[122] In April 1820, the *Patriote alsacien*, a newspaper sponsored by Voyer d'Argenson and edited by Charles-Philippe Marchand, was closed down for printing a fable entitled "*Le Bon Père*," about a father who would not allow his children any liberties. The metaphor was a common one at the time.[123]

The hypothesis that the "angélique amie" discussed here was a code for republican government or liberty is strengthened by the evidence of Lafayette's letters to Voyer d'Argenson, which likewise use the image of a young woman to represent liberty or republicanism. The code in these letters is more easily broken because the young woman is given a name: Marianne. After the ordinance dissolving the Chambers in September 1816, Lafayette concluded a letter to Voyer d'Argenson by noting that Marianne's health had improved, "although she is not completely cured."[124] In early 1817, Lafayette sent him some suggestions for the debate on the law of individual freedom. Toward the end of this letter he added: "Marianne ought to take advantage of this law to come out. Do you think I can do anything to help?"[125] And in another reference, this time from Chavaniac where he was spending the summer of 1817, Lafayette wrote that Auguste de Staël and Victor de Broglie "have taken it upon themselves to replace us for Marianne's affairs which were dragging on."[126] No lady named Marianne figures in the family circles or close friends of the Lafayette or d'Argenson families. During an era when mails were not secure, Lafayette and his friends used the term *Marianne* to disguise references to republican principles. In this fashion, they helped to establish in common parlance the practice of giving the name Marianne to the republic.[127]

General Durrieu, then, may have been prepared to support the liberals during the crisis expected to follow the king's death or in any attempt to suppress the Chambers. Similar contacts with others were doubtless made. Joseph Rey recalled that in the summer of 1819 General François-Roch Ledru des Essarts, commander of the Seventh Military Division stationed at Grenoble, had committed himself to a revolt. The plan had been dreamed up by a man from Grenoble, Jean-Baptiste Dumoulin, who was such a rabid Bonapartist that he had traveled to Elba to urge Napoleon to return to France.[128] Rey said that Lafayette consented to join this plot but that the plans were upset when General Ledru des Essarts was transferred from his command in July 1819. Lafayette's letters to Durrieu, then, could possibly have referred to this aborted uprising.[129]

Rey's story raises several questions, however. The impulse of this plot seems too Bonapartist to have secured the whole-hearted support of Lafayette.[130] One wonders if his encouragement of these generals stemmed from a desire to maintain contact with military men in case the expected confrontations occurred in 1819. This seems especially likely since Lafayette's letters to Voyer d'Argenson during the summer of 1819 give no hint of plotting. Instead, they focus on political questions and on plans for the coming session. Given their close collaboration on most matters, it seems unlikely that Lafayette would have acted without his friend's knowledge. Nor would he have acted without George, who spent part of the summer in Auvergne.[131] Any contingency plans for armed struggles he might have been making were, in any case, not needed immediately because the king survived. Lafayette's main focus therefore continued to be politics. And in the fall of 1819, the most important political issue facing the left was the whirlwind of reaction created by Grégoire's election.

5

The Fight for
the Election Law

In late August 1819, Lafayette welcomed Goyet to Paris and accompanied him to ministers' offices and government bureaus to press the claims of people seeking positions and benefits.[1] The attention that Lafayette and Constant showered on "the excellent Goyet" was proof of his value to liberal politics.[2] Mme de Broglie, on the other hand, found him distasteful: "Benjamin Constant is showing around Paris a certain Goget, a journalist from the Sarthe, whose behavior towards him is unseemly. This Goget said in front of him to M. Decazes: 'If I had been eligible, I would have had myself elected instead of M. Constant.'"[3] Lafayette and Constant recognized the contributions of people like Goyet, even if Mme de Broglie did not, and they listened to his political advice. In mid-September, Constant and Goyet visited La Grange, no doubt for long discussions about politics. There, they heard the news of Grégoire's election. Goyet did not favor abandoning Grégoire, whom he had visited several times during his stay in Paris.[4]

The election results led to a cabinet crisis, as the ministry considered giving up its accommodation with the left and seeking support on the right. The opening of the Chambers was delayed while the politicians negotiated and Elie Decazes organized a new ministry with himself at the helm. Lafayette was embarrassed to see among the new ministers Victor de Latour-Maubourg, the brother of his son-in-law Charles and of his old friend César. Victor's royalist sympathies contrasted sharply with the views of his brothers. Lafayette informed friends that he would have no influence with the new minister, despite family connections.[5]

The liberals were also in disarray. Some wanted to continue opposing the ministry, while others urged support of Decazes to prevent the formation of an ultra ministry.[6] At first the crisis did not seem serious, and they believed Grégoire would have no difficulty taking his seat in the Chamber of Deputies.[7] They changed their minds, however, when the government arrested two men who had hosted meetings of the *Société des amis de la liberté de la presse:* Antoine Gévaudan and Colonel Charles Simon-Lorière. They were charged with breaking the law forbidding regular meetings of over twenty persons without government authorization.

By these arrests, the government could with one blow destroy a dangerous political organization and force moderate liberals to repudiate the clearly illegal activities of their associates. Broglie, one of the founders of the society, publicly acknowledged that it was illegal, and Laffitte now began to argue that opposition should be more restrained. Rumors even circulated that Constant was negotiating with the government. He dismissed such nonsense as another example of the government's attempts to divide the left. Despite his distance from the *Société* in the last year, Constant now devoted his efforts to keeping all the members of the left behind the incriminated group.[8] Charles Comte complained that the government was now making a distinction between *libéraux* and *ultrà-libéraux*.[9] The arrests forced many liberals to rally to defend their right to meet with whomever they wished. But the arrests also indicated a government shift to the right. Expecting, therefore, that the government would soon attack the election law, some liberals thought it prudent to avoid a confrontation as well over Grégoire.

Many liberals urged Grégoire to resign before the Chambers opened.[10] The problem was that electoral imperatives conflicted with parliamentary maneuvers. If Grégoire resigned, something might be salvaged from the electoral law, and the dangerous precedent of expelling a legally elected deputy would be avoided. But voters would be discouraged. Would they next try to force out Constant or Hardouin, Goyet wondered, or any deputy who had supported the Acte Additionel?[11] Constant, who had been opposed to Grégoire's election all along, was persuaded by Goyet's political advice and never joined those asking Grégoire to resign. He told Albertine de Broglie that, if he came out against Grégoire, he would lose his own seat at the next election.[12]

Lafayette seemed strangely uninvolved. He spent October and most of November at La Grange, distracted by the hunting season and by his many guests, leaving the Sarthe's business in Constant's hands. He appeared to think that the fight over Grégoire was inevitable, that if he were denied his seat, twenty other departments would reelect him.[13] In fact, Lafayette never wavered in his support, though others, even Grégoire's friend Lanjuinais, eventually decided he should resign.[14] When Lafayette saw the abbé in Paris, he found him as unaware as he had always been of the political furor he had created.[15] Voyer d'Argenson exhorted him not to give in; and by the end of October, Grégoire had concluded that resignation "in the present circumstances would be an insult to the electorate of the Isère and a disastrous means of discouraging the friends of liberty in the departments."[16]

With Grégoire determined to hold on, the new session promised to be stormy, but Lafayette did not appear worried. He was encouraged by his ever-sanguine reading of public opinion, which seemed "very good, and purer than it has been since 91; our youth is excellent; it has no schemes to serve, no faction to humor, no bad record to defend, no hatred or predilection to satisfy; it marches straight to liberty . . . without at all provoking the faults of despotism and oligarchy, but taking advantage of them in the interests of the European revolution." The younger generation would stand firm, but he was less certain of his fellow deputies of the left. He thought that "the column of the left will be attacked on two points: whether it will be broken, whether it will be cut higher or lower, that I cannot predict, and I don't get involved in it, having neither the facts, nor the tactics, nor even the influence *intra muros*. I hope only that three or four friends will arrive early, and I will be very happy to talk with them."[17] He admitted here his unfitness for the kind of coalition building that might hold the left together, and he did not seem to expect it to emerge intact.

The crisis facing the Chamber, he believed, had been engineered by the "crowned heads of Europe" meeting at Carlsbad. They were forcing Decazes to propose changes in the election law. Because he saw the crisis as the result of an international conspiracy rather than as what it no doubt really was (merely Decazes's attempt to keep himself in power), Lafayette believed that it was imperative to reorganize the National Guard so that the country could defend itself.[18] But this issue, as well as others he thought important (local administration and habeas corpus), had to be put aside until the Grégoire affair was over and the intentions of the new government were clearer.

Meeting at Laffitte's, the liberals decided to ask Grégoire once again to resign. Lafayette fought this decision till two in the morning but to no avail.[19] The delegation sent to Grégoire included such staunch liberals as Voyer d'Argenson, Dupont de l'Eure, Manuel, and Martin de Gray, and their presence shows the willingness even of some on the far left to reach an accommodation that would preserve some of their influence in the Chamber. Mindful of Goyet's instructions, Constant did not attend the meeting. When Grégoire again refused to resign, the left decided not to fight for his admission if they could have the election declared invalid on a technicality.[20]

During the stormy session of 6 December, Constant, as spokesman for the left, vigorously opposed Grégoire's expulsion on the grounds of "unworthiness" but left open the possibility of annulling his election. By such moderation, he hoped to reconcile several members of the center and ensure a majority to protect the election law.[21] This careful maneuvering failed when the chair asked for the votes of all those wishing to exclude Grégoire for whatever reason. The left insisted uselessly that one could not exclude a deputy who had not been legally elected, but their objections were brushed aside, and they did not pursue them.[22]

The left sacrificed Grégoire to a larger purpose, defending the Charter and the election law. Such a strategy was not surprising, since many had not favored his election to begin with. At a large meeting at Laffitte's on 29 November, the deputies had decided unanimously that defending the law would be their primary goal during the new session. Lafayette went along with this decision, though he had some reservations about the Charter and the election law, which he considered deficient when weighed against the principles of his "declaration of 11 July 89." He would have liked an improved Charter, but he was convinced "that the interest as well as the wish of the nation is, at this time, to meddle with neither the Charter, where many rights are recognized and many national interests are guaranteed, nor the law of elections, whose results should reassure the friends of liberty, as much as they worry its enemies."[23] One principle outweighed another. The origins and provisions of the Charter and election law might be faulty, but if public opinion favored them, he was unwilling to challenge them.

Another principle also dictated defense of the Charter. He had always held that constituted authorities could not amend "at their pleasure the social compact."[24] Lafayette seemed ready to accord the status of "social compact" to the Charter. George explained the logic: it might be the "work of the king," but it "belongs to us as much as to him, now that he has given it to us, and that we have accepted it by recognizing it and by submitting ourselves to it as the legal power actually protective of our liberties."[25] If the Charter was the social compact, then neither the legislature nor the king had the right to change it. Liberals were more and more inclined to sustain the Charter as a way of protecting minimum rights from the attacks of ultra-royalists.

While waiting for the government to present its legislative proposals, Lafayette and his friends asked their associates throughout the country to send petitions in favor of maintaining inviolate the election law and the Charter.[26] Their time was also occupied by the *Société des amis de la liberté de la presse* case, scheduled to begin on 11 December. The list of witnesses read like a roll call of prominent liberal politicians, even though many of those who appeared in court to support the group's right to meet had not been active in the meetings of the previous year. Their line of defense was that no real organization (as defined by the law) existed. There were no rules and no membership requirements. Each meeting was managed by the host, who sometimes delegated someone else to preside.

On 18 December Lafayette testified that he had been at Gévaudan's house but never at Simon-Lorière's.[27] When asked whether he believed article 291 of the Penal Code was applicable to these meetings, Lafayette responded truculently, "That article is so incompatible with any constitutional regime, that in applying it to these meetings, or to any other of this kind, I would have assumed I was contradicting the Charter and ridiculing the government."[28] The speech by the defense attorney, Saint-Albin Berville, likewise stressed the incompatibility of the political system established by the Charter with laws prohibiting meetings without government permission. The court found that an unauthorized association did indeed exist, and the society was dissolved. The two men were fined two hundred francs and assessed court costs.[29]

Despite the show of unity during the trial, the left was actually divided and unsure of the response they should make to the government's attacks. Benjamin Constant complained that jealousy (presumably Laffitte's) prevented regular and serious meetings. Constant invited people to his house on Fridays, but lamented that the presence of women precluded serious discussion of tactics. The newspapers continued in a state of disarray; the editors had asked the politicians for direction but received no guidance.[30] Characteristically, Lafayette was less worried than Constant about these divisions on the left. He assured Goyet that the disagreements were minor.

> Some opinions and behavior are more forceful than others; some believe more than others in the corrigibility [of the government]; some are more fearful than others of going too far; but on the election law for example, and on maintaining the Charter, nobody in the société Laffitte will stay behind. A large part of the société Ternaux, if I'm not mistaken, will follow. The small movements of pride of which you speak will always be sacrificed to a large and positive public interest.[31]

One of the difficulties in formulating a response to the government, according to Lafayette, was that every day brought a different rumor regarding its intentions, depending on the progress of negotiations with the ultras.[32] Meanwhile, petitions had poured into the Chamber in support of the electoral law, and the deputies spent much of their time dealing with them. Lafayette received petitions from all over the country, not merely from the areas with which he normally communicated.[33] He sent copies of some of them to journalists, so that articles could be written about them.[34]

The government and the right protested that these petitions were the work of the *comité directeur* of Paris and that collective petitions (signed by several people) should not be allowed. As proof of these accusations, Etienne Pasquier produced a letter from Goyet to the farmers of the Sarthe that enclosed a model petition. Pasquier called Goyet's letter seditious, especially his warning that feudal rights might return and national lands might be lost. Constant retorted that the Sarthe had special reasons to be concerned because of the oppression they had suffered under a prefect whom "M. le ministre knows quite well."[35] By a vote of 117 to 112, the Chamber decided not to act on these petitions. This vote was interpreted as a straw vote on the maintenance of the election law, and the left was heartened to notice that a change of only three votes would have reversed the result. They grew especially interested in filling the seats still vacant from the last election, but the government understandably delayed calling for by-elections.

Since the government was still having trouble putting together a new electoral law to present to the Chambers, the left decided to use the time to present proposals of their own.[36] Lafayette, of course, chose as his subject the reorganization of the National Guard. At the Second Restoration, the National Guard had been put under the command of the comte d'Artois, who controlled the institution through "inspectors," all of whom were his supporters. In 1818, the administration of the National Guard had been given directly to the ministry, and Monsieur was stripped of command. Though the guard was no longer in the hands of the ultras, its subordination to the government and the survival of Napoleonic regulations conflicted with Lafayette's expectations for a genuine citizen militia.[37]

The continuing problem of the organization of the regular army had been dealt with in 1818 with the passage of an army bill. The Bourbon regime had distrusted the loyalty of the army, interpreting the return of Napoleon during the Hundred Days as basically an army conspiracy. In their attempt to repay the loyalty of returning royalists and to reduce the inflated Napoleonic army, the new government had angered veterans by appointing new officers and by placing twenty thousand soldiers on the inactive list at half pay. These so-called *demi-soldes* were watched suspiciously by the authorities, who were worried that they might join conspiracies against the government.[38] A new war minister, Laurent Gouvion Saint-Cyr, appointed in 1817, was determined to provide for a more reliable army. His legislation called for a return to partial conscription, established a reserve, and instituted a system of promotion to eliminate favoritism. His achievement was widely viewed as a successful attempt to reconcile the old imperial army with the monarchy and had garnered the support of the left.[39]

Despite this victory over the ultras (who thought the new legislation dangerously democratic), Lafayette was still not satisfied and agitated for a citizen militia to guard against the possible abuses of a standing army. Lafayette's speech quoted at length an ordinance issued by Louis XVIII in March 1815 calling the National Guard to the defense of the country and promising to preserve the Charter as a "rallying point and sign of alliance of all Frenchmen." His proposal was rejected by the Chamber on what the *Censeur* called two doubtful voice votes.[40]

Lafayette's speech put forward an issue of interest to the far left, but it did so in a sober and uncontentious fashion. During this period, Lafayette was cooperating with other men on the left to try to ensure a majority for maintaining the electoral law, despite his personal view that they had little chance of succeeding. Their desire to conciliate moderates dictated even staying away from a banquet held in Paris on 5 February 1820 to celebrate the anniversary of the passage of the electoral law. At first Lafayette had promised the organizers that he would attend and bring along other deputies as well. But, as he explained later, "unfortunately, our society of the left got it into its head that all demonstrations of this kind would lose us votes from the center. And after fighting as much as I could in favor of our going to this dinner, we were entreated by almost the entire *réunion Laffitte* and by all the individuals of the *réunion Ternaux* that we have encountered, not to attend this banquet." Nearly a thousand people did attend, but only six deputies were there. Lafayette consoled himself by noting that it was "a good rule, in politics as in other things, to decide, when in doubt, against one's personal interest."[41]

Goyet thought the deputies should have been at the banquet. He also advised Lafayette that, to avoid giving the impression of having been corrupted by the government, he should publish a formal protest before taking part in any discussions of the draft legislation that were contrary to the Charter. Moderation was useless, Goyet believed. "The only resource of the liberal party is national energy. Will the deputies allow this energy to decline? Shouldn't they rather sustain it?"[42] Many of the deputies did not feel the same sense of urgency. After all, the left had won the most recent elections, petitions were pouring in for the preservation of the election law and the Charter, and the opposition was confused and divided over what to substitute for the current system. Even a slightly modified election law would still give liberals great opportunities to win elections, and the moderation they were displaying during the crisis might enhance their stature within the Chamber.

The strategy of parliamentary maneuver failed miserably for a reason that none of them could have foreseen. On 13 February, on the night before the government's proposal was supposed to be presented to the Chamber, an assassin killed the duc de Berry, the only member of the royal family who could continue the dynasty. The resulting sympathy for the royal family and the outrage at the event made possible a more drastic change than the government had heretofore contemplated. Moving decisively to the right, the ministry presented not only a proposal for a new election law but also for laws limiting individual freedom and imposing press censorship. Not long afterward, Decazes was forced from office, and the reluctant duc de Richelieu took his place at the head of a new ministry.

Two days after the assassination, Lafayette dined at Constant's home before going with him and other members of the Chamber's official delegation to offer their sympathies to the king. The delegates had been chosen by lot. When Lafayette's name was picked, Constant recounted, a royalist, Nicolas-François Bellart, had exclaimed, "Heaven is just." After hearing this anecdote, the poet Béranger remarked ironically that Bellart must have been thinking of Lafayette's defense of the royal family before the Convention. Lafayette responded dryly, "That must have been his thought." Ultras always insisted on Lafayette's guilt in the demise of Louis XVI, while liberals resented the ingratitude of the royal family for the sacrifices Lafayette had made in their behalf.[43]

Lafayette labeled the latest legislative proposals "evidently counterrevolutionary" and advocated vigorous responses from the deputies of the left, though it was not obvious what they could do.[44] One portion of the left continued to hope that their moderation could win over enough votes to make a majority to defeat the new measures. There were even some negotiations with the new government in hopes that the legislation would be withdrawn, but it was all in vain.[45] As usual, Lafayette saw the struggle in European terms and thought little could be accomplished in the Chamber.

> *I believe in the connivance of the Holy Alliance, mysti-cal at first and then become political at Aix-la-Chapelle. Everywhere privileges and rights are meet-ing head-on; but liberty will triumph without any doubt. Meanwhile, there is a big gap dividing what one would like and what one can accomplish here. As to the Chamber, should a very small number, a kind of patriotic Mountain separate itself off from the rest of the left?*

Lafayette believed that only a small fraction of the left would be willing to declare publicly (as Goyet had recommended) that the proposed legislation was contrary to the Charter. In the mean-time, negotiations might salvage the threatened laws, but he doubted that "the aristocracy" would allow a compromise to survive for long. He recognized that he had better stay out of the negotiations in which he felt he was "not good for anything except delivering a few definite sine qua nons."[46]

Pessimistic about what could be accomplished in the Cham-ber, Lafayette turned his attention increasingly to resistance. On 22 February he wrote to Goyet, "liberty will finally triumph. I wrote in the past to the first consul: 'The French people knew its rights too well to have forgotten them forever.' Now that it has remembered them, and that it has known in turn the excesses of anarchy, despotism and oligarchy, it will know how to oppose them with a wise and firm resistance."[47] These hints of resis-tance increased as the three bills made their way through the Chambers and as any hopes of salvaging part of the electoral system faded.

The first occasion for measuring the intentions of the Chamber and of the new government came on 2 March, when a group of petitions favoring the maintenance of the Charter was considered. The reporter for the committee, Lafayette's friend Dupont de l'Eure, announced that 442 new petitions bearing more than fifty-two thousand signatures from seventy different departments had arrived since the last petitions were presented to the Chamber in the middle of January. Although the earlier ones had been rejected by the Chamber, the committee once again recommended that the petitions be sent to the committee working on the election law. Despite speeches of support by Jean-Emmanuel Jobez, Lafayette, and Daunou, the petitions were again rejected.[48]

Lafayette said that he and Constant had decided that he would speak because Constant had spoken during the last petition debate and because "a very considerable number of the petitions" had been addressed to Lafayette.[49] But Constant was not satisfied with Lafayette's effort, complaining that the vanity of those who wanted to see their speeches printed in the *Moniteur* had prevented a genuine debate and had made it impossible to answer the objections of their opponents. The liberals could have won, he thought, if they had tried to sway the undecided instead of delivering set speeches.[50] Lafayette obviously had a different idea of the purpose of the debate, for he had made little effort to respond to the opposition, commenting that their arguments were so weak as to require no refutation. He had urged the Chamber not to impede the communication of their countrymen with their representatives. The demands in the petitions were no more seditious than were the demands in 1792 to "maintain with firmness, and without reservation, the social compact of the time, and not to deviate from the fundamental principles that assure the liberty of nations."[51] His emphasis on principles and provocative reference to the Revolution indicate that he had abandoned any hopes of compromise and persuasion within the Chamber.

He continued to invoke these principles, particularly the Declaration of the Rights of Man, in speeches opposing the three laws to change the electoral system and to restrict individual and press freedom. By drifting away from the principles established by the Revolution, Lafayette believed, the government was inevitably leading the country to violence and disruption because such a departure from the basic principles of constitutional government would have to be met with resistance. Privately, he told Goyet that he hoped that, unlike the response in 1793, the country would see the necessity of refusing to obey illegal ordinances or pay arbitrary taxes.[52]

Lafayette's speech during the debate on the law of individual freedom recalled the early years of the Revolution, when, according to Lafayette, the enemies of liberty had used allegations of crimes to attack freedom. Later, supposed crimes likewise became the excuse for passing the first Law of Suspects, the precursor of the Terror. The nation should have resisted that law vigorously. Now that the ministers, and indeed "all the cabinets of Europe," were decrying certain "pernicious doctrines," he wondered whether they meant the Declaration of the Rights of Man. The victims of the Terror, far from blaming the declaration for their misfortune, had appealed to it for relief from oppression. He concluded,

> *all the evils of France have been produced, much less by the perversity of evil men and the exaggeration of madmen, than by the hesitation of the weak, compromises with the conscience, and postponements of patriotism. Let each deputy, each Frenchman show what he feels, what he thinks, and we are saved! . . . The question has been set out clearly: on one side, the Revolution accomplished with all its moral, political and material advantages; on the other, the counterrevolution to be accomplished with its privileges and its perils. It is up to the Chamber, it is up to France to decide.*
>
> *Sirs, thirty-three years ago at the Assembly of Notables of 1787, I was the first to call for the abolition of lettres de cachet: I vote today against their reestablishment.*[53]

Lafayette's speech opposing the law on press censorship threatened revolution more expressly and praised the recent revolt in Spain. In January 1820, Spanish troops scheduled to sail for America to put down independence movements in the colonies had rebelled, and the revolt soon forced the king to reestablish the liberal Spanish constitution of 1812. Events in Spain confirmed Lafayette's belief that public opinion in Europe was moving in the direction of constitutional government, yet the French government was headed in the opposite direction. "Thus, while European liberty is making giant steps forward, and France wishes to and should remain at the head of this great development of human dignity and capacities, a government, which can no longer be reproached for hypocrisy, intends to drag you along in its retrograde movement, and widens more and more the gap which separates it from the nation."

He warned Frenchmen that demolishing the barriers against arbitrary government would leave no guarantees for "any of the advantages that the Revolution had created . . . in the last thirty years." Deliberately choosing examples that would taunt his opponents, Lafayette argued for the usefulness of a free press in scotching rumors or neutralizing alarming and seditious reports. The current rumor, that foreign troops were preparing to march across France to fight "the noble emancipation of the magnanimous people who already, on our border, call us their friends and come to fraternize with us," was certainly not credible. Though some tried to connect press freedom with the assassination of the duc de Berry, Lafayette recalled a time during the Empire when rumors were circulating that Berry intended to lead an invasion of France. If there had been no "press censorship, an article in a newspaper would have been sufficient to frustrate these foul schemes." As for Spain, it was in the tradition of the France of 1789, when soldiers identified with their fellow citizens. In Spain, too, the soldiers were demanding the constitution "derived *from the general will of the people.*" France could also maintain its liberties, if it rejected the law on censorship, canceled the projected election bill, and created the promised institutions. His conclusion was plain: "may the Charter be respected, because *to violate it is to dissolve it, it is to dissolve the mutual guarantees of the nation and the throne, it is to return to the complete original independence of our rights and duties.*"[54] Lafayette was here threatening revolution, and it was no slip of the tongue. He told Goyet, "The last sentence is very explicit. I will speak once more concerning the election law, after which speaking would be inappropriate."[55]

Lafayette had abandoned hope of persuading his fellow legislators to reject the new laws, and his speeches were now aimed at encouraging French and foreign liberals. If they had followed Goyet's advice and retired from the Chamber when the laws they considered unconstitutional were discussed, Lafayette argued, few would have followed them, and their gesture would have been soon forgotten. By remaining, their speeches had served "the cause of humankind and of our nation."[56] He was pleased that his speech was circulating in Spain and spreading "our sentiments of fraternity and of liberal Holy Alliance to the people which has so nobly recovered its liberty."[57]

By the spring of 1820 Lafayette had begun to make plans to resist what he saw as the unconstitutional measures of the government and the counterrevolutionary activities of the Holy Alliance. The government, already suspecting him of leading a Europe-wide revolutionary conspiracy, assumed that the liberal opposition was behind the recent assassination and was planning further assaults on the regime. Starting immediately after the assassination, police agents regularly intercepted the correspondence of Lafayette, Constant, and Goyet and sent it to the so-called *cabinet noir* where it was copied.[58]

Although they were not to blame for the assassination, which was the work of a lone individual, some members of the opposition did turn to illegal conspiracies after the assassination when legal opposition seemed no longer possible. A dramatic indication of this change lies in the surviving correspondence from Lafayette to Voyer d'Argenson. In contrast to the many long letters filled with political news from 1818 and 1819, only two or three short notes exist from 1820, and there are none from 1821 and 1822. They obviously destroyed the incriminating correspondence to prevent its being used against them by the authorities.

The increasing difficulty of mounting a legal opposition became quickly evident when the new press laws went into effect at the beginning of April. Political newspapers were required to submit all articles for prior censorship. The censorship commissions allowed facts to be reported, but opinions could not appear. This interpretation of the law meant an end to the most popular journals of opinion, the *Minerve* for the left and the *Conservateur* for the right. The commissions frequently disallowed articles in daily newspapers. When the opposition fought back by publishing the censored items as pamphlets, they were taken to court. The podium of the Chamber of Deputies, whose proceedings could be freely reported, became even more valuable as a way of getting a message across.[59]

To protest the new laws and to provide a rallying point for their supporters throughout the country, some liberals organized a subscription to aid victims of the law allowing arbitrary arrest.

Lafayette was the president of the committee, which included all the prominent deputies of the left.[60] The authorities immediately began proceedings against the newspapers that had carried the subscription notice, along with all members of the committee who were not peers or deputies. On 18 April, the committee members who had escaped indictment wrote an open letter to the *procureur général*, Bellart, demanding to be included as defendants in the legal action. If Bellart were genuinely convinced that their actions were illegal, they argued, it was his duty to demand authorization from the Chambers to include them in the indictment.[61]

The government dropped its charges against the members of the committee, a decision Lafayette believed was prompted by the protests of the deputies and peers. But the victory was short-lived, as they were eventually included with the cases pending against the newspapers.[62] Lafayette worried about the outcome and even more so about the fate of the liberals in the provinces who had opened subscriptions and might yet be arrested under the new laws. When the case came to trial in late June, the jury acquitted the signers of the subscription but found the journalists guilty of "provoking disobedience to the laws" and gave them all prison sentences and fines.[63]

Debates became more heated as the liberals used the podium of the Chamber of Deputies to accuse the ultras of illegal influence. On 25 April, the Chamber debated a petition from a lawyer at Nîmes named Madier de Montjau, who feared the recurrence of the 1815 persecutions in the department of the Gard, commonly called the White Terror, during which ultra-royalists had attacked their liberal opponents, especially Protestants.[64] He alleged that, after the assassination, circulars with instructions had been sent from an ultra *comité directeur* in Paris to ultras in the south of France.[65] Calling attention to this correspondence was, of course, the purpose of the petition. Lafayette believed that the discussion had shown without doubt the existence of two governments, "today united." The legal government was subject to manipulation by the ultras.[66] Benjamin Constant called this ultra network "the hidden Government which wants to lead us to counterrevolution."[67]

By the time the debate on the new electoral law began on 15 May, Lafayette was convinced that the old law could not be saved and was contemplating what the liberals should do after defeat.

139

Once again, Lafayette and Benjamin Constant differed sharply. Constant hoped that a properly conducted debate could sway enough deputies, but "the difficulty is in conducting it, and there are men who, out of good intentions and out of principle, can hurt us vitally."[68] Lafayette believed Constant's hopes were illusory. The liberals, he thought, should do something "energetic," but he did not yet know what they would do.[69]

Some doubt about the outcome existed at first. The Richelieu government had substituted a new bill, still more favorable to the right, for the one introduced by Decazes immediately after the assassination.[70] It called for two-step elections in which arrondissement colleges (made up of those paying three hundred francs in taxes) nominated candidates, and departmental colleges (composed of the richest one-fifth of the electors) selected the deputy from among the nominees. The ability of the arrondissement colleges to influence the outcome was further reduced by the stipulations that the nominations of each arrondissement college equal the number of deputies to be elected in the department and that each arrondissement list be different. In a department electing four deputies and consisting of four arrondissement colleges, for example, the departmental college would have a choice from among sixteen nominees. The liberals would then have to come up with sixteen candidates instead of four and would have scant hope of excluding all government candidates. It seemed likely that such an unwieldy electoral system might be defeated in the Chamber of Deputies.

The position of the liberals was presented by the famous orator General Sébastien Foy, who maintained that the bill would create an aristocratic despotism and would violate the Charter, leading to unrest in the country. True supporters of the king and the Charter must oppose it. Debate continued for eleven days before the Chamber began to consider the specific features of the bill. Lafayette's turn to speak came during the discussion of the first article, which provided for a division of the electorate into arrondissement and departmental colleges.

His speech on 27 May, the longest of his career in the legislature to date, had little to do with the subject: he scarcely mentioned voting. It was less a contribution to the debate on the election law (the results of which he deemed a foregone conclusion) than it was a rallying cry for those already contemplating insurrection. He explained the principles justifying revolt, identified the enemy, and warned of the dangers ahead. He had hoped that the Charter would be maintained by "the various parties" and that all would protect "institutions that would lead us peacefully to the possession of all the social guarantees; my expectations were deceived. Counterrevolution is in the government; they want to establish it in the Chambers."

He next embarked on a lesson in constitutional principles. Certain natural rights could not be violated by any power, not even by "an entire nation." Basic constitutional powers might be modified. Indeed, Lafayette said, he had been the first to proclaim this tenet at the Constituent Assembly; and he had been the most recent to proclaim it from that very podium, on 6 July 1815. But the social compact could not be revised by ordinary legislation "and even less in defiance of circumstances and of evident public opinion from all sides." The Charter, he argued, despite its origins and its imperfections, had become genuinely popular because it guaranteed fundamental rights. But these rights were now being destroyed, and the promised laws to organize municipal government and the National Guard were being postponed. Because the next election would have brought a sufficient number of right-thinking deputies to make all these things possible, the electoral law itself was being attacked. The proposed law, he complained, would establish a second chamber of nobles.

He responded to criticism of his membership on the committee to aid victims of the law of individual freedom by proclaiming the constitutionality of these activities. "Despotism, under whatever form it may take, is the most insolent of revolts, . . . arbitrariness is the most scandalous and most lasting of public disorders!" In response to those who attacked "factious committees," Lafayette recalled some of the disorders of the Revolution, caused, he charged, by counterrevolutionary groups, who joined "the other categories of perverse or misguided disorganizers, to make the Revolution hateful by making it deviate from its original generous impulse." Such counterrevolutionary groups still existed, as Madier de Montjau's petition courageously showed. There was still time, he concluded, to

> return to the national, constitutional, peaceful and
> generous paths. . . . Our contemporaries are tired of

141

> *revolutions, glutted with glory; but they will not allow*
> *themselves to be robbed of dearly won rights and inter-*
> *ests. Our youth, the hope of the country, better edu-*
> *cated than we were, enlightened by its own*
> *intelligence and by our experience, ignores factions,*
> *listens to no prejudices, is amenable only to honorable*
> *intentions and generous measures; but it desires free-*
> *dom with an ardor that is well thought out and there-*
> *fore more irrepressible.*

Threatened by the loss of "all the useful results of the Revolution," young people would be compelled "to take up the sacred fasces of the principles of eternal truth and sovereign justice, principles applicable to all free governments, and beside which all other combinations, personal or political, can be, for a people of common sense, nothing but secondary considerations."[71]

In this early call to revolt, Lafayette showed the way to overcome the problems of forging a coalition for insurrection. The potential recruits had different political goals: a Napoleonic style of government, a republic, a constitutional monarchy. They included former Napoleonic soldiers, young students and soldiers, journalists, businessmen, and politicians. Lafayette called them to rally around the tricolor flag: "the symbol of emancipation and glory that Louis XVI accepted from the hands of the nation, which his august successor was proud to carry, and whose least important claim is to have waved over all the capitals, received the homage of all potentates, and knocked down before it all flags, from the most powerful to the most insignificant for more than twenty years."[72] They would rally around the tricolor, a symbol they could all agree upon, but leave the substantive content of the symbol deliberately vague. Their first goal would be to topple the government. The nation would then choose the definitive form of the new government, which, as Lafayette said in his speech, was a secondary consideration once the principles had been established.[73]

By the time of his speech at the end of May, Lafayette was definitely focusing on resistance to the government. Charles Goyet apparently destroyed a letter written by Lafayette on 30 May, perhaps because in it Lafayette revealed too explicitly the purpose and meaning of his speech.[74] Minister of Justice de Serre read Lafayette's speech as a call to insurrection and re-

142

sponded immediately by recalling the old accusations against Lafayette's actions during the Revolution. He asked whether Lafayette realized that after getting the masses riled up "not only can one not always stop them when they run into crime, but that one is often forced to follow them and almost to lead them." He objected to Lafayette's praise of the tricolor flag, which at the current time could be only "the colors of rebellion." Furthermore, de Serre charged, Lafayette had declared to the nation, "in his name and in the name of several of his colleagues, that he believed himself released from the oath given to the charter! . . . is that not an appeal to revolt and a manifesto to justify it? And doesn't this show you your duties toward an opposition that makes you listen to such words and assumes such traits?"[75]

Lafayette did not bother to respond to de Serre's speech, but Constant did, for it clearly threatened the coalition he was still trying to create against the new election law. He assured the nervous moderates that Lafayette's words had been misinterpreted, that he meant only that the tricolor flag deserved the respect of the nation as a symbol of what France had done in the past. His remarks on sovereignty referred only to the right of all nations to modify their fundamental law in certain established ways. Nobody, Constant disingenuously assured the Chamber, supported "sovereignty of the people, that devastating torrent whose ravages and excesses we have all seen." Finally, he reminded the Chamber of Lafayette's courageous defense of Louis XVI in 1792.[76]

Criticism of Lafayette continued, this time by Goyet's nemesis, Etienne Pasquier, now serving as foreign minister. Pasquier assured the Chamber that, on the much-debated issue of Lafayette's leading the crowds during the Revolution, he was not "blaming the intentions of my honorable colleague, I am blaming his impotence; I deplore his long and constant weakness." He also faulted Lafayette's appeal to the youth of the country, who had neither the "enlightenment" nor the experience to be brought into such a serious matter.[77] The discussion had strayed from the subject of the election law to personal attacks on Lafayette and questions about his character. The government apparently thought it necessary to combat his reputation for incorruptibility and to associate him more intimately with the disorders of the Revolution. In the process, they were labeling all of those on the left, even the moderates, as the party of dangerous and irrespons-ible rebellion.[78]

Despite these attacks, the left did well on the first vote on the election bill. On 30 May, the Chamber had to decide which of two amendments to consider first. The decision to debate the Jordan amendment first, favored by the left, passed by one vote (128 to 127) because Chauvelin was carried from his sickbed to the floor of the Chamber. The victory proved illusory, however, because the Jordan amendment (providing for no departmental colleges and for direct election of one deputy by each arrondisse-ment college) was subsequently defeated by ten votes. This mar-gin of support for the government's side continued throughout the debate.[79]

Meanwhile, though, Chauvelin had become a hero, and noisy demonstrations dominated by students greeted him and other deputies of the left as they made their way into and out of the Chamber each day. The attention of the nation was focused on these debates. Excitement in Paris was heightened by the simultaneous trial in the Chamber of Peers of Louis-Pierre Louvel, the assassin of the duc de Berry. The crowds milling around the Chamber of Deputies included government supporters, as well as liberal suppor-ters. Troops were sent to keep order. In one of the disturbances, the troops killed a young student named Lallemand.

Both sides now interrupted debate on the election law to accuse the other of fomenting the disruptions. On 5 June, Con-stant informed the deputies that he had been warned that Lafa-yette would be attacked upon leaving the Chamber. A young man had been overheard declaring, "We'll make him cry *Vive le roi!*" Then an older officer answered, "Keep still. It's not a question of making them cry *vive le roi*; let us surround them, and don't budge."[80] Lafayette explained that he had luckily avoided the "ambush" because he and George had gone to plead with the police for the release of several young men whose only crime had been to cry "*vive la charte.*"[81] Other deputies of the left accused the troops of attacking those who cheered for the Charter and of directing rowdies to assault them instead of keeping the peace. Bloodshed, they warned, was increasing dramatically. Govern-ment speakers charged the left with inciting revolution, and the left charged the government with causing unrest by its uncon-stitutional policies.

In the midst of this tumult, the debate on the election law continued. The government seemed certain to win. Their support increased, in part, no doubt, because the unrest in the streets prompted some of the more timid deputies to support the existing government. But support increased as well because of developments in the debate and because amendments to the original proposal had changed it substantially. Article one, establishing a two-tier college system, passed. When article two, stipulating the composition of the departmental college, was brought up for discussion, Antoine Courvoisier proposed an amendment to increase the number of deputies, to require the new deputies to be elected by departmental colleges made up of one-fourth of all electors, and to have the old deputies elected by arrondissement colleges, each college to elect one deputy. Since this proposal would have preserved the principle of direct election, Constant indicated that he would support it, just as the left had similarly been willing to compromise on the Jordan amendment. Courvoisier, however, hesitated to go ahead with the amendment unless the government approved it. When de Serre did so, all seemed in place for a compromise.

The next day Courvoisier sought to clear up a potential misunderstanding. He had not intended that members of the departmental colleges also vote in the arrondissement colleges. De Serre rejected this interpretation because it would make the arrondissement colleges too democratic. Courvoisier then retracted his amendment, which was taken up immediately by another deputy, Antoine Boin. The Boin amendment established the principle that gave the law its nickname: the "Law of the Double Vote." It passed by the comfortable margin of 119 votes (185 to 66), with support from many moderates. It preserved the principle of direct election, even though it would result in a substantial number of new members in the Chamber who would be chosen by an extremely restricted electorate, and it would give the top one-fourth of the electorate two votes apiece.[82]

The Boin amendment became a test of loyalty to liberal principles, and the gap between Lafayette and Benjamin Constant can be gauged by some liberals' suspicions that Constant had voted for it. His attempts to maintain a majority to defeat the original bill, his willingness to compromise, and his failure to speak against the Boin amendment (unusual for Constant, who regularly led the debate for the left) had convinced some liberals that he had defected to the ministerial side. Lafayette assured a correspondent that Constant had indeed voted against it.[83] Passage of the complete electoral law came on 12 June, by a vote of 154 to 95.[84]

The passage of a new electoral bill had not been a foregone conclusion in early 1820; because it was not, Lafayette had cooperated with his political associates to save the election law. He had still pinned his hopes on liberal victories at the polls, which would then make further advances in the Chamber possible. The assassination of the duc de Berry transformed the political landscape and brought on Lafayette's decision to conspire against the government. Had there been no assassination, he might have confined his opposition to the bounds of the established political system. True, Decazes intended to propose a new election law even before the assassination, but how the Chamber would have received it was not at all clear. Even after the murder of the duc de Berry, when fear of revolution was at its height, provisions passed with only narrow margins until the government compromised on important questions. An electoral-law debate carried out in a calmer atmosphere might have ended differently, and Lafayette's response to it might not have been the same.

The fear of seeing the Decazes ministry replaced by a more conservative one had already led many liberals to dampen their opposition. Broglie had disavowed his former colleagues, Laffitte was having second thoughts, and Constant tried to play down the radicalism of his friends' ideas. Conspiratorial projects were doubtless bandied about. One proposal to replace Louis XVIII with the prince of Orange was reportedly discussed in late 1819. But Lafayette, who was supposed to consider the political ramifications, dragged his feet and the idea came to nothing.[85] Lafayette's attention then was concentrated on politics, on trying to save the election law.

An essential part of Lafayette's political faith was that the government should reflect the views of the nation as expressed through elections. He hoped that liberals would someday come to power in the ministry. But that event now seemed unlikely. The government was essentially declaring that genuine parliamentary government would not be allowed in France. Its policies, he believed, were definitely unconstitutional.

146

The drama surrounding the debate on the electoral law and the intensity of the nation's interest in the outcome was significant as well in Lafayette's turn to conspiracy. If changes had come about slowly, if there had been no assassination followed by a sharp turn to the right, it might have been more difficult to galvanize opinion to see the changes in the law as dangerous and counterrevolutionary. Without his sense that the overwhelming majority of the country felt that the legislation was illegal, Lafayette might have hesitated to move to conspiracy.[86]

Lafayette was concerned not only with events in France but also with those in the rest of Europe. He worried about the Holy Alliance, reactionary policies in Germany, and unrest in England. When the revolution in Spain broke out, he perceived a connection between events in France and the rest of the world, including South America. France, he believed, should set the example, as it had done in the past. But it seemed to be moving backwards. Despite his dissatisfaction with the Charter and with the electoral law, he was willing to support them because the French people seemed content with them and because they could provide a platform for future development. But the attack on the Charter in France would have serious consequences in the rest of Europe, where the idea of constitutionalism was struggling to survive. He was not held back by public opinion this time: the experience of recent elections and the petition campaign had convinced him that public opinion was on his side.

Lafayette did not automatically resort to conspiracy. He was more a revolutionary than a conspirator. Although he had conspired to overthrow Napoleon, he preferred revolutions in the eighteenth-century style: public movements entered into with broad support from the populace for purposes spelled out clearly and openly. His mythmakers during the Restoration propagated an image of him as the man of order and probity during the Revolution of 1789. He wanted to be remembered, then, as a revolutionary, not as a secret conspirator. A conspiratorial cell was distasteful to him because legitimate revolution required that the purposes of the revolutionaries be those endorsed by the people. His preparations to overthrow Napoleon during the Hundred Days were clandestine, but even then he wanted to act with the cooperation of the legislature, as the speech demanding permanent session makes clear.

147

The circumstances of the 1820s drove Lafayette to attempts to undermine the government. He chafed at the secrecy. His scarcely veiled threats on the floor of the Chamber of Deputies contrasted with the more purposefully oblique utterances of men like Manuel, who was conspiring just as seriously but who did not proclaim his intentions so openly. Lafayette seemed to relish the danger and the excitement of more public confrontation. Perhaps he felt transported back to the days of his youth, to his American adventure, when as a young man of nineteen he became a renowned fighter for liberty. Now Lafayette was sixty-two. He was getting old. He may have wondered whether this was his last chance to introduce liberty to France and to Europe. His real hopes lay with the next generation, as his frequent references to the virtues of youth indicated. The demonstrations by the young students in favor of the election law had brought them into contact with the parliamentary leaders and had cemented an alliance that made conspiracy possible. And such conspiracy was necessary, he felt, because of the strength of the reactionary forces arrayed against them, not only in France but in the rest of Europe too. They were fighting an international conspiracy poised to snuff out all expressions of liberalism.

6

The Call to Revolution

L afayette paid less attention to the Chamber and more to plans for conspiracy once the distasteful electoral law passed. Yet by remaining in the Chamber, Lafayette and the rest of the liberals lost any opportunity to proclaim forcefully their objections to what the Chamber was doing. Goyet, for one, thought they should dramatize their view that the law was unconstitutional by boycotting the Chamber, but this move was impractical, as only twelve liberals would have joined the boycott.[1] They did not participate actively in the proceedings either, and at one point Lafayette had to defend himself against charges that he was skipping sessions of the Chamber. The problem was that, while continuing to function somewhat halfheartedly as a deputy and political leader, Lafayette was at the same time pursuing conspiracies that proclaimed the futility of politics. And these conspiracies, in turn, would contribute to the liberals' failure at the polls.[2]

The government, which was rightfully suspicious of Lafayette, increased its surveillance of his family, friends, and political allies. Martial Sauquaire-Souligné, a native of the Sarthe and correspondent of Goyet's, was arrested in Paris on 7 June 1820. Meanwhile in Le Mans, the authorities searched Goyet's house. Two weeks later, an agent dispatched from Paris seized the letters Goyet had received from Constant, Lafayette, and other political associates and sent them to the minister of justice. Perhaps to inform Lafayette and Constant that incriminating letters had been destroyed, Goyet rather pointedly told them that his correspondence, "like your letters, contains nothing criminal."[3]

Lafayette visited Sauquaire-Souligné in jail but could do nothing to gain his release. The government intended to use his case to implicate Lafayette and Constant in illegal activities. Sauquaire-Souligné was almost certainly involved with some of the Paris groups plotting insurrection in the summer of 1820, and a government spy reported that Lafayette visited Sauquaire-Souligné regularly. Lafayette nevertheless gave the impression that he hardly knew the man, despite his residence in Paris and their mutual friendship with Lanjuinais and with Goyet.[4]

The government harassed other friends and political associates of Lafayette and his son. Antoine Bonne Chevant, George's correspondent in the Haute-Loire, was denounced to the authorities.[5] Charles-Philippe Marchand, who had acted as courier to Le Mans in 1818 and was now the editor of a liberal newspaper in Alsace called the *Patriote alsacien*, modeled on Goyet's *Propagateur*, was arrested in April. He had fashioned an allegory satirizing a "good father" who did not allow his children any liberties.[6] Liberal newspapers suffered under the new censorship regulations, some closing down, others merging.

While defending themselves in court, liberals worried about the coming elections, the ultimate source of their strength. Rumors circulated during the summer of 1820 that the Chamber would be dissolved and general elections called.[7] Goyet made plans for either eventuality: a general election or the election of only the new deputies at the departmental level. He wanted to make sure that Constant and Lafayette stayed in the Chamber. Meanwhile, the government was busy drawing the boundaries of the new arrondissement districts for their own benefit. They abandoned the idea of a general election and shrewdly decided to postpone the fall elections until after the birth of the posthumous child of the duc de Berry. It proved to be a boy who could continue the Bourbon dynasty. This "miracle child" seemed a providential sign and stimulated widespread sympathy for the royal family and support for the government.

If elections had been called that summer, Lafayette and George would probably have delayed their plans for an uprising and concentrated instead on electing liberals to the Chamber. In August, George canceled a trip to Auvergne, citing pressing business that kept him by his father's side. But, he explained, if elections were called, "no business . . . would keep me here and I'd leave in an instant."[8] Elections, though, were deferred, and the plans for conspiracy continued. By the time of the fall campaign, the government at last had proof of its frequent accusations that the left was disruptive, disloyal, and irresponsible.

The conspiracies had disastrous effects on liberal political fortunes in France. Yet Lafayette persisted in lending his name and his money to these enterprises, which appear in retrospect to have had no chance of success. His willingness to sacrifice immediate political possibilities for the uncertainty of violent measures can probably be traced to the European context of these events. In July, a military revolt in Naples, in imitation of the one in Spain, forced King Ferdinand IV to accept a constitution on the model of the Spanish Constitution of 1812, and in August, a military revolt occurred in Portugal as well. Lafayette was encouraged to see what could be accomplished by so few people. "Several regiments were necessary for the restoration of the *Cortès*: one hundred fifty men managed the *Naples* business. . . . it took only three drunks in *Berlin* to stir up a crowd and make the king of *Prussia* remember a few things."[9]

In a long letter to Jefferson, Lafayette characteristically saw recent events in Europe as approaching the aims they had shared during the course of their long lives. "The Great Work of General Enfranchisement to which You and I, My dear friend, Have devoted ourselves So Many Years Ago, is progressing through innumerable obstacles of despotism, privilege and every kind of political, sacerdotal, personal aristocracy." They had been fighting these same enemies in various guises — "Under the Mask of popular Licentiousness, or the glittering Seductions of Military Glory." But now, things looked hopeful. Frenchmen, he informed Jefferson, had applauded the changes in Spain and Naples. "There is also Sympathy Between the German and french Nations," he remarked. Although Lafayette continued to be suspicious of Great Britain, the enemy of both the American and the French Revolutions, and found the British generally "averse . . . to Mingle with an extensive Common interest," he was now agreeably surprised to find some sympathy between "Us and the liberal part of the British Empire."[10] He worried that France, which constituted "a kind of political Head Quarters for liberalism," might now let others down. "Much attention is paid to Her debates as if there was an instinctive universal Sentiment that on her Emancipation depends the solidity of Every other Succès in Europe. Yet when our Neighbours Have Gained ground we found ourselves Materially defeated, altho' the Struggle Has Greatly advanced our Moral Maturity." Opinion in France was improving, especially among the new generation, which, he assured Jefferson, was "Remarkably More Enlightened than You Have known them, they Have Risen above the Spirit of faction, and Care very little about dynasties, Generals, and even Secondary forms of Government. They are generally Republicans. Jacobinism and Bonapartism are to them objects of disgust."[11] Lafayette here reiterated a conception of republicanism as something different from a government without a king. Jacobinism, with its tyrannical tendencies, did not fit his definition. Republicanism was almost synonymous with liberty, with the cause of the early years of the French Revolution and its concerns for the rights of the individual. Guarantees of those rights could be possible under either a monarchical or a republican form of government, and thus he was willing to work with people of various backgrounds to rid themselves of the government that had proved unwilling to respect those rights.

Lafayette pinned his hopes on young people with whom he came into contact through old friends, through George's acquaintances, and through young writers and journalists who looked to the old revolutionary for inspiration and financial backing. For example, two natives of the Auvergne who came to Paris to study, Bonne Chevant's nephew Grenier and a young man named Salveton, became part of the Lafayette circle and were eventually arrested in one of the plots.[12] George praised them highly: "The young aristocrats are outshone by the young men of the Third Estate. A wonderful generation of defenders of liberty is growing up."[13] Another acquaintance from Auvergne, named Triozon, was with the student Lallemand when he was killed.[14] Sons of old political friends were members of the student groups in Paris who carried out the conspiracies, and Lafayette met many young men who demonstrated for Professor Bavoux in 1819 and for the electoral bill in 1820. Lafayette received a petition signed by a group of young people in Le Mans praising the liberal deputies, and he sent it to the *réunion Laffitte*, to Ternaux, and to journalists.[15] Goyet called him "the friend of French youth."[16]

The first public knowledge of the abortive conspiracies came on 20 August 1820 when the *Moniteur* reported that the government had foiled a plot by rebellious troops to march on the royal palace and to proclaim a Bonapartist monarchy.[17] This attempt, known as the conspiracy of 19 August 1820, certainly existed, though its aims were not exclusively Bonapartist. The plotters intended to catch the government off guard by staging several *pronunciamientos* on the Spanish model in various regiments throughout the country. The government arrested twenty-two men during the night of 19–20 August and made further arrests later in the month. Predictably, the government's informers reported that Lafayette was a guiding member of the conspiracy, that he headed a committee of liberal deputies, while other committees of Bonapartists and students were also involved.[18]

In addition to active soldiers, the conspirators included young men from Paris who met at the Bazar Français, a business run by former army officers discontented with their forced retirement. Many of the students were members of a Masonic lodge, the *Amis de la vérité*, which was used as a front for their conspiracies. The young people kept in touch with political leaders through the mediation of radical journalists and lawyers, many of whom were former members of the dissolved *Société des amis de la liberté de la presse.*[19] Joseph Rey recalled that he went to La Grange to obtain Lafayette's support only two weeks before the plot was scheduled to take place. But Rey was not the only contact between the plotters and Lafayette, who undoubtedly had several sources of information among the students and military men involved. Although his exact role is not clear, Lafayette certainly knew about and supported this conspiracy.[20]

After the discovery of the plot, Lafayette helped some of those implicated to escape and gave them financial assistance, which constituted a great drain on his (and his family's) resources.[21] At the end of September, George wrote to an old American friend, Daniel Parker. George begged Parker to repay money he owed and described his own plight. "Shall I go to Paris, then I must go not in our own house, but in another corner of the city so as not to meet with creditors who shall crowd upon me when they will know I am in town. It is impossible for me to go to Auvergne because I have no money to pay my seat in the stage, and the moment is not distant when perhaps I shall not have anymore credit for to procure the necessary dress to my wife and children." In October, Lafayette borrowed money from his son-in-law Charles de Latour-Maubourg.[22]

Once the news of the failed coup appeared in the press, liberal politicians were faced with the awkward task of minimizing the political damage in the coming elections. The deputies had already left Paris as soon as the Chambers had adjourned at the end of July, and they traveled to their home districts to prepare for the elections and to maintain the enthusiasm generated by the petition campaigns of the previous winter. There they were greeted with banquets and serenades, which became for the liberals the equivalent of the royalist ceremonies used with such good effect to win over the crowds.[23] In 1820 these serenades were especially important in countering the effects of the celebrations following the 29 September birth of the "miracle child." Liberals could hardly deplore the happy event, but the politicians tried to create reasons for their supporters to congregate and hoped that their demonstrations would rival those hailing the miraculous survival of the royal line.

The authorities, who suspected the liberal deputies of spreading revolution throughout the country, naturally followed their travels anxiously. The officials assumed all too willingly that any opposition activity was conspiratorial and dangerous, even much that today would be considered legitimate political organizing. Because the right for groups to meet freely was denied, indeed, they were difficult to distinguish. Contemporaries often mistook political opposition for subversive movements, and historians have had corresponding difficulties with interpretation. For example, liberals often referred to committees that coordinated their electoral activities. Their conservative opponents assumed that there existed an all-powerful *comité directeur* in Paris that dictated policies to the provinces. But the term *comité directeur* was also used to describe an alleged committee that plotted insurrection in France or one even more powerful that coordinated revolution throughout Europe. The *comité directeur*, then, could refer to either a legal or an illegal group, depending on the way it was used. But the distinction was not always maintained.

Reports by the authorities describing travel by liberal deputies always assumed that their purposes were subversive. Usually, however, preparations for the coming elections explain the meetings and banquets. In the wake of the conspiracy of 19 August, though, even electoral banquets could seem subversive and dangerous.[24]

The dilemma faced by the liberals in 1820 can be illustrated by their activities in Lyon. When word came that Lafayette's friend and fellow deputy Corcelle would be arriving, a subscription was launched for "a serenade, a banquet & festivities." But his appearance was delayed, probably because of his involvement in the 19 August conspiracy. When he finally arrived in the area, the prefect was glad to report that the idea of giving him a dinner had been abandoned. "The sensible liberals, friends of order who because of their commercial livelihood have the most influence, had the good sense to feel that it would be best to avoid everything that might inflame passions, embitter rivalries, and be the cause, or the pretext, for commotions. They managed to moderate the original fervent enthusiasm of the deputy's most ardent partisans."[25]

To retain their voters, liberals needed to mark their ideological position clearly, to prove their independence, and to encourage their supporters to vote despite the obstacles put in their way by the government. But the conservative elite who made up the electoral colleges were easily frightened by hints that political differences might lead to revolution. The liberals could win, as Goyet had shown, by making the officials look arbitrary and irresponsible, by persuading the voters that they had more to fear from the capture of the government by the ultras than from any other political group. But with the beginning of the conspiracies and in the aftermath of the assassination, the government could convincingly accuse the liberals of being the real threats to tranquillity.

Goyet recognized this problem immediately. Ordered to Paris on 12 August for questioning in the Sauquaire-Souligné case, he feared he would be arrested upon his arrival.[26] The authorities, already aware of plans for conspiracy later in the month, were trying to discover the ties between the leaders in Paris and their presumed coconspirators in the provinces. Goyet arrived in Paris a few days after the news of the 19 August conspiracy had broken. Returning to Le Mans shortly afterwards, he was distressed to see that the conspiracy was being blamed on liberalism. "It is up to us who have never conspired, who will never conspire, to defend the Charter by our writings," he told Constant. "Sooner or later enlightened public opinion will accomplish what conspiracies will never be able to do."[27]

155

To recoup from this disastrous episode, Goyet thought that Constant and Lafayette ought to tour the Sarthe. He knew that Lafayette's involvement in the affair of 19 August might make him hesitate to make the trip. But, he wrote Constant in veiled language, Lafayette's reasons for staying home were not "valid. . . . The harvesting will be finished. He will have returned home to oversee the wine and cider making." The "harvesting" presumably meant the arrests of the conspirators, whom Lafayette could no longer help. But when Lafayette explained why he did not want to come, Goyet prepared to invent excuses for his absence: his age or an indisposition would explain the cancellation.[28] These letters show that Constant had taken no part in the recent conspiracy because Goyet did not suggest that similar pressing reasons might prevent Constant's visit. However, both Goyet and Constant were well informed about the scheme.

Lafayette and Constant did finally decide to make the trip. Although some liberals in the Sarthe thought their coming was ill-advised, Goyet had insisted.[29] When the authorities learned of their plans, they naturally assumed that the deputies intended to incite revolution in this notoriously unmanageable department. Local residents prepared the usual elaborate ceremonies to welcome the visiting deputies. Musicians of the National Guard were to greet them on their arrival, and some sixty young people hired horses for the ride to La Ferté-Bernard, their first stop in the Sarthe. Goyet produced pamphlets extolling their virtues and tried to calm fears by insisting that their visit would be peaceful.[30] On the other hand, the new prefect was determined to keep the public demonstrations to a minimum. He distrusted the authorities in La Ferté-Bernard, so he sent the head of the *gendarmerie* of Mamers to the city to maintain order.[31] At La Ferté-Bernard on Saturday, 23 September 1820, the richest residents and the officials of the town joined to offer the deputies a banquet.

Lafayette and Constant were scheduled to arrive in Le Mans on Sunday afternoon, accompanied by groups of young people. But on Saturday, Goyet was amazed to discover that, contrary to his earlier assurances of not interfering with their plans, the prefect had ordered the municipal authorities of Le Mans to forbid all public gatherings either on foot or on horseback. Those who disobeyed would be immediately arrested.[32] Knowing that it was too late to stop the young people who were coming from various parts of the department and fearing that they would be arrested, Goyet rushed to La Ferté-Bernard to persuade Lafayette and Constant to start for Le Mans right away. They left at midnight and arrived in Le Mans at 4:00 A.M. The prefect had thus succeeded in preventing any substantial public display of enthusiasm for the arrival of the two liberal deputies.

When the young people on horseback rode into Le Mans on Sunday, the regiment on duty in the city had been mobilized to stand guard in the square to prevent their demonstration. The young riders entered the square but dispersed quickly when the commander approached them. That evening, they held a banquet under a tent; toward the end of the meal, Constant and Lafayette made an appearance. More important was the appearance of the deputies at a banquet of adult voters the next day, attended, according to Goyet, by "the 130 principal merchant proprietors." Lafayette and Constant had planned to visit the prisons, but orders were given that no one was to enter without prior written permission, so they were turned away. They did visit the *école d'enseignement mutuel*.[33]

Their stay in Le Mans proved peaceful. The prefect, of course, attributed the tranquillity to his precautionary measures, as well as to the indifference of the people of Le Mans. The only incident was a cavalry officer's shouting insults at Lafayette outside the home where he was staying. Since the purpose of the visit was to rally support for liberal politics, not to cause violence, the government's display of force might have been a mistake. One official pointed out; "The two deputies and their ardent partisans whose pride must have suffered from the indifference of the great mass of the inhabitants of Le Mans, will not fail to say that the military preparations stifled the enthusiasm of the inhabitants."[34]

On Tuesday, 26 September, after dinner with Le Mans liberals at the home of his fellow deputy Hardouin, Lafayette departed for La Grange, escorted by twenty young people, some of whom followed him as far as La Ferté-Bernard. There, another cscort joined him and went as far as Nogent-le-Rotrou on his route home. Though Lafayette may not have known it, there was good reason to cut short the trip to the Sarthe: his friend and fellow conspirator Colonel Charles Fabvier had been arrested in the early-morning hours of 26 September. This arrest was more serious than the previous ones because Fabvier had extensive knowledge of the conspiracy, having acted as a link between the lower and upper levels of the organization. His arrest threatened to give proof of Lafayette's involvement in the conspiracy.[35]

Constant, after remaining in the Sarthe a few days, headed for Saumur in the neighboring department of Maine-et-Loire. With evidence of Lafayette's involvement in the conspiracy mounting, with rumors that further armed attempts were to be made in the west, government suspicion of Constant's intentions seemed justified. Yet there were compelling political reasons for his trip. Maine-et-Loire was scheduled to hold arrondissement elections in 1820, and Goyet had already been sending emissaries there to help organize the liberals. Constant's trip was part of this effort at organization, though the avowed purpose was to show Mme Constant the area of the Loire.[36]

At Saumur, Constant and his wife stayed at the home of the man who would be the liberal candidate in the elections of 1820. As they were seated at dinner with about a dozen guests, several cadets from the cavalry school at Saumur appeared in front of the house to denounce Constant and cheer for the Bourbons. Originally intending to leave Saumur the next day, Constant declared that he would stay longer to avoid giving the impression that he had been intimidated by the cadets. On Sunday the demonstrations continued. This time they were marked by death threats and pistol shots. Constant's defenders went to get their own guns. The mayor and the sub-prefect now intervened, asking Constant to leave before violence worsened. Constant insisted that the mayor write a letter asking him to leave, making it clear that he had not caused the disturbances.

At midday on Monday, 9 October, Constant and his wife ostentatiously walked across Saumur through sympathetic crowds to take their places in a coach heading for Baugé.[37] On their way back to Paris, they stopped at La Grange, where Constant wrote a pamphlet about the trip to the Sarthe that he hoped would "be useful for the elections."[38]

All sides were apprehensive about the upcoming elections because the new departmental and arrondissement colleges would be used for the first time. The government had carefully manipulated the arrondissement districts to undermine liberal influence. Goyet's hometown of Montfort, for example, had been taken out of the Le Mans district to prevent his voting in the same college as his old acquaintances.[39] The arrondissement of Brioude in the Haute-Loire had been broken up, no doubt to dilute the influence of the Lafayette family.[40]

In the summer, Lafayette had been pleased to see that, despite the changes in the election law, the government still hesitated to dissolve the Chamber because it was "even now . . . not sure of a large majority."[41] But by the fall, the possibilities of liberal victories had become more remote. The liberals faced divisions in their own ranks and were burdened with the conspiracy. They suggested that the conspiracy was invented by the authorities or egged on by their "agents provocateurs" and hoped that the voters' suspicion of the government would lead them to discount its seriousness.[42] Dupont de l'Eure reported that, in his department, "They do not believe at all . . . in the latest conspiracy. The ministry has lost all rights to public confidence."[43]

By their attempts to deny the existence of the plot, the liberal politicians revealed the incompatibility of conspiring and trying to win elections at the same time. Their majorities had been forged by combining opponents of the Bourbon Restoration with more moderate voters who feared that government policies would cause unrest. But if unrest were to come from the left, the moderates would abandon the liberals. As arrests continued throughout the early 1820s, it became less and less likely that voters would attribute everything to government manipulation.

In Seine-et-Marne the government and the ultras were working harmoniously together. "The same is not true of the liberals," Lafayette explained, "who are having more trouble agreeing, not having the means which power gives and finding themselves labeled seditious in the bargain."[44] The sub-prefect of Meaux confirmed that the liberals were in disarray. Taken aback by the August conspiracy, they tried to explain it away as a momentary aberration of a few officers "more scatter-brained than dangerous."[45] To gain votes, Lafayette seemed ready to compromise by adding to the liberal list for the departmental college a man identified with Decazes.

The elections disappointed the residents of La Grange. George had hoped to win election as an arrondissement deputy in the Haute-Loire, though some of his friends talked of promoting him in the Haut-Rhin as well.[46] In the Haute-Loire, George had a slight lead on the first round (145 votes to his opponent's 144).

Then the government rallied its forces and compelled its employees to write their ballots in plain view, and he lost.[47] Although liberals won about half of the seats at the arrondissement colleges, it was less than they had hoped for. The new departmental colleges, dominated by the richest people in each department, offered fewer opportunities, though the liberals won a few seats in these uncongenial circumstances (in the Vosges and in the Haut-Rhin, for example).[48] The balance of power in the Chamber was altered substantially by the addition of the 172 new deputies, many of whom had sat in the *Chambre Introuvable.*[49] The departmental college in Melun, which Lafayette attended in mid-November, followed the standard pattern. After hearing the president of the college remind them that only the royal family could assure tranquillity, the 277 voters in attendance gave their support to two experienced politicians, one of whom had been a member of the *Chambre Introuvable.*[50]

Some reasons for the left's failure can be glimpsed in Dupont de l'Eure's description of the results in the Eure, where he was the only liberal reelected. He blamed the results on the "treachery of the ministry and the violence of its agents." In other words, this time the government had mounted vigorous opposition to the left. But he mentioned as well "the weakness of a rather large number of *patriotes* who, by abstaining from voting, gave the victory to the ministerials united with the ultras."[51] Some of these stay-at-homes, though dissatisfied with the liberals, were still unwilling to vote for their opponents. Others now feared the increased power of the government to harass and jail them under the laws passed the preceding spring.

Such fears were not altogether unfounded. On 4 November 1820, Goyet was ordered to appear in Paris before the *juge d'instruction* in the Sauquaire-Souligné case. He suspected that the date of his appearance, 15 November, was chosen to prevent his being in Le Mans on the thirteenth and fourteenth during the meeting of the departmental electoral college. Goyet also assumed that he would be arrested when he arrived in Paris, even though the ministry of justice had earlier concluded that there was no evidence that an incriminating plan to overthrow the government (found among Sauquaire-Souligné's papers) had ever been communicated to anybody else.[52] This time he was merely questioned, but immediately after his return to Le Mans on 13 December, he learned that the court had ordered him into custody, though he was still not charged with a crime.[53]

Goyet returned to Paris, but instead of submitting to the authorities, he went into hiding to prepare his defense. Lafayette arranged for him to stay with the duc de Gaete, and George, who visited him regularly, engaged Joseph Mérilhou as his lawyer. As the case dragged on with no resolution, Benjamin Constant shouldered the greater burden of helping Goyet, since the attention of both Lafayettes was necessarily focused on the trial of the 19 August conspirators being conducted by the Chamber of Peers.[54]

Goyet was exasperated at Sauquaire-Souligné, who seemed more eager to make a name for himself than to be acquitted. He worried that Sauquaire-Souligné would make intemperate revelations that would destroy both their cases. There had never been any understanding between them to do anything illegal, Goyet insisted, and his most convincing proof of this was that their correspondence had been carried out exclusively by mail and not by private messenger. Since the government had no evidence that Goyet had conspired, he was finally accused of the crime of "nonrevelation," that is, of having knowledge of criminal activity and not informing the authorities. In February 1821, still waiting for trial, Goyet presented his case in a pamphlet entitled *Accusation de non révélation*, which was meant to reassure his friends in the Sarthe who were beginning to fear that he was guilty and that they would be implicated as well.[55]

The deputies of the Sarthe tried to induce the court to set a date for the case.[56] Sauquaire-Souligné also petitioned the Chamber of Peers on "6 February 1821, 246th day of my captivity," to complain that he had originally been incarcerated under the exceptional laws and was now being held under a specific charge but that he had still not been brought to trial.[57] Goyet begged Lafayette to accompany Mme Goyet to the court to have the case put on the new calendar for March.[58] On 2 March, ten days before the trial was to begin, Goyet called on Mérilhou, Constant, and Lafayette, then surrendered for imprisonment at the Conciergerie.[59]

It soon became clear that the main purpose of the trial was to publicize the contents of the seized correspondence between Goyet and the two deputies and to insinuate that they too were part of a conspiracy. The authorities had been reading Goyet's letters since at least February 1820, in the aftermath of the assassination.[60]

Both deputies were called as witnesses. Benjamin Constant insisted on the letters being read in their entirety, saying that his words were taken out of context. Lafayette took a more confrontational tone. He acknowledged that the excerpts were indeed from his letters and added that he had repeatedly expressed the same sentiments in the Chamber of Deputies. "Should these opinions ever need any clarification in the general interest, it is at the rostrum of the Chamber that it would be appropriate for me to comment." The presiding judge chided Lafayette for persisting in these views and for dragging the accused, "by the erroneous principles of your correspondence, to the dock." Lafayette responded, "My respect for the court will not allow me to say in this courtroom what I think of the presiding judge's rebuke." He then reminded the court that, if the authorities wished to bring charges against a deputy, they could present the case to the Chamber for its approval, and he invited them to do so. As the judge continued to lecture Lafayette on the dangerous nature of his pronouncements and called his views "destructive of public order," Lafayette retorted, "You have that opinion; I have another; Europe will decide between us."[61] Interestingly, the unrepentant deputy called Europe, not France, his judge. After a five-day trial, the two defendants were acquitted.

Coinciding with the Goyet case was the potentially more serious trial in the Chamber of Peers of those arrested because of the conspiracy of 19 August. George complained bitterly of living "in the midst of criminal trials, royal prosecutors' indictments, and judicial abuse of all kinds. That is our current curse."[62] These trials claimed more of Lafayette's attention than did the new session of the Chamber, which began on 19 December. He spoke only twice during the session of 1820–1821.[63]

The evidence in the trial of the 19 August conspirators began to be considered on 28 December.[64] The crucial question was how widely to cast the net. Would the investigation be limited to those military men actually captured, whose conspiratorial activities were clearly established, or would the search be widened to include those who had promoted the plot, especially such deputies as Lafayette and Voyer d'Argenson, whose names were continually linked to the revolt?

Many in the Chamber of Peers (most notably the more moderate peers newly created during the Decazes ministry) were disinclined to pursue the high-ranking generals and politicians rumored to be involved. Others feared that attacking popular and prominent deputies might backfire and do more damage to the government than would merely leaving them alone. The prosecutor, however, was eager to widen the investigation. The Chamber delayed by debating procedure, trying to find a way out of the difficulty.

A key figure in the maneuver to spare the liberal deputies was the duc de Broglie, who wanted to save his stepfather, d'Argenson, and his good friend Lafayette. Wishing neither to pursue them nor to neglect his duty as a member of the Chamber of Peers, Broglie decided to keep their names out of the proceedings. He began by going to them and asking them to tell him nothing about what they had done. "If I knew from you, from outside the trial, the real truth, I would lie in denying it or in altering it; I will not be lying in my role as judge, by knowing only what I should know, and by putting the facts as presented by the prosecution, in the most favorable light." Broglie knew the importance of Colonel Fabvier, "in some way, the link between the politicians and the men of action, between the leaders of the left and the military." He feared that Fabvier's boldness and impetuosity would lead to indiscretions if he were questioned sharply by the prosecution. His aim, then, was to remove Fabvier from the list of the accused. The rest of those in custody could give only hearsay testimony regarding the prominent politicians and generals.[65]

Colonel Fabvier's case came up for discussion on 10 February, and Broglie was able to convince his colleagues to drop it. The rest of the trial offered no further dangers for Lafayette and his political friends.[66] Lafayette was not called as a witness, and after deciding not to pursue the highest-ranking conspirators, the Chamber of Peers handed down light sentences to the men who had attempted to carry the conspiracies into action. The only people condemned to death were in flight. Of the twenty-nine accused who were in custody, twenty-three were acquitted. The remaining six were found guilty of "*non-révélation de complot*": five were sentenced to five years in prison, one to two years in prison.[67]

Lafayette did his best to help the defense. In May he discovered some potentially damaging information about the vicomte de

163

Montélégier, the commanding officer who had first heard the confession of the government's star witness, Bérard. Lafayette passed the information along to the defense lawyers in the hope that it could be used to impugn Montélégier's honesty.[68] When the trial was almost over, a colonel named Maziau (who had been tried in absentia) was taken into custody. Lafayette put Mme Maziau in touch with peers who might be sympathetic to her request that he be tried speedily. Eventually, the peers handed him a lenient sentence, too.[69]

The indulgence shown the conspirators seems to have emboldened Lafayette. Both of his contributions to debate in the Chamber of Deputies followed a judicial victory in the Chamber of Peers. His first speech came shortly after Fabvier's case was dropped, his second after Fabvier successfully completed his testimony as a witness.

The first speech protested French policy toward Naples. The Richelieu government had been trying unsuccessfully to steer a moderate course on Italy. Austria intended to move into Naples to put down the revolt, which threatened their hegemony on the Italian peninsula. When the issue was discussed at the Congress of Troppau in the fall of 1820, the French government championed the alternative of joint action by the powers. They hoped to forestall increased Austrian influence in the area and to sponsor a compromise in Naples based on the French Charter. Metternich and Alexander rejected the French proposals. The powers instead issued an uncompromising repudiation of change and endorsed Austria's right to intervene alone in Naples to help the king "to consolidate his power so as to offer guarantees of calm and stability to Naples and to Europe."[70] If the Naples revolt were suppressed, then it was only a matter of time, liberals feared, before Spain would experience the same fate.

The French policy was rejected by both sides. The Neapolitan revolutionaries preferred the radical Spanish Constitution of 1812 to the French Charter, and the powers meeting at the Congress of Laibach in January 1821 once again endorsed Austria's decision to put down the revolt. Challenged on the issue in the Chamber, the ministry was caught in the uncomfortable position of having to defend a policy it had never favored.

Because foreign policy was not normally an area of responsibility for the Chamber, the left had to contrive an occasion for discussion.[71] Lafayette managed to speak about the issue in the context of a debate on the accuracy of the minutes of the previous session. He argued that the deputies had the right to ask whether the policies of the government were "contrary to the interest, the security, and the honor of our country." The Constituent Assembly, he reminded the deputies, had endorsed the principle "that the French nation would never employ its forces against the liberty of any people." Despite protests that he was straying from the subject, Lafayette continued to complain that the minutes had not reflected the true sentiment expressed.

> *We should regard as an important protest what has been said about measures taken to consolidate social order, in other words, measures analogous to what occurred in the partition of Poland, the treaty of Pilnitz and the manifestoes of Coblentz . . . (lively exclamations on the right.) Yes, gentlemen, the manifestoes of Coblentz. What we have been saying for twenty-five years, why should we not repeat it today?*

Amid further protests and interruptions, Lafayette concluded by urging his fellow deputies never to mount the podium without saying: "Let us not destroy Neapolitan independence!"[72]

Lafayette ignored the French government's attempts to seek an alternative solution in Italy and pictured their acquiescence in the Laibach decisions as tantamount to wholehearted endorsement. He saw the struggle in Manichaean terms: "The friends of liberty were never in such perfect sympathy as in this moment of European crisis; ours is a holy alliance which is well worth the other one."[73]

In March, French liberals were heartened by news of revolts in Piedmont and in Greece. But in that same month, the Austrians marched into Naples and easily reestablished the monarchy of Ferdinand IV. Lafayette held out hope for northern Italy and thought that "Italian liberty, though subdued is not extinguished; the nation is stirred by a sense of nationality and by a need for independence."[74] These vain hopes were soon dashed, as the Austrians crushed the revolution in Piedmont and as Italian refugees headed toward Spain.[75]

After the failure of the conspiracy of 19 August 1820, the French revolutionaries had apparently decided that they needed to create a better-organized conspiratorial network with procedures to protect secrecy.[76] Inspired by the Carbonarist organization in Italy, which had played an important role in the events in Naples, the French Carbonarists created *ventes* or cells. The members of one *vente* were given no information about the extent of the organization or its numbers and knew only one agent from a higher *vente*.[77] Secret rituals and symbols encouraged loyalty to the organization.[78]

Because Lafayette believed that "European liberty Chiefly depends on the interior politics of France," he was ready in the spring of 1821 to join this Carbonarist conspiracy to overthrow the French government.[79] He was consistently identified as a member of the directing committee, called the *haute vente* or *vente suprême*. The exact nature of his authority, however, is not clear, for the students and former soldiers who founded the Carbonari insisted that they retained leadership, that Lafayette was given the title of honorary president, and that he was no more than "the instrument and ornament" of the association.[80] The organization brought together students and soldiers, as well as politicians, all of whom understandably deemed their contributions as central and indispensable. The view that Lafayette was merely a figurehead probably stemmed from the students' desire to magnify their youthful accomplishments and from Lafayette's reluctance to take blame for what turned out to be disastrous conspiracies. Though he never denied his participation, he did not consider it among his life's greater achievements. Charles de Rémusat remarked that in later years Lafayette's way of speaking about the conspiracies "in a brief and playful manner" indicated "a little embarrassment, a certain desire to diminish the importance of them and give them the least possible place in his history."[81]

The section in his posthumous *Mémoires* entitled "Sociétés Secrètes. 1821–1822," consists of only four documents.[82] These pieces are, unfortunately, undated. Other letters alluding to conspiracies exist, but they are too few to construct a detailed chronology of his activities, and they are understandably vague about the operations. For these reasons, the question of the composition of a directing committee is fraught with difficulties.

The first document reproduced in the *Mémoires* referred to many groups throughout the country working for the overthrow of the Bourbons. Lafayette hoped that they could coordinate their efforts. "If in the current crisis, in the measures taken that I am aware of in several places throughout France, and in the means of advancing those measures, a common, homogeneous, national direction can be agreed upon, then our country, the whole of Europe, will be saved; if not we risk being nothing but the instigators of the enslavement of peoples, and the playthings of all domestic and foreign intrigues."[83]

In the second document in the *Mémoires*, Lafayette reported that several deputies who had received requests for support had decided to pool their resources to create a committee of seven.[84] This kind of organization was similar to contemporary attempts at political organization that worked through the spheres of influence and networks of associates cultivated by each deputy. National inspiration was important, but a close look at electoral politics has shown the importance of local leaders as well, people who were often jealous of their independence. It is safe to assume that military conspiracies were subject to the same pressures. And the necessity for secrecy surely aided local independence also.[85] Despite Lafayette's prominence in the national leadership of the Carbonarist movement, the areas where the movement drew its strongest support were not those in which his political influence was very great. He had personal or political ties to Paris, Auvergne, and the departments of the Sarthe and Seine-et-Marne. Except for Paris, none appears to have been a major center of Carbonarist activity.[86]

The third document was addressed to a committee that spoke in the name of a Carbonarist congress. Lafayette was here assuring them of his adherence to the principles adopted by the congress: (1) that the organization would be based on the principles of election and federation; (2) that the aim was the recovery of natural rights and of national rights as proclaimed in 1789 and that the choice of the form of government would be left up to the nation; (3) that to facilitate the expression of the national will they would adopt the electoral law of 1791; and (4) that they pledged themselves not to favor any dynasty or party. These tenets reveal that the Carbonari felt compelled to smooth over the usual differences among their members until their revolution had succeeded.[87]

It also seems clear that Lafayette, whether as an individual or as a member of a committee of deputies, was not dictating to the rank and file. Instead, in their own organization they followed the vague principles of the congress, namely, that the will of the people would rule. Lafayette was undoubtedly a Carbonarist leader, but how this position translated into specific authority is unclear. The specter conjured up by the ultras of a Parisian *comité directeur*, which oversaw all opposition movements in France and in Europe, is certainly inaccurate.

The fourth letter in the *Mémoires* reveals an attempt to create a more centralized leadership, but one deputy objected to the assumption of greater powers by their committee. This letter was apparently written quite late, when repeated failures might have induced the politicians to try to exert greater control. Before then, the need to draw as many participants as possible into the conspiracies probably dictated a large central committee, including the young student founders, the prominent politicians, as well as important journalists and lawyers who acted as agents throughout the country.[88]

Although his authority was limited, Lafayette was more than a figurehead. If the revolts were to have any chance of success, participation could not be limited to students and sergeants. Lafayette's social stature enabled him to recruit fellow generals and politicians. In May 1821, for example, he tried to enlist a general into the conspiracy. The letter he wrote on that occasion sheds light on Lafayette's political views and suggests that other letters of this kind must have been written but were destroyed because of their compromising content.

> *Counterrevolution no longer hides; it is located on the throne, in the chambers, in the courts, in the administrative and military headquarters; it relies on internal governance and on its intrigues with arbitrary governments; its advances are rapid, they will invade in turn all that the nation has gained since 1789 until resistance arises; but from the moment of that resistance, counterrevolution will be defeated because we have on our side the immense majority of the nation, proprietors, nonproprietors, old army, new army, neighboring*

*peoples, and because a great patriotic act would be
imitated everywhere in France.*

He had been willing to cooperate with the new government until
he discovered its bad intentions. Then he had expressed his views
clearly in the Chamber. The importance of France's acting to
preserve liberty in Europe weighed heavily in Lafayette's argument.

> *Liberal Europe is displeased with us; the Peninsula,
> brought back to liberty, is convinced that she cannot
> maintain it without our help; Italy, and especially
> Piedmont would rise up as soon as France demanded
> its rights; the German people have completely changed
> their attitude towards us since recognizing that with-
> out French liberty there was no hope of liberty for
> them. If owners of national lands, younger sons, farm-
> ers, artisans, soldiers of the old army still employed in
> the current regiments, enemies of privilege, adver-
> saries of the Old Regime and of noble distinctions will
> just read attentively our censored newspapers, the
> trials in* cours d'assises, *the debates in our Chamber,
> they should be able to see plainly where we are
> headed.*

He had tried to reach his goals by peaceful means, "but when
resistance to oppression, to the enterprises of despotism and
aristocracy seemed indispensable to me, it became for me a right
and a duty." He was convinced that "in order for the French people
to be free, they have merely to wish it, and that the first step
towards its deliverance will be as effective as it is (in my conscience) just and glorious."[89]

Lafayette confidently expected people throughout France to
rise against an oppressive government as soon as the signal was
given. The proof that such a sentiment existed he found in the
election returns and in the Chamber of Peers, whose members
might not join the conspiracy but had shown by their leniency
that they did not completely disapprove of it either. Lafayette once
again imagined that others held the same degree of interest and
enthusiasm for his cause that he did. As an Auvergne correspondent told him after reading one of his speeches, "You always

commit the generous error of comparing the French people to the heavenly tribe of your own family which was born of and lives by virtues alone."[90]

This confidence might help explain the anomaly of the Carbonarists never having planned for extensive fighting.[91] They seemed mesmerized by the example of the Spanish *pronunciamiento* and by their faith that they represented the overwhelming sentiment of the nation. Censorship perhaps helped to lead them astray. They did not believe the widespread professions of attachment to the royal family following the birth of the duc de Bordeaux because critics of the government had no corresponding right to public expression. Had such criticism been freely expressed, the liberals might have been better able to compare the strength of the opposing sentiments.

In spite of his own generally hopeful attitude, Lafayette knew that the failures of the revolutions in Italy had disheartened many liberals in France. In the late spring of 1821, he resolved to give one more speech to try to raise the spirits of his countrymen. It was aimed at those outside the Chamber since he could have little effect on the majority of deputies.[92] The occasion was a debate on the budget, but the date was significant: the anniversary of the large demonstrations in favor of the election law that had led to the death of Lallemand. Demonstrators numbering in the thousands marked the anniversary.[93]

On 4 June, while the excitement was at its height, Lafayette delivered what was universally interpreted as a call to insurrection.[94] His long and carefully prepared speech, appreciably better than his standard effort, testified to the importance of what he had to say.[95] He began by declaring that the large budget deficit stemmed from the mistakes of previous governments. France, instead of settling for the costly treaty with its conquerors, should have called on the energy of its population to rid itself of the enemy. The murmurs that this remark provoked in the Chamber were repeated after almost every subject he broached, and cries of horror from the right and bravos from the left punctuated his speech. Lafayette questioned whether the deputies were justified in voting for the scandalously expensive government, considering that its direction was "evidently contrary to rights and to the wishes of almost all the taxpayers." He urged citizens to learn what things the government had a right to ask of them "and therefore what they had a duty to resist." They should recognize critical moments when "the boldness and the intrigues of those factions can be put down only by the courageous and active resistance of good citizens." At this point, the right accused Lafayette of inciting insurrection.

In his speech he contrasted the new France with the old and defended the results of the French Revolution more forcefully than he had heretofore. He opposed appropriations for foreign affairs conducted in a manner contrary to "*la France nouvelle.*" Where was France, he asked, "in this division of Europe between two flags, on one side despotism and aristocracy, on the other, liberty and equality which we were the first to proclaim?" Lafayette expressed gratitude that the government at least had not cooperated "in the aggression of the satellites of Troppau and of Laibach." Nonetheless, the government had done even less than the British to distance itself from the policy of the allied powers. Lafayette reminded the deputies that it was not merely his own "personal disbelief in the dogma of divine right" that prompted him to label these policies un-French. After all, well before 1789, the "era of the European revolution, when we, American soldiers, were honored with the names of *insurgents* and *rebels*, which the English government called us by virtue of the *social order* also, Louis XVI and his ministry had expressly recognized the sovereignty of the United States, founded on the principles of their immortal declaration of independence."

These principles, proclaimed by the Constituent Assembly and accepted by the king, were confirmed by the Charter, Lafayette continued. They should not be confused with the excesses of the era of the French Revolution:

> the murders, the calamities which we all loathe,
> which we all deplore, are no more the revolution than
> Saint-Bartholomew was a religion, and no more would
> you call monarchical the eighteen thousand judicial
> murders of the duke of Alba. The revolution, as you
> well know, is the victory of right over privilege; the rev-
> olution is the emancipation and the development of
> human potential, the restoration of peoples; and that is
> so true, that the friends of liberty have always been
> and are still hated by the adversaries of the revolution

171

in proportion to the efforts that they have made to pre-
vent its being sullied by crimes and disfigured by ex-
cesses.

His speech touched briefly on several subjects dear to him: appropriations for *enseignement mutuel*, abolition of the slave trade and improved relations with Haiti, reform in the army and the National Guard. When he broached that last predictable subject, it was greeted with laughter in the Chamber. The way the army was being treated, he noted, would make one believe that some wished to return to the ancien *régime*, that they missed "the time when the regiments were created by recruiters, the title to employment by a genealogist, and . . . the plans of campaigns by the mistress of the king."

The last part of the speech continued his denunciation of the *ancien régime*, lately the subject of praise and nostalgia in some circles. Lafayette told Goyet that he had decided to "refresh the memory of the old people and to give some idea to the young of this *ancien régime . . .* which we are accused of having foolishly destroyed."[96] He evoked the excessive power of the Church, courts staffed by venal judges, a chaotic and unfair financial system, unequal provinces with different laws. What, he asked rhetorically, do we miss from this regime? Taxes imposed arbitrarily by a king and his finance minister? The capitation tax or sales taxes? The criminal justice system with its torture? Religious intolerance, which reduced a great portion of the population to living in common-law marriages? Tithes and feudal privileges? *Lettres de cachet*? Offices without functions?

Frenchmen, that was the ancien régime, *whose de-*
struction has made you as unaware of the advantages
of the Revolution as you are of the air that you breathe,
whose reestablishment was the avowed purpose of the
emigration to Coblentz and the coalition of Pilnitz, and
whose spirit continues to drive that more or less hid-
den government of the court, before which the minis-
ters are nothing, and which, since 1814, said
officially: "Let us enjoy the present, I'll answer for the
future."

Lafayette thus alluded to Louis XVIII's brother, soon to be Charles X, who was popularly believed to have uttered that complacent statement and whose power in the government had dramatically increased. Lafayette said that he had hoped that barriers had been erected to prevent the resurrection of the *ancien régime*, but

> *this hope is completely destroyed; not only do I admit it, but I believe I must declare it, and after having, since the last session, pointed out the counterrevolution's invasion of all our rights and the new order of duties which, in my opinion, would result for us; after having fought within the established institutions the dogma of parliamentary omnipotence, today that the counterrevolution has got hold of them, and at the point to which we have arrived, I limit myself to recognizing openly the powerlessness of those institutions to save the nation.*

The call for action outside legal channels could hardly have been made clearer.

Benjamin Constant felt compelled to defend Lafayette from charges that this was a call to insurrection and tortured his colleague's arguments to make them seem less seditious. His proposal that Lafayette's speech be printed at the expense of the Chamber met defeat almost as a matter of course. Constant explained to Goyet that he had offered it merely as a way of showing his adherence to what Lafayette said, since he knew it had no chance of being approved.[97]

The speech attracted just the attention that Lafayette wished. His adversaries, he noted proudly, had begun to call it a "manifesto." He soon exhausted the fifteen hundred copies of the speech that he had had printed, and he had it reprinted.[98] It was translated into English and published in London, thus achieving another of Lafayette's goals: international notice.[99] His words could have little impact in the Chamber itself, but as he told James Monroe, "part of it may fructify elsewhere."[100] Lafayette was especially pleased that the Austrian authorities took his speech seriously enough to attack it in print. Lafayette announced proudly that an Austrian paper, edited by Metternich's close associate Friedrich von Habsburg Gentz, had declared him "guilty of disrespect to the crowned heads of Europe, and of seditious appeal of the nation to arms."[101]

Lafayette boldly asserted his antagonism to the established governments in Europe and called on others to join in what he saw as a war between privileges and rights. His outspokenness led many to assume that he was the head of the famous *comité directeur*, which allegedly coordinated all the revolutionary activity breaking out in various parts of Europe in 1820 and 1821. In 1821, for example, Metternich told Czar Alexander that it was at Paris "that the great furnace exists . . . for the most vast conspiracy that has ever threatened the whole of society."[102] After the outbreak of the revolt in Greece, Alexander hesitated to go to war with the Turks to help his fellow Christians because he feared that, by supporting rebels against any authority, "the Paris directing committee will triumph and no government will be left standing."[103]

The truth was somewhat different. Although Lafayette kept himself informed about events in the rest of Europe and encouraged revolutionaries, no *comité directeur* in Paris coordinated all of the revolutions. The coordination of the Carbonari's activities within France was a less than successful effort, and the resources for a Europe-wide system certainly were not available. Some attempts at communication were made. Joseph Rey, for example, recalled trying to create ties with German revolutionaries, and Victor Cousin was in touch with possible revolutionaries in Switzerland and Germany.[104] But in 1821 Lafayette's direct contacts with other revolutionaries were not extensive. He did seem to know about plans for revolution in Piedmont before it actually occurred; but, though he occasionally remarked hopefully on developments in Germany, nothing ever happened there.[105] On the other hand, he showed no interest in Greece until after the revolution had broken out there, and he seemed to have had no advance notice of the revolutions in Spain and Naples.[106] His contacts with revolutionaries from other countries increased greatly after the failures of the early revolts sent many into exile.

Lafayette's focus was primarily on France because he saw success in France as essential for success in the rest of Europe. If France could defeat counterrevolution, then it could support revolutionaries elsewhere. But success in France had to be the first step. Politics in France having failed to preserve proper constitutional government, Lafayette abandoned it for revolution. In the rest of Europe, political solutions were even less likely because the parliamentary systems were less developed. Lafayette tended to see two starkly opposed sides to most questions. By not backing European revolutionaries, the French government was on the wrong side. He ignored the substantial difference between the French government and that directed by Metternich, for example. He dismissed the differences between the governments headed by Richelieu and Villèle. Slight advances within France seemed irrelevant to him if the destruction of the other European revolutions continued apace. Politics as usual in France might produce a slight improvement, but it could no longer achieve a liberal majority that could put the weight of France behind other European revolutions. The new laws passed in 1820 had made a parliamentary victory impossible. His goal, then, on the European level, could not be reached through ordinary politics in France. Instead of leading and inspiring the revolutions occurring throughout Europe, Lafayette's decision to adopt revolution and to abandon politics was the result of the European revolutions. Their precarious existence made him much less willing to compromise with the conservatives in his own country.

Popular engraving reproducing the portrait of Lafayette painted by his friend
and fellow conspirator, Ary Scheffer. Many engravers and lithographers
used the Scheffer portrait as a model. This engraving was published by
Goodrich and Hopkins in New York in 1825.

Mme de Staël. Her book on the French
Revolution praised Lafayette's actions.

Louis XVIII. His Charter provided the
basis for the surprisingly vibrant political
life of Restoration France.

Alexander I of Russia. The reluctance of
his support for the restoration of the
Bourbons encouraged Lafayette
to seek his aid.

Jeremy Bentham. His ideas inspired radical
reformers in many countries. (Courtesy of the
Lilly Library, Indiana University)

Singry.

Lith. de Langlumé.

Le Général Lafayette.

(Député du Département de la Sarthe.)

" Ainsi tandisque la liberté Européenne marche à pas de géant que la France veut et
" doit rester à la tête de ce grand développement de la dignité et des facultés humaines un
" gouvernement auquel enfin, on ne peut plus reprocher l'hypocrisie, prétend vous entraîner
" dans son mouvement rétrograde; et agrandit de plus en plus l'intervalle qui le sépare de la
" nation. " (Séance du 23 Mars.)

In this popular lithograph, Lafayette is identified as a deputy of the department of the Sarthe. The text is a quotation from his speech of 23 March 1820, which criticized the government for reactionary policies and threatened revolution.

Benjamin Constant. Lafayette's fellow deputy of the Sarthe
and close political ally.

View of La Grange, Lafayette's country home in the
department of Seine-et-Marne.

The execution of the Four Sergeants of La Rochelle, 21 September 1822. The
four young soldiers convicted of Carbonarist conspiracy became heroes
to the left and the most famous martyrs of the cause. (Courtesy of the Lilly
Library, Indiana University)

The expulsion of Manuel from the Chamber of Deputies on 4 March 1823. The deputies of the left of the Chamber are shown reacting with indignation to the actions of the troops.

French troops march through the Pyrenees. This lithograph of a scene from the French entry into Spain in 1823 was produced by the talented lithographer Charlet. His sympathetic depiction of imperial soldiers made an important contribution to the Napoleonic legend.

Frances Wright. The young Scotswoman shared Lafayette's enthusiasm
for the United States, became his close friend, and joined in his
conspiratorial dealings with other European revolutionaries.
(Courtesy of the Lilly Library, Indiana University)

7

The Conspirator

Lafayette had always been hostile to Great Britain, yet during the Restoration it remained Europe's most liberal nation. His father died in battle against the British, who stood as France's traditional enemy from the Old Regime through the revolutionary and Napoleonic eras. Lafayette's own public career was forged in America's struggle against the British. There, he acquired his fundamental dislike of the British constitutional system, far inferior in his eyes to the American. Early in the Restoration, he predicted that, when "Old despotism" died, "the Civilized world . . . will Be divided Between the British and American doctrines. The lat[t]er I Hope will prevail."[1]

Lafayette preferred limitations on legislative power to British "parliamentary omnipotence."[2] When the ultra government of 1823 sought to replace the Charter's five-year term for deputies with one lasting seven years, Lafayette criticized the proposal as a violation of his country's fundamental document and as an import from Great Britain. The notion that the two Chambers and the king had the right to make such constitutional changes had also been borrowed from across the English Channel, according to Lafayette. This doctrine of "the omnipotence of the three powers" was contrary to the Charter and to true constitutional government.[3] The American Constitution provided the proper model for separation of powers, Lafayette believed. His friend Destutt de Tracy had criticized Montesquieu's assertion that the British enjoyed separation of powers, and Lafayette endorsed the criticism. Destutt de Tracy asserted that the British were "enemies" of his "economic, . . . political and philosophical principles."[4]

Unlike Lafayette, many French liberals were inspired by the British example and hoped to emulate it in France. François Guizot, for example, believed that American institutions were entirely inappropriate for Europe. He saw the United States as an "infant society," whose government would not work in the old societies of Europe.[5] Guizot admired the Charter of 1814 as an embodiment of the spirit of the Revolution but only of a particular faction in the Revolution: the Charter "was the victory of one of the liberal sections of 1789 over its rivals as well as its enemies, a victory of the partisans of the English Constitution over the framers of the Constitution of 1791, and over the republicans as well as the supporters of the ancient monarchy."[6] Under the Charter, he believed, the gains of the Revolution had been allied with the monarchy, and both had gained.

As a supporter of the Constitution of 1791, Lafayette differed with Guizot over the value of the Charter, a difference reflected in Lafayette's opposition to the Decazes ministry, in which Guizot served. But as the ministries moved to the right, Guizot, too, was thrown into opposition and eventually into cooperation with Lafayette. The first signs of this realignment appeared in the fall of 1820, when Guizot's book *Du gouvernement de la France* asserted that the king had adopted the Revolution by promulgating the Charter. Its appearance at election time signaled Guizot's break with the new authorities, who had already removed him from his post at the ministry of the interior. Guizot's turn to the left became even more pronounced when his history lectures at the Sorbonne were closed down in 1822.[7]

In the political climate of the early 1820s, Guizot looked more liberal than he had a few years before, and so did the British. Lafayette now developed closer ties with sympathetic British radicals. But despite these friendships, he still could not shake his deep-seated suspicion of Britons. In 1823 he commented, "In England both Whigs and Tories are tenacious of a double aristocracy, their own with respect to the Commoners, that of their island over all the countries of the earth. There is, I am told, more liberality among their Radicals; but hitherto we must take them at their word, as power is elsewhere, and they do nothing to obtain it."[8]

Lafayette had always had a few friends in England—the anti-slavery advocates William Wilberforce and Thomas Clarkson, for example, as well as Charles James Fox and Lord and Lady Holland. His British acquaintances became especially useful in the 1820s in aiding French radicals to flee the Bourbon government. In 1821, for instance, a young writer named Benjamin Laroche ran afoul of the French authorities because he intended to publish the letters of the abbé Grégoire. Lafayette asked Alderman Wood, a partisan of Queen Caroline in her battles with the new king, George IV, to help the young man.[9]

Another of Lafayette's English friends was Sir Robert Wilson, once described by the duke of Wellington as "a very slippery fellow."[10] Wilson's dashing exploits during the Napoleonic wars had included making himself an advisor to Czar Alexander and to the court of Austria. His Whig friends at home relied, often unwisely, on his questionable expertise in military matters. Though his judgment was sometimes faulty, he was generally acknowledged a charming man and a courageous adventurer. His ties to Lafayette probably dated from the time of Wilson's connivance in the dramatic rescue of the comte de Lavalette, who had been arrested after the Second Restoration for complicity in the return of Napoleon. In December 1815, Lavalette escaped from prison by dressing in his wife's clothes and walking out the door. Wilson provided the prisoner with a British passport and accompanied him across the border. The French authorities later captured Wilson and his two English accomplices and sentenced them each to three months in prison. The punishment was mild, but both the British and French governments wished to hush up the incident. The French government did not really deplore Lavalette's escape because it spared them from having to put to death another Bonapartist. General Ney's execution had caused sufficient ill will.[11]

By June 1821, Lafayette and Wilson (now a radical and supporter of Queen Caroline) were confederates in the European struggle to overthrow conservatism. In light of the coalition of Laibach, Lafayette wrote him, friends of liberty everywhere needed to become more united. The person carrying his letter, a man named Baud, could enlighten Wilson further about "patriotic affairs in France."[12]

Lafayette also trusted Baud with a letter to Frances Wright. She had recently published a book entitled *Views of Society and Manners in America*, and Lafayette liked her flattering picture of the United States and offered his help in getting the book translated into French. This communication began an important and emotional relationship for Lafayette.[13] The Scottish-born Wright, called "Fanny" by her friends, was twenty-five years old in the summer of 1821. Her mother and her father, a linen merchant, died when she was two years old. Fanny and her younger sister, Camilla, were raised by their grandfather and their strict young aunt in circumstances that were not very congenial. Her brother, raised by other relatives, died when Fanny was fourteen, making the two sisters heirs to a sizable fortune. Two years later, Fanny read a book that changed the course of her life: a history of the American Revolution by Carlo Giuseppe Guglielmo Botta.[14] She was so taken with the image of a land of freedom that she resolved to visit it someday. She kept her thoughts to herself, however, for this was the era of the War of 1812, when the British and the Americans were once again at war.[15] Her study of America continued when she went to live with her great-uncle, James Milne, professor of moral philosophy at the University of Glasgow.

In 1818, after both sisters had come of age, they decided to travel to the promised land of America. Supplied with letters of introduction from a friend, Fanny explored America and wrote a book in the form of letters to this same close friend.[16] Their two-year trip to the United States was made memorable by the performance in New York of Fanny's first play, *Altorf*, and the start of important friendships, including one with Charles Wilkes, a New York banker and nephew of the notorious John Wilkes.

Publication of her book opened further opportunities for Fanny. Her naturally exuberant nature and tall, striking looks made her noticed wherever she went. Her bold proposals and keen intellect earned her the admiration of many distinguished people. An example of the impact that Fanny had on her contemporaries was the reaction of the philosopher Jeremy Bentham. Cerebral and determinedly rational, Bentham lived a quiet life devoted to propounding his schemes for Utilitarian reforms. Yet after reading Fanny's book, he wrote to the American minister in England: "I want to talk with you about Miss Wright. I am in love with her, and I suspect that you are." He invited her to stay with him when she was in London, and she eagerly took up this invitation.[17] Bentham said of her: "She is the Sweetest and Strongest Mind that ever was Cased in a female Body."[18]

Through her friendship with Bentham, Fanny entered the world of reform and reformers in England and Europe. One of Bentham's devoted followers and an enthusiast of the Spanish and Greek revolutions, Lieutenant Edward Blaquière, had already been contemplating the translation of Fanny's book into French before she received the communication from Lafayette.[19] To oversee the translation and to meet Lafayette, Fanny, accompanied as usual by her devoted sister, Camilla, made her way to Paris. She was so eager to see Lafayette that she headed for La Grange soon after arriving, only to discover that he had left for Paris. Lafayette's family received her warmly "but were in despair at the absence of the General," she told Bentham in a letter revealing her romantic sensibilities, as well as the intimacy into which she immediately entered with these two older men.

> *I determined to return next day, to meet him here, which I did. You will say again, "giddy goose," why did you set off for La Grange, without having written beforehand? There are reasons for everything, great philosopher. I had found a letter in Paris notifying the approach of some English friends, who were coming to see all the sights of this gay city, in the short space of ten days. Civility, therefore, constraining, for this period, my presence in Paris, I was obliged to seize the only day that remained to me before their arrival, for my journey into the country. Returning late at night, I sent a note, early the following morning, to General La Fayette, who soon answered it in person. Our meeting was scarcely without tears, (at least on my side,) and whether it was that this venerable friend of human liberty saw in me what recalled to him some of the most pleasing recollections of his youth, (I mean those connected with America,) or whether it was only that he was touched by the sensibility which appeared at that moment in me, he evidently shared my emotion. He remained about an hour, and promised to return in the evening, (he was engaged to dine with Constant). . . . We held an earnest tête-à-tête until after midnight. The main subject of our discourse was America, although we wandered into many episodes and digressions.*

188

*The enthusiasm and heart affection with which
he spoke of our Utopia, the high respect he expressed
for the character of its people, the ardent love of liberty
which breathed through all his discourse, found, I
need not say, an answering note of sympathy in me.
He told me he had been particularly interested by the
allusions in my work to the history of the American
Revolution: "you made me live those days over
again."*[20]

This dramatic meeting was the beginning of an intimate friendship, with Fanny and Camilla spending months at a time at La Grange. Fanny acted occasionally as a courier for Lafayette and his friends in their conspiratorial schemes. The affection between the young female radical and the old revolutionary general was based first of all on their mutual fascination with the United States. Neither could find any faults with it, except for slavery. They must have been struck as well by the coincidences of their lives. Both had become enthralled with America when quite young and rather impulsively determined to go there to see it for themselves. They shared a birthday, 6 September. Both had lost their fathers at the age of two, and both had been raised among people who were not sympathetic to their aspirations. Lafayette had taken George Washington as his model, as a sort of adopted father, and he constantly referred to himself as Washington's adopted son. Fanny immediately called herself Lafayette's adopted daughter and took him as a model. On the morning following their meeting, she wrote in raptures: "Ah, what a day for me yesterday was! . . . How happy and proud I am of your friendship and of that adoption which unites my destiny to yours for life!"[21]

Fanny was especially susceptible to the idea of kindred spirits, of exceptional souls who found each other in the midst of the ordinary creatures of this world. At the time of her trip to America, she had written a poem addressed to Lord Byron's *Childe Harold*, claiming kinship with him.

*Start—but 'tis truth. There is a soul on earth,
Twin-born, the same, the counterpart of thine;
As strange, as proud, as lonely from its birth—
With powers as vast. Harold, that soul is mine!*[22]

Fanny was eager to find someone with whom she could share her enthusiasms, someone whom she could admire and emulate, someone who would appreciate her desire for fame and her love of liberty.

Fanny's appearance revived Lafayette's memories of his own youthful zeal. He turned sixty-four in September 1821 and must have begun to doubt whether his dreams of liberty for Europe would come true during his own lifetime. He pinned all his hopes on the rising generation and eagerly embraced young conspirators. He accepted willingly the discipleship offered by Fanny. Lafayette was susceptible to the charms of young ladies and had always valued female companionship. In addition to his devoted wife, he had enjoyed the friendship of Mme de Simiane and of Mme d'Hénin. He also maintained close ties with the wife of Destutt de Tracy and with her daughter, George's wife.

Stendhal, who frequented the salons of Destutt de Tracy's circle in the early 1820s, described Lafayette as a "hero of Plutarch," eager to perform "any great deed which presented itself." While waiting for such heroic events, though, he took the opportunity, despite his age, of squeezing from behind the petticoats of the pretty young girls, "and that often and without too much embarrassment." Stendhal, though given to rather acid pen pictures, nevertheless saw too the greatness of the man. "For me, accustomed to Napoleon and to Lord Byron, I could add to Lord Brougham, Monti, Canova, Rossini, I recognized right away the greatness of M. de Lafayette and went no further."[23] The young women, Stendhal pointed out, also recognized the hero and often reciprocated Lafayette's attentions.

A difference exists, of course, between playful flirtations and a serious affair. It is doubtful that the relationship between Lafayette and Fanny Wright was of the latter kind, but it was not playful either. It was serious and intense, described always between themselves in the language of familial relationships. Fanny wrote to him, "You know I am your child—the child of your affection the child of your adoption. You have given me the title & I will never part with it. To possess the title was the highest of my wishes—to deserve it is my proudest ambition."[24] Lafayette generally referred to her as "*ma bien aimée Fanny.*" But in one letter, he added, "*la tendre fille de mon choix.*"[25] To others, he described his ties to the two sisters as paternal: "*j'ai pour elles une paternelle affection.*"[26]

190

In the sophisticated world of Paris, extramarital relationships were not uncommon. Lafayette himself had long associated with Mme de Simiane without causing scandal. But the persistent use by Lafayette and Fanny of the terms of the father-daughter relationship would seem to preclude a sexual relationship, and the great gap in their ages also makes it seem unlikely. Fanny's infatuation with someone else during a trip to London in 1822 and Lafayette's continued interest in and support for her after her marriage likewise suggest that they were devoted friends but not lovers.[27]

Whatever the exact nature of their relationship, she was certainly important to Lafayette at this time. Because she idolized him, she contributed to an atmosphere in which he reigned as the great man, unchecked by the criticism of equals. His children revered him and followed his lead. His young associates helped to draw him into their conspiracies against the government. The contrary advice of Mme de Simiane, always more conservative politically, was apparently no longer present. Surrounded by younger people who looked up to him, Lafayette became even more deeply involved with impractical plots and visionary international revolutionaries.

In the summer of 1821, what Lafayette called "our colony" at La Grange included Virginie and George and their families. Several members of Anastasie's family were absent, visiting Célestine, Anastasie's eldest daughter, who had married one of Lafayette's fellow deputies, the baron de Brigode, and lived with him in Flanders. That summer Célestine gave birth to Lafayette's first great-grandchild.[28] In the fall, Fanny and Camilla came for a long stay. Fanny basked in the warmth of this family circle, describing the "sweet hours" she passed there. "I must pass many more there my good friend and (receive the threat for a prophetic one) *shall* pass many more there. Hitherto my life has had so little pleasure in it, that I am sure there must now be a great deal in store for me."[29]

Lafayette entered eagerly into plans for the translation of Fanny's book into French. Even before her arrival in France, Fanny had sent Lafayette a corrected copy, which he passed on to the translator Jacques-Théodore Parisot. Lafayette sent another copy to Albert Gallatin, calling it "a phenomenon indeed from a British pen."[30] Lafayette had suggested a few revisions for the sake of accuracy and now enlisted Gallatin's help in correcting other errors.[31]

Lafayette continued his work on behalf of Fanny's book when Parisot's translation appeared in early 1822. He suggested to Marc-Antoine Jullien, the editor of the *Revue encyclopédique*, that he publish a review by Thierry along with J.-C.-L. Simonde de Sismondi's notice of the English edition.[32] He corresponded with Sismondi and Etienne Dumont (Bentham's translator) about the possibility of an Italian edition as well.[33] Lafayette marshaled his considerable influence to make the book a success because it promoted the reputation of the United States but also because he was interested in the author, an interest he proclaimed in all of these communications.

The promotion of Frances Wright's book shows the usefulness of Lafayette's network of friends and political associates in various countries. Numerous connections reinforced their ties, as the historian and economist Sismondi illustrates. Sismondi was a close friend of Jullien and of Dumont, a fellow Swiss and the popularizer of Bentham's ideas on the Continent. Having been in Mme de Staël's circle, he thus knew well the Broglies and Constant. He was also a cousin by marriage of the Garnett sisters—another tie to Frances Wright. During her tour of the United States, Fanny had met the Englishman John Garnett, who had settled his family in New Jersey. Taking a keen interest in scientific experimentation, Garnett had educated his daughters in a more serious fashion than was the custom of the time, and they soon became Fanny's close friends. After her husband's death, Mrs. Garnett and her daughters, Julia, Harriett, and Fanny, moved to France and once again into the orbit of Frances Wright. She stayed with them at Paris, when not visiting La Grange.[34]

Many of the people in this network of international reformers had ties to Jeremy Bentham. Lafayette's first contact with Bentham came in 1789, when the English reformer sent him advice concerning the Estates General in the form of a pamphlet entitled *Essay on Political Tactics*.[35] Bentham did not approve of the Declaration of the Rights of Man, calling it "the *ne plus ultra* of metaphysics." The French, he thought, had been "deluded by a bad example—that of the American Congress."[36] Natural rights theory was at odds with Bentham's Utilitarian doctrine, "the greatest happiness of the greatest number," with its emphasis on compromise and calculation. Bentham, who despised appeals to higher laws for their abstraction and for their potential for misuse, devoted his life to clarifying and simplifying the law. Statute law, he argued, was better than the irrationalities of the common law. Although not originally a supporter of democracy, Bentham came to believe that democracy offered the only means of bringing about the reforms that he wanted, reforms being blocked by monarchs and entrenched self-serving parliamentarians. Under the influence of James Mill, Bentham became a radical and an advocate of parliamentary reform. His earlier fears about revolutionary democracy had been assuaged by the example of the United States, where democracy had not led to disorder.[37]

Despite their original differences on the French and American Revolutions and their fundamental disagreements about the question of natural rights, Lafayette and Bentham now became allies in a fight against conservatism, eager to work together on subjects of common concern. One of these subjects was the revolution in Spain and the fate of the Spanish colonies. Bentham had been advising liberals in those countries and sending legislative suggestions.[38] Lafayette and Bentham also promoted liberal economic theory and educational reform. The economist Jean-Baptiste Say, Lafayette's friend and the father-in-law of Charles Comte, one of the editors of the *Censeur européen*, regularly corresponded with Bentham.[39]

In the summer of 1821, when Bentham's friend John Bowring went through France on his way to Spain, he brought with him some of Bentham's writings and a letter of introduction to Lafayette from Clarkson. Lafayette thanked Bentham for his gift and predicted a "happy result" for "the cause of liberty to which you have been so attached and on which you have thrown so much light," if the "patriots of several nations" will sustain it vigorously. Fortunately, he continued, the model of the United States existed to confound the fears of critics, and he was pleased to hear that Bentham shared his opinion of the "utility of spreading by all possible means the American work of your friend, so distinguished in every respect."[40]

As plans for international cooperation increased, Lafayette began to work even more closely with military men whose contribution to the conspiracies would be crucial. The accommodation with Bonapartists became especially marked after the news of

Napoleon's death reached Paris on 5 July 1821.[41] In his last days, Napoleon had tried to destroy Lafayette's reputation. He denounced Lafayette "to posterity" along with Talleyrand and Marshals Marmont and Pierre Augereau for having incited the Chambers to rebel against him. Napoleon condemned Lafayette's lack of patriotism, accusing him falsely of having "deserted to the Prussian camp." Lafayette had always pointed proudly to his refusal to sit in the Napoleonic senate. Bonaparte now asserted that he had never offered Lafayette a senate seat and that if he had Lafayette would surely have accepted it since his financial situation was precarious. Napoleon said that he had never received any letter explaining Lafayette's vote against the life consulate; indeed, he had not known of his vote.[42] Other evidence of these events exists, so Napoleon's final comments on Lafayette can be seen as a desire to wound his old adversary rather than to set the record straight.[43] Napoleon was clearly bothered by Lafayette, despite his scorn for his political principles. Lafayette and others, he sneered, were "still exactly as they were in 1791, with their utopias, their English notions, their bills of grievances and States-General. All they see in the Revolution of 1789 is a mere reform of abuses, and they refuse to admit that it constituted, all in itself, a complete social rebirth."[44]

Napoleon's last words on St. Helena were unknown in France and therefore had no effect. In fact, Lafayette's cooperation with Bonapartists increased when, shortly after the news of the death arrived, he acceded to Colonel Fabvier's request to deposit a petition before the Chamber of Deputies calling on the British to return Napoleon's body. Lafayette first submitted the petition (signed by several former Bonapartist officers) to the approval of Dupont de l'Eure, Manuel, and General Foy, then presented it to the proper committee on 14 July 1821, too late for it to be acted upon.[45]

The death of the emperor brought no major changes to the Carbonarist conspiracies. The chances of returning Napoleon to power had always been extremely remote, and Bonapartists willingly worked with others for the overthrow of the government, leaving the question of future institutions to be decided later. Napoleon's death did, however, make even liberals like Lafayette less worried about working with the Bonapartists.[46]

Lafayette's attention was now focused on conspiracies, and he took scant interest in the elections in the fall of 1821. Despite well-merited fears about their chances, the left seemed unprepared to contest these elections to renew one-fifth of the Chamber. As late as July, Constant asked Goyet whether he favored organizing a committee in Paris to prepare for the elections.[47] Goyet answered gloomily that their supporters were abandoning politics for military plots and warned that increased military influence would be disastrous for the future of liberalism.[48] Furthermore, he noted, participation by the left in debate over clearly unconstitutional laws discouraged voters because it lent an air of legitimacy to obviously illegal proceedings that the left could not prevent.[49]

After the predictable liberal defeat, Lafayette seemed unconcerned, noting that the losses were few because liberal deputies up for reelection in 1821 were so few to begin with.[50] Hardly anything could be accomplished in the new Chamber, "but the little that will be said should be direct and to the point."[51] He now neglected ordinary politics in favor of conspiracy. No letters from Lafayette to Goyet survive for the period from October 1821 to October 1822. They apparently destroyed some letters to prevent seizure by the authorities, but they also wrote to each other less frequently. Lafayette was not being asked to intercede for constituents or to help his political friends.[52] He did at least attend meetings of the new session, which opened on 5 November, but he favored the defeatist strategy of opposing the Richelieu government and allowing it to be replaced by an avowedly ultra ministry. He reasoned that, once the nation realized the evils of the right, the success of the left would follow quickly.[53] And the ultras would be easier to overthrow by violence.

The government first became aware of the Carbonarist plots in December 1821, when they got wind of a conspiracy at the cavalry school at Saumur. The atmosphere there had obviously changed since the demonstrations against Benjamin Constant fourteen months before. An active secret society, the *Chevaliers de la liberté*, was now subverting the cadets. The important agents managed to avoid arrest, but several military men arrested by the government provided information about the plots. When the authorities also learned of preparations to subvert the garrison at the fortified city of Belfort on the eastern side of the country, they became convinced that the society at the cavalry school in the west formed part of a national network of conspiracy.

The rising at Belfort had been carefully planned. Voyer d'Argenson and his fellow deputy of the Haut-Rhin Jacques Koechlin, a textile manufacturer and mayor of Mulhouse, had given asylum and jobs at their establishments in Alsace to several men implicated in the aborted 19 August 1820 conspiracy.[54] The deputies had borrowed money to finance the schemes, and the new men had established Carbonarist cells in the area.[55] Students traveled from Paris to take part in the revolt scheduled for the end of December. But at the last moment, just as the plans went into operation, army officers discovered the plot.[56] They arrested a few participants, though some of the most important organizers escaped. Continuing investigations convinced the authorities that the events in the east were part of a national movement with ties to liberal deputies in Paris, but they had only circumstantial evidence.

Lafayette had expected to play an important part in the Belfort uprising. In late December he went to La Grange for the traditional commemoration of the death of his wife, Adrienne, on Christmas Eve. Instead of returning to Paris, he left for Belfort accompanied by George and his servant Bastien.[57] His arrival on 1 January would be the signal for the revolt and for announcing the establishment of a provisional government. From their stronghold in Alsace, the revolutionaries hoped to draw other soldiers and other regions of the country to join them. The original plan had called for Lafayette to arrive earlier, on 29 December, but for some reason, the outbreak was delayed, perhaps until Voyer d'Argenson and Koechlin, who were on the scene, felt confident that all was in place. Lafayette waited until he received assurances from Ary Scheffer, who made a hurried trip to La Grange, that he was indeed expected in Alsace. The delay meant that the plot was discovered before Lafayette could arrive.[58]

Two young men, Saint-Armand Bazard and François de Corcelle (the son of the deputy), left Belfort and intercepted Lafayette to warn him away from the city. Lafayette's carriage then turned off toward the town of Gray, where he visited the liberal deputy of the Haute-Saône, Alexandre Martin de Gray, to concoct a plausible excuse for the trip.[59] Corcelle next headed south to warn others, including Arnold Scheffer, who had traveled to Lyon to coordinate an uprising there.[60] The conspirators still needed to dispose of incriminating evidence remaining at Belfort. George

196

Lafayette had sent a carriage there containing his own uniform and one of his father's to be worn at the time of the revolt. Ary Scheffer and a friend drove the carriage from Belfort to Mulhouse. The Koechlins then took charge, paying a hotel keeper to take it to Basel, where one of their political friends burned it.[61]

The location of the Belfort conspiracy points to the importance of Voyer d'Argenson in the early Carbonarist plots. He had the resources and the connections in Alsace to bring about the revolt. Lafayette trusted d'Argenson and continued to work closely with him as they moved from legal to illegal activities.[62] But as prominent as he was in the region, d'Argenson was not enough; Lafayette's participation was considered essential. The conspirators, modeling their revolt on the recent one in the Spanish army, needed a general who could lead the subverted troops.[63] Lafayette's reputation also guaranteed him a place in the provisional government to be established after the revolt. One historian writes that Lafayette was "the center to which all projects and all communications led."[64] Yet he was not the only leader, and he did not exercise strict control over the Carbonarist organization.

The few surviving documentary fragments in which Lafayette commented on the conspiracies mentioned a group of seven deputies who oversaw the Carbonarist plots. Three were those most deeply involved at Belfort: Lafayette, d'Argenson, and Koechlin. Manuel, Dupont de l'Eure, and Corcelle were also Carbonarists, but the seventh deputy is not as easy to identify. Some sources mention General Jean Demarçay, a close friend of d'Argenson's. Others frequently mentioned are Antoine Bourreau de Beauséjour, George Washington Lafayette, and Pierre-François Audry de Puyraveau.[65] It is possible, too, that the membership of this committee of deputies varied and that those on the committee were not the only Carbonarist deputies.

After Belfort, more conspirators were arrested at the southern port of Toulon, where Captain Fidèle-Amand Vallé had arrived to recruit among the sailors and soldiers. A similar conspiratorial cell was uncovered at Nantes in the west. Meanwhile, Lafayette called on his international connections to help those who had escaped the government's grasp.

At the end of January 1822, Frances Wright left France for England, ostensibly to oversee the second edition of her book about America. But she had another purpose: to carry messages and money to French conspirators in hiding there. She was undoubtedly well informed about the Carbonarist plans. On the original date of the Belfort conspiracy, 29 December, Fanny wrote to Lafayette from Paris, hinting at the momentous events in which he was involved.

> *Time at present hangs heavy on my hands and on my heart, and it seems as if the burden could alone be lightened by discoursing with a friend. I mean not however to call your attention from important matters to my idle words. Throw them aside till you have some moments of leisure—or perhaps of weariness;—then possibly they may serve to banish some anxious thoughts. . . . I anxiously await the post of tomorrow wch will bring me tidings of my good friend. . . . Write to me my friend—my father. One word will suffice—but let me know that word soon & often.[66]*

In London she scurried from office to office, seeing people and arranging accommodations for the exiles. The needs of the revolutionaries took precedence over her own. On 7 February she wrote to Lafayette,

> *I have been all day talking about house rents, powers of attorney, and heaven knows what, with heaven knows who, and heaven knows where. I trust, however, I shall soon see my friend's affairs arranged. I have, as yet, attended little to my own. Next week I hope to be free to set about them. I have a copy of the second edition of our book, Views of Society and Manners, by me, but have scarcely looked into it.[67]*

Even as Lafayette and Fanny aided exiled conspirators in England, further plots in France were creating new victims to worry about. The resulting trials were bringing unwanted attention to the clandestine activities of some liberal deputies.

In late February 1822, during the military trial of the Saumur conspirators, General Jean-Baptiste Berton made an unsuccessful attempt to raise the revolutionaries in the western departments. Calling himself "the general commanding the National Army of the West," Berton organized an insurrection in the town of Thouars, then headed north to Saumur, accompanied by Lieutenant Honoré-Edouard Delon, the man who earlier had subverted the troops at Saumur and had escaped arrest. The authorities met Berton and his small band at the edge of Saumur and prevented their entry into the town but somehow allowed the rebels to escape unharmed. Although arrests of Saumur citizens in league with Berton were subsequently made, the military leaders were not found.

Shortly afterwards, other arrests more directly implicated Lafayette and his friends in the unrest in the west. On 4 March, the authorities at Nantes arrested Colonel Jules-Louis Alix, who was on his way to La Rochelle. Discovered on him were records of his visits during the last few months with many suspected persons, including Beauséjour, d'Argenson, Mérilhou, and a General L (presumably Lafayette). Alix was apparently the courier between the western departments and the leadership in Paris. His trip to La Rochelle, officials soon discovered, was related to the presence in that city of the 45th Regiment, recently transferred from Paris, where many of its members had been brought into the Carbonarist conspiracies. Under harsh questioning, a man named Goupillon confessed that he had been inducted into the organization, and his disclosures led to the arrest of the Four Sergeants of La Rochelle, the most famous martyrs of the Carbonarist revolts. These four men (named Bories, Pommier, Goubin, and Raoulx) intended to join Berton's group in the west and provided the government their best hope so far of tying the military conspirators to the liberal leaders in Paris.

Naturally, the opposition was not waiting for hard legal evidence before making the connection between Lafayette and the events in the western departments. On 1 March, just days after Berton's attempt on Saumur, a conservative paper printed a spurious declaration presumably from Berton urging "honest *Carbonari*, unemployed Bonapartists, convicts *libérés ou liberaux*" to join him in the area of Saumur. The notice added, "They should, before leaving, apply to General la Fayette, who will give them marching orders, and to the banker in charge of paying their campaign expenses."[68] The banker referred to was Jacques Laffitte, widely, but erroneously, suspected of providing the finances for the disturbances.[69]

From the beginning, then, suspicion focused on Lafayette. Hatred and mistrust of the liberals were so intense now that, when a series of unexplained fires broke out in the departments around Paris, a royalist newspaper asserted that the arsonists were acting on orders issued by Manuel, Constant, Foy, and Lafayette from the podium of the Chamber of Deputies. The newspaper charged that "the *comité directeur* in order to punish the common people for not having listened to it, is burning their cottages and their crops."[70] Liberal papers retorted that only the party that wished to destroy constitutional government would be interested in such violence.

April brought the execution of the first Carbonarist conspirator, one of the young men arrested at Saumur. At about the same time began the trial of Captain Vallé, arrested at Toulon. The jury sentenced Vallé to death.[71] Meanwhile, the authorities were taking a long time in carefully preparing the case against the Belfort conspirators. That trial did not begin until late July.

While French authorities conducted trials of conspirators within the country, they began to receive information about more extravagant conspiracies bringing together revolutionaries from various countries. French and Italian exiles now congregated in London, where the plots were hatched and organized. Frances Wright's trip to England at the end of January provided important contacts for Lafayette with these exiles. One person she got in touch with was Joseph Rey, who had left France after the 19 August 1820 conspiracy and had arrived in England in the summer of 1821. He devoted his exile to study, especially the works and ideas of Jeremy Bentham.[72] But Rey was also useful in England for helping to coordinate the departures of foreign liberals eager to fight in Spain. It was likely that Fanny Wright discussed Spain with Rey, as well as with Bentham, with whom she spent many evenings.

She met with radical Englishmen, including those who frequented the home of Thomas and Fanny Trollope. Fanny Wright had become acquainted with the Trollopes in Paris in the fall of 1821, when they had visited their old family friends, the Garnetts. The Trollopes now provided hospitality for Fanny Wright and helped her revolutionary causes. The correspondence they maintained with the Garnetts became an important avenue of communication among the liberals, who hoped that letters passing between a London barrister's family and a widow with several daughters would be unlikely to raise the suspicions of the French police.[73]

The most important person Fanny Wright met in London was the exiled Neapolitan revolutionary, General Guglielmo Pepe, introduced to her by another new acquaintance, the radical Major John Cartwright. As a youthful hothead, eager to distinguish himself in the military, Pepe fought on the side of the French against Ferdinand IV of Naples. In 1811 he led a Neapolitan brigade in Spain. He followed King Joachim (Murat) to fight on the side of the Austrians, but he and other generals demanded without success that the king issue a constitution, hoping to make Murat an independent Italian monarch. With the return of the Bourbon King Ferdinand IV, Pepe was temporarily cashiered, but he was reinstated in 1818. From his position as general in the army, Pepe played a leading role in the revolution in Naples in 1820. Suspicious of the Italian Carbonari, Pepe hoped to use the citizen militia, which he had helped to organize, to force the king to accept a constitutional monarchy. When a Carbonarist rebellion began, he acted swiftly to put himself in control of the situation.[74]

Pepe's role in the Neapolitan revolution was reminiscent of Lafayette's in the French Revolution. Caught between the Carbonari (with their desire for greater change) and the Muratist generals (with their fear of disorder), Pepe, like Lafayette, found it impossible to mediate forever between the two sides. The moderate ministry feared Austrian intervention and wanted to present the events in Naples as merely a change in government, not as a revolution at all. Pepe, though, believed that the popular enthusiasm for the revolution, which the Carbonari fostered, should be kept alive. In fulfillment of a promise he had made, once the king had solemnly accepted the constitution, Pepe resigned his command of the constitutional army. But the threat of foreign intervention made it impossible for him to continue this noble imitation of Cincinnatus. Though Pepe wanted to stave off the Austrian advance, his effort was undermined by a dispirited militia and by his fellow army officers, who hoped to preserve their influence after the expected Austrian victory. Following the disastrous defeat at Rieti, Pepe went into exile.[75]

Pepe traveled first to Spain where he met refugees from the revolution in Piedmont and watched the progress of the Spanish revolution. Believing that lack of coordination among revolutionary groups was a major cause of their failures, he founded the "Constitutional Brothers of Europe" in an attempt to "open communication between the most enlightened patriots of the different cities in Europe." Accompanied by Lieutenant Colonel Vincenzo Pisa, another Neapolitan refugee, Pepe made his way through Portugal to England, where he immediately entered radical circles sympathetic to his cause. There, he met Fanny Wright, and through her, he began a correspondence with Lafayette. One of the first things he did was to recruit Lafayette into his Constitutional Brothers of Europe.[76] Lafayette agreed wholeheartedly with Pepe on the need for cooperation among liberals and thought such collaboration especially important for Italy. Indeed, Lafayette was an early and fervent promoter of Italian unification. He wished that "Piedmontese, Milanese, Florentines, Romans, Neapolitans, Sicilians would be first of all *Italians*. All physical and moral circumstances point to that confederation which cannot fail sooner or later to be substituted to the conceptions of what is called the Holy Alliance."[77]

Fanny was greatly impressed by Pepe, whom she described to Lafayette as "a fine, warm-hearted patriot but," she continued, "a very crude legislator. It is not every country that is blessed with a Lafayette. . . . His creed, however, is a good one as to the outline, and the filling up may be mended, though I doubt if the head be as deep as the heart is warm." She asked Lafayette to send a French translation of her book about America, so that Pepe might read it.[78]

Fanny's interest in Pepe grew into more than mere admiration. Her letters to Lafayette were filled with descriptions of their growing intimacy, while she continued to assure Lafayette that her love for him had not wavered. "My new friend . . . is sitting beside me at this moment writing a letter to Paris, which he wishes me to send by the portfolio of the ministry. I enclose it. He is gone. Oh, I am very much interested in him more than is reasonable."[79] Later she told Lafayette, "Our friend . . . always begs me to tender to you the assurance of his highest consideration and esteem. Your name is often in his mouth, as it must be in that of all noble men. I say 'our friend' because I can never have a friend that is not yours, and because he entertains for you every possible sentiment of esteem and high consideration."[80] Shortly before leaving London, Fanny anticipated being once again at Lafayette's side, revealing to him

*all the secrets of a heart which, believe me, will never
hide anything from the best friend that ever existed.
. . . What goodness, what adorable goodness is yours
to me. . . . Oh, my friend, my brother, my father . . . Believe me, no new friendship, however dear it may be,
is capable of replacing this sentiment, at the same
time so tender and so reverent that you have permitted
me to consecrate to you.*

    *I know when I place myself again at your feet,
you will be merciful to your young friend, if she has
had the error of inspiring a passionate feeling in a soul
of flame, and of being incapable of remaining insens-
ible to his virtues, to his misfortunes, to his great qualities combined with so much "noblesse" and manly
beauty.*[81]

Fanny Wright, the intimate friend of both Bentham and
Lafayette, had now fallen in love with a younger man, but one as
famous as they were. Indeed, Pepe's life story bears remarkable
similarities to Lafayette's. She particularly admired Pepe's romantic impetuosity and his devotion to revolution. "He has a
noble soul and a sweet nature . . . but I see in him a sanguineness
of temper and a contempt of danger which makes me apprehensive lest he should some day run upon the enemy's spear too
hastily. I would, however, that men of this character were more
numerous among your countrymen, and in the world at large. The
game cannot now be won by longheaded calculations. We want
hands of steel and heads of flame."[82]

    After having delayed her departure from England because
of "*faiblesse de coeur*," Fanny finally sailed for France in early
April, apprehensive about the future of her relationship with
Pepe.[83] Her fears were warranted, for though she saw Pepe at least
twice more, he seems to have lost interest in her after he left to
fight in Spain.[84] When Pepe returned to London in the spring of
1823, Lafayette chided him for his neglect. "You can have no
doubts about the fond interest with which we speak of you, our
friends and I: not that we do not have cause to reproach you for
your silence. . . . Politics is a fine thing when it is directed toward
our goal; but friendship also claims its rights."[85] Lafayette's tone
is that of a "paternal friend," who, seeing Fanny's grief, hints to

Pepe that he owes her a letter. Lafayette must have been distressed to witness Fanny's unhappiness, for her exuberant nature was not the kind to suffer in silence.

Why did this romance end? Pepe gave one clue in his memoirs. Despite the importunities of his family, he said that he never wished to marry.[86] If Fanny's relationship with Pepe followed the pattern of her possessive attachments to Bentham and Lafayette, Pepe might well have resisted her smothering affection. The loss of this friendship helps, too, to explain the increased tenacity with which Fanny clung to Lafayette, an attachment that would cause a crisis within the Lafayette family. It is also possible that Fanny misinterpreted Pepe's interest in her. Perhaps he saw her primarily as the friend of Lafayette, the person who could open channels to the revolutionaries in France. Pepe's conspiratorial letters during the spring of 1822 refer to Lafayette by the phrase *"l'amico della signorina"* ("the young lady's friend").[87] After the failure of the grand enterprise they contemplated that year, Pepe might have lost interest in Fanny Wright.

Lafayette and his associates were concocting a scheme that would further the goals of liberalism from the Balkans to Spanish America. By the winter of 1821–1822, though the Italian revolutions had been defeated, the Spanish and Portuguese revolutionaries were still in power, and the Greeks were still fighting the Turks. Lafayette had followed the fortunes of the Spanish revolutionaries from the beginning. His interest in Spanish America had naturally attracted him to a revolt which had broken out among soldiers being gathered to put down the American independence movement. In early March 1820, he had been briefed on the progress of the revolution and on the intentions of General Rafael Riego and the other leaders to establish a provisional government. Lafayette learned that General Francisco Espoz y Mina had joined forces with the revolutionaries. Although Lafayette had been suspicious of Mina for his ties to the British while in exile in Paris during the early years of the Restoration, he now concluded that Mina was acting in good faith by joining the "constitutionals."[88]

After the Austrians had put down the revolutions in Italy, Lafayette feared that Spain too was becoming "an object for Counter Revolutionary intrigues from every part of Europe."[89] As usual, he saw the fate of other countries tied to that of France. He wrote Jefferson that, though Spain and Portugal were "Constitutionally Governed," the "Counter Revolutionary party" in Europe was promoting plots there that threatened the stability of the new regimes.[90] The Spanish political situation was difficult at best. After General Riego had proclaimed that the liberal Constitution of 1812 was reestablished, King Ferdinand VII had been forced to accept the new institutions, but having overturned the Constitution once already, he was unlikely to submit happily to its limits on his power. Moderates whom he had forced into exile or prison returned, hoping to work for constitutional revisions that might bring about a compromise between the king and the radicals. Led by Francisco Martínez de la Rosa and the count of Toreno, this group dominated the new Cortes, the Spanish parliament.[91] But outside of the assembly, many patriotic societies sought to awaken a democratic commitment to the new institutions and warily watched the actions of the king and his government for signs of lack of devotion to the new order. When General Riego was transferred from the command of his army, his supporters in Madrid interpreted the move as antirevolutionary, and his appearance in the capital produced excited demonstrations in his favor. The government then began to close the societies from which the *exaltados* (radicals) received their support.[92]

In the spring and summer of 1821, Lafayette and Benjamin Constant met in Paris with Toreno. His reports that the radicals' suspicions of the government were forcing liberals to take essentially illiberal actions to safeguard the new order made Constant fear that the situation in Spain was precarious.[93] Lafayette reported simply that Toreno gave reassuring reports about developments in Spain and put the blame for the disorders occurring there on the manipulations of royalists.[94] From other contacts in Spain, Lafayette must have known that the ranks of the liberals were becoming more and more divided. Ferdinand VII was seeking help from Louis XVIII to defeat the radicals.[95] The moderates who cooperated with him were viewed with suspicion by the *exaltados*. Even the *exaltados* became divided, when a group of Freemasons created a new secret society known as the *comuneros*.[96] When he came to power in the spring of 1822 as the leader of a moderate ministry, Martínez de la Rosa was the avowed enemy of the democratic *comuneros* and committed to a policy of revising the constitution to make it palatable to the king and to the foreign powers whose antagonism threatened the Spanish experiment.

In the winter of 1821–1822, the attention of the foreign powers was focused as well on the continuing revolt in Greece. Russian concern for their coreligionists was creating worsening relations between Russia and Turkey, which pointed to war between those countries. Metternich tried to dissuade Czar Alexander from going to the aid of the Greeks, arguing that war would introduce instability throughout Europe and set off uprisings in several countries. Lafayette was convinced that Metternich's efforts to prevent war would fail because war fever in Russia was too strong for Alexander to ignore.[97] And while the European powers were preoccupied with an eastern war, Lafayette, Pepe, and others intended to launch simultaneous operations. Pepe, working in London with Sir Robert Wilson and an Italian general named Maceroni, was buying guns and ammunition, outfitting ships, and recruiting soldiers in Ireland. From England, this expedition would go to Spain to pick up Italian exiles who had gathered there, then head for southern Italy. They anticipated that Austrian troops would be withdrawn from Naples because of the eastern war and that they could then easily conquer the country. Meanwhile, French Carbonarists were to back them up by launching an uprising in France. They hoped to have the support of the Spanish and Portuguese as well.[98]

In furtherance of this plan, Wilson had traveled to France in January 1822.[99] Pepe's friend Vincenzo Pisa headed for Spain, stopping on the way to consult with Lafayette in Paris.[100] One of Pisa's responsibilities was to try to subvert the French troops posted on the border of Spain. The ostensible purpose of the troops was to provide a *cordon sanitaire* to prevent the spread of an epidemic of yellow fever from Spain into France. Preventing the spread of dangerous Spanish revolutionaries seems a plausible objective as well. Lafayette had suspected for some time that the French government meant to use these troops as an invasion force to put down the Spanish revolution.

The grandiose plans of the revolutionaries required money, but in the spring of 1822 they were confident that funds would be forthcoming from a surprising and unlikely source: the faraway Spanish-American republics struggling to establish their independence. In 1819, Simón Bolívar had appointed Francisco Antonio Zea, the first vice president of Colombia, as an agent to Europe to restore Colombian credit and to secure further desperately needed foreign loans. Zea arrived in London in 1820 and met Lafayette in 1821 on a visit to France. Having managed to float several loans, Zea used the money to finance an unsuccessful mission to Spain to secure independence. In the spring of 1822, Zea negotiated a substantial loan of two million pounds from British bankers and, apparently without the knowledge of his government, undertook a bold scheme to use the money to win recognition of his country's independence.[101] If French revolutionaries persuaded their friends in Spain to recognize the independence of Colombia, Zea would provide 100 million francs for military assistance to the Spanish government and the foreign revolutionaries. Part of the money would be used to subvert the French troops gathering on the Pyrenees.[102]

Lafayette entered into these schemes wholeheartedly, envisioning a way to overthrow the government in France, establish the revolutionary government in Spain on a solid basis, reconquer Italy, establish Spanish-American republics, and help the cause of the Greeks all at the same time. To get off the ground, the plan required at least two things: a war between Russia and Turkey to distract the European powers, and the willingness of the Spanish government to grant independence to its colonies.

The first requirement was effectively destroyed by Metternich, who bombarded Alexander with warnings not to go to war and who sent police reports confirming that war would unleash revolutionary forces throughout Europe. In late February and early March 1822, war seemed imminent, but by mid-May, Metternich had effected a compromise between Russia and Turkey.[103] As late as 27 May, Pepe still believed that war was inevitable, and he waited in London for its outbreak and for the money that Lafayette assured him he would be receiving from Zea.[104]

But Zea's money depended on Spanish recognition of Colombian independence. The moderate ministry of Martínez de la Rosa was unwilling to risk the unpopularity that acknowledging the loss of the American colonies would entail. When news arrived of President James Monroe's message to Congress of 8 March 1822, proposing that the United States recognize Spanish-American independence, the Spanish government instructed its ambassadors to protest this measure vigorously. Though several proposals were presented in the Cortes favoring recognition, the ministers would agree only to sending agents to investigate and to begin commercial negotiations with the de facto governments.[105]

Support for acknowledging the independence of the American nations was more likely to come from radicals than from the Martínez de la Rosa government. José Moreno Guerra, for example, wrote a pamphlet before the start of the spring 1822 session of the Cortes insisting on the need for American independence. His work, which was immediately translated into French, criticized the moderate governments as venal and servile.[106] He accused them of wanting to rule in imitation of the corrupt British system, whose leaders disdained public opinion. One of their important errors was to refuse to face the truth of the American problem: "either the Americans have the wish to remain united to Spain; or the Spanish government has the force required to compel them."[107] When envoys from Colombia appeared proposing negotiations, the government answered evasively. They were unwilling to make the best deal they could, yet nothing concrete was being done to win America back. Moreno Guerra defended the *exaltados* by arguing that the people should be told the truth about the problems they faced. The only enemies of Spain, he insisted, were within Spain: "the war in the Orient and the situation of France shield us from all foreign danger."[108] The new Cortes, he insisted, must face the issues of supporting the constitution and arranging the country's finances to recognize that Spain no longer owned the American colonies. Moreno Guerra's recipe for saving the Spanish revolution sounded remarkably like that of Pepe and Lafayette.

Lafayette was, of course, happy to see the United States taking the lead in promoting Latin American independence and hoped that they would do more, particularly in the cause of the Greeks. Americans had apparently been involved in these schemes all along, as Lafayette's dealings with Pepe demonstrate. During the spring of 1822, Pepe waited in London for the arrival of Zea and the money. His letters used the cover of a commercial correspondence, pretending that "Don Guglielmo" (Zea) owed him money, which he needed before he could leave with his shipment of Irish cloth to buy French wines. The "friend of the signorina" (Lafayette) was his associate in this business venture and kept assuring him that, when Don Guglielmo arrived, Pepe would be entirely satisfied.[109] In the meantime, Lafayette was securing letters of introduction for Pepe to Americans in London and Madrid. He asked Gallatin whom to address in Spain and wrote letters introducing Pepe to Richard Rush, the American minister in London.[110] The Americans seemed well informed. In a letter to President Monroe in July, Lafayette mentioned casually that "Mr Zea is in England," without further explanation or identification.[111]

In the spring, while Zea was in Paris, he had been entertained at a dinner given by what Lafayette called "the Commerce of Paris and a few deputies."[112] Zea had called attention to his cause by issuing a circular to the ministers of the European powers, threatening to end their commerce with the Spanish-American republics if they did not immediately recognize their independence.[113] This ploy was no more successful than his contacts with the Spanish government had been.

The revolutionaries apparently hoped that their combined operations could be launched at the end of May.[114] Spies reported that an uprising among the French troops on the Spanish border had originally been scheduled for 22 May but had been postponed.[115] Pepe's departure from England seemed imminent in May. Frances and Camilla Wright made a hurried trip to England and met Pepe at Dover to hand over documents sent by Lafayette.[116] Several days later, Pepe informed Pisa that he had letters for various gentlemen from the United States, and he still expected war.[117]

Also in May, Voyer d'Argenson traveled to London. Historians have generally suspected that fears about what might be revealed during the trial of the Belfort conspirators had prompted Voyer d'Argenson to flee the country while the trial was under way. Broglie gave that explanation for his willingness to help his stepfather by approaching Mathieu de Montmorency, the foreign minister, and asking him for a passport for d'Argenson. Montmorency and d'Argenson had been close friends as young men, and Broglie hoped that a residue of goodwill would bring him to accede to the request. Though Montmorency was startled by the suggestion, he ordered the passport delivered without asking any questions.[118] Accompanied by Broglie and Auguste de Staël, Voyer d'Argenson crossed the English Channel. The two young men paid a courtesy call on the French ambassador in London, François-René Chateaubriand, but d'Argenson did not make an appearance.[119] Montmorency's willingness to give Voyer d'Argenson a passport is surprising: the authorities must have suspected that his trip would put him in contact with Pepe and his confederates.

Pepe waited in England, but "Don Guglielmo" still did not arrive. By the beginning of June, Lafayette doubted that war would break out. "There are ten fold the Materials which at an other period would Have precipitated Russia Upon Turkey, and all Christian potentates Upon each other. But the fear of western Emancipation, and the Concerns of despotism and privilege Are foremost in all those legitimate and Aristocratic Heads."[120] By the end of June, Pepe had given up plans for an expedition to Italy. It was clear by then that Spain would not recognize the Spanish-American republics and that the Carbonarist organization in France had lost much of its usefulness because of repeated failures and arrests. At the beginning of July, Pepe's principal agent in Paris, Gabriele Cobianchi, warned in time, barely managed to escape the police and flee to Switzerland. One of his associates had been supplying the authorities with accurate information about the plans of the Italian refugees.[121]

Wilson now announced that it was necessary to forget Italy to concentrate on Greece.[122] When Pepe finally arrived in Portugal in August, he had to turn the attention of the Italian exiles there from plans of reconquering Italy to ways of helping Spain keep its constitutional government. In July a poorly organized revolt of the Royal Guards in favor of Ferdinand VII had failed, discrediting the Martínez de la Rosa government. A new ministry headed by an *exaltado*, Evaristo de San Miguel, came to power. But the policies of the new government differed little from the previous one. They sought a compromise that might satisfy the British and keep them from supporting the efforts of the other European powers. The Spanish royalists were now in open revolt, fighting the Spanish army from strongholds in the countryside. The new government also had to contend with the growing dissatisfaction of the *comuneros*, who deplored the wishy-washy policies of the government.

Lafayette and Pepe still hoped to do something to help the cause of Spain, but the grandiose projects of the spring had to be put aside, in part because the French Carbonarist organization suffered more reverses in the summer of 1822. By the autumn, the heady hopes of the conspirators would be replaced by disillusionment and grief.

8

Reverses

A lthough Lafayette was preoccupied in the spring of 1822 with plans for European conspiracies and worried about arrests of conspirators in France, other politicians on the left faced continuing political challenges. There were more elections than usual in 1822. Despite a reactionary ultra government that had come to power in January, the liberals won two new deputies at by-elections to fill vacancies in Paris early in the year.[1] Lafayette was particularly pleased with the election of General Etienne-Maurice Gérard, who had served under Marshal Bernadotte.[2] For the other Paris vacancy, the liberals hoped to elect Augustin de Schonen, a *conseiller à la Cour Royale* and a leading member of the Carbonari. He was also an accepted member of the Tracy-Lafayette circle, who would marry Claude de Corcelle's daughter in 1824.[3] At the last minute, however, Schonen discovered that his taxes had been lowered, so he no longer qualified for election. The liberals settled instead on Antoine Gévaudan, one of the men arrested in the case of the *Société des amis de la liberté de la presse.*[4]

The government, now headed by Villèle, decided to hold two regular elections in 1822 to solve a persistent budgetary problem that stemmed from the customary timing of elections. Normally, annual elections were held in the fall, which meant that the new session of the Chambers began so late in the year that not enough time remained to pass the budget for the following calendar year. Each year, then, the Chambers were obliged to grant temporary taxes, an arrangement satisfactory neither to the government nor to the Chambers. By holding an election in the spring, a summer session could approve taxes and budgets for 1823. Then, after elections in the fall, another session could begin.

Lafayette was too distracted by other matters to pay much attention to the spring elections, which produced ten liberals out of the twelve deputies chosen in Paris. Liberals did not fare as well in the rest of the departments, though Lafayette was surely pleased at the choice in the Haut-Rhin. Voting in the midst of the preparations for the trials of the Belfort conspirators, the electors settled on George Washington Lafayette.[5] The major disappointment was Corcelle's loss in Lyon. Lafayette commented later that if the news of Corcelle's defeat had arrived in time in the Haut-Rhin George would have stepped aside in favor of the older man, but arrangements there were already too far along.[6]

The summer session of the Chamber began on 4 June, and the discouraged liberals were greeted with news of more trials and of the execution of Captain Vallé at Toulon. On 17 June, General Berton was finally arrested at Saumur in an operation that brought criticism of the authorities' methods but gave further indications of the connections between Lafayette and the conspirators. A sergeant named Wolfel acted as a government secret agent. Recently posted to Saumur, Wolfel presented himself to the local conspirators as an envoy of Lafayette's, whose confidence he had apparently gained. At Saumur, he cultivated the friendship of a wine merchant named Baudrillet and a surgeon named Grandmesnil, pretending to share their Carbonarist views.[7] Wolfel agreed to help recruit soldiers for a planned uprising under Berton's direction, and he asked to meet the general. Baudrillet introduced Wolfel to Berton at a farm outside of town. With the help of four soldiers (whom he had described as recruits), Wolfel arrested Berton, Baudrillet, and the owner of the farm, and escorted them back to Saumur. Grandmesnil managed to escape.[8] Under interrogation, Baudrillet confessed that Grandmesnil had recruited him for the conspiracy and had taken him to Paris to meet General Lafayette.

Two weeks later another undercover operation netted Lieutenant Colonel Joseph-Augustin Caron. This case provided even more opportunities for the left to decry agents provocateurs. Colonel Caron, who had been implicated in the 19 August 1820 conspiracy, was now in the area of Colmar plotting to free the prisoners from the Belfort conspiracy of January 1821, who were still awaiting trial. Government spies made contact with him, encouraged his schemes, and provided him with troops (carefully chosen for their reliability). On 2 July, the detachment got under way with cries of "Vive l'Empereur!" and Caron gave them an inspiring speech. Caron, however, appeared to have second thoughts and suggested heading off to search for more support or for more money. At that point he was arrested.[9] Alsatians were outraged. Caron's goal, after all, was not insurrection but merely a rescue of his friends. The rest of the operation, planned by the authorities, appeared to be an attempt to trap Alsatians into committing illegal acts.

On 22 July, the day the trial of the Belfort conspirators opened, the actions of the officials in Alsace offered matter for heated debates in the Chamber. The next day, in his first speech of the year, Lafayette denounced what had happened. He saw no reason to repeat his colleagues' criticism of the trial, conducted by a military court at Strasbourg rather than by a civil court at Colmar. But he felt compelled to express the pain he experienced "on seeing that a police scheme, a trap laid for the honest inhabitants of the Haut-Rhin, perhaps even for the prisoners, . . . has been celebrated, as our most glorious feats of arms were in former times." Counterrevolution was triumphing everywhere, manifesting "that horror of equality which was always its principal motive." Now openly undermining judicial guarantees, when these guarantees were gone, it would announce "that all the liberties, all the advantages won from the *ancien régime* by the national revolution of 89 . . . were only illegitimate, temporary and removable usurpations."[10]

The carefully prepared trial of 23 defendants in custody and 21 others in absentia presented 184 witnesses. The prosecution showed a great deal of evidence of travel that could be explained in no satisfactory manner other than as conspiracy, but hard evidence tying these people together into a conspiracy was lacking. The skepticism of the Alsatian jury and the hostility of the general population could not be overcome. All of the accused were found not guilty of conspiring, while four were (illogically) found guilty of nonrevelation of conspiracy.[11]

On 1 August, while the Belfort trial was taking place, an indictment was handed down in the case against General Berton and his accomplices in the west. The prosecutor had spread his net as widely as possible, mentioning several liberal politicians in his accusations. The indictment pointed to Berton's announcement of a provisional government consisting of Foy, Auguste-Hilarion Kératry, Benjamin Constant, Voyer d'Argenson, and Lafayette. Berton had allegedly declared that Grandmesnil went frequently to Paris to see Foy, Lafayette, Laffitte, and Constant. The prosecutor said a witness had confirmed that Grandmesnil made such trips, that he identified himself to the famous leaders

> *with the help of Carbonari membership cards; . . . that the marquis de Lafayette paid for his trip; that he received instructions from these gentlemen for the new operation against Saumur. . . . Furthermore, it is proven that this individual introduced to the marquis de Lafayette, last May, one of the most important agents of the new conspiracy; that the marquis de Lafayette told Grandmesnil, at the time that he bade him farewell: "Come on! courage, my dear Grandmesnil."[12]*

Because this dramatic accusation inevitably mixed fact and fantasy, those deputies unjustly accused immediately took the podium of the Chamber to deny their guilt.[13] When Lafayette's turn came, he slowly approached the podium and spoke, as one historian put it, "with the calmest tone, and with that slightly disdainful grace which neither the ordeals of the Revolution, nor the long solitude of the dungeon of Olmütz, had been able to obliterate."[14] His entire comment was:

> *Whatever may be my habitual indifference toward partisan charges and hatreds, I think I should add today several words to what my honorable friends have said. During the course of a career devoted entirely to the cause of liberty, I have constantly merited being the object of the ill will of the adversaries of that cause, under whatever form, despotic, aristocratic, anarchical, they chose to fight it or distort it. I do not at all complain, then, though I have the right to find a trifle cavalier the word* proven, *which M. le procureur du roi used in regards to me; but I join my friends in demanding, as forcefully as we can, the largest publicity, within this chamber and before the nation; it is there that my accusers and I, in whatever rank they may be*

214

placed, can tell each other, forthrightly what we have been blaming each other for during the last thirty-three years.[15]

In spite of the danger he was in, Lafayette refused to lie and to proclaim his innocence. The accusations, he suggested, were ultimately political and would be most appropriately answered before the bar of public opinion. He was not ashamed of what he had done and seemed indifferent to these judicial proceedings insofar as they touched him personally.[16]

The charged scene in the Chamber of Deputies almost became more dramatic. The deputies of the left had defended themselves by pointing out that the only evidence for the prosecutor's accusations rested on the alleged conversations of Grandmesnil, a man whom the prosecutor could not produce and probably would not produce. They were suggesting, in other words, that Grandmesnil was an agent provocateur in the pay of the government. This line of reasoning caused great consternation to Grandmesnil, who happened to be in the Chamber of Deputies at the time, having come there to meet George Washington Lafayette and another deputy who were to help him escape. Outraged at this accusation, he almost ran forward to defend himself, and only George's restraining arm prevented his dangerous disclosures. Grandmesnil henceforth suffered from the suspicions of other Carbonari. When he sought refuge in Normandy, the cells there would not help him until they received a letter from George testifying to his loyalty.[17]

The prosecutor's hopes of ensnaring Lafayette were soon dashed. Baudrillet, who had confessed to meeting the general, had second thoughts. When pressed for details at a later interrogation, he described Lafayette as a short man in his fifties with long black whiskers.[18] When the trial opened on 25 August, the secret agent, Wolfel, testified to meeting Lafayette in Paris and to hearing Grandmesnil recount his own links to the Parisian political leaders. But Baudrillet stuck to his erroneous description of Lafayette. The judge pointed out to the jury that the "witness has an interest in conveying the impression that he was not in contact with M. de Lafayette. That is why he changes his first description today, and why he wants to reveal only a part of the truth."[19]

Berton insisted that he had been participating in a peaceful demonstration in favor of the Charter and the king without any intention of causing a rebellion. He undertook his second trip to the area, he asserted, to warn the inhabitants against falling for the machinations of Grandmesnil, whom he also labeled an agent provocateur. The prosecution, on the other hand, continued to tie the actions of the defendants to a wider network of conspiracy. Special care was taken to try to show Constant's connections to the area by stressing his disruptive visit to Saumur in the fall of 1820. In the process of testifying about that incident and suggesting that Constant had used the occasion to organize a conspiracy at Saumur, the sub-prefect recollected that at his suggestion Constant had agreed to leave the town. But, "instead of leaving early in the morning, as he had been asked to do, he found excuses for staying; he said that *madame* (this was a woman whom he wanted to pass off as his wife, but who was far from being that), that madame had been so moved by the events of the previous evening, that she was indisposed."[20] This gratuitous slur became the excuse for great polemics and led to consequences more serious than the silliness of the remark might lead one to expect.

Although the prosecution was unable to produce sufficient evidence to try the implicated deputies, it convinced the jury that most of the accused were guilty. Of fifty-six men brought to trial (forty in person and sixteen in absentia), six (including General Berton and Dr. Caffé of Saumur) received the death penalty; Colonel Alix and thirty-one others received prison sentences; eleven were given death sentences in absentia; only two were acquitted. After an unsuccessful appeal, Berton was executed in early October. Two of the condemned had been pardoned, but two others were also executed. Dr. Caffé committed suicide on the morning of the day he was scheduled to die.[21] Benjamin Constant offered to renounce his candidacy in the fall of 1822 in exchange for clemency for Caffé. "I believe the man is innocent. I believe and I fear that the support he gave me, in 1820, are the cause of his condemnation." His proposal arrived too late.[22]

The prosecutor in the trial of the four sergeants of La Rochelle also sought to link the accused to a European conspiracy, directed by the *comité directeur* of Paris. The young soldiers had broken down under questioning and had described their initiations into secret societies, but they could provide little specific information about other cells. Their confessions led to the arrest of a Parisian schoolteacher named Hénon, who acknowledged meeting one of the sergeants at a Masonic lodge and belonging to an intermediate *vente centrale* which transmitted information to the *haute vente* through the lawyer Baradère.[23] On the stand, however, the accused retracted their confessions, saying that they had been extorted from them. In the end, the jury was convinced of the guilt of the soldiers. The Four Sergeants received the death penalty, while the links to upper levels, Hénon and Baradère, were freed. The fate of these four young men, who faced death courageously, captured the public imagination as no other victims of the Carbonarist trials would. Many popular books about them have appeared throughout the years, and two cafés in Paris still bear the name "Aux Quatres Sergeants de La Rochelle."[24]

An attempt to rescue them failed. Lafayette must certainly have known about this attempt since those involved were his friends and fellow conspirators. He had already called on his English and American acquaintances to aid escaped revolutionaries. For example, on 8 April, Lafayette wrote a letter to Sir Robert Wilson recommending François Chauvet, "a good citizen of Saumur, . . . in exile for having, with rare devotion, walked alone through the street, a tricolor flag in his hands, inviting his fellow citizens to join Gen. Berton."[25] On the same day, Lafayette also recommended him to William H. Crawford in the United States.[26] When Chauvet finally found his way to England, he stayed with Bentham's associate John Bowring.[27]

The effort to rescue the Four Sergeants of La Rochelle was apparently hatched in August when Colonel Fabvier met with Wilson in London. Wilson had, after all, had a hand in the escape of the comte de Lavallette in 1816. John Bowring was also enlisted. On his return to France, Fabvier, with the help of some medical students, arranged to bribe the concierge of the prison. Unfortunately, the concierge informed his superiors, and when one of the students came to pay the first installment, he was arrested. An investigation soon led the police to Fabvier and to his accomplice, Colonel Dentzel, who were both arrested in early October.[28] The police also arrested John Bowring and discovered letters on him from Italian refugees and other suspicious people, including Benjamin Constant. There was not enough to prove

Fabvier's guilt, but Dentzel was condemned to four months in prison. Bowring was released after Jeremy Bentham asked George Canning, the British foreign secretary, to intercede on his behalf with the French authorities.[29]

In August 1822, Lafayette and Fabvier were also trying to help Italian refugees detained in France, including the count of Santarosa, who had led the Piedmontese defense against the Austrians and had escaped eventually to Paris. He lived there under an assumed name (Conti) and became a friend of the liberal philosopher Victor Cousin, who was an intimate of liberal politicians and an apparent dabbler in revolutionary conspiracies.[30] When the ultra government came to power in January 1822, Santarosa sought refuge in the home of one of Cousin's friends in Auteuil. In March, at the height of international fears about an eastern war and revolutionary conspiracies, the French government arrested him and two other Italian exiles under the law making it illegal to travel in France with fraudulent passports.[31] Authorities rounded up other exiles the next day and searched Cousin's house. Hoping to find connections between these men and the conspiracies in France, they focused their interrogation of Santarosa on his ties to Lafayette, Fabvier, and others.[32]

Unable to convict the exiles of crimes, the government would normally have deported them on the charge of irregular passports, but the government in Piedmont asked that they be kept in France, away from General Pepe in London. Santarosa and his two friends were committed to "surveillance" in the town of Alençon, despite the authorities' concerns about the town's proximity to Le Mans and to Charles Goyet.[33] Though some liberals feared that public association with the exiles might do them more harm than good, in early August Lafayette advocated discussing their plight in the Chamber to pressure the government to release them. Colonel Fabvier, on the other hand, proposed a more radical solution: spiriting Santarosa out of the country.[34] Lafayette was relieved to hear from Cousin that the effort made in the Chamber had been appreciated, although they had still been apprehensive that someone might express "sentiments sufficiently *proven*," that is, something that would tie the exiles to the French conspiracies. Lafayette's "*proven*" referred to the use of that word in the indictment issued in the Berton case. The speakers had tried to enumerate "the most striking facts. . . . Publicity is all we can produce."[35]

Liberal deputies accused the government of abusing its authority to issue passports in order to deny freedom of movement to liberals. Despite having been cleared by the French courts, the Piedmontese refugees still found themselves deprived of their right to move freely.[36] Santarosa, annoyed by the government's suggestion that the exiles acquiesced in these restrictions out of gratitude for France's hospitality, published a letter of protest in the *Contitutionnel* of 18 August. After this daring gesture, he expected arrest and at last agreed to Fabvier's proposal to flee the country. Fabvier's trip to England in August, then, might also have included projects to free the Italian refugees. When the police learned of his plans, they sent Santarosa further inland and south, to Bourges. The government eventually decided that it would be best to send the troublesome refugee out of the country. In October 1822, he left for England.[37]

By the fall of 1822, the French government could breathe easier about conspiracy. No Carbonarist prisoners had been rescued. With the execution of General Caron on 1 October, the Carbonarist trials had resulted in eleven deaths and the imprisonment and flight of many more. The movement could not long survive such disasters. In fact, the Carbonarist organization as an active conspiratorial movement had probably ceased to exist.[38] During the summer of 1822, several attempts were made to preserve the network. Lafayette's associates Arnold Scheffer and Schonen, for example, traveled extensively around the country meeting with Carbonarist groups. According to the police, Scheffer was at a meeting in Lyon in June and again in the middle of July. In early August he was in Nancy, but the authorities were expecting him to go on to Bordeaux for a large Carbonarist meeting on 17 September.[39] A Carbonarist congress was held in Paris during the summer as well. Lafayette communicated with the delegates, but these efforts to maintain the enthusiasm of the conspirators in the face of division and rancor brought on by persistent defeat did not succeed.[40] Many young men now left France to fight in Spain.

Lafayette's participation in the Carbonarist plots has been criticized on several grounds. An early and persistent complaint has been that the Carbonarist leaders escaped arrest while the young men they lured into the conspiracies paid with their lives. As early as the Saumur trial, when the deputies had called the prosecutor a coward for mentioning their names without giving them the opportunity to clear themselves, he had responded, "The cowards and traitors are those who hurl into the abyss simple and gullible men, and who then disown them! The cowards and traitors are those who sleep, while the unfortunate monarch that they should protect struggles under the sword of the assassins! those who corrupt the youth of the schools, by their destestable sophistry!"[41] Such an argument distorts the true nature of the Carbonarist coalition. It was not simply a matter of leaders corrupting youth but a more complicated relationship in which rebellious young people were seeking generals to assume leadership posts and prominent people to further their cause. Lafayette's was the most famous name they could attract.[42]

The leaders escaped arrest because the government never managed to secure the evidence to convict them. With a few exceptions, those with inside knowledge of the Carbonarist movement loyally held their tongues when arrested or interrogated. And those who did talk had limited knowledge of the leadership. By preserving strict legal procedures in its prosecution of the accused, the government allowed some of the guilty to escape but ultimately proved even to skeptics that those condemned were genuine conspirators.

The charge of cowardice seems especially unwarranted in the case of Lafayette, whose fellow conspirators sometimes accused him of taking unnecessary risks, of being too willing to undertake schemes that were not well thought out, and of trusting too readily all those who sought his help. The charge might be more appropriately leveled at Voyer d'Argenson and Manuel, whose hesitations and fears, according to some of the youthful conspirators, meant the Belfort plot was unmasked before it could be carried out.[43] Neither was Lafayette cowardly about proclaiming his political faith. He made little attempt to hide his involvement and challenged the authorities from the podium of the Chamber of Deputies to institute proceedings against him.

Compelling political considerations no doubt made the government hesitate to bring formal charges against famous deputies like Lafayette or Benjamin Constant or Manuel. A well-publicized trial concluding with their vindication would have been more damaging than having them at large, especially since the failure of the conspiracies made their effectiveness as revolutionary leaders seem less serious as time went on. The battle between the government and its enemies was being fought on several fronts. Not only were the Carbonarists being defeated and sentenced to jail or condemned to death but the liberals were losing at the polls. The power of the liberals to sway the population ultimately derived from their positions as deputies. The podium of the Chamber of Deputies gave them an essential vantage point from which to spread their ideas without the restrictions placed on speech by the laws of the Restoration.

As the rather conservative electorate began to understand the reality of the subversion, to see that the disruptions were the work of genuine revolutionaries, not merely agents provocateurs, it rejected liberal candidates. All liberals were tainted by association, whether they had conspired or not. These losses, in turn, made potential revolutionaries more fearful because they could no longer count on the protection of powerful people. Defeating the left at the polls also helped to defeat the Carbonari, making it less essential to bring the leaders to trial. By early 1823, the left was in retreat on all fronts, and even fears about the loyalty of the army were put to rest.

Lafayette's decision to conspire was based on faulty judgment. His optimism about public opinion led him to believe that liberal success at the polls would translate easily into a successful overthrow of the government. It led him to believe that those who voted in favor of candidates who supported his brand of constitutional government would be willing, as he was, to take risks for it, that if the tricolor flag were displayed, the vast majority of the country would flock to it. He seemed to believe that most Frenchmen shared his outrage at the policies of the new ultra government and would not stand for their continuation. This failure to understand the true complexion of public opinion meant defeat, not only for the Carbonari but also for liberal politicians. He may have been right that most of the population favored constitutional government, but they surely wanted to maintain it through legal and nonviolent means. The Carbonari, perhaps overly influenced by the recollection of Napoleon's return in the Hundred Days and by the recent example of Spain, hoped that if they could win over a part of the army, the rest would follow and their opponents would give up. They never seemed to believe that much fighting would be required.[44] Yet they were opposing a government that had considerable means of fighting back. Armand Carrel, a youthful participant in the conspiracies, reflected on them from the perspective of 1830 and summed up their collective delusion.

Why did we have the mad idea that a government supported by laws and by the weight of inertia of 30 million men could be overturned by the plots of law students and second lieutenants? . . . If you are honest, you have to admit that it was not the clashes at Belfort, Colmar, and Saumur, which bore fruit for our cause and prepared the wonders of last July; that those wonders, on the contrary, are due to an entirely opposite order of ideas; that we had to wait until there were no more conspiracies in the country before the government ceased being supported by the interests of and the need for order of the immense majority of the nation.[45]

Lafayette's actions within France were influenced as well by his perceptions of an international struggle between liberalism and reaction. He was willing to make even foolhardy efforts because he believed the fate of liberty in other countries depended on progress within France. French Carbonarism was to him only one part of a much larger struggle in which revolutionaries fought conservative European powers. The ultra government in France, he assumed, would support the powers of the Holy Alliance to block freedom. It was vital to establish a "liberal alliance" to counter the Holy Alliance. Therefore, he encouraged Spain and the new Spanish-American republics, and he urged the United States to send aid to the Greeks. He overlooked the fact that, though ideologically Americans might sympathize, their national interest dictated not becoming involved. Lafayette seemed to expect nations to make foreign-policy decisions based on ideology, and he recognized only two sides: those who favored liberty and those who opposed it.

When the European powers faced the issue of Spain, they fell into disagreement, contrary to Lafayette's expectations. Alexander I championed allied intervention. But when the revolution in Spain was discussed at the Congress of Verona in 1822, the powers agreed only to send a joint communiqué expressing their concern. England refused to be a party to that proposal, and France insisted on acting independently of the others.[46] The Congress of Verona had immediate repercussions for French politics because it coincided with the fall elections.

The chances of the left, already undermined by the failures of the conspiracies, were further diminished by foreign-policy issues. Though the government feared that rumors of armed intervention in Spain would hurt the ministerial candidates, talk of war seemed instead to make the voters hesitate to entrust their future to those trying to subvert the French army.[47] In the fall of 1822, the left also faced a concerted government campaign, which made genuinely free elections impossible. Etienne Pasquier recalled that the elections were in the hands of a minister of the interior who believed that "anything was lawful to assure the triumph of his party, of what he called 'the good cause.'"[48] The stakes were particularly high because those standing for reelection had won their seats in the large liberal victory of 1818 and included some of the left's most visible deputies, among them Lafayette, Constant, and Manuel. Lafayette doubted whether he could be reelected in the Sarthe, despite Goyet's assurances to the contrary.[49]

Constant was so depressed at liberal prospects that he allowed himself to be inveigled into a duel. It stemmed from Constant's account of a demonstration held on the anniversary of the death of the student Lallemand. A royalist journalist named Forbin criticized his article, and their mutual recriminations led to an unusual duel fought sitting down because Constant's lameness prevented the traditional pacing. They each fired twice but missed. Goyet and others in the Sarthe scolded Constant for having taken such a chance. Goyet warned him that if he fought another duel the voters would reject him utterly.[50] Constant confessed that he was motivated by despair at the political prospects.

> I'm over 50 years old, I have devoted my life to liberty,
> I have neglected my fortune, worn down my health,
> abandoned my literary pursuits, and given up the rep-
> utation which they might have earned for me, all in or-
> der to see men who I believed shared the same cause
> going to sleep or becoming discouraged, and the world
> fallen prey perhaps for a long time to the vilest scoun-

223

> *drels who ever inhabited antechambers and wore gilt*
> *suits.*

The future appeared to hold in store only the scaffold or exile. He would do his duty to the end, "but an event which would rid me of it sooner would be welcome."[51]

Lafayette, too, seemed to some to be courting martyrdom. Laffitte suggested as much to Royer-Collard in a conversation held at the beginning of August 1822, when the Chamber was heatedly debating the accusations lodged against the deputies by the prosecutor in the Berton trial. Royer-Collard wanted to come to their defense, but he asked Laffitte whether he was certain that Lafayette was not conspiring. Laffitte responded that he most probably was and that he wanted to be accused of it. Royer-Collard asked, "Is he crazy?" On the contrary, Laffitte replied, he is "the wisest, the most reasonable, the sharpest man you would ever meet." His actions sprang from his convictions, Laffitte explained. "Insurrection according to him is the most sacred of duties." But what does he want? Royer-Collard insisted. "I'm not sure. Lafayette is a monument wandering around in search of its pedestal. If on the way he should find the scaffold or the chair of president of the Republic, he would not give two cents for the choice between them." When he described the conversation to Lafayette, Laffitte recalled, the general laughed loudly and agreed that it was true.[52]

The news of arrests and trials for conspiracy considerably hindered political organizing. Goyet warned that people would hesitate to serve on a local electoral committee for fear of being hauled into court or having their papers searched, yet such committees were essential.[53] Since liberals could not hope for a majority in the Chamber, Goyet proposed aiming for quality instead of quantity, by making sure the incumbent deputies, the ones the government most wished to defeat, were reelected. He suggested that each be a candidate in more than one district or department simultaneously.[54] Constant, Manuel, and Lafayette all did so.

The government, Goyet predicted, would try a new tactic: arresting a candidate and then spreading the word that an indicted man was not eligible. Indeed, Benjamin Constant landed in court immediately before the November elections. The train of events leading to his arrest began with the sub-prefect of Saumur, who testified in the Berton trial that Constant had traveled there with a woman who was not his wife. Constant was traveling with Mme Constant, but their marital status was ambiguous in some people's eyes. Mme Constant had been married twice before. She divorced her first husband, and her second husband, having become a devout Catholic, came to consider their marriage null. She married Constant after her first husband's death and after her second husband testified that their marriage no longer existed, though they had never gone through divorce proceedings.[55] Constant angrily defended himself by charging that the sub-prefect had lied in his testimony and that the prosecutor had libeled him by accusing him of conspiring. The authorities then brought Constant to court for insulting public officials.

The fiasco probably cost Constant the election. He first appeared in court on 30 October, and though that trial was postponed, another began on 6 November. Elections took place on 13 November. On 19 November he was found guilty and sentenced to one month in prison along with a five-hundred-franc fine and court costs.[56] Other tactics employed against the liberals included the usual attempts to remove their supporters' names from the lists of voters and to intimidate their associates. For example, two liberal notaries in the Sarthe had their papers searched. No printer in Le Mans proved willing to brave the harassment that was a certain consequence of publishing Goyet's pamphlets. A more damaging tactic was used against Lafayette: voiding his eligibility to run for office by removing him from the list of voters paying one thousand francs. Fighting to get back on the list took up a great deal of Lafayette's time. His son George came to his aid and had to "face all the little tricks of five or six administration employees who would like to prove that my father lives on air, and that he possesses nothing in the world not even any revenue."[57] Whatever the outcome of George's struggle, the electors, of course, might hesitate to vote for a man whose eligibility had been questioned.

Since he had qualified to be a voter and a deputy in 1818, in 1822 Lafayette presented only certificates from mayors showing that his status had not changed. Expecting harassment, he was not surprised when the sub-prefect requested specific documentation that he had paid enough taxes to qualify for the list of arrondissement voters. After providing that proof, he was asked to do it again because the certificates of the mayors and tax collectors were not on the same piece of paper. When he had acceded to that request, he was next asked for property titles, which, Lafayette insisted, were not required by law and which, furthermore, it would be impractical to demand of all voters.[58] He then learned that his name had been removed from the list of taxpayers of Bernay and Courpalay because of questions concerning his inheritance of La Grange. Adrienne de Lafayette had left her husband as much of her property as the law allowed, that is, half the inheritance during his lifetime.[59] A technicality required his children to sign official notices surrendering for his use half the property left by their mother, and, though Adrienne had died in 1807, they had not done so until this current challenge. The prefect therefore maintained that Lafayette had become *legal* owner only eight days previously. Not having been in possession of the property for an entire year as the election law specified, he could not count the taxes toward his eligibility. Lafayette had been using the property, no one heretofore had questioned his right to it, and he had appeared as the owner on tax rolls, but the prefect argued that these things were irrelevant. The prefect discussed the issue with a delegate from the central government on 20 October 1822, and then all the documents were sent to the minister of the interior.[60] The prefect asked the minister of the interior for a quick decision because the final lists had to be posted by 31 October.[61]

The government must have concluded that the legal grounds were flimsy because Lafayette was reinstated on the lists. Suspecting rightly that the decision had been made in Paris and not in the prefectural council, the appropriate body according to the law, Lafayette asked the prefect for copies of the extracts of the deliberations of the council. He was told that official notice was given only in the case of denial.[62]

Before the outcome was known, Lafayette had argued that the issue of the La Grange inheritance was specious: his other lands in Seine-et-Marne and in Brittany, along with his personal property, were themselves sufficient for eligibility.[63] However, the authorities had made no distinction in their reports between property acquired by Lafayette in his own right and property derived from the inheritance. Therefore, to be able to count any of it toward eligibility, Lafayette had to prove his right to count all of it.[64]

A comparison of his taxes in 1818 and in 1822 is difficult because of the way the authorities changed the reporting. Since no question of eligibility was raised in 1818, Lafayette had not bothered to report taxes paid in Brittany. After passage of the Law of the Double Vote in 1820, giving the vote in the departmental college to the top one-quarter of the taxpayers, Lafayette and other electors felt obliged to show more than a minimum level of eligibility. In 1818, Lafayette reported total taxes of 2,299f 06c. In 1822, the total was 3,679f 93c.[65]

Lafayette wrote to Goyet in the middle of October to reassure him about his eligibility.[66] Lafayette had not written to him in months. He seemed more interested in being elected from Seine-et-Marne, where his chances were better, than in Goyet's Sarthe. Goyet ran Constant in two arrondissement colleges in the Sarthe: Mamers (noted as a liberal stronghold) and La Flèche. Lafayette was presented in Saint-Calais, where Goyet thought he might do well despite the conservatism of its *chef-lieu.* In fact, the gerrymandering of districts had made Saint-Calais more attractive to liberals by the addition of the canton of Montfort, which contained Goyet's hometown.

Neither Constant nor Lafayette was successful in the Sarthe. The government recognized that in the smaller arrondissement districts the voters would hesitate to elect an outsider as their only deputy. In 1818 Lafayette had won as the fourth candidate after three local men had already been chosen. Now the government's publicity stressed their candidates' family and economic ties to the area.[67] The authorities spent lavishly in contesting this election because "it was a top priority to oppose and to paralyze the influence and the schemes of certain individuals already too well known from their successes in 1818 and 1819."[68]

Despite defeating all of Goyet's candidates in the Sarthe, the authorities were not yet rid of Lafayette, who was elected by the arrondissement college of Meaux in Seine-et-Marne. La Grange was not in that arrondissement, but this prosperous region had the reputation as the most liberal portion of the department. In 1820, the sub-prefect in a detailed report had described dominant political opinion there as "constitutional royalism." "Pure royalists" were few and isolated, exercising little influence on the rest of the population. Constitutional royalists formed "the great majority of the inhabitants endowed with some knowledge, . . .

almost all the salaried or nonsalaried public functionaries, the major part of the well-off proprietors, many *fermiers*, *cultivateurs*, merchants, and among the individuals devoted to industrial arts, almost all those who are able to understand the mechanism of our government."

Ultra-liberalism was also well represented. "Several public functionaries" espoused that position, "as well as almost all the attorneys and a large part of the notaries." Other partisans included "*fermiers*; all the owners of émigrés' property, a part of the owners of church property," as well as those who suffered economically by the fall of Napoleon. The ultra-liberals were especially dangerous because at Meaux as elsewhere they were "the most able and the most in accord about making their disastrous doctrines triumph."

Fermiers, who abounded in this prosperous wheat-growing region, were described as independent minded, extremely liberal, and democratic.

> *The men of that profession have in general a great element of pride; having almost all received in the collèges a beginning of education, they parade the half-knowledge they possess and esteem themselves able to discuss all questions. Having become rich, far less by their efforts than by purchasing all sorts of national lands during the Revolution, they think nothing is above them, see in society only their equals and are surprised at not being placed in the first ranks yet.*[69]

Meaux's liberalism stemmed in part from a substantial group of independent farmers whose ownership of national lands made them fearful of the extreme right.[70] Another factor, though not specifically mentioned by the sub-prefect, may have been Meaux's Protestant population. Protestants, too, had reason to fear a resurgent conservative right with strong ties to the Catholic church.[71]

Meaux was the only arrondissement in Seine-et-Marne described as divided in its opinions. Less likely to follow docilely the directions of the authorities, the inhabitants there were willing to listen to other leaders and were exposed to sources of information outside the official channels. In February 1822, the sub-prefect reported that, though there were few public expressions of political opinion, many still leaned toward the opposition, especially "in the intermediate class and among rich farmers who frequently have dealings with the capital." Calls to revolt from the Chamber of Deputies had made things even worse, he added.[72]

To defeat Lafayette at Meaux, the government ran the most liberal of the incumbent deputies, Mesnager de Germigny.[73] Nevertheless, Lafayette's chances looked good from the first meeting on 13 November, when the provisional bureau was not chosen as the permanent bureau. The next day the voters heard the president of the college urge them to choose someone devoted to the king and his dynasty. The president suggested that enemies of the king threatened to revive the horrors of the revolutionary Terror but predicted that together they could destroy these "criminal plots by surrounding the throne with our love and our respect." The references to the aborted Carbonarist plots did not succeed in defeating Lafayette. He received 169 votes to Mesnager's 136 and was the only liberal chosen from the four arrondissement colleges in Seine-et-Marne.[74]

A week later, Lafayette went to Melun for the meeting of the departmental college. On the evening before the election, both royalists and liberals met to settle on candidates for the two seats. The sixty-five liberals agreed on their first candidate, a man named Bejot fils, but were split on the second.[75] Forty-three supported Benjamin Constant, but twenty-two others opted for a resident of Seine-et-Marne named Baillot.[76] The preparatory meeting, meant to smooth over divisions, failed. Constant received only thirty-seven votes, one of those presumably from Lafayette. The winners were ultras. The prefect reported proudly that four out of five deputies of the department were precisely the men whom the minister of the interior would have chosen himself. "I hope that this consideration will console you for the fifth, who will certainly not be reelected if the proceedings which resulted in this scandal can be annulled."[77]

The prefect's suggestion confirmed what Benjamin Constant had suspected even before the election, that the government might try to annul liberals' elections on one pretext or another: Lafayette's because of the evidence in the Berton trial, Constant's because he was himself on trial, and Manuel's because he had suggested that the Bourbons were looked upon with "repugnance" when they first returned to France.[78] Constant's fears proved groundless. The victory of the royalists was so overwhelming that expulsion of the liberals probably seemed superfluous. The left managed to retain only eight of the seats up for reelection.[79] Constant himself lost. Manuel's victory in the Vendée, where he won in two arrondissements, appears to have been more a rejection of the ultras, who dominated local government and threatened violence against the opposition, than an endorsement of the liberals.[80]

The most serious loss was certainly Benjamin Constant's. Lafayette was surprised at the magnitude of his defeat. He somehow remained convinced that public opinion was improving, though this improvement would not be reflected in the Chamber. He explained the losses by citing the government's use of illegal methods "to obtain choices that I believe [are] completely at variance with public opinion."[81]

Between the elections of the fall of 1822 and the opening of the new session, Lafayette spent most of his time at La Grange. He had time to think back on his life. Camilla and Fanny Wright were staying there while Fanny began her biography of Lafayette, which she never completed. Sir Charles Morgan also inquired about publishing Lafayette's memoirs. The old general confessed that he was guilty of "a genuine error; not having taken advantage of my leisure, under the imperial regime, to collect a lot of materials." Having left unanswered many absurdities written about him, Lafayette now found them accepted as the truth and would have liked to repair those errors. But he shrank from "publishing during my lifetime memoirs in which I would be the principal subject." As usual, he stood ready to help "historians of the two revolutions of America and of Europe."[82] Now sixty-five years old, Lafayette was more concerned about his historical reputation than ever before.

When he looked toward the future rather than the past, Lafayette contemplated the coming session and the issue of Spain, which would surely dominate it. Ignoring the decision made at Verona, Louis XVIII announced at the opening of the Chambers on 28 January 1823 that the French army would soon march into Spain to preserve the throne for the grandson of Henry IV.[83] Although Lafayette interpreted the intentions of the French government as advancing the aims of the Holy Alliance, the eastern powers did not see things the same way. The French had been trying without success to persuade Ferdinand VII to accept a constitution on the model of the French Charter. Their attempt to spread French constitutional monarchy elsewhere seemed dangerously liberal to Metternich.[84]

Lafayette and his associates in France now faced a crisis in Spain and had no effective way of dealing with it. By the end of 1822, the Carbonarist organization was, for all intents and purposes, defunct and the liberal leadership badly split. Among those actively plotting, two groups took shape: one around Manuel, the other around Lafayette. Part of the difference was personal. Manuel was coldly rational and calculating, and his eloquent speeches in the Chamber were designed to exasperate the opposition without revealing much of his own sentiments. Lafayette, on the other hand, was always praised for his simplicity and directness, his openness and charm. Charles de Rémusat, who knew both men well, has left a keen image of Manuel:

> Basically, the only eminent man who took a serious role in conspiracy was M. de Lafayette. He and Manuel were certainly the two men in France who, during that time, most attracted the attention and the confidence of the men of action who wanted a revolution. However, they differed considerably and conducted themselves very differently. Manuel, at that time, was more committed than anyone to the notion of overthrowing [the government]. He was . . . a coldly passionate spirit, master of his actions and of his words, who enjoyed extreme but practical ideas, scorning the aspirations of a speculative mind, and the vague plans of an enthusiastic one. He was courageous, not incapable of dedication, but he wanted his courage to benefit himself and intended to devote himself only advisedly. . . . The democratic instincts of an energetic mind, the vulgar habits of an uncultured intelligence made him a revolutionary rather than a liberal. . . . This was a disposition likely to lean toward Bonapartism and, for a long time, he thought it politic to use Bonapartism in the interest of the revolution. . . . His means and his goal decided in this direction, his mistrustful and sus-

picious personality, his rather clever patience, [and]
his rather casually acquired reputation as Fouché's pu-
pil did not make him very congenial to Lafayette,
whose popularity among the zealots he always chal-
lenged, while always leaving him the perilous posi-
tion. . . . He knew all the plots, discouraged none and
went so far as to relinquish his name to the conspira-
tors, but never his person. He did not help them much;
he never disowned them. He told me several years lat-
er: "I don't believe very much in conspiracy in France, I
believe in insurrection." That statement rang true.[85]

Manuel was not one of Lafayette's close friends. Lafayette was personally closer to Constant and Voyer d'Argenson, even to Ternaux, than he was to Manuel. Only rather businesslike references to Manuel appear in Lafayette's correspondence. They planned meetings on political matters and cooperated to help constituents or supporters, but one does not sense a warm personal friendship.[86] Béranger, the celebrated liberal poet, was struck by the absence of praise of Manuel in Lafayette's *Mémoires*. "Except for the speech pronounced over his grave, whose inclusion was obligatory, there is only a slight appraisal of his old colleague. I thought I perceived there a little of the old grudge."[87] Béranger was himself always aloof from Lafayette, refusing to visit him at La Grange and fearing to become a part of his coterie. His distance was, he remembered, almost instinctive. Yet he nonetheless recognized "the purity of Lafayette's intentions and the immense services he rendered to liberty. . . . it is hard to find in such a long political career, crisscrossed by so many opposite events, a more steadfast integrity, a firmer attachment to the most generous and patriotic principles. He is a statue which could with profit be placed before the leaders of our era and maybe for many eras to come."[88]

One of Manuel's close friends was the Napoleonic veteran Colonel Charles Fabvier, who like the Manuel faction in general, was more sympathetic to Bonapartism than was Lafayette.[89] Fabvier and Lafayette had been friends for some time and collaborated in the Carbonarist conspiracies, but Fabvier had always harbored doubts about the organization and its aims. He followed Lafayette to Belfort in January 1822, but he did so with misgivings.[90] The substance of the debates within the secret Carbonar- ist organization is necessarily unknown, but it appears that Fabvier consistently wished to rely more on the army than did Lafayette. Manuel's willingness to ignore constitutional niceties in favor of getting results made Lafayette suspect that he lacked commitment to a properly republican form of government. Manu- el saw himself as practical and realistic, less trusting and more effective than Lafayette, Voyer d'Argenson, and their friends. Manuel's calculated prudence had spared his being named by the prosecutor in the Berton trial, even though he was certainly involved in the conspiracies.[91]

By the summer of 1822, after the failures of the conspir- acies, these divisions grew more pronounced. Before Fabvier's trip to England in August, Lafayette complained that he and his friends were not being adequately apprised of events. He told Fabvier that he was surprised that "seeing us every day, those of our colleagues who knew your ideas, did not propose that we confer together before our separation. My friend had recently seen the two indicated by you. I recently had a long talk with M. at the moment of his departure on a subject similar to that. He said not a word to me about it."[92] Fabvier's friend, presumably Manuel, was not cooperating with Lafayette.

The fear of an invasion of Spain caused greater disagree- ments. In December 1822, Fabvier left for Spain without inform- ing Lafayette of his plans. He apologized by saying that leaving in that way had been painful,

> *but when it is a question of my country and the great*
> *cause of liberty, I know how to sacrifice my affections.*
> *You have admitted into your confidence men who do*
> *not have mine. You know that my confidence cannot*
> *be coerced. Many sad examples have made us very*
> *suspicious. You know that you have been given proofs.*
> *I have proof of the immorality of your agents on several*
> *points. From that to the rest is an easy step, which I*
> *think has been crossed by several of them.*

He urged Lafayette to endorse his plan of action in Spain, assur- ing him that he was not an Orléanist. "You know that I am not for

233

anyone. What France wants, that is my law." And he reiterated his personal attachment to Lafayette.

> *I told you that my personal inclination was to stay by your side. But next to you, General, I was convinced that we would create victims without success. Here is an opportunity to put right so many misfortunes. . . . In a word, think of history, of your glorious deeds, that should be crowned by the most useful of all. Afterwards, count forever on the submission of him whom you were pleased to call your son and who was so pleased to hear you do so.*

He begged Manuel and others to dissuade Lafayette from trusting incompetents and unreliable emissaries and to depend on him to coordinate the liberal effort in Spain.[93]

The criticism and personal recriminations hurt Lafayette deeply, and he poured out his disappointment to Voyer d'Argenson in a letter whose rare candor and passion provide a contrast to his generally polite and guarded communications.

> *My dear friend, I am charged with summoning you for today at noon at Manuel's. He is inviting several deputies: you, me, Koechlin, Dupont, the Saint-Aignans, Caumartin, Beauséjour. George is excluded. He [Manuel] persists . . . with more ardor and tenacity than ever on that plan which was discussed only after those who could participate had left, and those they wanted to exclude had made other commitments. I will undergo a new cross-examination, a new reprimand, and unfortunately, I have no new success to announce to them, no personal submission to make. Two years ago all the patriots were unanimous in my favor; they have deprived me of the friends they could take away from me; I refuse to quarrel with those who have refrained from reviling me; I offer the simplest and most straightforward means of overcoming as best we can the inconveniences that we all deplore; but I must do what I said I would not do, submit to a definite direction, where my name may be useful but where my opinion*

will be every morning treated as inaneness, my actions as foolishness and my alleged agents as contemptible beings, the men they did not succeed in turning against me as beggars or spies, and my son as you see, and in the last analysis I'll almost have a falling out with colleagues whom I love and esteem and to whom I have given only signs of affection and deference. After having been treated at the age of nineteen like a man by people who were twenty and forty years older than me, I am treated at sixty-six like a child by people who have spent twenty years less than I have in private life and thirty-seven years less in public life.[94]

The unusual anger shown by Lafayette was one sign of the deep divisions among the conspirators, who differed over tactics and were separated by generations. Lafayette's preferred way of agitating for change in a more or less open attempt to win the hearts and minds of the people seemed out of date. Governments now were organized to fight revolutionary movements, and revolutionaries were beginning to develop the tactics of secret organizations. But Lafayette bridled at relying exclusively on the army or at maintaining complete secrecy. To a veteran of eighteenth-century revolution secrecy seemed hypocritical or immoral. The way to fight despotism, Lafayette had learned, was for virtuous, independent men to stand up to the tyrant. That is what the Americans had done. The French Revolution, too, had shown the power of the people to defeat their enemies. Now, despairing of the Spanish government's intentions, Lafayette hoped for a national uprising supported by foreign exiles.

Lafayette's apparent rejection of Fabvier's mission in Spain showed as well that he understood the ideological divisions existing among the Spanish themselves. By now, the more radical *comuneros* were openly distrustful of the San Miguel government. In October 1822, when a new society of *comuneros* called the *Landaburiana* held its initial meeting in Madrid, Pepe presided at the meeting.[95] In January 1823, Lafayette wrote the members of the secret society into which Pepe had inducted him to assure them of his devotion and to restate his political philosophy. They should all work together, he believed, so that all nations might recover

> *their natural and social rights, indispensable to all*
> *free government, [and] have the possibility of choosing*
> *and regulating by themselves the constitutional forms*
> *which best suit them. This exercise of true sovereignty*
> *can take place only through representation emanating*
> *from the mass of the nation; it can be effectively pro-*
> *tected only by the general arming of the citizens; this*
> *is the French doctrine of '89, these are today the virtu-*
> *ous and persevering practices of your heroic nation.*[96]

This emphasis on action by the people and on reliance on a citizen militia to protect the nation had long been a part of Lafayette's philosophy. The leaders of the *Landaburiana* society shared his views. On 15 December 1822, Moreno Guerra (who had recently returned from a trip through Europe) gave a speech to that group emphasizing the importance of resurrecting the patriotic societies, of rejecting moderation, and of using the threatened invasion of Spain to consolidate the revolution by exciting the revolutionary enthusiasms of the people.[97] Those leaders in Spain who were trusted by Lafayette and his friends emerge clearly in a work about Spain written by a Piedmontese refugee, Count Pecchio, and published in London in February 1823 by Edward Blaquière, the friend of Bentham and Bowring. Pecchio's work is in the form of letters written between May 1821 and August 1822, to which Blaquière has added notes. Blaquiere describes Moreno Guerra and Romero Alpuente as leaders of the *comuneros*, as patriotic, wise, and devoted to liberty. By contrast, when Pecchio praises Martínez de la Rosa, Blaquière notes that his early enthusiasm proved unwarranted.[98] By 1823, Lafayette and his friends sided with the most radical Spanish faction.

Fabvier's letters back to France criticized Lafayette's reliance on untrustworthy emissaries, and this criticism obviously had some validity. The most important Frenchman acting for Lafayette in Spain was apparently Commandant Caron, who went by the name "Legras." Fabvier complained about Caron's puerile vanity, his boasting about his connections, and about his participation in Carbonarist activities.[99] Caron had been attached to the French army and stationed at Marseilles. He managed to escape before the arrests of Vallé and others took place there.[100] Lafayette had sent letters of introduction for him to Riego in early 1822.[101]

But beyond the issue of who was to be trusted or who was more competent loomed the issue of how best to promote the Spanish cause. Lafayette differed with Fabvier, not only over tactics but also over ideology. He would never take sides with those in Spain who opposed Spanish-American independence. And Fabvier would soon discover that the San Miguel ministry could not be trusted to keep its word and to provide him assistance.

Fabvier's plan called for inducing the French soldiers to revolt while they still stood on French soil, and he assured the Spanish government that many of the officers were on their side. Like the Spanish troops that had been gathered for the reconquest of Spanish America in 1820, they would be susceptible to calls from their generals to revolt, Fabvier believed. Once he and his associates had control of the army, they could march back across France, thus saving both France and Spain from the forces of reaction. But the success of this plan depended on the coup taking place on French soil. The soldiers would not desert the French army once hostilities had broken out on foreign soil.[102]

The liberals in the Chamber, meanwhile, fought a losing battle to prevent French intervention in Spain. Although Lafayette did not take part in the debate, he played a prominent role in the most dramatic incident of the session: the expulsion of Manuel. On 26 February 1823, Manuel argued that intervention would not help Ferdinand VII. He cited the case of the Stuart kings of England, whose cause was hurt by French support, then said, "Do I need to add that the dangers of the French royal family became far more grave when foreigners invaded our land, and that France, revolutionary France, feeling the need to defend herself by new forces and new energy . . ." The rest of his sentence was drowned out by a storm of protests from deputies who accused him of justifying regicide. Prevented from resuming his speech, Manuel wrote to the president of the Chamber during the adjournment that followed that his sentence would have continued: ". . . set in motion the masses, stimulated popular passions, and brought on thus terrible excesses and a deplorable catastrophe in the midst of a noble resistance."[103] The Chamber refused to listen to his explanations and on 3 March voted his expulsion.

The next day, Lafayette and the other deputies of the left accompanied Manuel as he marched into the Chamber. When he refused to leave, a detachment of the National Guard was sent in to remove him. At that point Lafayette confronted them with the cry, "What! Would the National Guard lend itself to such a service!" After this reproach from the old revolutionary commander of the National Guard, the leader of the detachment, a Sergeant Mercier, ordered the men to withdraw, and regular police were given the task of escorting Manuel out of the Chamber.[104] Manuel was followed by the deputies of the left, who did not return for the rest of the session.

Mme de Broglie witnessed the dramatic scene from the public benches of the Chamber and recalled that Lafayette had risen "and, with a paternal air, motioned to him to withdraw. He found himself again, all of a sudden, back thirty years ago."[105] Lafayette, too, made the connection to the Revolution: "I admit that the conduct of the National Guardsmen in the critical moment of 4 March took me back to the sensations of 89."[106] Manuel and the young National Guard sergeant became the heroes of the hour.[107] When a National Guard colonel disavowed the actions of Mercier, Lafayette responded with a public letter reminding him that the

> National Guard was instituted by the conquest of and
> for the maintenance of liberty, legality, and legal order.
> . . . Born enemy of despotism, aristocracy and anar-
> chy, it has defended the authorities established by the
> nation; it has protected persons, property, opinions. . . .
> It would have had the good fortune of saving King
> Louis XVI, if the faction of privileges on the inside and
> on the outside had permitted him to be saved once
> again by the patriots.[108]

Lafayette saw the expulsion of Manuel as part of an ultra conspiracy to destroy the legislature.[109] After all, rumors had circulated at the time of the elections that liberals would be excluded. He and sixty-one other deputies of the left signed a protest, and most of them boycotted the rest of the session. Lafayette wrote a public letter to his constituents at Meaux explaining his own withdrawal. He told them that he had planned to speak out against "an ungodly, senseless war, condemned by all the feelings, all the wishes of the French people, and where our soldiers, now the auxiliaries of the inquisitors and monks of the army of the faith, find themselves fated to fight against their own cause." The interruption of Manuel's speech had been premeditated. Lafayette dismissed out of hand the Chamber's attempt to justify the exclusion by reference to the practices of the United States Congress. In the United States, he reminded them, there were frequent elections on every level, and the people lived free and secure, "without thrones, courts, nobility, superfluous or unpopular taxes, police, *gendarmes*, and disorder." In France, on the other hand, "there are no longer either municipal and administrative elections, or any of the other popular elections, or freedom of the press, or properly constituted juries, or representation emerging from the bosom of the nation; those guarantees of 89 and 91 whose reestablishment would have been easy and swift no longer exist." The deputies' alternatives were to leave their posts or to stay on, but staying would mislead the voters into thinking that a legal Chamber existed. They decided to denounce "a system which is inducing France to embark upon an unjust foreign war in order to consummate the domestic counterrevolution and open our territory to invasion."[110]

Because the letters of protest from the liberal deputies were not delivered at the podium of the Chamber, they did not enjoy exemption from the censorship laws. The one signed by George Washington Lafayette and his fellow deputies of the Haut-Rhin was lithographed and distributed surreptitiously.[111] In July, Koechlin's secretary was sentenced to three months in prison and fined three hundred francs for having distributed the letter. When the deputies protested that they were the authors and ought to be tried instead of him, the authorities agreed, but the trials were delayed until after the elections of early 1824.[112]

While these political struggles were going on, the French army was gathering at the Pyrenees. A veteran general had been sent to rouse the officers, and progress was being made.[113] But they needed money. Later, Lafayette told an American friend that if Jacques Laffitte had been willing to supply the money they could have succeeded. Two regiments of guards began to "show symptoms of revolt" on their way to Spain. When he approached Laffitte for money, the banker hesitated to become involved. Finally, Lafayette proposed that, the next time they met in private, Laffitte should put a million francs on the mantle. Lafayette would take it without Laffitte's seeing him do so and, thus, keep him out of it altogether. But Laffitte refused.[114]

The French liberals apparently did finance the purchase of supplies in England that were then sent by ship to Spain, along with volunteers to fight.[115] Joseph Rey was helping to coordinate the efforts of the French refugees in England, and Sir Robert Wilson left for Spain in early April. In the end the efforts failed. Fabvier gathered a force of around one hundred fifty French and Italian refugees across the Bidassoa River from the French army. They waved the tricolor flag, sang the Marseillaise, and urged the French soldiers to turn around. As the famous Béranger song put it: "Brave soldiers, here's the order of the day: Attention! About Face!"[116] But when the commanding officer ordered the French troops to fire on Fabvier's men, they did so without hesitation, killing some dozen or so Frenchmen, who, according to Fabvier, stood with arms on their shoulders refusing to fire upon their countrymen.

Discontent did not permeate the French army in 1823 as it had the rebellious Spanish army in 1820. The Saint-Cyr army law, written in 1818 by a moderate ministry, was still in force. The army was well paid, and former Napoleonic officers were being reintegrated into it. Many of the officers and men doubtless disapproved of invading Spain and restoring its king to power, but they were not opposed to a campaign that would give them opportunities for advancement. After the Carbonarist failures of the preceding year, they would be unlikely to put stock in hopes for successful revolt. Many soldiers sympathized with the liberal cause (just as did many civilians), but not many were willing to risk their lives and their careers for an ephemeral dream.[117] Lafayette had to watch unhappily as the French army successfully defeated the Spanish constitutionalists and regained absolute power for the Spanish king.

The foreign liberals fighting in Spain now turned to the last European struggle, Greece. Some, including Fabvier and Santarosa, would go there to fight. Lafayette had been interested in Greece all along, though Spain and Italy had necessarily occupied more of his attention. He had met with several Greek agents. In August 1821, he had introduced two of them, Piccolo and Polychroniades, to Gallatin, who warmly endorsed their cause as "that of the civilized world against barbarism, of Christianity against the intolerance of fanaticism, of liberty against tyranny, and of national independence against foreign usurpation."[118]

Lafayette's letters to American friends had pleaded the cause of the Greeks. "This classic nation and interesting cause are now an object of unfeeling and selfish speculation for the cabinets of Europe on whatever side they may find it their profit to act. To the United States alone they may look for honest and efficient support."[119] He urged President Monroe to send American ships to the Mediterranean to protect the Greek revolution: "A few friendly ships, a trifling loan of money would render them immense service."[120] After consulting Gallatin, Lafayette advised the Greek agents that a loan from the United States government was out of the question, but he encouraged them to try to procure a private loan in the United States and offered to provide letters of introduction.[121] He valued disinterested help from the United States. England, he believed, was against Greece because of "the advantage they have over England in the cost of their navigation; an ungenerous policy, and even unenlightened, which that government has too often been accused of and justly."[122]

Lafayette's prejudice against Great Britain remained as strong in the 1820s as it had been in the 1780s. He faulted Britain for small-minded greed and for denying support to liberals elsewhere. The English refused to take a position in the international war between rights and privileges. On the issue of Spain, he told Lady Morgan, "England will remain neutral, they say, and indeed [the English] are attached to both privileges and rights. Which complicates the question, as respects sentiment; but your ministers will decide it according to commercial and political interest."[123] He disapproved of deciding policy by calculations of commercial advantage rather than by commitment to ideology, though he occasionally used economic arguments to persuade others. And he idealistically believed that the United States would be immune from such crass considerations. Lafayette himself seems to have been so indifferent to economic motives that he willingly spent enormous sums of money to further what were surely lost causes to begin with. He helped refugees of all European revolutions.

Greece kept the hope alive, but Lafayette's promotion of the Greek cause in America shows how much he now looked to the United States as the savior of liberalism. Revolutionary efforts had failed in France and in Europe, and the next elections would make that failure even clearer. He consoled himself by writing to his American friends. One of these friends, apparently well informed about Lafayette's affairs, warned him that his "exalted virtues and patriotism" might lead to his enemies' vengeance and urged Lafayette to seek asylum in the United States before it was too late.

> *Do not let your love of country force you to cling to her until everything noble great & useful shall be buried in the ruins of fanaticism and crime. If you tarry too long in devoted France you will not have it in your power to appear again as her champion when honest men and honest measures shall prevail. Here you will be received with open arms as the friend of Washington, the early defender of our rights and liberties and the proud chief & head of the liberal party of all countries.*[124]

He might have failed in Europe, but in America Lafayette was loved. In the spring of 1823, a new fort was completed in New York and named for him. An expatriate Frenchman, General Simon Bernard, announced the news to Lafayette and told him how solicitous all Americans had been for him. "Words fail me to paint their generous thoughts about you, the wishes they raise to heaven for your happiness, the admiration which they profess for your private virtues and your political courage." Bernard was moved to tears at the thought of the contrast between Lafayette's reputation in the United States and his situation in France.[125] Lafayette must have been equally moved and gratified. He looked longingly toward America, but duty kept him in France, as long as there was any hope of making a difference.

9

An Asylum of Liberty

Lafayette spent the summer of 1823 with his family at La Grange as usual. The customary throngs of visitors appeared, among them Fanny and Camilla Wright and his old friend the comte de Ségur.[1] In September, the Trollopes, who came from England to visit the Garnetts, met Lafayette for the first time, and they, too, were invited to La Grange. Indeed, Lafayette played an important role in their trip to France.

Mrs. Trollope's journal records their arrival in Paris on 3 September. Fanny and Camilla came to Paris to greet them, followed soon by Lafayette. At a dinner party at Fanny Wright's, Lafayette entertained the company with stories of Louis XVI's entry into Paris in 1789 and of his own imprisonment in Austria. Another Englishman, Major Frye, joined the group on 6 September. At a party on 9 September, Lafayette, who had brought along five young Greeks, was the only Frenchman. The Trollopes dined with Lafayette again on the twelfth, when they were joined by several Americans, including Charles Wilkes of New York, a close friend of Frances Wright's. The next morning, Lafayette escorted the Trollopes to La Grange, keeping up a pleasant conversation along the route. "We talked much of Pepe—of Fanny Wright—of the revolution of the various scenes in which he had himself been a principal actor—nothing can exceed the graceful unaffected simplicity with which he speaks on these occasions—ready to give you all the information you wish, but without the slightest appearance of wishing to speak of himself."

Upon arrival, they sat down to dinner with the inhabitants of La Grange, twenty-one in all, waited upon by six servants. "The dinner was excellent, and served in a very agreeable style though not à l'anglaise—the second course consisted of vegetables and meat dishes all served in silver. Then followed an excellent dessert and some very fine wine . . .—then followed coffee. The whole occupied about two hours and a half—We then all adjourned to the Lawn." They spent the evening in the salons on the second floor, conversing in both English and French.[2]

After dinner on the next day, Sunday evening, they went to a "*fête de village.* . . . It was delightful to watch the good man, looking like the father of the hamlet dispensing his smiles around. All the young people from the chateau joined in the dance." The next evening M. de Ségur read a recent play about Clytemnestra. The rest of their days at La Grange were similarly arranged. They walked in the gardens, conversed with Lafayette about his adventures, heard Ségur's tales of his days as ambassador to Russia, read another play, listened to music, and danced. More visitors arrived, including his Carbonarist colleague, Augustin de Schonen.[3]

This detailed picture of life at La Grange would have delighted the police, whose efforts to uncover Lafayette's actions proved frustrating. Spies in Seine-et-Marne complained to the prefect of police that it was difficult for them to learn anything because there were no royalists in the neighborhood, "even among the priests."[4] They were able to report that a party of English or American people (including Washington's nephew) had been at La Grange hunting in August and that Ségur and his family were the only visitors still remaining at the beginning of September, but they could not discover who came and went during the following month. The prefect of police was especially eager to ascertain the identity of an English major who had allegedly arrived from Cadiz with news of Spain, but despite their investigation, the authorities never uncovered the identity of this person.[5]

The police reported that Frances Wright had arrived at La Grange on 19 September, while, in fact, she was still in Paris. The explanation for this error can be found in Mrs. Trollope's diary. Fanny had written that she would be arriving then and a carriage was sent to pick her up, but she did not come. The police, having no doubt read the mail and seen the carriage, assumed she had arrived.[6] Mrs. Trollope's detailed diary shows how undependable and fragmentary police reports often were.[7]

The government ordered surveillance of La Grange because they were still worried that Carbonarist sympathizers were plotting action in Spain or in France. In fact, though Lafayette followed the events in the Peninsula closely, he and his friends could do little to influence them. Lafayette now began to devote more time to matters other than conspiracy. He tried to reconstitute his library by calling in books and papers that had been borrowed.[8] He wrote to a bookseller about updating the scientific works in his collection and completing his run of the *Moniteur* by acquiring the index volumes. He contemplated selling some books to raise the funds to buy the latest publications, for example, Sir Walter Scott's new novel, *Quentin Durward*. He considered subscribing to the *Encyclopédie moderne* and buying the Michaud biographical encyclopedia, though he thought it was too long and too imbued with "party spirit."[9]

Lafayette felt compelled to sell some of his books because his support for revolution and his aid to revolutionaries in exile had left him short of funds. In August he borrowed fifty-two hundred francs at 5 percent interest from one of his political supporters in Meaux, Charles Petit. About two weeks later, he borrowed another large sum from him: forty-eight hundred francs.[10] He had often discussed the confused state of his Louisiana lands with his American acquaintances, but now he told James Monroe that a settlement of the case was essential, "some additional private expenses, not unconnected with the difficulties of the time, having made it desirable for me to obtain in Europe a loan upon that mortgage."[11]

Former revolutionaries continued to make their way to asylum in England, and Lafayette supplied them with letters of introduction. Frédéric Degeorge, a former Carbonarist, headed for England, as did Charles Comte, forced to leave Switzerland because the French government pressured the Swiss authorities to deport him.[12] Meanwhile, he also did his best to help defeated Spaniards. When General San Miguel was captured and brought to France, Lafayette considered enlisting the aid of the duc d'Orléans. Though Lafayette ostentatiously distanced himself from Orléans and never visited him during the Restoration, he and Orléans had friends in common who could pass on the request. Ary Scheffer taught drawing to the duke's children, and Laffitte was on friendly terms with him. Lafayette also knew the duke's secretary.[13] As for General Riego, Lafayette could only watch helplessly from afar as he was defeated and then executed. Riego sent his wife a lock of hair and the tie he was wearing on the day he was executed. She divided these relics in half and sent one portion to Lafayette, who kept them piously at La Grange.[14]

The result in Spain showed the triumph of ignorance over enlightenment, according to Lafayette.

> *Now every thing on Spanish ground is in dreadfull confusion. Every man that can read and write is Constitutional; the remainder who form a great majority are slaves to monkish superstition, many of them living on plunder; the few taxes that can be had have been restored to the church; both armies are disbanded; a wild beast, the king, is let loose, and no authority, not even his own, is obey'd except in the way of mischief.*[15]

And, as usual, he blamed the British as much as the other powers. He warned his American correspondents not to believe "that in this business of the Peninsula Great Britain has acted a more honest part than any other of the antiliberal cabinets."[16]

Articles in the American press urging Lafayette to seek refuge in the United States had sparked rumors in France that he would soon be going to the New World. But his sense of duty compelled him to remain in Europe. To his old friend, President Monroe, who had urged him to come, Lafayette repeated how much he would enjoy revisiting the United States. But, he added,

> *you must be sensible of certain public duties which, while they are common to all who on this side of the Atlantic have engaged in the cause of European freedom are particularly binding for one of its earlier promoters, the more so as in some cases a voluntary absence from the political field of action, as long as such an action may be supposed to exist might be interpreted for discouragement and . . . submission to aristocratical and arbitrary power, an induction which everyone ought as much as possible to avoid. Yet I more and more look forward to the day when, with a safe conscience, it shall be my happy lot to find myself on American ground.*[17]

246

He put his decision more colorfully to another friend. "But as long as duty or even honour point out the field of action, can an old herald of the charge now sound the retreat?"[18]

The duties to which Lafayette referred certainly included promoting the election of liberals to the Chamber. By the middle of November, he had learned that the government intended to dissolve the Chamber and call for general elections.[19] Standing for reelection at Meaux required Lafayette to spend more time in Seine-et-Marne.[20] At the end of December, he was at La Grange recuperating from an attack of gout and worrying about the tactics the government would use in the coming elections.[21]

As in the last elections, the government used the courts to discredit liberal deputies. They still threatened to bring George and his fellow deputies of the Haut-Rhin to court for their protest of Manuel's expulsion. And Lafayette himself was soon forced to appear in court as a witness in a case involving former conspirators. François Chauvet, one of the participants in the Saumur plot, had escaped to England with letters of introduction from Lafayette.[22] Chauvet found work as a teacher and fought in Fabvier's army in Spain. His wife, who had joined him in England, served as a courier between France and England before the French invasion of Spain. In March 1823, she passed through Calais accompanied by a four-year-old girl and by a woman said to be Fabvier's mistress. The police arrested her and found that among the many letters she was carrying was one addressed to Lafayette. Purportedly written by a language teacher on friendly terms with the general, the letter was apparently signed "Philipps."[23] The correspondent was, in fact, Lafayette's old friend Joseph Rey, who was using his middle name "Philippe."[24]

The trial of Mme Chauvet was delayed while the police tried to induce her to confess. Lafayette suggested the delay was timed to affect the upcoming elections. The government, he said, wanted to wait for "the opportune moment for judicial insults and threats that they proposed to address to several patriots, notably to my son and me."[25] Accused of nonrevelation, Mme Chauvet was brought to trial on 7 February 1824, after eleven months of imprisonment.[26] Elections were scheduled to begin on 26 February.

Lafayette was the first witness called in the trial. Questioned about the letter addressed to him, he testified that, though he had known two men named Philipps, neither one was a language teacher. The judge pointed out that the correspondent seemed to be on intimate terms with Lafayette since he discussed his health and personal affairs. Lafayette responded evasively that he had been confronted with so many documents fabricated by spies that he had learned not to pay attention to them and not to say anything that might compromise other people. He refused to offer any information, and his testimony soon ended. Mme Chauvet was acquitted.[27]

Being hauled into court was only one of the many problems that the liberals faced before the elections in February. A general election forced them to run candidates in all districts simultaneously, and they had trouble finding enough men willing to run. A committee organized in Paris to coordinate the choices made on the local level lacked real authority and proved rather ineffectual. Even within the Lafayette family, differences of opinion arose. Apparently at the instigation of the electoral committee, George Washington Lafayette wrote to his political friends in the Haute-Loire to suggest that they choose his father as their deputy. His suggestion revealed the desperate position of the liberals. If not reelected in the Haut-Rhin, George himself might have turned to the Haute-Loire, where he maintained his political residence and which he had twice represented. But, obviously, his father's reelection was more important than his own, and George feared Lafayette would not be successful at Meaux. There, George charged, the government was padding the rolls with unqualified electors and with voters who were actually residents of Paris. Under the circumstances, then, he would make way, he wrote, for the "veteran of liberty."[28]

Lafayette disagreed completely with George. Many practical reasons dictated his son's candidacy, not the least of them that George's chances there were better than his own. Voters expected Lafayette to be elected at Meaux and to choose that district over one in the Haute-Loire if elected from both. He acted from sound reasons of public interest, Lafayette insisted, and not from mere paternal pride or from a desire to have his son protected by the immunity provided by a seat in the Chamber, though such protection might be needed in perilous times. But George continued to disagree.[29] Lafayette in this case demonstrated keener political sense. George did not succeed in persuading the voters of the Haute-Loire to vote for his father, nor was George reelected in the Haut-Rhin.

In Paris Lafayette attended the American dinner in celebration of Washington's birthday before heading for Seine-et-Marne to vote at the arrondissement college at Provins. He stayed at the home of Etienne-François-Marie Boby de la Chapelle. Though his host's father-in-law, Jacques-Germain Simon, was hoping to be the liberal candidate, Lafayette was pledged to throw his support to the moderate Mesnager de Germigny in fulfillment of a deal worked out with the voters of Meaux.[30] Simon won the preliminary balloting among the liberal voters, but, as Lafayette had predicted, he lost the election to the incumbent ultra deputy, who was also president of the electoral college. One of the techniques the government used to ensure that its employees voted correctly was to insist that they hand in their ballots unfolded to the president of the college. When a Provins voter objected to a ballot's being submitted that way, the bureau ruled that though the relevant ordinance stipulated that ballots should be handed in closed, nothing prevented an elector from declining to do so if he chose.[31]

While Lafayette was voting at Provins, the electors of Meaux were denying him reelection, choosing instead, by a vote of 184 to 161, the government candidate, François Pinteville-Cernon, a resident of Meaux and president of the electoral college.[32] Lafayette believed his loss resulted from government fraud.[33] Another possible explanation is that the government was successfully wooing away liberal supporters. An indication that this was occurring was the surprising appointment of Clement Petit to the provisional bureau of the electoral college (chosen by the government until the college elected a permanent bureau). Clement Petit, the *maître de la poste aux chevaux* at Meaux, had served, along with his brother Charles, as a key liberal political activist in Meaux.[34] Now he had changed sides. By judiciously using their powers to harass and to appoint men to government office, the government could win converts.

Liberals in Seine-et-Marne were discouraged in 1824. When the departmental college met at Melun, the Petit brothers were notably absent.[35] Liberals had been soundly beaten everywhere, at both the arrondissement and the departmental levels. Only thirty-four liberals were returned, which constituted only 8 percent of the new deputies.[36] They had been unable to combat the government's combination of increasingly sophisticated use of powers of censorship, manipulation, and appointment to office, plus its enhanced reputation, which stemmed from the successful military expedition to Spain. The liberals, on the other hand, were saddled with a record of inept and ruinous conspiracies and identification with European liberalism, which was in retreat on all fronts. Finally, though the decision of some liberals to boycott the end of the 1823 session could be justified on both practical and ideological grounds, some voters must have doubted the wisdom of voting for deputies who might not remain in the Chamber.

Lafayette was unhappy to see that Manuel had not been vindicated by reelection somewhere. His old constituency in the Vendée chose three liberals, but he was not among them. Nor had he won in Paris, where Lafayette hoped the voters would elect him as a mark of their approval of the liberals' stand at the time of his expulsion. Paris did elect Benjamin Constant, despite the disapproval of Laffitte, who, according to George, feared that his election would be interpreted as a "hostile choice."[37] Constant's election did not go unchallenged, however. The credentials committee of the Chamber tried to exclude him on the grounds that he was Swiss, not French. This objection was finally put aside, and Constant once again took his place as the major liberal spokesman in the Chamber.

In spite of the magnitude of the defeat, Lafayette fought on tirelessly. He immediately launched an effort to collect evidence of illegal activities on the part of the government, hoping to prove that the elections did not represent the true sentiment of the electors. Thus, he would "exonerate electoral France in the eyes of the people and of foreigners from a part of the reproaches which will be leveled against it."[38] In Meaux, he pointed to "the refusal by the prefect to give cards to over forty electors, to register them, and even to return their documents to them, and then the eliminations of the last days with the introduction of newcomers."[39] Seventy-four liberal voters had been removed from the rolls, while twenty-eight government supporters had been added to the lists at the last moment, he charged. Proving that the electoral results were tainted by fraud was important to Lafayette because he continued to believe that the cause of European liberty was dependent on the French. "English aristocracy" would not promote European liberty, and southern Europe had shown that it could not lead the way.[40] As for Germany, its "patriotism and philanthropy evaporates in romantic ideology."[41]

Of course, Lafayette thought the United States was the mainstay of liberty worldwide. So with the depressing electoral results in France added to the already-bleak picture in the rest of Europe, Lafayette turned inevitably to America. He told Jefferson, "Every account I receive from the United States is a compensation for European disappointments and disgusts."[42] His interest in visiting the scenes of his youth could now be indulged without neglecting pressing duties at home. Defeated in Europe, Lafayette would continue the struggle indirectly in the New World. By going to America, he could focus attention on a republican government that worked, on a society that prospered under a system of freedom. Its example might help to revive the cause of liberty in Europe.

Lafayette's visit to the United States was, from the beginning, more than a nostalgic personal trip. In January 1824, the Congress of the United States issued an official invitation and offered to send an American ship to transport him. This unusual gesture and the extraordinary trip which followed were part of an American debate over the proper role of the United States in the worldwide struggle between what Lafayette called *rights* and *privileges*. The United States was especially worried that the European powers, after defeating liberalism in Europe, would turn their attention to the New World, restore Spain's control over its former colonies, and then attempt to destroy republicanism in North America as well.

James Monroe and the officials in his administration had been deliberating the American response to this European threat. An old friend of Lafayette's, Monroe shared his analysis of recent history. He, too, viewed the American Revolution as the origin of liberal movements in Europe and aspired to do something to help those movements succeed. American officials were inevitably influenced by their friendship with European liberals, such as Lafayette. And Lafayette had been warning Monroe that the only disinterested power that could genuinely help the liberal movement in Greece was the United States. By the summer of 1823 Monroe considered it time for the United States to "take a bolder attitude . . . in favor of liberty" than in the past. When he asked Jefferson's advice about such a policy, Jefferson recommended

251

caution, saying that nations seeking independence should not expect help from the United States.[43] In the fall of 1823 Monroe presented to his cabinet the original draft of the presidential message that would enunciate the Monroe Doctrine. The draft included criticism of the French incursion into Spain and proposed sending an American minister to Greece.[44]

Monroe's inclination to help the Greeks was probably strengthened by advice from Albert Gallatin, who had left his post as minister to France the previous spring and visited Washington, D.C., in the fall. In his letter of resignation to Monroe, Gallatin revealed disaffection with the ultra ministry.

> *I beg leave to refer to my public letter for a view of the general affairs of Europe & will only add that I am heartily sick of them, and that, since the change of ministry here, although there has been no alteration in the usual civilities and formal treatment, it is impossible unless I conceal my opinions, that the same species of intercourse should subsist between me and them as with their predecessors. I understand too well the language and have mixed too much with the statesmen of this country to be able to preserve perfect silence and neutrality on general questions, such as those of Spain & of the Greeks.*[45]

On these questions, Gallatin and Lafayette were in perfect agreement. The Frenchman expected Gallatin to promote their views among his American colleagues. In a letter of October 1823, Lafayette remarked to him, "It has been confidentially written to me from Washington that our wishes respecting the destination of an American squadron might soon be fulfilled. I am ardently expecting the realisation of those hopes and know you must have been, and will continue to be highly serviceable in this business so often anticipated in our patriotic conversations."[46] Ten days later he repeated the sentiment. "I long to see the American flag where in our joint opinion it ought to ride, friendly and disinterested, amidst the intrigues of European politics."[47]

Despite Gallatin's promotion of the Greek cause in Washington, the final version of the president's message differed from the first draft. Secretary of State John Quincy Adams had successfully argued that the United States should not become embroiled in European affairs.[48] Instead, the Monroe Doctrine marked out two spheres of influence. America would not interfere in Europe, but in return it warned European nations not to interfere on the American side of the Atlantic. Lafayette greeted the message as "admirable. . . . It has cheered every liberal mind, and is seriously felt where it ought to strike. The effect of it on both sides of the channel is very remarkable."[49] But the Greeks had not been entirely forgotten. Daniel Webster introduced a resolution calling for funding to send an American agent to Greece. This proposal, tantamount to a recognition of the Greeks, was debated in Congress during January 1824; at the same time, the resolution inviting Lafayette was being passed.[50]

Although Monroe had changed his policy on the Greeks and therefore opposed Webster's resolution, he favored the invitation to Lafayette. He was concerned about Lafayette's safety, and his discussions with Lafayette's friend Gallatin had probably helped to persuade him. Circumstantial evidence that Monroe was behind the congressional invitation is provided by a speech given by Andrew Stevenson of Virginia. He read excerpts from Lafayette's letter to "a distinguished citizen" in which Lafayette expressed a desire to revisit the United States. The letter was, in fact, to James Monroe, though Stevenson understandably neglected to read portions in which Lafayette explained the weighty obligations that prevented his leaving France.[51]

After issuing the Monroe Doctrine warning the powers of the Holy Alliance not to move into the Western Hemisphere, the government of the United States feared it might be obliged to take up arms to enforce those threats and was therefore unwilling to do more in support of the Greeks. But many American citizens sympathized with the Greeks, and the winter of 1824 was the high point of enthusiasm for the Greek cause.[52] By inviting Lafayette, the Americans could express support for liberalism in Europe without the attendant diplomatic complications that a more direct action would create. Newspapers advocating recognition of the Greeks compared their plight to that of the United States in 1776.[53] As a veteran of struggles for liberty on foreign shores, Lafayette could be expected to promote the Greek cause in America and to show by his example the importance of standing up for republican liberty.

This last effect of Lafayette's visit might have been of interest to the American government because they feared that broad public support for military intervention in the affairs of Spanish America did not exist in the United States.[54] Though historians have disagreed about the seriousness of the threat by the European powers to reconquer Spanish America, the Americans certainly took it seriously. It was in this atmosphere of trepidation and debate over the American role that Congress's invitation to Lafayette was issued.[55] The trip was in several respects an official, rather than a purely personal, visit and was viewed that way by both Americans and Frenchmen. For example, a Bostonian forwarded to Monroe a copy of a letter to Lafayette, in which he offered Lafayette his hospitality while in the United States. He hoped his offer might "prevent the necessity of any other arrangement at that City, on the part of the Government."[56]

Lafayette looked forward to seeing the new American minister, James Brown, who would be bringing him the congressional resolutions.[57] Arriving in France in April, Brown found Lafayette eager to make the trip. His "health and spirits appear to be renovated by the marks of respect which he has received from the American people." But Brown learned that the invitation was not greeted favorably by all. "From some quarters hints have been given that these attentions spring rather from hostility to the reigning family than from a desire to confer honor on the General."[58]

At first Lafayette did not raise with the new American minister the most serious impediment to his accepting the invitation: his lack of money.[59] But soon, Lafayette was consulting daily with Brown, who was doing what he could to help him raise sufficient funds.[60] Lafayette's financial difficulties were not settled until June. He sold some of his sheep and with the help of the American consul, Isaac Cox Barnet, secured loans from two American citizens to cover his immediate obligations. Thomas Jefferson, who knew of Lafayette's reduced circumstances and knew what the trip would cost, urged Monroe not to let him go back to France empty-handed.[61] James Brown gave Monroe the same advice, noting that the United States should reimburse Lafayette for the loans he had made, especially since he had turned down the expensive American offer to send a ship to fetch him. And Brown expressed an idea that would be one of the major themes of Lafayette's trip: they should do this to prove that "Republics are not ungrateful."[62]

While Lafayette worked to solve the problems standing in the way of his American trip, the plight of former revolutionaries continued to engage his attention. For instance, he tried to help the Spanish General José María Torrijos during his confinement to the town of Alençon. In April 1824, he met with a judge from Alençon named Clogenson and promised to send money to Torrijos, who was now being permitted by the French authorities to move to London.[63] He also provided letters of introduction for Pepe, who was contemplating going to the United States.[64] And the sister of one of the Four Sergeants of La Rochelle sought Lafayette's aid. This woman was married to a man named Bidault who worked for a royalist millowner near Blois. Though the Bidaults were royalists too, the sister had stood by her brother, taking him provisions in prison. For this loyalty her husband lost his job. Lafayette wrote to a friend from the Sarthe, asking him if he could give them employment. "Their misfortune," Lafayette pointed out, "is that all their old acquaintances are more or less counterrevolutionary."[65]

In the spring of 1824, Lafayette also had to cope with a worrisome dispute over a potentially embarrassing book. To help him deal with the author, Lafayette relied on the advice of Jean-Pierre Pagès de l'Ariège, a journalist and close friend of Benjamin Constant's. Pagès had worked on several Parisian papers, most notably the *Minerve* and the *Renommée*. By 1824, though continuing to work as a journalist on the *Constitutionnel*, he now devoted himself more to the *Encyclopédie moderne*, directed by Eustache-Marie-Pierre-Marc-Antoine Courtin, which began publication in 1823. While in the United States, Lafayette tried to persuade his American friends to subscribe to Pagès's new encyclopedia.[66]

The problem for which Lafayette sought Pagès's help concerned an author named Regnault-Warin, who in February 1824 was planning to publish a life of Lafayette. Many years earlier, this author had contemplated such a work, but Lafayette had opposed the appearance of a biography during his own lifetime, especially one that gave the impressions that he might have cooperated in its writing or publication.[67] He objected strenuously to the title: *Mémoires pour servir à la vie du Général LaFayette, et à l'histoire de l'Assemblée constituante*, and he asked Regnault-Warin to change it.

A month later Lafayette discovered that the changes he had requested had not been made. Indeed, the book had already appeared, part of a series of memoirs of figures of the Revolution. Lafayette's worst fears were realized. The words *pour servir à la vie* appeared in very small type, thus giving the casual observer the impression that these were the general's own reminiscences. The title on the spine of the first volume was even more deceptive: "*Mémoires relatifs à la Révolution française/I. Général La Fayette.*"[68] Seeing that he could not stop the publication, Lafayette asked the publisher to issue an explanation and sent Regnault-Warin the text of a statement that he wanted placed in the newspapers to disavow his cooperation with the project.[69]

Lafayette enlisted the help of Pagès, explaining that he was particularly afraid that, like Adolphe Thiers, the author might have used a "certain letter of my friend Lally which has been pursuing me for thirty years without my being able to subscribe to it, for my own sake, or disavow it, for his sake."[70] The letter was written during the turbulent days of July 1792, shortly before Louis XVI's arrest by the Jacobins. Concerned for the king's safety, Lafayette had offered to provide an armed escort for the king's move from Paris to the safer town of Compiègne, which was within the distance prescribed by law for the king's residence during sessions of the assembly. To help his friends persuade the king to go along with the plan, Lafayette jotted down some notes. His friend Lally-Tolendal then used them as the basis for a letter to Louis XVI, presumably from Lafayette. Lally-Tolendal's political views were always more conservative than Lafayette's, and in trying to make his proposals as attractive as possible to the king, he expressed views to which Lafayette objected, especially the implication that he would use the army to threaten the legislature and that he would countenance the king's move beyond the area to which he was restricted by law. The letter came to light in 1795, when Lally-Tolendal sent it to the king of Prussia in an attempt to enlist his help in obtaining Lafayette's release from prison. Lafayette later questioned the authenticity of the letter as printed in 1795, but whether completely accurate or not, disavowing the sentiments in it would require criticizing his good friend, and that Lafayette did not want to do.[71]

Lafayette and Pagès failed to arrive at a compromise with Regnault-Warin, who refused to publish the disclaimer they requested. Instead, he published an article in the *Pilote ministériel* defending his work. Lafayette feared that Regnault-Warin's defense might include mentioning some notes Lafayette had given him years before and of which Lafayette now had only a vague recollection. The controversy had not ended by the time Lafayette embarked for the United States, and Pagès was deputized to continue the efforts to get satisfaction from the difficult, though sympathetic, author.[72]

Pagès also coordinated the effort in France to derive the greatest publicity from the American trip. To supply liberal writers at home with frequent dispatches, Lafayette took a secretary with him to the United States. The rest of his party consisted only of the devoted and invaluable George and the servant Bastien. The person selected for the post of secretary, Auguste Levasseur, had been an officer in the 29th Regiment stationed at Neuf-Brisach and deeply implicated in the Belfort conspiracy. Lafayette was pleased with his selection, commenting in one of his first letters home, "We congratulate ourselves more every day for our association with Le Vasseur, who is truly excellent and full of merit with a very pleasant personality."[73] Levasseur kept a journal of the trip and supplied information to Pagès, the center of the news network in Paris. Pagès made sure that all those who had been promised information actually received it and oversaw publication of a book about the trip.[74] The trip was planned, from the beginning, to revive political prospects back home and to publicize the lessons that Lafayette believed the United States could teach Europe.

Lafayette's confidence in Pagès was also important in helping him through a serious family crisis immediately before his trip. The crisis sprang in part from concern over Lafayette's image, but it was more deeply personal and revealed the disquieting effect Fanny Wright had on the normally hospitable and placid Lafayette clan.

Fanny intended to accompany Lafayette to America. In early April, she, Camilla, and their friend Julia Garnett traveled to England, probably to visit friends and relatives before she and Camilla departed for the United States. Her intentions, however, met with the disapproval of the Lafayette family. A noticeable coolness had invaded the relations between Fanny and the family. One sympathetic witness told Fanny that, had she experienced the ill-treatment that Fanny and her sister were forced to endure, she would not have remained in the house.[75] During the fall of 1823, her visits to La Grange had been less frequent than in previous years. Fanny, though, was used to having her own way and was confident of the important place she held in Lafayette's affections. Obstacles might exist, but she had no doubts that she would be going to the United States at the same time as Lafayette.

While Fanny was in England, Lafayette was assailed with problems, most notably the serious illness of his sister-in-law, Pauline de Montagu. Her condition became so critical that he was convinced she would die. Lafayette spent at least one long agonizing night by her bedside. His granddaughter Mélanie de Lasteyrie was ill at the same time, and he divided his time between the two sickrooms, with frequent stops at home to see if letters had arrived from Fanny.[76] His loved ones recovered, but other worries continued. His family's opposition to Fanny's plan increased. And in London, shortly before leaving for a visit to Scotland, Fanny learned that rumors were circulating that she and Lafayette were lovers. Though her first reaction was to ignore such gossip, she decided that the only way their friendship could continue on its former basis was to regularize it in such a way that they could travel together freely without fear of society's censure.

Fanny said that, when her letter describing the situation reached Lafayette, he suffered "a very violent seizure which, after depriving him for some time of sense, was followed by vomiting to an alarming degree of violence. He continued unwell for two days." He turned for help to Pagès and to Madame Charles de Lasteyrie, the wife of Virginie's brother-in-law. "Madame Charles," as she was called in the correspondence, became Fanny's special advocate and friend in the difficult days that followed.[77]

As soon as Fanny heard of Lafayette's illness, she abandoned her visit to Scotland, left Camilla behind, and hastened to France. Her meetings with Madame Charles and with Lafayette were emotional and painful. Fanny was bewildered by the resistance to her suggestions for solving the problem and seemed unaware of the magnitude of the demands she was making on this close-knit and proud family. Her first suggestion, that Lafayette formally adopt the two sisters, Madame Charles immediately branded as impossible because of the opposition of the family.

At her first meeting with Lafayette, Fanny was struck by the signs of wear that his face still showed. Though she dreaded causing him undue anguish, the strained relations had to be discussed. Lafayette told her that when he had described to Pagès the rumors Fanny had heard and asked him "on his honor to state if he had ever heard such reports or any thing like such etc. [he] solemnly affirmed to the contrary, adding 'I am astonished first at its being said, but far more at its being listened to. The difference of ages & yet more your known virtues & *honor*.'" Pagès thought adoption was a sensible alternative, and Lafayette recoiled from explaining that family animosity made it impossible.

Fanny broached the even more delicate subject of marriage, but Lafayette told her, as had Madame Charles, that a promise made to his wife on her deathbed precluded his marrying. The vow, he assured her, was voluntarily given, because when he sensed that Adrienne feared that he might marry a longtime friend (Mme de Simiane), he responded to his wife's fears by promising Adrienne that he would never remarry. Lafayette said he would find it impossible to go back on this promise, made in the presence of many witnesses.[78] Fanny, far from being sensitive to the enormity of what she was suggesting, felt instead that the family's objections to her traveling with Lafayette were doing him irreparable harm. She believed that her absence would shorten his life. "Were he 20 years younger or had he near him one being with whom he could exchange thoughts I should think this fear . . . exaggerated but with my knowledge of his sensibility of the deep rootedness of his affection of the feeling of his confidence in F. & of the moral desert in which he would be left, I feel as certain of this fact as if I saw it passing before my eyes."[79] Lafayette begged her to talk to Pagès and, if he approved, to meet with George. She saw Pagès, but nothing was settled. Lafayette left for La Grange at the end of May, and Fanny headed for Le Havre to spend some time with the Garnetts. From there she wrote to Camilla, "The coming voyage which has now lost for my paternal friend every charm seems yet to hold out the only prospect I say not of happiness & peace for both . . . but of occupations & relief from things & people now odious. I have in part engaged in the event of his being constrained to remain in that country & of his son's return that we should then join him."[80]

Fanny surely exaggerated her importance in Lafayette's life. She might have found some members of the family odious, but it is difficult to believe that Lafayette saw them in the same light.

Fanny was important to him, but George was essential. George's devotion to his father was recognized by all. The historian Achille de Vaulabelle came to know George when they both sat in the National Constituent Assembly of 1848. At that time, he wrote, George was an old man, "but age had neither cooled his heart nor weakened his convictions: his eyes would become moist and his voice would tremble with profound emotion each time he pronounced the name of his father; each of his votes testified, furthermore, to an unshakable loyalty to the principles of the first years of his life. A calm and sweet disposition, an honest and upright heart, a firm conscience." George's life was devoted to sacrifice without seeking fame or notice. He passed through life quietly, "leaving a profound impression of respect" with those who knew him.[81]

By contrast, Fanny Wright would become a notorious advocate of radical and controversial ideas. The normal effect produced by her magnetic personality and sharp intelligence was heightened by her absolute conviction of the rightness of her cause and by her willingness to ignore society's conventions. She was certain that her friendship with Lafayette was honest and useful to him, but she failed to appreciate his obligations to and his need for others besides her. Lafayette enjoyed the stimulation of such a devoted and intelligent disciple as Fanny, but she was certainly not the only person in his wide circle of friends whom he could trust and talk to. He wanted her to remain his intimate friend, but he understood the need to include her on terms approved by his family. Unlike Fanny, who was held back only by her often-tardy and halfhearted considerations of Camilla's desires, Lafayette was not free to do as he pleased. The trip to America, after all, was more than a sentimental journey of a private citizen. It was designed to revive the liberal cause and his personal reputation. Flaunting society's strictures at the outset (no matter how unfair they might be) would surely not help to make the trip a success.

Lafayette's family and friends had come to fear her increasing influence. As Fanny explained to Camilla,

> It appears that there have been mischief makers and busy bodies at work—of whom too we knew little, perhaps nothing. Meddling politicians jealous of my sup-

> *posed influence who had asserted to the son that noth-*
> *ing was done or said without my approbation, etc. &*
> *that our father was held in leading strings—silly & ill-*
> *natured women who supposed intentions of another*
> *nature & the Lord knows what—All this operating*
> *upon little minds & petty jealousies produced all &*
> *more than we saw. Fully convinced that they have*
> *wounded the feelings & marred the happiness of our*
> *father they are now as anxious to cement the tie as*
> *they were before to break it.*

Now convinced that Lafayette needed Fanny by his side, the family was willing to approve of her going, as long as she and Camilla sailed on a separate ship. Virginie wrote to Fanny urging her to do so, as did Madame Charles. Fanny found this arrangement totally unsuitable. She pointed out to Lafayette that everybody would know that she and her sister were going to America to be with him.

> *Our intimate connexion is too well & universally*
> *known in both hemispheres—No, . . . might I give an*
> *opinion it is this—If our union is to continue, it can*
> *only do so with honor to you & without prejudice to us*
> *by your assuming openly & avowedly the air & char-*
> *acter of a protector. You must be our father not in a*
> *doubtful & covert way but in an open & manly one.*
> *. . . Forgive me then if I say that if you & yours ap-*
> *prove, I will call my Camilla to me. I will place her un-*
> *der your protection we will assume together the place*
> *of your children, we will call you father, we will be*
> *with you as children, & despising & confronting slan-*
> *ders which thus met in the face will slink away, we*
> *will go & stay & return with you. If not, . . . late as it is*
> *to renounce engagements which my heart will ever ac-*
> *knowledge to be more sacred than any ever made on*
> *earth, we must part.*

But, she continued, even their parting would lead to gossip. People would say that his family had objected to her presence or that they had quarreled.[82]

261

Pagès once again became the mediator in the dispute, and Fanny wrote him a long letter summarizing her position. Finding excuses or subterfuges, she argued, would be to acknowledge that there was something to the rumors,

> *that there is something to hide. . . . I am ready to make any sacrifice, I recognize my obligations toward my father, as I believe his obligations toward me are more sacred than any other, but the more sacred they are, the less they must be shrouded in mystery—and I confess to you that it is impossible for me to act in a manner repugnant to my character and which in my own eyes would be giving up the dignity of innocence and virtue. . . . I will gladly take the place of a daughter with the express consent and approbation of the family but I do not want to follow him as I don't know what and begin again the same life that I have already been dragging out for far too long.*

Moreover, the issue of her proper role would not have been solved, she protested, and upon their return the same questions would again be raised.[83]

The dispute stood at this juncture in the middle of June. Meanwhile, Lafayette's plans were finally taking shape. He had borrowed money and made arrangements to embark at Le Havre on the *Cadmus*, one of the packet boats that ran regularly between France and the United States. The captain, Francis Allyn, had heard that Lafayette intended to travel on the *Stephania*, but its scheduled departure date fell before he was prepared to leave. At the end of June, only two American ships that could accommodate passengers were at the port of Le Havre: the *Don Quixotte* and the *Cadmus*. Because Lafayette "disliked the name of the former," no doubt contemplating the number of jokes the name would inspire, Allyn offered him the use of the *Cadmus*, if another ship could be found to replace it on its regularly scheduled departure date of the first of July. The *Spartan* filled in for the *Cadmus*, and Allyn then waited until Lafayette was ready to sail, with the sole stipulation that it must be before 15 July. Allyn offered to transport Lafayette and his party free of charge, fully expecting he would be reimbursed for his services by the American government.[84] They were hoping to sail by 10 July, though Allyn thought it might actually be a day or two later.

Pressed by time, by the importunities of Lafayette's family and friends, by her genuine fears for Lafayette's well-being, and by Camilla's advice not to abandon Lafayette, Fanny finally gave in and promised to follow Lafayette to America on another ship. Lafayette was much relieved, explaining to Pagès that her original view had been "founded on the loyalty and purity of her character, and on her hatred of devious means when there is nothing to hide; but she will give up that opinion if it is not that of her friends."[85] Fanny waited in Le Havre for Camilla's arrival from England, then dashed with her to Paris.

On 11 July, the day before his intended departure for Le Havre, Lafayette was in the midst of last-minute preparations when he received the surprising news that Fanny and Camilla had arrived in town. He wrote feverishly to Pagès, explaining his difficult circumstances. "The entire family, my doctor, two or three friends have been with me since seven o'clock. They are at the Vauban Hotel, 366 Rue St Honoré. Much good might come from this for all of us; go to see them right away." He would try to delay his departure for a day, "but, my God, why didn't they arrive three days ago." The uncharacteristic "*mon dieu*" revealed the agitated state of Lafayette's mind. The departure was delayed, and when the Lafayette family met with the two sisters on the following morning all harsh feelings dissolved, so much so that they were invited to La Grange to rest for a few days before returning to Le Havre. Now Lafayette felt convinced that "both dear Fanny and Camilla will not fail to come to the United States."[86] The awkwardness of traveling separately, which Fanny had been so loath to announce to her friends in England, was now explained as the consequence of Camilla's late arrival in France and the impossibility of completing their arrangements in time to depart with the general.[87]

Lafayette arrived at Le Havre on 12 July 1824 to a reception prepared by the citizens of the town. Young people wearing black jackets and white coats, some on horseback, greeted him and accompanied him to the gates of the town, but the authorities would not allow the demonstrations to proceed inside. The sub-prefect apologized to his superiors for having failed to stop the demonstrations, explaining that his efforts were bound to fail in a town containing so many foreigners and resident American businessmen.[88] That evening Lafayette stayed at the home of a merchant, M. Philippon, where groups gathered to cry "*Vive Lafayette.*" The next morning he made several visits, then returned to M. Philippon's house where a considerable crowd had already collected. His way to the dock was lined with crowds as well. By 1:00 P.M. he was on board the *Cadmus*, to the great relief of the authorities.[89]

The crowds at Le Havre were merely a foretaste of the public attention that would surround Lafayette during the next fourteen months. Lafayette's trip to the United States, a remarkable celebration of the liberal ideal and the grandest tribute ever paid by the country to any individual, had finally begun.

Afterword

During the early Restoration, Lafayette was at the center of a network of European liberals who were desperately trying to find a place for their brand of politics in an exasperatingly conservative age. They fought for their cause with both legal and illegal means. But the ultimate result was failure.

Despite his general confidence in public opinion, Lafayette appears to have concluded from his experiences during these years that the French people were not prepared to follow him into agitation for rapid changes in the French government. The Carbonarist conspiracies failed dismally, and with them, the strategy of using violence as the means to political change. After he returned from his American trip in 1825, Lafayette supported a broad coalition of those on the left, who pledged themselves to effective electoral politics and to ostentatiously legal maneuverings.

By stressing the determinedly legal quality of the opposition, this new, more moderate coalition was able to raise the specter of illegal actions by the king. Such a strategy not only reconciled them with the rather conservative electorate, which had supported liberals in the earliest years of the Restoration, it also boxed the king into a corner. Constantly monitored and suspected of harboring desires to sweep away constitutional guarantees, the inflexible Charles X was bound to make an ill-considered move. And when he did so in 1830, the left was able to step in as the guardian of constitutionality, order, and the rights of the people. The Revolution of 1830, a victory for the left, came only after the ineffective tactics of the conspiracies of the early 1820s had been decisively abandoned.

Lafayette returned from America prepared to accept the policy of legality and of cooperation with moderates. The extravagant celebrations of the trip satisfied his vanity. After the rewarding experiences in the New World, he could be more patient in seeking the accomplishment of his goals in the Old World. But the

265

trip reconfirmed his belief that eventually Europe would follow the road to liberalism carved out by the Americans. It might take longer than he had hoped, but his commitment to an American style of republican government was as firm as ever.

His particular devotion to the American tradition distinguished Lafayette from some of the other supporters of liberalism in Europe. He saw the struggles in Europe as continuations of the struggle for liberty that had begun in the New World in the 1770s. Historians' neglect of Lafayette's career in the early nineteenth century has resulted in neglect as well of the way the American example was used by European radicals.[1] It provided a model of republicanism that worked, an example of a revolution that resulted in an orderly system of government and a prosperous economy, and an effective counterpoise to the dictatorial Jacobin republic in France. Liberalism inspired by the American example was more radical than liberalism inspired by the English model of parliamentary supremacy. But, as René Rémond has shown, the image of America during the Restoration (closely tied to the image of Lafayette) was derived from the classical ideals of the eighteenth century and would not survive long.[2]

Before 1824, ideological differences among those on the left were not as pronounced as they became later. The left opposed aristocracy and privileged orders, emphasized the rights of the people and the importance of constitutions, and preached civic virtue and industry. Later, after the disappointments of the failed conspiracies, many of Lafayette's associates, from Frances Wright to Voyer d'Argenson, began to reexamine their beliefs. Voyer d'Argenson started to focus on economic reform, eventually becoming a socialist. Others turned to Saint-Simonianism. Not having experienced the reassurances of the American trip, they felt more keenly than did Lafayette the failures in Europe and came to believe that a more radical restructuring of society would be needed before their dreams would succeed.

The years between 1814 and 1824 provided links among advocates for change in many countries. Lafayette often mediated between these groups and continued, until his death in 1834, to see his own role in international terms. The cosmopolitan tone of Lafayette's advocacy of liberalism, inspired by the American example, sustained by his belief in French energy, and committed to the establishment of liberalism everywhere in the world, would not long survive him. As believers in national rights became more narrowly nationalistic and leftists became more determinedly international, Lafayette's brand of liberalism fell into disfavor. Eighteenth-century republican ideas began to die out, and it became increasingly difficult for people to understand the nature of Lafayette's conception of constitutional monarchy.

But if the political battles of the early nineteenth century are to be understood, Lafayette's beliefs and activities must be remembered because he was often at the center of concern. He was frequently singled out for vilification or praise. His life was cited in opposition to that of Napoleon and of Charles X, not for what he had done so much as for what he symbolized. Historians have often labeled Lafayette ambitious and, because he failed to attain power, have concluded he was a failure. But the people in his own day did not see him in that light. Opponents believed him dangerous and disruptive. Supporters found him principled and consistently brave. To both sides, then, he personified the liberal ideal, an ideal still so daring that it provoked men to arms.

Notes

Works Cited

Index

Notes

Abbreviations

AG Papers	Albert Gallatin Papers, microfilm edition
AN	Archives Nationales, Paris
AP	*Archives parlementaires de 1787 à 1860*
Catherwood	Martin P. Catherwood Library, Cornell University
Chinard	Gilbert Chinard, ed., *The Letters of Lafayette and Jefferson* (Baltimore: Johns Hopkins Press, 1929; Paris: "Les Belles Lettres," 1929)
Correspondance	Benjamin Constant and Goyet de la Sarthe, *Correspondance, 1818-1822*, edited by Ephraïm Harpaz (Geneva: Librairie Droz, 1973)
Dean	Dean Collection, Department of Rare Books, Cornell University Library
Galpin	Archives de la Famille Galpin
GWL	George Washington Lafayette
LG Papers	Louis Gottschalk Papers, Special Collections, University of Chicago
Lilly	Lafayette Manuscripts, Lilly Library, Indiana University
LPP	Lafayette Papers Project, Cornell University
Mémoires	Gilbert du Motier de Lafayette, *Mémoires, correspondance et manuscrits du général Lafayette*, publiés par sa famille (6 vols.; Paris: H. Fournier aîné, 1837-1838)

Note on Translations and Spelling

All quotations from *Correspondance*, Galpin, and *Mémoires* have been translated by the author. Other translations by the author are indicated in the notes by the notation "(trans.)." Lafayette frequently wrote to American and English correspondents in English. His sometimes-awkward English syntax and spelling have been reproduced as written. Like others of his time, he was consistent about neither capital-

271

ization nor punctuation. To avoid confusion, I have imposed modern standards of capitalization on documents written by Lafayette.

Introduction

1. Etienne Charavay, *Le Général La Fayette (1757–1834)* (Paris: Société de l'Histoire de la révolution française, 1898), pp. 396–429. Chantal de Tourtier-Bonazzi, ed., *Lafayette: Documents conservés en France* (Paris: Archives Nationales, 1976), p. 26. Gottschalk's biography was published by the University of Chicago Press and the last two volumes were co-authored by Margaret Maddox. The titles and dates of publication are: *Lafayette Comes to America* (1935), *Lafayette Joins the American Army* (1937), *Lafayette and the Close of the American Revolution* (1942), *Lafayette Between the American and the French Revolution (1783–1789)* (1950), *Lafayette in the French Revolution through the October Days* (1969), *Lafayette in the French Revolution from the October Days through the Federation* (1973).

2. For example, in one book an eight-page chapter covering the period from 1815 to 1821 is misleadingly entitled "The Phase of Abortive Conspiracies." Lafayette began active conspiracy only at the end of that period. His election in 1818 is mentioned without indicating which district he represented, and his defeat in 1824 is recorded, but not his having become a deputy of another district in the meantime. Maurice de LaFuye and Emile Babeau, *The Apostle of Liberty: A Life of La Fayette*, trans. by Edward Hyams (New York: Thomas Yoseloff, 1956).

3. "La Fayette, whose ideas and habits had not changed since the Old Regime. To tell the truth, his thought was less rapid than ever, except when it was a question of chasing some skirt. He was always ready to bless any adventure that he was asked to sponsor, although it might mean seeking refuge at the last moment in inaction" (trans.). André Jardin, *Histoire du libéralisme politique de la crise de l'absolutisme à la constitution de 1875* (Paris: Hachette, 1985), p. 248. His goals were not explained in the sections dealing with the French Revolution either, where he was mentioned only in passing.

4. Ruth F. Necheles, *The Abbé Grégoire, 1787–1831: The Odyssey of an Egalitarian* (Westport, Conn.: Greenwood, 1971), p. 213; Jean Vidalenc, *La Restauration (1814–1830)* (Paris: Presses Universitaires de France, 1973), p. 122; Thomas D. Beck, *French Legislators, 1800–1824: A Study in Quantitative History* (Berkeley: Univ. of California Press, 1974), p. 66; James H. Billington, *Fire in the Minds of Men: Origins of the Revolutionary Faith* (New York: Basic Books, 1980), p. 192; John Simpson Penman, *Lafayette and Three Revolutions* (Boston: Stratford, 1929), p. ii.

5. The only book on Jacques-Antoine Manuel was published in 1877: Ed. Bonnal (de Ganges), *Manuel et son temps, étude sur l'opposition parlementaire sous la Restauration* (Paris: E. Dentu, 1877). No biographies of his close political associates Laffitte, Voyer d'Argenson, or Dupont de l'Eure exist. Georges Weill, "D'Argenson et la question sociale," *International Review for Social History*, IV (1939), 161–169, describes d'Argenson's intellectual development and conversion to socialist ideas, but his role as a politician has not been studied. Most popular biographies of Lafayette do not mention his association with d'Argenson, one of his best friends.

6. Alan B. Spitzer, *Old Hatreds and Young Hopes: The French Carbonari against the Bourbon Restoration* (Cambridge: Harvard University Press, 1971).

7. David G. Chandler, *Dictionary of the Napoleonic Wars* (New York: Macmillan, 1979), p. 233.

8. Billington, *Fire in the Minds of Men*, pp. 192–193 and footnote 3, p. 573. Agénor Bardoux, *Les Dernières Années de La Fayette* (Paris: C. Lévy, 1893) was published in a small edition and is now quite difficult to find.

9. Tourtier-Bonazzi, *Lafayette*, p. 26. (trans.).

10. Charles de Rémusat, *Mémoires de ma vie* (3 vols.; Paris: Plon, [1958–1960]), II, 243, 253–254.

11. For an example of a historian who characterizes Lafayette as mediocre largely on the grounds that "he wrote little," see Patrice Gueniffey, "Lafayette," in François Furet and Mona Ozouf, eds., *A Critical Dictionary of the French Revolution*, trans. by Arthur Goldhammer (Cambridge: Belknap Press of Harvard Univ. Press, 1989), p. 225.

12. See Lloyd S. Kramer, "America's Lafayette and Lafayette's America: A European and the American Revolution," *William and Mary Quarterly*, XXXVIII (April 1981), 228–241.

13. For an anlysis of the evidence on these events, see Gottschalk and Maddox, *Through the October Days*, pp. 329–387.

1. The Hundred Days

1. André Maurois, *Adrienne: The Life of the Marquise de La Fayette*, trans. by Gerard Hopkins (New York: McGraw-Hill, 1961), 385–387, 413–414, 422. This biography is especially valuable because Maurois is the only historian who has had access to the archives at La Grange. However, this work ends at the death of Adrienne in 1807.

2. Born in 1757, he celebrated his fifty-seventh birthday on 6 September 1814. Henry Crabb Robinson, *Diary, Reminiscences and Correspondence*, ed. by Thomas Sadler (2 vols.; London: Macmillan,

1872), I, 232, describes meeting Lafayette in September 1814: "his reddish complexion clear, his body inclining to be stout. His tone of conversation is staid, and he has not the vivacity commonly ascribed to Frenchmen. There is apparently nothing enthusiastic about him."

3. The two brothers, Charles and César (1758–1831), shared Lafayette's political views. A third brother, Victor (1768–1850), differed sharply, becoming minister of war in 1819.

4. Lafayette to Bonaparte, 20 May 1802, cited in Charavay, *Le Général La Fayette*, p. 386 (trans.).

5. Maurois, *Adrienne*, p. 436.

6. Emmet Kennedy, *Destutt de Tracy and the Origins of "Ideology"* (Philadelphia: American Philosophical Society, 1978), pp. 184–191.

7. *Mémoires*, V, 298. Jacquemont's son, Victor, was a frequent visitor at La Grange during the Restoration. See chapter 3.

8. *Mémoires*, V, 302.

9. *Mémoires*, V, 304.

10. *Mémoires*, V, 296, 305. Lafayette to Jefferson, 14 Aug. 1814, in Gilbert Chinard, ed., *The Letters of Lafayette and Jefferson* (Baltimore: Johns Hopkins Press, 1929; Paris: "Les Belles Lettres," 1929), p. 341. Lafayette to Lord Holland, 14 Apr. 1814 in *Mémoires*, V, 483.

11. *Mémoires*, V, 307.

12. Lafayette to Masclet, 23 April 1814, Huntington Library, HM9412, photo at LG Papers (trans.).

13. Cited in Paul Bastid, *Benjamin Constant et sa doctrine* (2 vols.; [Paris]: Librairie Armand Colin, 1966), I, 264 (trans.).

14. Marcel Reinhard, *Le Grand Carnot*, vol 2, *L'Organisateur de la Victoire* (Paris: Hachette, 1952), p. 298.

15. General Dupont. Lafayette to Masclet, 23 Apr. 1814, Huntington Library, photo at LG Papers.

16. Lafayette [copy] to Lord Holland, 24 Apr. 1814, Dean (trans.).

17. Lafayette to Comte d'Artois, 15 Apr. 1814, *Mémoires*, V, 308.

18. Gottschalk, *Lafayette Comes to America*, pp. 47–48.

19. Philip Mansel, *Louis XVIII* (London: Blond & Briggs, 1981), pp. 16, 23.

20. *Mémoires*, V, 327–328; Mansel, *Louis XVIII*, p. 114. The duc d'Ayen was Adrienne's father and the prince de Poix was her sister's brother-in-law, as well as a Noailles relative. See the genealogy chart in Stanley J. Idzerda, ed., *Lafayette in the Age of the American Revolution* (5 vols.; Ithaca: Cornell Univ. Press, 1977–1983), I, xliv–xlv.

21. Jean-Yves Coppolani, *Les Elections en France à l'époque napoléonienne* (Paris: Editions Albatros, 1980), pp. 66, 91, 96, 129–130. Napoleon intended these colleges to be intermediary bodies between the government and the citizens, a sort of aristocracy.

22. Lafayette to [Gallois, April 1814], AN 138 AP 213 (trans.).

23. On the creation of the cockade, see Gottschalk and Maddox, *Through the October Days*, p. 176.

24. Lafayette to Jefferson, 14 Aug. 1814, Chinard, p. 345; Achille Charles Léonce Victor, duc de Borglie, *Souvenirs du feu duc de Broglie, (1785–1870)* (4 vols.; Paris: Calmann Lévy, 1886), II, 256. *Mémoires*, V, 308.

25. Mansel, *Louis XVIII*, p. 206.

26. *Mémoires*, V, 309. The duc d'Orléans (1773–1850), son of the duc d'Orléans who voted for the death of Louis XVI, fought with the revolutionary armies and was in exile during the extreme phase of the Revolution and during the Empire. He was next in line for the throne after the sons of the comte d'Artois. Influenced by English political ideas, he was promoted as a candidate for the throne by some opposition leaders during the Restoration and ascended to the throne as Louis-Philippe in 1830.

27. Lafayette L[copy] to Albert Gallatin, 25 May 1814, New York Historical Society, photo at LG Papers.

28. AP, vol. 12, p. 7. Alexander's declaration was dated 31 Mar. 1814.

29. Lafayette L [copy] to William Crawford, 26 May 1814, Brown University Library.

30. Albert Gallatin to James Monroe, 3 June 1814, in Henry Adams (ed.), *Writings of Albert Gallatin* (3 vols.; New York: Antiquarian Press, 1960), I, 625; James F. Hopkins (ed.), *The Papers of Henry Clay* (9 vols. to date; Lexington: Univ. of Kentucky Press, 1959–1988), I, 906.

31. Lafayette's access to La Harpe was perhaps facilitated by family connections. One of La Harpe's closest friends, Charles de Lasteyrie, was the brother of Lafayette's son-in-law. A copy of Crawford's memorandum is in the Albert Gallatin Papers, New-York Historical Society, "Reflections upon the War between the United States & England." Copies of Lafayette's covering letter to "Monsieur," 22 May 1814, are in the Thomas Jefferson Papers, Library of Congress and in the New-York Historical Society. The letter is printed in Chinard, pp. 347–348. From what Lafayette wrote in *Mémoires*, V, 309, it is clear that this letter is to La Harpe. Lafayette continued his interest in the American cause, meeting with James A. Bayard, another American commissioner, on 9 and 10 June, and with Gallatin on 27 June 1814. Lafayette asked Bayard whether, in the event efforts for peace failed, the United States would welcome the help of French soldiers as volunteers in the war. *Papers of James A. Bayard, 1796–1815*, vol. 2 of *Annual Report of the American Historical Association for 1913*, p. 510.

32. Lafayette L[copy] to William Crawford, 26 May 1814, Brown University Library.

33. Alexander feared that without this pressure Louis XVIII might renege on his promise. Allen McConnell, *Tsar Alexander I: Paternalistic Reformer* (New York: Thomas Y. Crowell, 1970), p. 127.

34. Lafayette to Jefferson, 14 August 1814, Chinard, p. 343.

35. Lafayette to [Lanjuinais?], mercredi soir [1818?], Benjamin Franklin Papers, Yale University (trans.). This letter, commenting on a "tableau comparatif" which the authors had lent him was apparently addressed to Lanjuinais and Jullien, who published in 1818 a prospectus announcing a work on comparative constitutions. The work never appeared, though Lanjuinais did publish a book on constitutions: *Constitutions de la nation française, avec un essai de traité historique et politique sur la Charte* (2 vols.; Paris: Baudouin frères, 1819). See review of *Collection des constitutions, chartes et lois fondamentales des peuples de l'Europe et des Deux Amériques* par MM P.-A. Dufau, J.-B. Duvergier, et J. Guadet in *Revue Encyclopédique*, vol. 25, Jan. 1825. The Lanjuinais and Jullien project may be the one referred to in the *Constitutionnel* of 3 Sept. 1817, to be entitled *Recueil des constitutions des différents peuples, ou Droit public intérieur des nations*, to be written by two peers "known for their noble independence" (trans.). Bastid, *Benjamin Constant*, I, 315.

36. Lafayette to Jefferson, 14 Aug. 1814, Chinard, pp. 342–344.

37. Lafayette to Jefferson, 14 Aug. 1814, Chinard, pp. 343, 345.

38. The generals were Charles Lefebvre-Desnouettes and the Lallemand brothers, Frédéric-Antoine and Henri-Dominique. Joseph Fouché, *Mémoires* (2 vols.; Paris: Le Rouge, 1824), II, 216, says that Lafayette was to be part of the provisional government following their successful coup, but Fouché has probably exaggerated the extent of the plot. Louis Madelin, *Fouché, 1759–1820* (2 vols.; Paris: Librairie Plon, 1923), II, 319–326, does not mention Lafayette.

39. Benjamin Constant, *Journaux Intimes* ([Paris]: Gallimard, 1952), pp. 406, 410, 420, 433; 27 July, 16 Sept., 25 Oct. 1814, 20 Feb. 1815 (trans.).

40. Constant, *Journaux intimes*, p. 434, 2 Mar. 1815 (trans.).

41. Benjamin Constant, *Mémoires sur les Cent Jours* ([Paris]: Jean-Jacques Pauvert, 1956), p. 53.

42. *Mémoires*, V, 353.

43. Lafayette to Crawford, 8 Aug. 1816, Special Collections, University of Chicago.

44. Those planning an armed revolt to overthrow the government were not doing so in behalf of Napoleon. In fact, Lafayette believed that it was rumors of such plots that prompted Napoleon to launch his expedition. *Mémoires*, V, 354–355. See Henri Houssaye, *1815* (32d. ed.; 3 vols.; Paris: Parrin, 1900), I, 118–121, for a description of these plots. At

the time it was assumed that these men were in complicity with Bonaparte, but the latest assessment is that Lafayette's description is essentially correct. Guillaume de Bertier de Sauvigny, *La Restauration* (3d ed.
rev.; Paris: Flammarion, 1974), p. 88.

45. *Mémoires*, V, 313, 332, 325. The minister was M. Ferrand,
who made the remark when introducing a bill to return to the émigrés
confiscated lands still held by the government and not yet sold. Prosper
Duvergier de Hauranne, *Histoire du gouvernement parlementaire en
France, 1814–1848* (10 vols.; Paris: Michel Lévy frères, 1857–71), II,
292–294.

46. Constant, *Mémoires sur les Cent Jours*, p. 58.

47. Emile de Perceval, *Un Adversaire de Napoleon: Le Vte Lainé
et la vie parlementaire au temps de la restauration* (2 vols.; Paris:
Librairie Ancienne Honoré Champion, 1926), I, 329–337; *Mémoires*, V,
371–372; Constant, *Journaux intimes*, p. 435; Houssaye, *1815*, I, 329.

48. *Mémoires*, V, 372. Pierre-Louis-Jean Casimir, duc de Blacas
d'Aulps (1717–1839) had joined Louis XVIII in exile. His handling of
affairs during the First Restoration made him so unpopular that he was
removed from power at the beginning of the Second Restoration. He
served as ambassador to Naples, negociated the concordat of 1817, and
followed Charles X into exile after 1830.

49. *Mémoires*, V, 371.

50. *Mémoires*, V, 365.

51. Lafayette to [Mme de Simiane], [1815–1816], *Mémoires*, VI,
17.

52. Benjamin Constant, *Recueil d'articles 1795–1817*, ed. by
Ephraïm Harpaz (Geneva: Droz, 1978), pp. 149–152. Constant's erratic
behavior during this period is partially explained by an obsessive and
hopeless passion for Mme de Recamier that dominated his attention.

53. Ephraïm Harpaz, "Une lettre inconnue de Benjamin Constant
à Napoleon (30 avril 1815)," *Revue de la Bibliothèque Nationale*, I (Mar.
1982), 34, footnote 26.

54. Lafayette to Mme d'Hénin, 15 May 1815, *Mémoires*, V, 499.

55. Constant, *Journaux intimes*, p. 439, 1 May 1815. Constant,
Mémoires sur les Cent Jours, p. 123.

56. Lafayette to Benjamin Constant, 9 April 1815, *Mémoires*, V,
406–412.

57. *Mémoires*, V, 414–415.

58. Lafayette to Mme d'Hénin, 29 June 1815, Dean (trans.). This
portion of the letter was not printed in *Mémoires*. Lafayette to Dupont de
Nemours, 30 Oct. 1815, Hagley Museum and Library, photo at LPP.

59. *Mémoires*, V, 418.

60. Houssaye, *1815*, I, 545–546; *Moniteur*, 23 Apr. 1815.

61. *Mémoires*, V, 422.

62. The decree calling for elections was issued on 30 April 1815. *Archives parlementaires*, vol. 14, p. 386. Lafayette to Benjamin Constant, 3 May 1815, *Mémoires*, V, 424. The electoral system of the Hundred Days is described in Coppolani, *Elections*, pp. 131–146.

63. Seine-et-Marne elected seven representatives. The others were: Duc Charles de Plaisance, Gouest, Lefeuvre, Hattaingais, Guyardin, and Simon. AP, vol 14, p. 381.

64. He also protested the oath required of electors because it was unclear whether the constitution to which they swore allegiance was the old constitution or the new one in the process of being ratified by the people. *Mémoires*, V, 425–426. Lafayette to Mme d'Hénin, 15 May 1815, Dean.

65. Lafayette was willing to aid in matters of foreign affairs. At Joseph Bonaparte's request, he arranged for the departing William H. Crawford to take a confidential message to London at the end of April. *Mémoires*, V, 422; Crawford to Lafayette, 15 May 1815, Dean.

66. This anecdote comes from *Esquisse historique sur les Cent Jours, et fragments inédits relatifs aux séances secrètes des chambres, à la marche du gouvernement provisoire, et aux négociations d'Haguenau* (Paris: Baudouin Frères, 1819). pp. 13–14 (trans.). Duvergier de Hauranne, *Histoire*, III, 50n, maintains that this work was based on notes by Lafayette and Lanjuinais. Of thirty-one sections describing different events of the Hundred Days, twelve were published in slightly different form in the section entitle "Chapitre III" of *Mémoires*, V, 441–481. This similarity, as well as the identity of the publisher, Alexandre Baudouin (a close political associate of Lafayette's), makes it extremely likely that the reports in this work came directly from Lafayette or his close friends. Benjamin Constant hints that this was the case: "It is readily apparent that it has been written from the Memoirs of an eyewitness. The facts are presented scrupulously and honestly. While recognizing the patriotism and lofty sentiments that characterize the author or authors of this brochure, I differ from them essentially . . . regarding the usefulness and results of the abdication; but the depiction of the meetings at Haguenau leaves nothing to be desired." Constant, *Mémoires sur les Cent Jours*, p. 205n (trans.). Emile Le Gallo, *Les Cents-Jours* (Paris: Librairie Félix Alcan, 1924), p. 439.

67. Constant, *Journaux intimes*, p. 441 (trans.).

68. Lafayette [copy] to [his family at La Grange], 8 June 1815, Dean (trans.).

69. Mme d'Hénin had been married in 1766 at the age of sixteen to the prince d'Hénin, but they had never really lived together as husband and wife. They were officially separated in 1784, and, before the Revolu-

278

tion, she had become linked with Trophime-Gérard de Lally-Tolendal, to whom she was devoted for the rest of her life. Eugène Welvert, "La Princesse d'Hénin," *Revue de l'histoire de Versailles et de Seine-et-Oise*, XXV (1922), 123–138, 232–243, and XXVI (1923), 93–104. Chateaubriand describes Lally-Tolendal's sentimental enthusiasm for the royal cause in his *Mémoires d'outre-tombe*. His statement that Lally-Tolendal spent his time in Ghent with "a lady who hastened from Paris out of enthusiasm for his genius," which presumably refers to Mme d'Hénin, is at least misleading, since their liaison was of long-standing. Cited in Edouard Romberg and Albert Malet, eds., *Louis XVIII et les Cent-Jours à Gand: Recueil de documents inédits publiés pour la Société d'histoire contemporaire* (2 vols.; Paris: Alphonse Picard et fils, 1898), I, xxxi (trans.).

70. Lafayette to Mme d'Hénin, 15 May 1815, Dean (trans.).

71. Lafayette to Mme d'Hénin, 29 June 1815, Dean (trans.). Lafayette's statement here that he would have won had he not interfered may, in fact, have been more optimistic than the occasion warranted.

72. *Moniteur*, 5 June 1815, report of session of 4 June. Lanjuinais (1753–1827) was a deputy of the Third Estate in 1789, an opponent of the Mountain in the Convention, an expert on law and constitutional questions, and a close political associate of Lafayette's during the Restoration. He had been named a peer by Louis XVIII in 1814. See Coppolani, *Elections*, pp. 393–397, for an analysis of the membership of the Chamber of Representatives.

73. Lafayette to [Lanjuinais], "lundi matin, 5 juin" [1815], Lilly.

74. Lafayette to [his family at La Grange], 8 June 1815, Dean. The other vice presidents were Flaugergues, Dupont de l'Eure, and General Grenier. Lafayette came in third in the voting. AP, vol. 14, p. 400.

75. Lafayette to [his family at La Grange], 8 June 1815, Dean (trans.). As printed in *Mémoires*, the personal invective has been removed and Benjamin Constant's name omitted. *Mémoires*, V, 504. André-Marie-Jean-Jacques Dupin, called Dupin aîné (1783–1865), was a lawyer who became famous as a defender of liberals under the Restoration. He was elected deputy in 1827, president of the Chamber from 1832 to 1840, and also served under Napoleon III. In his memoirs, Dupin denied Lafayette's claim that he was a member of Lafayette's party. He said that he did not know Lafayette at the time, and that even later he was not a member of that party whose aim he had never known. André-Marie-Jean-Jacques Dupin, *Mémoires de M. Dupin* (2 vols.; Paris: Henri Plon, 1855), I, 16. Lafayette perhaps used the term *parti* to mean one who favored his point of view on the question, and nothing more. See Duvergier de Hauranne, *Histoire*, III, 7–8, for this incident.

76. AP, vol. 14, p. 405; Duvergier de Hauranne, *Histoire*, III, 13 (trans.).

77. Lafayette to [his family], 8 June 1815, Dean (trans.).

78. Lafayette to [his family], 9 June 1815, Dean. *Mémoires*, V, 446.

79. Lafayette to [his family], 12 June 1815, Dean (trans.).

80. Lafayette to [his family], 12 June 1815, Dean (trans.). The latter portion was edited out of the *Mémoires*.

81. *Mémoires*, V, 451.

82. *Mémoires*, V, 452. Merlin de Douai had been named a *ministre d'état* with special responsibility for liaison with the Chamber. Duvergier de Hauranne states that the resolution regarding the National Guard was the least important of those that Lafayette proposed. But, in fact, it was quite important for him, for giving him a potential body of supporters during the jockeying for power. Duvergier de Hauranne, *Histoire*, III, 20, 37–40. Madelin portrays Lafayette as the dupe of Fouché, acting on his inspiration. Yet the proposal to call the National Guard was not Fouché's idea. Fouché managed to take advantage of some of the things Lafayette did, but Lafayette was acting in ways that were consistent with his own principles and aims. Madelin, *Fouché*, pp. 390–393. On the role of the National Guard during the transfers of power during this period, see Louis Girard, *La Garde nationale, 1814–1871* (Paris: Librairie Plon, 1964).

83. AP, vol. 14, p 504 (trans.). *Esquisse historique*, p. 45. Antoine Jay (1769–1854), former tutor of Fouché's children, was director of the *Journal de Paris* in 1812, deputy from the Gironde during the Hundred Days, and an important figure of the opposition during the Restoration, when he wrote for the *Constitutionnel*, the *Minerve*, and the *Biographie des contemporains*.

84. *Mémoires*, V, 453–454.

85. Lafayette to Mme d'Hénin, 29 June 1815, Dean.

86. AP, vol. 14, p. 518. On the first round the votes were: Carnot 324, Fouché, 293, Grenier 204, and Lafayette 142. On the second round Grenier received an overwhelming majority of 350. The original wording was that they would be chosen *"dans"* the Chamber; this was changed to *"par."* The two peers named were the duc de Quinette and Caulincourt.

87. *Mémoires*, V, 461.

88. Constant, *Journaux intimes*, p. 443, 22 June 1815 (trans.).

89. Duvergier de Hauranne, *Histoire*, III, 74. Lafayette's comment about the choices was, "The fear of the return of the Bourbons had once again led the Chamber to seek for very sad guarantees in the choice of members of the provisional government. That was the biggest error the representatives committed." *Mémoires*, V, 459.

90. Speech by Mourgues, 22 June 1815, AP, vol. 14, p. 514.

91. Benjamin Constant's journal says 24 June. *Mémoires* say 25

June. Houssaye, *1815*, III, 98, says 24 June. The other commissioners were Antoine de Laforest, General Horace Sébastiani, Marc-René-Marie de Voyer d'Argenson, and the comte de Pontécoulant.

92. Lafayette to Mme d'Hénin, 29 June 1815, Dean (trans.).

93. William H. Crawford to Lafayette, 15 May 1815, Dean.

94. Notes on AN CC^{22} Dr 610, Paris, 23 June 1815, "Instructions pour M.M. les Plenipotentiaires de la Commission de Gouvernement auprès des puissances alliées," in LG Papers; *Mémoires*, V, 471. Marc-René-Marie de Voyer d'Argenson, *Discours et opinions de Voyer d'Argenson . . . précédés d'une notice biographique et publiés par son fils . . .* (2 vols.; Paris: Bureau de la "Revue générale biographique," 1845–1846), I, 240–246, suggests that the aim of the expedition was to get concessions from the Bourbons, to explain that the Chamber had not expressly repudiated the Napoleonic succession for fear of revolts in the army, but that their intentions were clear by their choice of a provisional government instead of a council of regency.

95. See speech by Durbach, 22 June 1815, for an appeal to the Allies' declarations. AP, vol. 14, p. 515. Bertier writes that "La Fayette believed naively that he was going to play the glorious role of mediator between Europe and France." Bertier de Sauvigny, *La Restauration*, p. 110 (trans.). Lafayette's letters show instead that he would have preferred to stay in Paris, that he was not sanguine about the outcome of this expedition.

96. Elizabeth Longford, *Wellington, The Years of the Sword* (London: Weidenfeld & Nicolson, 1969), pp. 396–397.

97. Houssaye, *1815*, III, 181.

98. Houssaye, *1815*, III, 181–182 (trans.), describes this incident. He points out, for instance, that neither Lafayette's *Mémoires* nor the *Esquisse historique* attributes such sentiments to Blücher's aide.

99. Lafayette [copy] to Tsar Alexander I, 30 June 1815, Dean (trans.).

100. Lord Liverpool, in advocating a reduction of French territory, pointed to the danger that the government of the king, after the evacuation of the Allies, might be "*overturned, and be followed by a Jacobin or Revolutionary system, though not that of Buonaparte.*" Quoted in Sir Archibald Alison, *Lives of Lord Castlereagh and Sir Charles Stewart* (Edinburgh & London: Blackwood, 1861), vol. 3, 627. The *Esquisse historique*, p. 77, states that at Haguenau the representatives of the foreign powers gave positive assurances of "not wishing to interfere over the form of our government" (trans.).

101. Henri Troyat, *Alexander of Russia: Napoleon's Conqueror* (New York: E. P. Dutton, 1982), p. 233.

102. La Harpe to Alexander I, 23 January 1818, in Jean Charles

Biaudet et Françoise Nicod, eds., *Correspondance de Frédéric-César de La Harpe et Alexandre Ier*, (3 vols.; Neuchâtel: Baconnière, 1978–1980), III, 293 (trans.); I, 38.

103. *Mémoires*, V, 312. Benjamin Constant wrote simply: "Alexandre pas différent des autres." Constant, *Journaux intimes*, 16 July 1815. Lafayette finally met Alexander after the Allies entered Paris, but by that time it was impossible to affect the restoration of Louis XVIII. A spy watching the Elysée Palace, where Alexander stayed, reported that Lafayette went there several times in the week preceding 16 July 1815. See Ernest Daudet, *La Police politique: Cronique des temps de la Restauration d'après les rapports des agents secrets et les papiers du cabinet noir, 1815–1820* (Paris: Plon, 1912), p. 9. Lafayette [copy] to Alexander, 12 July 1815, and Lafayette [copy] to [Capo d'Istria], 17 July 1815, Dean.

104. Lafayette to Mme d'Hénin, 11 July 1815, Dean (trans.). The implication here is that they would have endorsed a king who would have accepted conditions, including apparently Louis XVIII.

105. *Mémoires*, V, 515–520.

106. Gottschalk and Maddox, *Through the October Days*, p. 81.

107. Joseph Fouché, *Mémoires* (New York: Merrill & Baker, n.d.), p. 261. For Fouché's actions see Paul Robiquet, "La Disgrace de Fouché," *La Révolution française* (July–Sept. 1920), 73, 193–224.

108. Lafayette to Dupont de Nemours, 30 Oct. 1815, Hagley Museum and Library, photo at LG Papers (trans.). *Mémoires*, V, 478.

109. Fouché, *Mémoires* (English ed.), pp. 267, 270.

110. The 5 July resolution was proposed by Dupont de l'Eure. Lafayette was named to the delegation to present the resolution to the allied sovereigns. Full text in *Mémoires*, V, 541–542; Duvergier de Hauranne, *Histoire*, III, 160.

111. *Moniteur*, 7 July 1815, p. 774 (trans.). Duvergier de Hauranne, *Histoire*, III, 160-161; Houssaye, *1815*, III, 316–317. The editors of Lafayette's *Mémoires* omitted this speech, perhaps because they believed it did not show Lafayette in a good light. See Lafayette [copy] to Capo d'Istria, 17 July 1815, Dean (trans.): "I'd like to think that the only sentence pronounced at the podium in the name of my colleagues and myself regarding the meetings at Haguenau will seem to you as measured as it is truthful." In this letter to the Russian representative at Haguenau Lafayette seemed to imply that he had reported what they *said*, not what they did. Copies of the declaration passed on 5 July and of the "Compte rendu par les plénipotentiaires, 6 July 1815," signed by Lafayette, Sébastiani, and Voyer d'Argenson are in the *Esquisse historique*, p. 101.

112. Typescript of Lafayette to Crawford, 4 Aug. 1815, LG Papers. The original of this letter, kept in Special Collections of the University of Chicago, has been lost. Benjamin Constant remarked in his diary on

Lafayette's great courage on this occasion. Benjamin Constant, *Journaux intimes*, p. 443, 8 July 1815.

113. Albert Gallatin to Thomas Jefferson, 27 Nov. 1815, in Adams, *Writings of Albert Gallatin*, I, 666.

114. Typescript of Lafayette to Crawford, 4 Aug. 1815, LG Papers.

115. See Ezio Cappadocia, "The Liberals and Madame de Staël in 1818," in Richard Herr and Harold T. Parker, eds., *Ideas in History* (Durham, N.C.: Duke University Press, 1965), pp. 182–198, for an example of liberals' reluctance (for political reasons) to countenance criticism of Bonaparte.

116. See Maurois, *Adrienne*, for Mme de Simiane's ties to the Lafayette family and for Adrienne's surprising willingness to accept Mme de Simiane as her friend. Charles de Rémusat wrote that, when he came to know the Lafayette family in the late 1820s, his mother-in-law (Emilie) "admired her still in memory. She was, I believe, a woman more amiable than witty, just as she was more graceful than beautiful. She broke definitely with Lafayette in 1814, although she had not been for a long time in tune with his opinions. But the Restoration made the disagreement more acute, and furthermore, she had for a long time been under the influence of the abbé de Montesquiou." Rémusat, *Mémoires*, II, 235 (trans.). Mme de Simiane was a close friend of Mme d'Hénin's and related to Talleyrand and Louis XVIII's minister of the interior, Montesquiou. Her brother, also a royalist, defended Lyon against Napoleon at the start of the Hundred Days. Maurois, *Adrienne*, pp. 352–353, 376. Houssaye, *1815*, III, 258–259.

117. Lafayette [copy] to the Duchesse de Broglie, 2 Oct. 1830, Archives de Broglie, in the LG Papers (trans.).

118. *Mémoires*, VI, 3, 6. This letter carries no addressee's name, but Mme de Simiane is the most likely recipient. Many earlier letters in *Mémoires* without name of correspondent are to her, and the circumstances discussed in the letter are consistent with their relationship.

119. This issue is discussed at length in notes he wrote after his release from Austrian imprisonment. See "Sur la démocratie royale de 1789 et le républicanisme des vrais constitutionnels," *Mémoires*, III, 191–215.

120. *Mémoires*, VI, 7–8, 12.

121. *Mémoires*, VI, 14.

122. Cited in Gordon Wood, *The Creation of the American Republic, 1776–1787* (Chapel Hill: Univ. of North Carolina Press, 1969), p. 55. Wood points out that the two phrases most often invoked were *liberty* and *public good*. He explains: "To eighteenth-century American and European radicals alike, living in a world of monarchies, it seemed only too obvious that the great deficiency of existing governments was precisely

their sacrificing of the public good to the private greed of small ruling groups." Wood, *Creation*, pp. 53–55.

123. *Mémoires*, VI, 19, 23.

124. *Mémoires*, VI, 27, 31–32.

2. Liberalism in Retreat

1. Lafayette to Humboldt, 9 July 1815, Archives Départementales de Seine-et-Marne 132F2.

2. Lafayette to Crawford, 21 Aug. [1815] and 7 Nov. 1815, Special Collections, University of Chicago. Lafayette to Jefferson, 8 Sept. 1815, Chinard, p. 375. Lafayette to Gallatin, 14 Dec. 1815, AG Papers, Reel 28. Lafayette [copy] to Madison, 11 Nov. 1815, University of Virginia Library. Lafayette [copy] to Crawford, 11 Nov. 1815, University of Virginia Library. The adventures of the French emigrants in the United States are recounted in Jesse S. Reeves, "The Napoleonic Exiles in America: A Study in American Diplomatic History, 1815–1819," *Johns Hopkins University Studies in Historical and Political Science*, series XXIII, no. 9–10 (Sept.–Oct. 1905), pp. 526-656.

3. Typescript of Lafayette to Crawford, 4 Aug. 1815, LG Papers.

4. Lafayette [copy] to [Capo d'Istria], 17 July 1815, Dean (trans.). The letter refers only to a *"femme malheureuse"* but a footnote in Lafayette's hand identifies her as the duchesse de St Leu, the title given to Hortense by Louis XVIII.

5. The meeting began on 22 Aug. 1815. Others elected were the president of the electoral college St-Cricq (also head of the customs service), Huerne de Pommeuse, and Clermont-Mont St Jean (both large landowners and nobles). AN C1303, Seine-et-Marne. Adolphe Hugues, *Le département de Seine-et-Marne de 1800 à 1895* (Melun: de E. Drosne, 1895), pp. 535–554.

6. See Arnaud Chaffanjon, *La Fayette et sa descendance* (n.p.; Berger-Levrault, 1976), pp. 290–295, 173.

7. Lafayette to William Crawford, 7 Nov. 1815, Special Collections, University of Chicago.

8. Paul Robiquet, "La Disgrace de Fouché," p. 315. Constant, *Mémoires sur les Cent Jours*, p. 224.

9. Lafayette to Jefferson, 21 Jan. 1816, Chinard, p. 379. See *Mémoires*, V, 541–542 for a copy of this declaration.

10. Lafayette to Crawford, 7 November 1815, Special Collections, University of Chicago. The National Assembly passed a bill reforming the court system on 9 October 1789. Lafayette had advocated such a change because he feared the National Guard would be unwilling to make arrests of people disturbing the peace if they were to be tried in these semimili-

tary courts which denied them a public trial and other procedural guarantees. Gottschalk and Maddox, *Through the Federation*, p. 13; *Through the October Days*, pp. 247–248, 320–321. Charles E. Freedeman, "Cours Prévotales," in Edgar Leon Newman, ed., *Historical Dictionary of France from the 1815 Restoration to the Second Empire* (2 vols.; Westport, Conn.: Greenwood Press, 1987), I, 275–276.

11. Lafayette to [Mme de Simiane, 1816], *Mémoires*, VI, 24. Lafayette to Jefferson, 21 January 1816, in Chinard, pp. 378–379.

12. Bertier de Sauvigny, *La Restauration*, p. 130.

13. Lanjuinais to Lafayette, 8 Nov. 1815, Dean. On this subject see Duvergier de Hauranne, *Histoire*, III, 278–279; and AP, vol. 15, pp. 117–118, 169–172, and 205–207.

14. Voyer d'Argenson, *Discours et opinions*, I, 212 (trans.); Broglie, I, 279–280.

15. AP, vol. 15, p. 99 (trans.). See Lafayette's comments on persecution of Protestants in *Mémoires*, V, 534, and in Lafayette to [Mme de Simiane, 1816], *Mémoires*, VI, 8.

16. Lafayette to Jefferson, 21 Jan. 1816, in Chinard, p. 379 and Lafayette to [Madison], 25 Jan. 1816, Historical Society of Pennsylvania, photo in LG Papers. The speech is in AP, vol. 16, pp. 13–17; Broglie was not given an opportunity to deliver his speech in debate.

17. On Broglie's trip, see his *Souvenirs*, I, beginning p. 337. Constant's paternity is discussed in J. Christopher Herold, *Mistress to an Age* (Indianapolis: Bobbs-Merrill Company, 1958), pp. 174–175.

18. Lafayette to Gallatin, 3 Sept. 1816, AG Papers, Reel 28; Lafayette to Alexandre Baudouin, 5 Sept. 1816, Bibliothèque de Versailles, typescript in LG Papers.

19. Winfield Scott to Lafayette, 28 Dec. 1815, Dean. Lafayette did not attend.

20. Lafayette to Jefferson, 16 Apr. 1816, in Chinard, pp. 380–381.

21. Lafayette to Gallatin, 14 July 1816, New-York Historical Society, AG Papers, Reel 28.

22. Parker had been associated with the bankers, the Baring brothers. Katherine T. Abbey, "The Land Ventures of General LaFayette in the Territory of Orleans and State of Louisiana," *The Louisiana Historical Quarterly*, XVI (July 1933), 370. See Stanislaus Murray Hamilton, ed., *Writings of James Monroe*, (7 vols.; New York: Putnam's, 1898–1903), I, xxviii, where a Daniel Parker is described as the owner of a ship, *The Empress of China*, in 1784. In France, Parker lived with the wife of Henry Preble, Commodore Preble's brother. The irregularities of this arrangement seemed to raise few eyebrows, as Parker was an accepted member of the American community in France, though at least one member of that community disapproved of him. See William Lee, *A*

Yankee Jeffersonian: Selections from the Diary and Letters of William Lee of Massachusetts, edited by Mary Lee Mann (Cambridge, Mass: The Belknap Press of Harvard Univ. Press, 1958), pp. 61, 264. One of Mrs. Preble's daughters was married to Joel Barlow's nephew. On Americans who made fortunes in the French Revolution, see Yvon Bizardel, "Un acquéreur de biens nationaux: Richard Codman de Boston," *Bulletin de la Société de l'histoire de Paris et de l'Ile de France*, vol. 92 (1965), 67–73. On Parker's investments in national lands see Louis Bergeron, *Banquiers, négociants et manufacturiers parisiens du Directoire à l'Empire* (Paris: Ecole des hautes études en sciences sociales, 1978), p. 86. George Ticknor who visited Draveïl in the summer of 1817 called it "a fine establishment, worthy of an English nobleman from its magnitude, its completeness, and its hospitality." George Ticknor, *Life, Letters, and Journals of George Ticknor* (2 vols.; Boston: Osgood, 1876), I, 146.

23. Lafayette to Gallatin, 18 Aug., 3 Sept., and 24 Oct. 1816; Gallatin to Lafayette, 6 Sept. 1816; Gallatin to Madison, 14 Sept. 1816; AG Papers, Reel 28.

24. See Abbey, "The Land Ventures of General Lafayette," pp. 359–373.

25. Jefferson to Lafayette, 17 May 1816, 23 Nov. 1818, and 8 Mar. 1819, in Chinard, pp. 381–383, 397.

26. Thomas Jefferson to Lafayette, 17 May 1816, in Chinard, p. 383.

27. See Le Gallo, *Les Cent Jours*, for example, who criticizes the Chamber for not being loyal to Napoleon.

28. William H. Crawford to Lafayette, 22 Apr. 1816, Dean; Lafayette to Crawford, 8 August 1816, Special Collections, University of Chicago. Crawford's opinions were perhaps influenced by his correspondence with George William Erving, who wrote to him from Paris in the summer of 1815 explaining why Napoleon had left his army. "The republican character of the house of representatives, & all its proceedings subsequent to his departure (probably he had also certain knowledge on the subject) instructed him of a certain danger, — it is the more probable that they were watching for an opportunity of dethroning him, since (as Lafayette says) the representatives beleived that he meant to dethrone them; this struggle has lost both him & them." Erving believed Napoleon's abdication was an error. George William Erving to William H. Crawford, 16 July 1815, William Harris Crawford Collection, Duke University. Erving was American minister to Madrid from 1814 to 1819.

29. Lafayette to Jefferson, 16 Aug. 1816, in Chinard, p. 384.

30. Lady Morgan to Lafayette, "ce samedi" [3 Aug. 1816], Dean (trans.). Although the letter is not dated, 3 Aug. 1816 is the likely date. Lafayette's invitation to them, dated 30 July 1816, is in a private collection; a typescript is in LG Papers.

31. Alexander von Humboldt to Lafayette, "ce mardi," [Aug. 1816], Dean.

32. Elizabeth Suddaby and P. J. Yarrow, eds., *Lady Morgan in France* (Newcastle upon Tyne: Oriel Press, 1971), pp. 139, 140, 142.

33. Lafayette to Gallatin, 3 Sept. and 15 Sept. 1816, AG Papers, Reel 28.

34. Ternaux (1763–1833) owned textile establishments which manufactured fashionable cashmere shawls. He experimented with the introduction of Asian breeds of sheep and goats into France. Lafayette often conferred with him about sheep raising. His estate at Saint-Ouen was described by Lady Morgan in *France*. See Suddaby and Yarrow, *Lady Morgan*, pp. 285–293. See entry by James K. Kieswetter in Newman, *Historical Dictionary*, II, 1038–1039.

35. Lafayette to Ternaux, 13 Sept. 1816, catalogue entry, sale of 26 Mar. 1971, Charavay, in LG Papers (trans.).

36. Lanjuinais to Lafayette, 28 Sept. 1816, Dean (trans.). Still without an election law, the government once again called the old Napoleonic colleges, and prefects once again could add to the lists of voters.

37. Lafayette to Voyer d'Argenson, 22 Sept. 1816, Université de Poitiers, no. 2 (trans.).

38. AN C1303, Seine et Marne. Lafayette's name is number 45 on the first round of voting for deputy and number 71 on the second round on 5 October 1816. The deputies chosen were St.-Cricq (the president of the college), Mesnager de Germigny, and Despatys.

39. Lafayette to Voyer d'Argenson, 24 Oct. [1816], Université de Poitiers, no. 35.

40. Voyer d'Argenson, *Discours et opinions*, p. 275.

41. Lafayette to Voyer d'Argenson, "mardi au soir" [Nov. 1816] and 21 Nov. [1816], Université de Poitiers, nos. 42 and 38.

42. Herold, *Mistress to an Age*, pp. 468–469. Benjamin Constant, *Oeuvres* (Paris: Gallimard, 1957), p. 788; Lafayette to Voyer d'Argenson, 24 Oct. [1816], Université de Poitiers, no. 35 (trans.).

43. Lafayette to comte de Suffren, 14 Dec. 1816, Lilly. Despite the help of a lawyer, Tripier, and of his aunt, the marquise de Lusignem, Lafayette had not succeeded in collecting this debt. Mme de Lusignem, whom Lafayette refers to as his aunt, was actually the second wife of the marquis de Lusignem, who had first been married to Lafayette's maternal aunt. L. R. Lusignem to Lafayette, 27 November 1816, Dean. Lafayette to Tripier, 26 Dec. 1816, Historical Society of Pennsylvania, photo in LG Papers. Idzerda, *Lafayette*, is helpful for sorting out Lafayette's friends and relations, especially the chart in vol. I, xliv–xlv.

44. Lafayette to Voyer d'Argenson, "lundi," Université de Poitiers, no. 74. Though this letter is undated, it appears to have been written in

1816 since all those mentioned were elected in 1816. Though Laffitte's name is not in the letter, there are reasons to think he is meant. He is described as "*notre excellent collegue*," probably a reference to his being in the Chamber of the Hundred Days. On 27 December 1816, Lafayette responded to a letter from Marc-Antoine Jullien: "Your letter of 21 December, Sir, dates from the day on which I was supposed to dine at M. Lafitte's before returning here. Our meeting did not take place; I was obliged to leave the next morning." Lafayette to Jullien, 27 Dec. 1816, photo in LG Papers of letter in Bibliothèque de Besançon (trans.). The undated letter notes that Lafayette picked out the day for the meeting and "chose Friday, intending to leave the next day." The dates and days match those for 1816 (trans.).

45. Voyer d'Argenson, *Discours et opinions*, pp. 295–296. *Mémoires*, V, 541 (trans.).

46. Jardin, *Histoire du libéralisme politique*, p. 234, notes Benjamin Constant's commitment to the three-hundred-franc contribution as a requirement for voting without showing the context of the political debate in which it was expressed.

47. Lafayette to Mr. Mercer, 26 Oct. 1816, in catalogue issued by Paul C. Richards, no. 190, item 371.

48. Lafayette AD—Notes for a speech on individual freedom, sent to Voyer d'Argenson, [12? Jan. 1817] (trans.); Lafayette to Voyer d'Argenson, "dimanche au soir," [12? Jan. 1817], Université de Poitiers, nos. 106 and 34. Voyer d'Argenson's speech, given on 15 Jan. 1817, did not incorporate any of Lafayette's ideas. Voyer d'Argenson, *Discours et opinions*, I, 304. Lafayette directed Voyer d'Argenson to Gallatin for the correct details on the American story.

49. Lafayette to Lady Morgan, 10 Feb. 1817, photocopy in Lafayette Mss., Lilly. Location of original unknown.

50. Though the word *indépendant* came to dominate the political discourse, Lafayette used the term *patriotique* to mean essentially the same thing.

51. Charles H. Pouthas, *Guizot pendant la Restauration: préparation de l'homme d'état* (Paris: Plon-Nourrit, 1923), p. 138.

52. Lafayette often used the word *party* to refer to intransigent royalists, presumably opposed to the "real" sovereign, the people.

53. Some Americans prided themselves on the absence if bitter party animosity during the presidential election of 1816. See, for example, Jefferson to Gallatin, 6 June 1817, AG Papers, Reel 29, in which Jefferson says he is pleased that there is "scarcely any agitation" in a presidential election now. See also Eliza P. Custis to Lafayette, 18 Feb. 1817, Dean: "party violence has greatly subsided & in a short time, James Madison leaves the chair of State, & James Monroe will succeed to it

without contest—all now seem disposed to live in peace & good fellowship & I hope they will continue so." See Richard Hofstadter, *The Idea of a Party System* (Berkeley: Univ. of California Press, 1969).

54. Lafayette [copy] to Crawford, 26 May 1814, Brown University Library.

55. Jefferson to Lafayette, 14 Feb. 1815, in Chinard, pp. 367–368.

56. Quoted in Duvergier de Hauranne, *Histoire*, III, 362 (trans.).

57. Bertier de Sauvigny writes that the name *indépendant* hid "all the enemies of the regime who dared not manifest their true allegiance: republicans, Bonapartists, Orleanists." Bertier de Sauvigny, *La Restauration* p. 145 (trans.). Lafayette's relationship to the Bourbons was more complicated than this.

58. Lafayette to Voyer d'Argenson, 26 Apr. [1817], Université. de Poitiers, no. 30. Lafayette's automatic assumption that proper political institutions are a prerequisite for prosperity can be seen in his suggestions to d'Argenson regarding a speech: "And since one is taking advantage of the opinion of free peoples, I will cite one which to judge by its public and private prosperity has not remained behind in social organization." Université de Poitiers, no. 106, Lafayette AD—Notes for a speech on individual freedom, sent to Voyer d'Argenson [12? Jan. 1817] (trans.).

59. See Félix Ponteil, *Histoire de l'enseignement, 1789–1964* ([Paris]: Sirey, 1966), pp. 191–194. See also M. Gontard, *L'Enseignement primaire en France de la Révolution à la loi Guizot* (Paris: Belles Lettres, [1959]).

60. AN F^{17} 11775—Enseignement Mutuel, Prefect to Minister of Interior, 4 Dec. 1817; Report by Prefect to Société pour l'instruction élémentaire, 26 Mar. 1817; Reports on state of schools sent by Prefect to Minister of the Interior; Minister of the Interior to the Société d'encouragement pour l'instruction élémentaire, 28 Feb. 1819. Other individuals who sponsored schools in Seine-et-Marne included the duc de Choiseul Praslin, M. de Greffulhe, and the comte de Mun. *Enseignement mutuel* would suffer a serious decline in the 1820s following ultras' control of the ministry.

61. GWL to Bonne Chevant, 4 Oct. 1818 and 21 Nov. 1818, Dean. See Lafayette to Sir Charles Morgan, 30 Oct. 1816, facsimile in *Lettres autographes composant la collection de Madame G. Whitney Hoff* (Paris: P. Cornuau [etc.], 1934), opp. p. 50, University of Chicago Rare Books, Z42f.H7. Here, Lafayette advises Morgan that the system would solve some of the problems in Ireland.

62. The young Jullien, son of a delegate to the Convention, Jullien de la Drôme, had been an ardent supporter of Robespierre and a friend of Gracchus Babeuf's, whom he met in prison after Thermidor. Jullien

backed General Bonaparte, believing that he was the savior of the republic. His disillusioned letter of protest after Bonaparte's calculated arrest of Jacobins in 1800 destroyed his chances for promotion, though he continued his position as an army commissioner. V. Daline, "Marc-Antoine Jullien après le 9 Thermidor," *Annales historiques de la Révolution française*, vol. 36 (1964), 159–173; vol. 37 (1965), 187–203; vol. 38 (1966), 390–412. Lafayette was interested in Jullien's campaigns for educational reform. Lafayette to Jefferson, 25 Feb. 1814, Harvard College Library, bMS AM. 1583 [photo at LPP]. At the Second Restoration, Jullien wrote articles promoting views which Lafayette shared: "Nécessité pour les députés . . . de se rattacher . . . au principe de la monarchie constitutionnelle et à l'observation rigoureuse de la charte" and "De la division des pouvoirs, considérée comme l'un des principes nécessaires de la monarchie constitutionnelle." Listed in Helmut Goetz, *Marc-Antoine Jullien de Paris (1755–1848): L'Evolution spirituelle d'un révolutionnarie* (Paris: Institut pédagogique national), p. 233.

63. *Manuel électoral*, p. 57 (trans.). Lafayette to Mme Jullien, 9 Oct. 1817, New York Public Library, photo at LG Papers [printed in Gaillard Hunt, *Fragments of Revolutionary History* (Brooklyn, N.Y.: The Historical Printing Club, 1892; reprinted by Arno, 1971), p. 64, but misdated as 1814]; Lafayette to Gallatin, "Thursday Morn" [1817], AG Papers, Reel 30. This revision never appeared. The *Manuel électoral* was reprinted without major changes for use in the elections of the following year.

64. *Censeur européen*, I, 346.

65. *Censeur européen*, II, 144 (trans.).

66. Comte and Dunoyer had published an earlier version of the *Censeur* beginning in the First Restoration and continuing through the Hundred Days, an enterprise that might also have had the backing of Voyer d'Argenson. In his memoirs, the duc de Broglie recalls that at that time he was already friendly with the editors. Broglie, *Souvenirs*, I, 294. Lafayette praised their patriotic devotion in his recollections of the First Restoration. *Mémoires*, V, 331.

67. "Notice historique" in J. B. Say, *Oeuvres diverses de J. B. Say*, ed. by Charles Comte, E. Daire, and Horace Say (Osnabrück: Otto Zeller, 1966; reprint of 1848 edition), pp. i–xviii.

68. Cited in *Censeur européen*, II, 179 (trans.).

69. Augustin Thierry, review of Jullien's *Manuel électoral*, *Censeur européen*, II, 164 (trans.).

70. The extent of these ties has not been previously understood. See Ephraïm Harpaz, "'Le censeur européen'; histoire d'un journal industrialiste," *Revue d'histoire économique et sociale*, 37 (1959), 185–218; 328–357; and Leonard P. Liggio, "Charles Dunoyer (1786–1862)

and French Classical Liberalism," *The Journal of Libertarian Studies*, I (1977), 153–178. Harpaz does not indicate the ties between Lafayette and Voyer d'Argenson and the editors of *Censeur*. The two politicians are mentioned only as potential candidates recommended in the journal and as members of a group that came to the aid of the arrested editors. Harpaz, " 'Le Censeur européen,' " pp. 330–331, 339n. Ezio Cappadocia, "The Liberals," p. 187, erroneously describes the *Censeur* as the paper expressing the views of the center of the Chamber and of the Chamber and of the *doctrinaires*. The paper's view on Mme de Staël were probably dictated by personal considerations. After all, d'Argenson's stepson was married to her daughter.

71. Harpaz, " 'Le censeur européen,' " pp. 205–206.

72. Thierry to Virginie de Lasteyrie, cited in A. Augustin-Thierry, "Augustin Thierry d'après sa correspondance," *Revue des deux mondes*, 6 (1 Nov. 1921), 153 (trans.). The letter was written in 1853 in response to Virginie's praise of Thierry's new book, *Essai sur le Tiers-Etat*.

73. *Censeur européen*, III, 9–192. They concluded that the book was the work of Bonaparte.

74. Lafayette had received a copy of this work in May from the editor, Franklin's grandson, before Thierry's visit to La Grange. This volume of the *Censeur* also included reviews of works by Lanjuinais, Bentham, and Benjamin Constant, and the beginning of Thierry's series on the English revolutions, based on books lent to him by Lafayette. See document at La Grange, "Liste des ouvrages envoyés a Mr Thierry," 15 Oct. 1818, notes in LG Papers.

75. See Harpaz, " 'Le Censeur européen,' " beginning p. 339 for an account of the trial. Harpaz, " 'Le Censeur européen,' " p. 213. Lafayette to Messieurs Treuttel et Würtz, 28 May 1817, photocopy at LPP of letter at Minnesota Historical Society. Lafayette to Voyer d'Argenson, 2 June 1817, Université de Poitiers, no. 5. Louis Gottschalk's notes of document at La Grange dated 15 October 1818: "Liste des ouvrages envoyés à Mr Thierry," LG Papers.

76. Lafayette to Voyer d'Argenson, 2 June 1817, Université de Poitiers, no. 5.

77. Invitation to Albert Gallatin, dated 28 June 1817, signed by John Rodman, P. E. Howard, B. E. Bremner, and I. Mosher, Jr., AG Papers, Reel 29. Lafayette to Gallatin, "Thursday Morn," [3 July 1817], AG Papers, Reel 30. GWL to Bonne Chevant, 25 Dec. 1816, 30 Jan., 15 Mar.. and 3 June 1817, Dean. George had been planning this trip since the previous December. He originally told Bonne Chevant he would arrive in Apr., but he was delayed until June. The original intention of the trip, then, was not to help alleviate the famine at La Grange as some writers have suggested. The source of this story is apparently Jules Cloquet,

Recollections of the Private Life of General Lafayette (London: Baldwin and Cradock, 1835), p. 241.

78. Ticknor, *Life, Letters, and Journals*, I, 139, 12 June 1817. Ticknor was also a guest at the dinner.

79. Lafayette to Voyer d'Argenson, 12 July 1817, Université de Poitiers, no. 47 (trans.).

80. Herold, *Mistress to an Age*, pp. 466–467. Lafayette to Voyer d'Argenson, 28 July 1817, Université de Poitiers, no. 48 (trans.).

81. Barante to Madame Anisson du Perron, 29 Aug. 1817, in Amable-Guillaume-Prosper-Bruguière Barante, *Souvenirs du Baron de Barante, 1782–1866* (6 vols.; Paris: Calmann-Lévy, 1890–1901), II, 294 (trans.).

82. Ticknor, *Life, Letters, and Journals*, I, 151–152. Lafayette to Comte de Mun, [3] Sept. 1817, Lilly.

83. Lafayette to Voyer d'Argenson, 18 Aug. 1817, Université de Poitiers, no. 6.

84. Lafayette was in Paris during the last week in January for much of February, for the first two weeks in April and again in the middle of June. There is no evidence on his whereabouts during most of May. He could have made another trip to Paris in the middle of May.

85. Duvergier de Hauranne, *Histoire*, IV, 221, for example, wrote that liberal politics in 1817 was directed by a committee made up of Laffitte, Manuel, Constant, and Lafayette. Vaulabelle's fuller description asserted that after the ordinance of 5 September, some liberals, "MM. Voyer-d'Argenson, Comte, Dunoyer and Gévaudan, among others, had gotten together during the last session at M. de la Fayette's. Others in the opposition, who had openly supported the government of the Hundred Days, like General Thiard and Benjamin Constant, soon swelled the ranks of the first group. The group became rather numerous; with the approach of elections, toward the month of August, the meetings multiplied. . . . They decided to get together in turn at the homes of la Fayette, Benjamin Constant, and General Thiard, all of whom lived on the rue d'Anjou, in the faubourg Saint-Honoré." Achille de Vaulabelle, *Histoire des Deux Restorations jusqu'à la chute de Charles X* (10 vols.; nouvelle ed.; Paris: Garnier Frères, [1874?], V, 422 (trans.). Though Vaulabelle's identification of a core made up of Lafayette, Voyer d'Argenson, Comte, and Dunoyer is obviously accurate, there are several problems with this description. Lafayette and Constant did not live in the rue d'Anjou in 1817. When in Paris, Lafayette usually stayed with his daughter Mme Charles de Latour-Maubourg at rue des Saussaies no. 9. He acquired a flat at rue d'Anjou no. 35 in the fall of 1818, and did not move to rue d'Anjou no. 6 (the house in which he died) until 1826. His daughter's home was just around the corner from the rue d'Anjou and would have provided no

obstacles to visits from friends in the neighborhood, but this inaccuracy calls into question the rest of the story, especially the description of increasingly frequent meetings as the elections approached. Lafayette's travels would have precluded such gatherings. Voyer d'Argenson was away from Paris all summer visiting spas for his health. Lafayette to Voyer d'Argenson, 2 June 1817, Université de Poitiers, no. 5 and Lafayette to René d'Argenson, 18 Aug. 1817, Université de Poitiers, no. 6.

86. Lafayette to Voyer d'Argenson, 12 July 1817, Université de Poitiers, no. 47.

87. Lafayette to Girot Pouzol, 11 Aug. 1817, photocopy at LPP, location of original unknown.

88. Pozzo di Borgo to Nesselrode, 7/19 Aug. 1817, in Charles Pozzo di Borgo (ed.), *Correspondance diplomatique du comte Pozzo di Borgo, ambassadeur de Russie en France, et du comte de Nesselrode depuis la Restauration des Bourbons jusqu'au congrès d'Aix-la-Chapelle (1814–1818)* (2 vols.; Paris: Calmann Lévy, 1890-1897), II, 184–185 (trans.).

89. Richelieu to Decazes, "ce mardi" [1817], Bibliothèque Nationale, N. A. Fr. 20280 (trans.). Richelieu's sister, Mme de Montcalm, wrote that Laffitte offered to drop Lafayette and Constant but insisted on Manuel, and so the negotiations failed. Armande Marie Antoinette, marquise de Montcalm-Gozon, *Mon journal, 1815–1818, pendant le premier ministère de mon frère* (Paris: Editions Bernard Grasset, [c. 1936]), p. 298. For George's version of this event, see GWL to Bonne Chevant, 11 Sept. 1817, Dean. He says merely that Laffitte turned down the request.

90. AN C1294A, Seine, 1817.

91. Lafayette to Sir Charles Morgan, 9 Nov. 1817, Lilly (trans.).

92. Lafayette to Voyer d'Argenson, 7 Oct. 1817, Université de Poitiers, no. 7 (trans.).

93. Pozzo di Borgo to Nesselrode, 21 Sept./3 Oct. 1817, in Pozzo di Borgo, *Correspondance diplomatique*, II, 235–236 (trans.).

94. Lafayette to Sir Charles Morgan, 9 Nov. 1817, Lilly.

3. Politics at Home

1. Lafayette to Jefferson, 10 Dec. 1817, in Chinard, pp. 391–393.

2. Lafayette to Lady Morgan, 12 Feb. 1818, Lilly (trans.).

3. On the family background, see Marthe Kolb, *Ary Scheffer et son temps, 1795–1858* (Paris: Boivin, 1937). Duvergier de Hauranne, *Histoire*, IV, 200–202. Arnold Scheffer's *Considérations sur l'état actuel de l'Europe* was strongly anti-British, blaming them for all misfortunes in France since 1789.

4. Lafayette to Voyer d'Argenson, 14 Dec. [1817], Université de Poitiers, no. 39 (trans.). On 10 August 1792, an uprising in Paris

deposed Louis XVI and made way for the Jacobin dictatorship. On 18 Fructidor (4 September 1797), the government of the Directory with the help of the army engineered a coup d'état against royalists and cancelled elections in forty-nine departments. The "civil list" refers to the portion of the budget under the king's control for supporting the court and providing pensions at his discretion. It was quite large during the reign of Louis XVIII. See chapter 9 of Philip Mansel, *The Court of France, 1789–1830* (Cambridge: Cambridge Univ. Press, 1988), pp. 175–184.

5. Lafayette to Arnold Scheffer, 14 Dec. [1817], in Jean Psichari, "Lettres inédites du général La Fayette," *La Revue, ancienne Revue des revues*, XLIII (1er et 15 décembre 1902), 531 (trans.).

6. Lafayette to Arnold Scheffer, 14 Dec. [1817], in Psichari, "Lettres," p. 531 (trans.).

7. C. A. Scheffer, *De l'Etat de la liberté en France* (Brussels: Demat, 1818), pp. 1–16.

8. *Moniteur*, 12 Jan. 1818, p. 48 (trans.).

9. Lafayette to Voyer d'Argenson, "mercredi" [probably 24 Jan. 1818], Université de Poitiers, no. 102 (trans.).

10. Lafayette to Arnold Scheffer, 12 Mar. 1818, Franklin D. Roosevelt Library, photo at LPP (trans.).

11. Sentence was handed down on 30 Mar. 1818. AN F⁷ 6659; *Moniteur*, 1 Apr. 1818, p. 401; Kolb, *Ary Scheffer*, pp. 73–79.

12. Promissory note for six-hundred francs signed C. A. Scheffer, 30 Mar. 1818, Dean. The presence of this note in Dean raises the possibility that Lafayette paid it off. Lafayette to Arnold Scheffer, 2 May 1818, and Lafayette to Ary Scheffer, 3 May 1818, in Psichari, "Letters," pp. 533–535.

13. Lafayette to Voyer d'Argenson, 9 Nov., 8 Dec., 14 Dec. 1817, Université de Poitiers, nos. 8, 27, 39. Thierry is referred to throughout as d'Argenson's "neighbor." The clue that this is Thierry appears in the first letter, where Lafayette asks about "a commentary on Montesquieu" that he believed he had lent this person at La Grange. Thierry's review of this book appeared in the *Censeur* in the spring of 1818. See note 75, chapter 2. Lafayette's scrupulous avoidance of the author's name points as well to an anonymous work.

14. *Le ministère vengé, ou Apologie victorieuse de la nécessité d'une législation de la presse, des lois, ordonnances et règlemens sur la presse, et de la loi du 9 novembre 1815, dans son application aux écrits: par un Constitutionnel salarié.* For proof that this was the work of Thierry, see Ephraïm Harpaz, "Sur un écrit de jeunesse d'Augustin Thierry," *Revue d'histoire littéraire de la France* (July–Sept. 1959), no. 3, pp. 342–364. Harpaz calls this "a real declaration of war on the ministerial attitude, concerned only with securing income and stifling

non-ministerial opinion." Harpaz, " 'Le Censeur Européen,' " p. 208 (trans.). The identity of the author must have leaked out because the notice of the pamphlet, which appeared in the *Censeur*, stated: "The author of this apology is M. THIERRY." *Censeur européen*, VI, 394.

15. He complained that he had not yet received the copy he had ordered. Lafayette to Voyer d'Argenson, 18 December [1817], Université de Poitiers, no. 28. The work was *Questions sur la législation actuelle de la presse en France et sur la doctrine du ministère public, relativement à la saisie des écrits et à la responsabilité des auteurs et imprimeurs* (Paris: Delaunay, 1817).

16. Benjamin Constant's turbulent relations with Mme de Staël are well known. At a dinner at Mme de Staël's, the American George Ticknor praised Pozzo di Borgo's wit to Schlegel, who responded that there was nobody equal to him but Benjamin Constant. Journal entry of 6 May 1817, in Ticknor, *Life, Letters, and Journals*, I, 130–131.

17. Despite the close friendship between Lafayette and d'Argenson, the latter's name rarely appears in biographies of Lafayette. See Broglie's perceptive description of his step-father's character in Broglie, *Souvenirs*, I, 100–101.

18. The journal was published at irregular intervals to avoid censorship.

19. John Russell, sixth Duke of Bedford (1766–1839). Lafayette to Gallois, "dimanche 3 mai" [1818], AN 138 AP213. Bedford to Lafayette, 27 Apr. 1818, Dean. Gallatin to John Quincy Adams, 4 May 1818, AG Papers, Reel 30. Destutt de Tracy to Jefferson, 11 Apr. 1818, in Gilbert Chinard, *Jefferson et les Idéologues* (Baltimore: Johns Hopkins Press, 1925; Paris: Presses Universitaires de France, 1925), p. 178.

20. See Gottschalk, *Between the American and French Revolution*, pp. 244, 263.

21. Gottschalk and Maddox, *Through the Federation*, pp. 251–257.

22. Ruth Necheles, *The Abbé Grégoire*, pp. 195–207.

23. Lafayette to Thomas Clarkson, 1 Sep. 1814, in Melvin D. Kennedy, *Lafayette and Slavery from his letters to Thomas Clarkson and Granville Sharp* (Easton, Pa.: The American Friends of Lafayette, 1950), p. 33. Lafayette to Thomas Clarkson, 28 Aug. 1815, Benjamin Franklin Papers, Yale University.

24. Gallatin to Lafayette, 30 Mar. 1818, AG Papers, Reel 30. The Swiss-born Gallatin complied with Lafayette's request, though he protested that they would be poorly written because in the last thirty-seven years he had written no more than fifty pages in French. See document at La Grange, "Liste des ouvrages envoyés a Mr Thierry," 15 Oct. 1818, notes in LG Papers. Charles Dunoyer, "Du projet de loi relatif à l'abolition de la Traite," *Censeur européen*, VII, 297 (trans.).

25. Lafayette [copy] to Pétion, "mai 1818," Dean. See obituary in *Minerve*, IV, p. 429. Montègre died on 4 September 1818 at thirty-eight years of age. He was described as a contributor to the *Dictionnaire des sciences médicales*. The *Journal des débats* (28 Dec. 1818) identified him as the *rédacteur* of the *Gazette de santé*. See also an obituary of 2 Jan. 1819. An entry on him appears in the *Biographie des hommes vivants*, (5 vols.; Paris: L. G. Michaud, 1816–1819), IV, 470. Montègre had been one of the men who tried to gain the release of Comte and Dunoyer in 1817. *Censeur européen*, IV, 311. As proof of his liberalism, Lafayette cited Montègre's membership in the society promoting *enseignement mutuel*, which he assumed the president also supported. Here Lafayette's republican sympathies led him astray, as Christophe was apparently a more enthusastic advocate of *enseignement mutuel* than was Pétion. See, for example, the descriptions of Haiti by W. W. Harvey, *Sketches of Hayti from the Expulsion of the French to the Death of Christophe* (London: F. Cass, [1971], reprint of 1827 edition).

26. Lafayette to Grégoire, 23 July 1818, notes in LG Papers of letter in private collection, Paris. For more on the suspicions of Pétion's intentions, see David Nicholls, *From Dessalines to Duvalier: Race, Colour and National Independence in Haiti* (Cambridge, G. B.: Cambridge Univ. Press, 1979), pp. 49–53, and Leslie F. Manigat, "Le Délicat Problème de la critique historique," *Revue de la Société haitienne d'histoire, de géographie et de géologie* (Oct. 1954), pp. 29–59.

27. Lafayette subsequently received a letter from Pétion's successor, General Boyer, acknowledging receipt of his letter and praising Lafayette as a defender of rights and of the independence of nations. Jean-Pierre Boyer to Lafayette, 15 Oct. 1818, Dean. This letter is catalogued at "1819" but it must be in error, since Boyer describes Montègre's death as recent and because Lafayette mentions receiving the letter from Boyer in a letter to Voyer d'Argenson dated 7 August, which from its other content can be logically dated to 1819. Lafayette to Voyer d'Argenson, 7 Aug. [1819], Université de Poitiers, no. 99.

28. Spitzer, *Old Hatreds*, pp. 28–32.

29. Lafayette to Fabvier, "lundi,' [Feb. 1818?], Benjamin Franklin Papers, Yale University. It is filed at [1822], but this is certainly in error.

30. Guillaune de Bertier de Sauvigny, *Le Comte Ferdinand de Bertier (1782–1864) et l'énigme de la Congrégation* (Paris: Presses Continentales, 1948), pp. 288–296.

31. Quoted in Roger Langeron, *Decazes: Ministre du roi* ([Paris]: Hachette, 1960), p. 182 (trans.).

32. Lafayette to Voyer d'Argenson, 14 July 1818, Université de Poitiers, no. 10 (trans.).

33. The minister of justice, Pasquier, maintained that the fear of

implicating highly placed people prevented a vigorous investigation. Etienne-Denis Pasquier, *Mémoires du Chancelier Pasquier* (6 vols.; Paris: Plon, Nourrit, 1893–1895), IV, 241–250. Charles-Guillaume Etienne wrote that the ministers could not "as they had during the last elections, depict the departments as preys to revolutionary influence; that would be to side with the authors of the *Note secrète*, which they have themselves consigned to public indignation." *Minerve*, III, 266 (trans.).

34. *Journal des débats*, 7 May 1818, p. 3.

35. Lafayette to Voyer d'Argenson, 4 May [1818] and 5 May [1818], Université de Poitiers, nos. 33 and 31 (trans.).

36. Mérilhou was a lawyer and active political organizer. Fayolle was the author of a brochure entitled "Lettre au Roi" which was seized by the police. *Censeur*, vol. 4, p. 300. Paul Bastid, *Benjamin Constant*, I, 314, suggests that this dinner was sponsored by the *Société des amis de la liberté de la presse* founded by "Tracy, Voyer d'Argenson, Broglie, La Fayette father and son and Benjamin Constant after the imprisonment of Chevalier, the director of the *Bibliothèque historique*, for an attack directed against the ministry. They met at the home of Broglie, Constant or Manuel. They also organized banquets. One dinner for four hundred people would be offered in May 1818 in honor of the deputies of the party" (trans.). It seems unlikely that this society sponsored the banquet. On the society, see below.

37. On criticism of Laffitte, see *Journal des débats*, 18 May 1818, p. 1. On liberal organization in 1818, compare the account of Vaulabelle, *Histoire des deux Restorations*, IV, 506: "We have already shown, on the occasion of the first elections to replace a fifth [of the Chamber], how the electoral committee of the *indépendants* had been formed. This committee had extended its contacts and strengthened its organization since the elections of 1817; the meeting place remained at the homes of General la Fayette, General Thiard, and Benjamin Constant; but the number of participants had increased" (trans.).

38. See invitation to Gallatin signed by Isaac Cox Barnet, Theo. Lyman, and Henry Preston, in AG Papers, Reel 30. Lafayette to Voyer d'Argenson, 14 July 1818, Université de Poitiers, no. 10 (trans.). An American who attended the dinner recounted that the restaurant was "decorated with great magnificence" and that Lafayette, as one of the honored guests, "sat in the middle of the crescent in which shape the tables were disposed." He believed Lafayette must be about forty-five years old; he was actually sixty. Franklin J. Didier, *Letters from Paris and Other Cities of France, Holland, &c. Written during a Tour and Residence in These Countries in the Years, 1816, 17, 18, 19, and 20* (New York: James V. Seaman, 1821), pp. 207–208.

39. Lafayette to Cadet de Gassicourt, 9 July [1818], Benjamin

Franklin Papers, Yale University. Lafayette to Albert Gallatin, 12 July 1818, AG Papers, Reel 31.

40. Victor Jacquemont to Achille Chaper, 4 Apr. 1825, in J. F. Marshall, ed., *Victor Jacquemont, Letters to Achille Chaper: Intimate Sketches of Life among Stendhal's Coterie* (Philadelphia: The American Philosophical Society, 1960), p. 96 (trans.).

41. J. B. Say to Bentham, 13 Oct. 1823, Louis Gottschalk's notes of Bentham Mss., portfolio 10, folder 19, in LG Papers. See Lafayette to Voyer d'Argenson, 4 May [1818], Université de Poitiers, no. 33 for what may be a reference to Comte's stay: "M. Charles is still here and so far is doing well" (trans.). Cloquet, *Recollections*, p. 180, says Comte was given asylum there. Harpaz, " 'Le Censeur européen,' " p. 343, reports Comte's flight from the authorities, but he does not report where he sought asylum. On the trial, see *Censeur européen*, VIII, 315–342, and X, 285.

42. Lafayette to Voyer d'Argenson, 14 July 1818, Université de Poitiers, no. 10 (trans.).

43. Lafayette to Voyer d'Argenson, 14 July 1818, Université de Poitiers, no. 10.

44. GWL to Bonne Chevant, 4 Oct. 1818, Dean (trans.). Lady Sydney Morgan, *Passages from my Autobiography* (New York: Appleton, 1859), p. 93. Lafayette to Victor Jacquemont, 4 Oct. 1818, in Pierre Maës, *Un ami de Stendhal. Victor Jacquemont* (Paris: Desclée de Brower, n.d.), p. 592. Lafayette to Sir Charles Morgan, "Monday morning," [7 Sept. 1818], in Morgan, *Passages*, p. 75. Henry Richard Vassal Fox, Lord Holland, was the nephew of the Whig politician Charles James Fox, who had championed Lafayette's cause during his imprisonment.

45. Notes of document at La Grange, "Liste des ouvrages envoyés à M. Thierry," 15 Oct. 1818, in LG Papers (trans.).

46. Lafayette to Victor Jacquemont, 4 Oct. 1818, in Maës, *Jacquemont*, p. 592. The *Journal des débats* of 6 Sept. 1818 noted her presence in Paris and remarked that they could no doubt soon expect to be again repaid for their hospitality by "very superficial and sometimes absurd judgments on our manners, our societies, our theaters, our literature, by epigrams against the most distinguished individuals who, after having opened their salons to the famous traveler, will then have the pleasure of seeing their names and their remarks circulate throughout Europe with variations and little instructive notes" (trans.).

47. Lafayette to Lady Morgan, 12 Feb. 1818, Lilly. One of Lafayette's friends, Mme Bignon, "indignant at the mutilations" in the translations that had already appeared, had translated the omitted portions which she intended to publish separately. The translator of *Florence Macarthy* and of *France* responded to criticism of his translations by accusing Lady Morgan of vanity and by saying that he had made changes

in his translations of Sir Walter Scott's works, too, because he knew what would sell. *Journal des Débats*, 8 Feb. 1819. Mme Bignon's translation of the omitted portions was subsequently published anonymously in Brussels. Though Lafayette did not mention her by name in his letter to Lady Morgan, he did say she was the lady mentioned to her by Dr. Montègre, and other correspondence makes it clear that this refers to Madame Bignon. Madame Bignon died during the summer of 1818. Lafayette to Voyer d'Argenson, 14 July 1818, Université de Poitiers, no. 10. Dr. Montègre to Lady Morgan, 22 Oct. 1817, in Lady Morgan, *Passages*, p. 156. Lafayette to Lady Morgan, 12 Feb. 1818, Lilly. Lafayette to Grégoire, 23 July 1818, typescript in LG Papers of letter in a private collection.

48. The pamphlet was published by the liberal editor Alexander Baudouin. In early September, Colonel Carbonel spoke to him regarding books and notes lent by Lafayette apparently for this project. The motto allows us to date the pamphlet since it is a quotation from Etienne's "Lettres sur Paris, no. 28," dated 6 October, appearing on 10 October 1818. *Minerve*, III, 458 (trans.). The work is at the Bibliothèque Nationale, Ln^{27}.10919, and its authorship was previously unknown.

49. Augustin Thierry to Lafayette, 10 Oct. [1818], Photo in LG Papers of Huntington Library, HM9427 (trans.). The letter is catalogued at 1820, but this must be an error because there were no elections in Seine-et-Marne in October 1820, nor was Lafayette running for election in 1820.

50. Lafayette to Ary Scheffer, 13 Aug. 1818, in Psichari, "Lettres," pp. 536–537. This contradicts the statement in Agnes Mongan, *Harvard Honors Lafayette* (Cambridge: Fogg Art Museum, 1976), p. 122, that by 1818 Ary "was already a familiar and favored figure in the Lafayette household at La Grange." Mongan's source is Kolb (*Ary Scheffer*) who makes this remark a propos of the painting done in 1822, not the earlier one.

51. Lafayette to Arnold Scheffer, 15 Oct. 1818, in Psichari, "Lettres," p. 538 (trans.). Psichari rendered a portion of this letter as *"publiée en même temps que l'original et présentée à la candidature de Seine-et-Marne,"* but presenting the lithograph as a candidate does not really make sense. I think Lafayette's handwriting here has been misinterpreted. It is more likely that he wrote: *"en même temps que l'original est présenté"*. On 6 October 1818, Ary Scheffer reported to Mme de Tracy that he hoped to bring her the lithograph of the general's portrait the next day (Dean). On 16 October, Lafayette reported that he had received the day before *"le paquet de M. Scheffer,"* perhaps the completed lithographs. Lafayette to Marchand, 16 Oct. 1818, LG Papers, photo of letter in a private collection. See also Lafayette to Arnold Scheffer, 17 Nov. 1818, in Psichari, "Lettres," p. 540. The lithograph prepared at this time was perhaps only of the head.

52. Morgan, *Passages*, p. 102. For another example of the use of portraits in a campaign, see Goyet to Benjamin Constant, 18 Jan. 1819, Benjamin Constant and Goyet de la Sarthe, *Correspondance, 1818–1822* ed. by Ephraïm Harpaz (Geneva: Droz, 1973), p. 28.

53. See Françoise Wacquet, *Les Fêtes royales sous la Restauration, ou L'Ancien régime retrouvé* (Genève: Droz, 1981) for a survey of royalist pageantry. The original of the Scheffer portrait is at La Grange. Scheffer made two copies of it in 1822: one is in Washington, D. C., and the other at the Fogg Art Museum at Harvard University. This likeness was the basis of a great number of lithographs and engravings. Mongan, *Harvard Honors Lafayette*, p. 122; Charavay, *Le Général La Fayette*, p. 614; Marc Miller, "Lafayette's Farewell Tour and American Art," in *Lafayette, Hero of Two Worlds* (Hanover: Univ. Press of New England, 1989), pp. 146, 175–191.

54. Rémusat, *Mémoires*, II, 227 (trans.).

55. See Marcus Cunliffe, *George Washington: Man and Monument* (Boston: Little Brown, 1958) on Washington's attempt to live up to a classical ideal.

56. Rémusat, *Mémoires*, II, 227–228 (trans.).

57. Stendhal, *Souvenirs d'Egotisme* (Paris: Le Divan, 1927), p. 56 (trans.).

58. Quoted in Langeron, *Decazes*, p. 214 (trans.).

59. Lafayette to Gallois, 3 Aug. [1818], AN 138 AP213.

60. Pozzo di Borgo to Nesselrode, 27 Aug./Sept. 1818, in Pozzo di Borgo, *Correspondance diplomatique*, II, 591.

61. *Minerve*, III, 422–423. Georges Ribe, *L'Opinion publique et la vie politique à Lyon lors des premières années de la Seconde Restauration* (Paris: Sirey, 1957), pp. 334–335, states misleadingly that the election was postponed because it was a by-election. The Basses-Pyrénées was also holding a by-election, but the college met there on the earlier date.

62. The departments of the Sarthe, Nord, Gard, and Finistère (all part of the second series) were scheduled for the twenty-sixth. In addition, by-elections to fill vacancies in Paris and the Rhône were also scheduled for the later date. *Moniteur*, 27 Sept. 1818, p. 1143; 3 Oct. 1818, p. 1167; *Conservateur*, I, 81.

63. Lafayette to Marchand, 16 Oct. 1818, LG Papers, copy courtesy of a private collector. Min. of the Interior to Prefect of Seine-et-Marne; 9 June 1818, 1 July 1818, 14 Sept. 1818, Archives Départementales de Seine-et-Marne, 3M23. AN F1C III Seine-et-Marne 4, "Elections-1818." Lafayette to Girot-Pouzol, 4 Aug. 1818, photo at LPP, location of original unknown. Lafayette to Gibert, 2 Oct. [1818], photo at LPP of letter at the Society of the Cincinnati, Anderson House Museum. Gibert is identified

as Mayor of Courpalay in documents filed in 1822 to prove Lafayette's eligibility. AN C1303.

64. Auguste-Jean Germain, comte de Montfort (1786–1821). *Nouvelle Biographie générale* (Paris: Didot, 1858), XIX, 240–241. He was first appointed prefect of Saône-et-Loire. At the Second Restoration he was named to Seine-et-Marne. His skillful handling of the election of 1818 earned him a peerage in 1819. He was removed as prefect after the fall of Decazes. Guizot pointed to the results in Seine-et-Marne as proof of his contention that government losses were attributable to maintaining ultra prefects who antagonized the local populations. Pouthas, *Guizot pendant la Restauration*, pp. 202–204. Rémusat, *Mémoires*, I, 332–333. Broglie, *Souvenirs*, II, 11.

65. GWL to Bonne Chevant, 4 Oct. and 21 Nov. 1818, Dean (trans.).

66. Draft of a letter from the Prefect of Seine-et-Marne to the Mayor of Melun, 28 Sept. 1818, Archives Départementales de Seine-et-Marne, 3M23.

67. The pamphlet was called *Réflexions d'un electeur*. AN F1C III Seine-et-Marne 4, "Elections-1818," Printer's bill. Printing costs, which included lists of voters, were 1,936.85 francs.

68. Charles de Rémusat to his mother, 20 Oct. 1818 and 25 Oct. 1818, in Charles de Rémusat, *Correspondance de M. de Rémusat pendant les premières années de la Restauration* (6 vols.; Paris: C. Lévy, 1884–1886), V, 28, 38 (trans.).

69. Duvergier de Hauranne, *Histoire*, IV, 482.

70. Morgan, *Passages*, p. 174. The duc d'Angoulême was next in line to the throne after his father.

71. Lafayette to Victor Jacquemont, 4 Oct. 1818, in Maës, *Jacquemont*, p. 592.

72. *Minerve*, III, 121–122, 331, 327, 241.

73. Lafayette to [unknown], "lundi matin" [Sept. or Oct. 1818?], Dean (trans.). This letter (which begins "*Je vous envoïe, mon cher collegue, une lettre pour M. Say, ami de M. Creary libraire anglais très recommandable*") can be dated to the fall of 1818 because it mentions the third edition of Lady Morgan's *France*. A likely date is 12 October. It might be to Benjamin Constant, who was trying to get an English publisher for his *Mémoires sur les Cent Jours*. Morgan, *Passages*, pp. 187–189. See also Lafayette to Marchand, 16 Oct. 1818, copy in LG Papers of letter in a private collection, where he expresses the same fear that planting will keep farmers away.

74. AN C1303 Seine-et-Marne; AN F1C IIISeine-et-Marne 4, "Elections-1818." Printed instructions sent from Minister of the Interior to Prefect of Seine-et-Marne, 26 Sept. 1818, Archives Départementales de Seine-et-Marne, 3M23. *Minerve*, III, 510, 545.

75. *Minerve*, III, 128, 616.

76. *Conservateur*, I, 294 (trans.).

77. For further analysis of this election, see Sylvia Neely, "Lafayette and Liberal Politics in the Early Restoration," Ph.D. Dissertation, University of Notre Dame, 1981.

78. GWL to Charles Goyet, 22 Oct. 1818, Galpin.

79. In a letter to the *Minerve* on 26 December 1818 (inserted in the *Propagateur*), Goyet said he began suggesting candidates in June. *Propagateur*, 1819, p. 613. The first reference to Lafayette in the *Propagateur* occurred in issue no. 20 which must have been published in July because the previous issue (no. 19) includes a description of the new prefect who was named on 8 July.

80. Lafayette to Marchand, 16 Oct. 1818, copy in LG Papers of letter in a private collection (trans.).

81. Goyet to Voyer d'Argenson, 27 Apr. 1818, Galpin.

82. The *Mercure* was the forefunner of the *Minerve*. Ephraïm Harpaz, *L'Ecole libérale sous la Restauration, le "Mercure" et la "Minerve," 1817–1820* (Geneva: Droz), p. 395. Goyet's friendship with Marchand might have originated when the *Censeur européen* reported on Rigomer Bazin's treatment in the Sarthe. Despite being freed by the courts, Bazin spent five months in prison in 1817 when Jules Pasquier arrested him under the law allowing jailing "disturbers of public order" without trial. Max Grignon, "Le parti libéral dans la Sarthe de 1815 à 1830," *La Révolution dans la Sarthe*, XXII (Jan.–Dec., 1927), 35. Harpaz, " 'Le Censeur européen,' " p. 346.

83. Sebastien Bottin, *Almanach du commerce de Paris, des départemens de la France, et des principales villes du monde* (Paris: Au Bureau de l'Almanach du Commerce, [1819]), p. 893. On Goyet, a good source of biographical information is the *Propagateur*. See also, *Correspondance*, p. 120. For a more thorough analysis of the election of 1818 and of politics in the Sarthe, see Sylvia Neely, "Rural Politics in the Early Restoration: Charles Goyet and the Liberals of the Sarthe," *European History Quarterly*, XVI (July 1986), 313–342.

84. On Etienne Pasquier, see James K. Kieswetter, *Etienne-Denis Pasquier: The Last Chancellor of France* (Philadelphia: American Philosophical Society, 1977).

85. In 1819, the title changed to *Propagateur de la Sarthe*. The run at the Bibliothèque Nationale lacks numbers 1, 5, and 26 of 1818, and number 37 of 1819.

86. Goyet to Benjamin Constant, 18 Jan. 1819, in *Correspondance*, p. 28.

87. Goyet to Benjamin Constant, 27 Jan. and 6 July 1819, in *Correspondance*, pp. 34 and 120.

88. Lafayette to M. Marchand, 17 October [1818], Private collection (trans.).

89. GWL to Goyet, 22 Oct. 1818, Galpin.

90. Goyet to Benjamin Constant, 27 Jan. 1819, in *Correspondance*, p. 34: "Le Mans contains 250 voters, out of which we can count on only 100 patriots at the most. Almost all the liberal voters live in the country, farmers or merchants and neither expect nor want favors from the ministers."

91. AN C 1290, Sarthe. For short biographical sketches of the two politicians, Jean-Pierre-Guillaume Delahaye de Launay (1751–1830) and Julien-Pierre-Jean Hardouin (1753–1833), see *Correspondance*, pp. 14-15. Pierre Thoré-Cohendet (1760-1829) was a rich merchant whose commercial ties made him influential throughout the department. For Pasquier's assessments of these men, see AN F[7] 4352[A], Sarthe.

92. *Propagateur*, 1819, p. 614 (trans.). In a letter to the *Censeur européen*, 25 July 1819, Goyet explained his tactics for the use of other liberal politicians.

93. *Conservateur*, I, 336 (trans.); Goyet to Benjamin Constant, 6 July 1819, in *Correspondance*, p. 120.

94. Duvergier de Hauranne, *Histoire*, IV, 479–487.

95. *Mémoires*, VI, 33. Charavay, *Le Général La Fayette*, pp. 412–413, apparently using this letter as a basis, came to the conclusion that there was a genuine chance of Lafayette's election in Paris: "*En 1818, les départements de la Seine et de Seine-et-Marne songèrent à lui offrir un siège; mais, sur l'initiative du publiciste Charles Goyet, celui de la Sarthe les devança.*" Contrary to the impression given by Charavay, the elections in the Seine and in Seine-et-Marne were completed before Lafayette's election in the Sarthe. Brand Whitlock, *La Fayette* (2 vols.; New York: D. Appleton, [c. 1929]), II, 186, repeated this misleading information. More recent biographers are not appreciably better. Peter Buckman, *Lafayette: a Biography* (New York: Paddington Press, 1977), p. 154, says only that he won in the Sarthe by 569 votes out of 1,055, after having been defeated in Paris the year before. De La Fuye and Babeau, *The Apostle*, pp. 243–244, give the vote totals and call it a "relative" victory. However, they do not indicate which department he represented. Olivier Bernier, *Lafayette: Hero of Two Worlds* (New York: E. P. Dutton, 1983), p. 289, notes that he was elected from Le Mans on 26 October 1818 (it was actually 30 October), but seems to believe that this election offered no real political challenge to the ministry: "Lafayette could not be more than a gadfly, irritating at times, but never politically dangerous." Etienne Taillemite, *La Fayette* ([Paris]: Fayard, 1989), p. 441, gets the order of these elections right and gives credit to Goyet's contribution, but states inaccurately that Lafayette was then elected in Seine-et-Marne in 1819.

96. Morgan, *Passages*, p. 174.

97. Langeron, *Decazes*, pp. 214–218 (trans.).

98. Broglie, *Souvenirs*, II, 90 (trans.).

99. Since political groups in this period were not disciplined political parties, it is difficult to state with precision what the exact numbers were, and historians often differ in their estimates. For an explanation of the totals here, see Neely, "Lafayette and Liberal Politics," 123–124. GWL said fifteen ultras had been replaced by fifteen *indépendants*. GWL to Bonne Chevant, 21 Nov. 1818, Dean. He gave liberal strength as forty; GWL to Bonne Chevant, 10 Feb. 1819, Dean.

100. Lafayette to his family, 1 Nov. 1818, in *Mémoires*, VI, 33–34. Confalonieri was in exile for participating in the 1814 Lombard independence movement against the Austrians. *Enciclopedia italiana di scienze, lettere ed arti* (n.p.: Istituto Giovannie Treccani, 1931-39), XI, p. 114.

101. Lafayette to Arnold Scheffer, 17 Nov. 1818, in Psichari, "Lettres," p. 539; Goyet to Benjamin Constant, 30 November 1818, in *Correspondance*, p. 13.

102. Lafayette to Monsieur Charolois, 11 Nov. 1818, Lilly (trans.).

103. Dupont de l'Eure to Lafayette, 2 Nov. 1818, Dean (trans.).

4. The Deputy of the Sarthe

1. He sold some sheep, but broke off negotiations to sell more because he decided that his flock was getting too small. Lafayette to Marcilly, 21 Nov. 1818, Dean. He was reading Boissy-d'Anglas's book on Malesherbes, and Lady Morgans' new novel, *Florence Macarthy*. Lafayette to [Boissy-d'Anglas], 28 Nov. 1818, Dean. Though the adressee is not given, it is certainly Boissy-d'Anglas whose book *Essai sur la vie, les écrits et les opinions de M. de Malesherbes* (Paris: Treuttel et Wurtz, 1818) was reviewed in the *Minerve*, IV, 145, in late November. Lafayette to Lady Morgan, 23 Nov. 1818, Lilly.

2. Quoted in Charavay, *Le Général La Fayette*, p. 413 (trans.).

3. Lafayette to Lady Morgan, "Wednesday morning" [9 Dec. 1818], in Morgan, *Passages*, pp. 243-245. Lafayette had extra tickets because he controlled all those to which the Sarthe delegation was entitled. Only one other member of the delegation was in Paris, Delahaye. Hardouin arrived later, and the fourth elected deputy, Thoré-Cohendet (who planned to resign), never came at all. Lafayette to Delahaye, 1 Dec. 1818, Lilly.

4. *Minerve*, IV, 296 (trans.).

5. *Conservateur*, I, 389 (trans.). The ministerial *Journal des débats* of (11 Dec. 1818) noted in its description of the royal session: "At the moment when M. le marquis de la Fayette arose to take the oath, a

304

general movement of curiosity was apparent in the hall" (trans.). He was the only deputy mentioned in the story.

6. In 1820, Lafayette's seat was in the fourth row, between Dupont de l'Eure and Grammont, according to a chart showing positions of all the deputies in April 1820. Bibliothèque Nationale Lc⁵⁵.16.

7. Albert Gallatin to John Quincy Adams, 6 Jan. 1819, National Archives, microfilm of AG Papers, Reel 31.

8. The original French reads *"pour qu'il reste patriote comme 4, il faut que nous le soïons comme 6."* Lafayette to Goyet, 17 Jan. 1818, Galpin.

9. Benjamin Constant to Goyet, 6 Feb. 1819, in *Correspondance*, p. 43.

10. Lafayette to Voyer d'Argenson, 2 June 1817, Université de Poitiers, no. 5 (trans.).

11. Lafayette to Jefferson, 10 Dec. 1817, in Chinard, p. 394.

12. "Affaires des insurgés d'Amérique," *Censeur européen*, VII, 300–311. This article (probably by Comte) appeared in a volume prepared while Comte was in hiding at La Grange.

13. Gallatin to John Quincy Adams, 4 May 1818, AG Papers, Reel 30. Lafayette's friend Destutt de Tracy also tried to interest Jefferson in the Argentine cause. Destutt de Tracy to Jefferson, 11 Apr. 1818, in Chinard, *Jefferson et les Idéologues*, p. 178. See Ricardo Piccirilli, *Rivadavia y su tiempo* (3 vols.; Buenos Aires: Ediciones Peuser, 1960), I, 234–235, for Rivadavia's report on his meetings with Lafayette and Gallatin.

14. Lafayette to General Dessole, 19 Jan. 1819, copy of a letter at La Grange in LG Papers (trans.). The letter is not in Lafayette's hand, but the signature is, as is the date. Rivadavia's friendship with Destutt de Tracy is described in Kennedy, *Destutt de Tracy*, pp. 237, 247–250, 303–304. Lafayette also arranged for the translation into French of the constitution of the Provincias Unidas del Rio de la Plata. Piccirilli, *Rivadavia*, II, 167.

15. Galpin. The letters from Lafayette to Goyet are in the possession of the Galpin family, whose ancestor, Augustin Pierre Galpin (1798–1860), was a close friend of Goyet's nephew, Ferdinand Bougard. See the *mémoire de maîtrise* analyzing these letters written by Dominique Parcollet under the direction of Maurice Agulhon at the Sorbonne.

16. Goyet to Benjamin Constant, 30 Nov. 1818, *Correspondance*, p. 13.

17. *Correspondance*, esp. p. 80; Galpin. "Mon excellent ami"; "Adieu, mon Ami. Pour la vie tout à vous"; "Mon cher Commetant"; and "Salut et sincère attachement."

18. Goyet to Constant, 22 Aug. 1819, *Correspondance*, p. 139.

19. Lafayette to Goyet, 22 Jan. 1819, Galpin. Broglie, *Souvenirs*, I, 134. René Bargeton, Pierre Bougard, Bernard Le Clère, and Pierre-François Pinaud, *Les Préfets du 11 Ventôse an VIII au 4 september 1870* (Paris: Archives Nationales, 1981), p. 239.

20. Goyet to Benjamin Constant, 27 Jan. 1819, *Correspondance*, p. 33.

21. Lafayette to Goyet, 28 and 29 Jan. 1819, Galpin.

22. Lafayette to Goyet, 14 Feb. 1819, Galpin.

23. Goyet to Benjamin Constant, 1 Feb. 1819, *Correspondance*, p. 38.

24. Constant to Goyet, 6 Feb. 1819, *Correspondance*, p. 43.

25. Constant to Goyet, 14 Feb. 1819, *Correspondance*, p. 45. Lafayette to Goyet, 9 Feb. 1819, Galpin; AP, vol. 22, p. 744.

26. Lafayette to Goyet, 14 Feb. and 17 Feb. 1819, Galpin.

27. Lafayette to Voyer d'Argenson, "jeudi" [Jan. to May 1819?], Université de Poitiers, no. 84 (trans.).

28. Joseph-François Michaud, *Biographie universelle ancienne et moderne* (reprint of 2d edition of 1854), vol. 35, pp. 137–138.

29. The ordinance of 24 July 1815 listed nineteen military men and forty-one civilians accused of complicity in the return. Many of these escaped into exile. In January 1816, the Chambers confirmed the king's ordinance and extended it by the Amnesty Law which exiled Napoleon's family and those regicides who "voted for the Acte Additionel or accepted positions or employment from the usurper" (trans.). J. B. Duvergier, *Collection complète des lois, decrets, ordonnances, règlemens, avis du conseil-d'état* (Paris: Guyot et Scribe, 1834–1918), vol. 20, pp. 14, 185.

30. Richelieu had earlier advocated breaking the "monstrous alliance" of the Bonapartists and liberals. Cappadocia, "The Liberals," pp. 196–197.

31. Benjamin Constant, "Session des Chambres," *Minerve*, V, 144–145, in Benjamin Constant, *Recueil d'articles: Le Mercure, La Minerve et La Renommée*, ed. Ephraïm Harpaz, (2 vols.; Genève: Droz, 1972), I, 703–712 (trans.).

32. Benjamin Constant to Goyet, 20 Feb. [1819], in *Correspondance*, p. 51.

33. Benjamin Constant in *Renommée*, no. 21, 5 July 1819, reprinted in Constant, *Recueil d'articles: Le Mercure, La Minerve et La Renommée*, II, 1245–1247.

34. GWL to Bonne Chevant, 10 Feb. 1819, Dean.

35. AP, vol. 23, p. 85.

36. Lafayette to Goyet, 26 Feb. 1819, Galpin. Constant to Goyet, 26 Feb. 1819, *Correspondance*, p. 53.

37. Lafayette to Goyet, 26 Feb. 1819, Galpin.

38. Quote from Laffitte's speech of 27 Feb. 1819, AP, vol. 23, p. 108 (trans.).

39. Lafayette to Goyet, 26 Feb. 1819, Galpin. On the left's adoption of the Charter, see Stanley Mellon, *The Political Uses of History: A Study of Historians in the French Restoration* (Stanford: Stanford Univ. Press, 1958).

40. *Mémoires*, VI, 34–38.

41. *Moniteur*, 6 Mar. 1819. Duvergier, *Lois*, vol. 22, p. 95.

42. Lafayette to Goyet, 3 Mar. 1819, Galpin.

43. Goyet to Benjamin Constant, 10 Mar. 1819, in *Correspondance*, p. 59. The term he used for the farmers was *cultivateurs*.

44. Lafayette to Goyet, 13 Mar. 1819, Galpin.

45. Goyet to Benjamin Constant, 22 Mar. 1819, in *Correspondance*, p. 63.

46. Lafayette to Goyet, 23 Feb. 1819, Galpin. The ministry was willing to allow Daunou's election in Finistère, even offering to name him president of the electoral college. Lafayette speculated that the enmity of the Pasquier brothers explained the government's lack of cooperation with the liberals in the Sarthe.

47. Lafayette to Goyet, 28 Mar. and 10 Apr. 1819, Galpin.

48. AN C 1290, Sarthe.

49. Broglie, *Souvenirs*, II, 82–83, recalled that in 1817 Manuel had tried to raise a subscription for those arrested under the press laws, but that this effort was abandoned when Laffitte refused his financial backing and when they concluded that it would be illegal anyway. The society came into existence the following year. This coincides with information presented at the trial of Simon and Gévaudan that the organization dated from Apr. 1818. *Procès de la Société dite les Amis de la liberté de la presse* (Paris: Librairie constitutionnelle de Brissot-Thivars, 1820), p. xxxix. Lafayette wrote to Lady Morgan in late 1818, "De Staël intends to visit you with Manuel tomorrow; he is very busy with his Society of the Press." [ca. 1 Nov. 1818], in Lady Morgan, *Passages*, p. 181 (trans.). Robert Brown asserts that a circular to raise a subscription was printed in November 1817 and signed by Victor Destutt de Tracy, Lafayette, Benjamin Constant, and Jacques Manuel. This attempt is perhaps the one cited by Broglie. Robert Brown, "Society of Friends of the Freedom of the Press," in Newman, *Historial Dictionary*, II, 997.

50. Lafayette to Goyet, 9 Mar. 1819, Galpin.

51. Duvergier, *Lois*, vol. 22, pp. 147–160, 165–167; Paul Bastid, *Les Institutions politiques de la monarchie parlementaire française (1814–1848)* (Paris: Editions du Recueil Sirey, 1954), p. 377.

52. Lafayette to Goyet, 24 Mar. and 28 Mar. 1819, Galpin.

53. Lafayette seconded amendments made by Constant and by

Manuel. Constant's amendment was to do away with the requirement that printers be licensed; Manuel's was to specify a date by which the requirement for security money would expire. AP, vol. 23, p. 730, and vol. 24, p. 218.

54. *Moniteur*, 28 Apr. 1819, p. 523. Also in *Mémoires*, VI, 38.

55. *Moniteur*, 29 Apr. 1819, p. 527 (trans.). The comtesse de Nesselrode, for example, wrote to her husband: "I hope you did not miss the letter that La Fayette wrote to M. Bellart and the latter's reply, which is charming, sharp, witty and in which he makes a point of calling him marquis." In Comte A. de Nesselrode, ed., *Lettres et papiers du chancelier comte de Nesselrode* (11 vols.; Paris: A. Lahure, [1904-1912?]), VI, 73–74 (trans.).

56. Arnold Scheffer was available to work on the *Censeur* because he had returned to and was in hiding in Paris, thus risking the sentence of imprisonment that had sent him into exile the previous year. Lafayette told Voyer d'Argenson that Scheffer "will leave his niche this evening to come to my house at nine o'clock." Letter dated "jeudi matin" [Spring 1819], Université de Poitiers, no. 69 (trans.). E. Hatin, *Bibliographie historique et critique de la presse périodique en France* (Paris: Firmin-Didot, 1866), pp. 318, 346, 327. *Correspondance*, pp. 89, 111, 102. See also, Marion Mouchot, "'Le Constitutionnel,' Contribution à l'histoire de la presse sous la Restauration," Thèse, Ecole des Chartes. Hervey is perhaps A.-C. d'Hervey, who wrote a pamphlet entitled *Réfutation du discours de M. le Vte. de Châteaubriant . . . sur le recrutement*.

57. Benjamin Constant to Goyet, 24 [26] May 1819, in *Correspondance*, pp. 102–103.

58. Goyet to Benjamin Constant, 31 May 1819, in *Correspondance*, p. 109.

59. Lafayette to Voyer d'Argenson, "jeudi matin" [Spring 1819], Université de Poitiers, no. 69 (trans.).

60. Lafayette to Voyer d'Argenson, "vendredi" [5 Mar. 1819] and "jeudi matin" [Spring 1819], Université de Poitiers, nos. 97 and 69 (trans.). The only "legislative" subscribers, according to Lafayette, were the two of them and Lanjuinais.

61. Frank E. Manuel, *The New World of Henri Saint-Simon* (Cambridge, Mass.: Harvard Univ. Press, 1956), pp. 208–210.

62. Lafayette to Goyet, 14 May 1819, Galpin.

63. Duvergier de Hauranne, *Histoire*, V, 132–141 (trans.). De Serre's statement affirmed that they would never allow the principle that regicides had a right to return. Individual regicides had, in fact, already received permission to return.

64. Several liberals later published remarks, which they had been prevented from presenting orally. Lafayette's argument for eliminating the

laws on exiles stressed the futility of laws by which "misled parties" persecuted each other alternately. When would these recriminations end, he wondered. *Mémoires*, VI, 40–42. The portions omitted from *Mémoires* can be found in AP, vol. 24, pp. 454–455. The printed version is listed in Stuart W. Jackson, *La Fayette: A Bibliography* (New York: Burt Franklin, 1968, reprint of 1930 edition), p. 154.

65. The *Conseil d'etat* eventually found in favor of Pont de Gennes, but against Montfort. *Propagateur*, 1819, pp. 508–512, 526–531, 560–569. Lafayette to Goyet, 17 and 22 Jan., 4 Feb. 1819, Galpin. Goyet to Benjamin Constant, 9 Aug. 1819, in *Correspondance*, p. 133. *Correspondance*, p. 111.

66. Lafayette to Goyet, 12 and 16 Mar. 1819, Galpin. The man suggested by the government, General Loverdo, was unacceptable to the liberals because he had fought on the wrong side during the Hundred Days.

67. Constant to Goyet, [23 Mar. 1819], 18 Apr. 1819, and [16 June 1819], in *Correspondance*, pp. 66, 79, 115.

68. Lafayette to Goyet, 17 Jan., 17 Feb., 18 Mar., and 4 May 1819, Galpin.

69. Lafayette to Goyet, 9 Mar. 1819, Galpin. See also his 1815 remarks on a constitution, which begin with local administration; *Mémoires*, V, 516.

70. Lafayette to Goyet, 10 Apr. 1819, Galpin. This excerpt (slightly altered) is also in *Correspondance*, p. 77, a reprinting of what appeared in the *Echo de la Sarthe* (17 Mar. 1821).

71. Benjamin Constant to Goyet, 18 Apr. 1819, in *Correspondance*, pp. 78–79.

72. Lafayette to Goyet, 14 May 1819, Galpin.

73. *Moniteur*, 4 June 1819, p. 721, "Séance du 2 juin."

74. *Mémoires*, VI, 44–51. The date in *Mémoires* is incorrect. The session was that of 3 June. The portions deleted in *Mémoires* can be found in the *Moniteur*, 5 June 1819, p. 724.

75. Goyet to Constant, 15 June 1819, in *Correspondance*, p. 114.

76. 29 May 1819, AP, vol. 24, 647–648 (trans.).

77. 10 July 1819, AP, vol. 25, pp. 660–661. The others were Chauvelin, Manuel, Benjamin Constant, Voyer d'Argenson, Guilhem, Daunou, Hernoux, and Corcelle. *Censeur*, 11 July 1819. Lafayette met with Bavoux in Paris in July. See Lafayette to Voyer d'Argenson, 16 July 1819, Université de Poitiers, no. 12. On this incident, see Alan B. Spitzer, *The French Generation of 1820* (Princeton: Princeton Univ. Press, 1987), pp. 35–47.

78. Franklin L. Ford, *Political Murder: From Tyrannicide to Terrorism* (Cambridge: Harvard Univ. Press, 1985), pp. 212–216.

79. Lafayette to Goyet, 20 July 1819, Galpin. Goyet to Benjamin Constant, 6 and 21 July 1819, in *Correspondance*, pp. 121, 125.

80. Lafayette to Voyer d'Argenson, "dimanche au soir" [13? June 1819], Université de Poitiers, no. 60 (trans.). Lafayette to [his family at La Grange], 17 June 1819, in *Mémoires*, VI, 52–53.

81. Seybert was in France in 1819 to put his son in school. Gallatin asserted that much of the work was composed of his own reports. Albert Gallatin [draft] to M. Becquey, 17 July 1819, AG Papers, Reel 32. Lafayette to Voyer d'Argenson, 16 July 1819 and 14 Dec. 1825, Université de Poitiers, nos. 12 and 16 (trans.). Albert Gallatin to Lafayette, 21 July 1819, AG Papers, Reel 32.

82. Adam Seybert, *Statistiques des Etats-Unis*, trans. by C. A. Scheffer (Paris: Librairie constitutionnelle de Brissot-Thivars, 1820), p. xiv (trans.). Seybert complained about the alterations and substitutions, and inserted a letter in the *Moniteur* disavowing the work. *Censeur européen*, 4 June 1820, and *Moniteur*, 29 May 1820.

83. *Censeur*, 25 Aug. 1819, pp. 3–4 (trans.).

84. *Censeur*, 22 Sept. 1819, pp. 3–4 (trans.). The articles were signed with initials "C. A." which stand for Scheffer's first two names: Charles Arnold.

85. Lafayette to Voyer d'Argenson, 16 July, 7 Sept., and 24 Oct. 1819, Université de Poitiers, nos. 12, 25, and 14. Lafayette to Madame Gardin, 19 Sept. 1819, Dean. *Censeur*, 16 Oct. 1819. Lafayette to Arnold Scheffer, "Lundi" [28 June? 1819], in Psichari, "Lettres," p. 541. *Censeur*, 23 June 1819, reported that Lafayette planned to bring up the questions of condemned writers at a secret session of the Chamber. This is, no doubt, the adjournment which Lafayette mentions in the letter to Scheffer, so Scheffer must have been in Paris by late June. See note 56 for this chapter. Reports of Féret's trial in *Homme gris* case are in the *Moniteur* of 17 and 23 May 1818. Lafayette counseled Féret to surrender, so that the reduction in his sentence could be presented to the king for his approval. Lafayette to Mme Gardin, 19 Sept. 1819, cited in Tourtier-Bonazzi, *Lafayette* p. 195.

86. Lafayette to Goyet, 20 July 1819, Galpin.

87. See, for example, *Censeur*, 1 July 1819, reporting the discussion at the meeting of the *Société des amis de la liberté de la presse* on the issue of "the compatibility of the duties of a deputy with those of a salaried agent who can be dismissed by the government" (trans.). On 29 July 1819, the *Censeur* reported that the voters of the Isère were demanding that Sappey, "a dubious candidate," pledge not to accept government office, a pledge Benjamin Constant had made earlier that year to the voters of the Sarthe (trans.).

88. Vaulabelle, *Histoire des deux Restaurations*, VI, 65. The

Censeur, however, used the term *liberal* all along, an indication perhaps of its emphasis on the principles of liberal doctrine.

89. Adolphe Robert and Gaston Cougny, *Dictionnaire des parlementaires français*, (5 vols.; Paris: Bourloton, 1890), III, 561. Lafayette to Voyer d'Argenson, [n.d.] [spring or early summer 1819], Université de Poitiers, no. 91 (trans.). Although Lafayette has written only "M. Lamb." it is probable that he is the person to whom Lafayette referred, since he is mentioned again in a letter of 7 Sept. [1819], Université de Poitiers, no. 25. *Correspondance*, p. 166n. Lambrechts had recently published a book critical of the proposed concordat of 1817, another possible reason for his choice as a candidate. "Candidats pour la Chambre des Députés (Elections de 1819)," at Bibliothèque Nationale Le⁵⁴.48. He was one of the authors of the Senate consititution rejected by Louis XVIII. Lafayette trusted his constitutional expertise. See above, chapter 1.

90. Before Lambrechts had chosen which department to represent, Lafayette received a letter from Alexandre Rousselin de Corbeau de Saint-Albin soliciting his support for the candidacy of his brother-in-law, the comte de Redern, to replace Lambrechts. He sent Lafayette information on Redern, but Lafayette explained that Lambrechts would not make his decision until he could meet with his colleagues. "One can say in advance that his opinion on that subject will be determined by the chances of success for an independent candidate; that is as well the view that M. d'Argenson will take." Lafayette to Alexandre Rousselin de Corbeau de Saint-Albin, 22 Oct. and 8 Nov. 1819, Lilly (trans.). Redern was not chosen a deputy in 1819. Lambrechts was elected in Bas-Rhin, according to the prefect, because the voters saw in him "a strong advocate" for free movement of goods and freedom of tobacco cultivation. Prefect, le Vte. Decazes, to Minister of the Interior, 15 Sept. 1819, Archives Départementales du Bas-Rhin, 2M13 (trans.).

91. Robert and Cougny, *Dictionnaire*, vol. 5, pp. 365–366. Lafayette to Voyer d'Argenson, 6 Aug. and 7 Sept. 1819, Université de Poitiers, nos. 13 and 25. Copy of Lafayette's letter dated 24 Aug. 1819, in Galpin. The publication is mentioned in the *Censeur*, 13 Sept. 1819. Tarayre, "De la Nature et de l'Organisation de la Force Armée qui convient à un gouvernement représentatif," *Censeur européen*, VI (1818), 1–29.

92. Lafayette to Voyer d'Argenson, 7 Sept. [1819], Université de Poitiers, no. 25 (trans.).

93. Abbé Henri Grégoire, *Mémoires de Grégoire*, ed. by H. Carnot (2 vols.; Paris: J Yonet, 1840), I, 412.

94. See Necheles, *The Abbé Grégoire*.

95. Ticknor, *Life, Letters, and Journals*, I, 130.

96. Grégoire, *Mémoires*, I, 251.

97. When an author sent Lafayette a book on religious issues, he

forwarded it to Lanjuinais and Grégoire, "the two men who are the most knowledgeable about the best time to use it." Lafayette to Girot-Pouzol, 4 Aug. 1818, photocopy at LPP, location of original unknown (trans.).

98. See Mellon, *The Political Uses of History*. Grégoire's work, entitled *Essai historique sur les libertés de l'église gallicane* was published in 1818 by the *Censeur européen*, an indication of his ties to this faction of the liberal coalition.

99. Goyet to Benjamin Constant, 2 Nov. 1819, in *Correspondance*, p. 183.

100. Grégoire to [?], 14 July 1819, in Grégoire, *Mémoires*, I, 209–211. The letter (possibly to Bérenger or to Duchesne, though the introductory text is not clear) mentions the correspondant's complaint that Grégoire has not answered the letters asking him to run. "The same reproach has been made to me by others, and especially by my old colleague and friend General Lafayette" (trans.).

101. Henry Dumolard, "Comment l'abbé Grégoire fut élu dans l'Isère," *Annales de l'Université de Grenoble* (1928), p. 254.

102. The two men who claimed to have first thought of electing Grégoire were natives of the Isère: Bérenger de la Drôme (so called because he had been a deputy for that department during the Hundred Days) and Joseph Rey. Alphonse-Marie Bérenger, dit Bérenger de la Drôme (1785–1866), favored Napoleon II during the Hundred Days but signed the protest at Lanjuinais's on 8 July. In 1818 he published *De la justice criminelle en France*. Another liberal coordinating the local effort was Jean-Pierre Dupont-Lavillette. According to the novelist Stendhal, who voted in the election, Dupont-Lavillette traded support for the moderate candidates Sappey and Français in return for commitments to Grégoire. Stendhal to Adolphe de Mareste, 1 Sept. 1819, in Stendhal, *Correspondance*, vol. 1 ([Paris]: Gallimard, 1962), 989–990. Jean-Pierre Dupont-Lavillette (1757–1827), a Girondist, was jailed till 9 Thermidor, became a deputy during the Hundred Days, and was exiled at the Second Restoration.

103. Rey's manuscript memoirs in the Bibliothèque de Grenoble offer interesting details of liberal activities during this period, though he exaggerates his own centrality to the movement. Rey wrote them in the late 1830s. Especially important is the manuscript entitled "Mémoires Politiques" (T3939), pp. 83–102. Rey's memoirs are summarized in Georges Weill, "Les Mémoires de Joseph Rey," *Revue historique*, vol. 158 (Jan.-Apr., 1928), pp. 291–307. An evaluation of the accuracy of these memoirs is in Spitzer, *Old Hatreds*, pp. 213–218. See also H. Dumolard, "Joseph Rey de Grenoble (1779–1855) et ses mémoires politiques," *Annales de l'Université de Grenoble*, (1927), pp. 71–111; and Richard Morris, "Joseph Rey of Grenoble, 1779–1855: Reformer, Educator, Humanitarian," Ph.D. diss., University of Iowa).

104. The chronology is not clear, but Rey's meeting with Lafayette apparently took place after Lafayette's election in the fall of 1818 since Rey says Lafayette promised to speak of it to "some of his colleagues in the Chamber of Deputies." Joseph Rey, "Mémoires Politiques," Bibliothèque de Grenoble, T3939, pp. 102–103, 112–113 (trans.).

105. Rey claims that under the influence of the Union, the *Société des amis de la liberté de la presse* was founded in 1819 and that the Union members secretly controlled the activities of the *Société*. In fact, that organization was already well established by 1819, and though its purposes and procedures were changing rapidly, it is not clear that the Union members controlled it. Of the twenty members of the Union listed by Rey, only thirteen appeared at meetings of the *Société* during 1819, according to a spy's report. AN BB[30] 192, dossier 1. Rey himself was clearly an important member of the *Société*. After he was removed from the Paris bar, the *Société* discussed his difficulties at one of their meetings. But the evidence of Rey or the Union being the directing body of this organization is lacking. Vaulabelle described a steering committee composed of the journalists and editors Cadet-Gassicourt, Cauchois-Lemaire, Châtelain, Brissot-Thivars, Larrèche, Chevallier, and Reynaud, as well as the lawyer Mèrilhou. Vaulabelle, *Histoire des deux Restaurations*, V, 59. Since newspapers were essential to liberal organization, a steering committee dominated by journalists (as described by Vaulabelle) seems plausible. Furthermore, the men he listed appear frequently in Lafayette's correspondence, perhaps indicating greater importance in liberal circles than Rey, whose name would certainly have cropped up if the Union, which he created, had been as important as he remembered. Unfortunately for our ability to sort out this relationship, letters from Lafayette to Rey, mentioned in the cover letter to file T3958 at the Bibliothèque de Grenoble, are no longer in the collection. Only letters from the late 1820s remain.

106. Staël attended only one meeting between April and October 1819, according to a spy's report. AN BB[30] 192, dossier 1.

107. *Procès de la Société dite les Amis de la liberté de la Presse*, pp. xxv–xxvi.

108. In a letter of 13 December 1819, he remarked that he had learned only the previous evening of a decision taken "*dans le conseil de la* Société de la Presse, *chez M. Manuel.*" *Mémoires*, VI, 57.

109. Dumolard, "Comment l'abbé Grégoire," p. 254.

110. Joseph Rey, "Mémoires Politiques," manuscript in Bibliothèque de Grenoble, T3939, p. 83 (trans.). The last sentence was lined through in manuscript, apparently part of the editing process for the publication of the memoirs in the *Patriote des Alpes*. Rey states categorically that a "*comité directeur* of the liberal movements, that is com-

pletely centralized, acting regularly, and giving a single impetus to its various collaborators" did not exist. What organization existed came through newspapers, especially the *Constitutionnel* and the *Censeur européen* (more principled than the former, according to Rey); through lawyers, notably Mérilhou, Odilon Barrot, Mauguin, Berville, and Barthe; and through electoral committees "established under the influence as well of the Parisian press, which alone in those days enjoyed some independence, and which would designate in its columns all the candidates chosen by the liberals of the departments, and those it wished itself to suggest for their vote. At first this organization was very incomplete, and yet it already wielded some influence in the elections of 1817; and especially in those of 1818." Joseph Rey, "Mémoires Politiques," Bibliothèque de Grenoble, T3939, pp. 67–73 (trans.)

111. Goyet to Benjamin Constant, 21 July 1819, and Benjamin Constant to Goyet, 6 Aug. 1819 in *Correspondance*, pp. 125, 130. For more on this subject, see Goyet to Benjamin Constant, 18 Oct. 1819, in *Correspondance*, p. 160. Goyet believed Hardouin's loyalty was bought by the ministry with *lycée* scholarships for his nephews. Goyet to Benjamin Constant, 21 Oct. 1819, in *Correspondance*, p. 164.

112. Barante, *Souvenirs*, II, 383 (trans.).

113. The proposal was apparently introduced by Léon Thiessé, editor of the *Lettres Normandes*, an influential provincial newspaper. *Correspondance*, p. 128. See Lafayette to [his family at La Grange], 7 July 1819, in *Mémoires*, p. 53, on early departures of deputies toward the end of the session.

114. *Censeur*, 11 Aug. 1819, p. 2 (trans.).

115. Benjamin Constant's letter of 25 July 1819, *Renommée*, reprinted in Benjamin Constant, *Recueil d'articles: Le Mercure, La Minerve et La Renommée*, II, 1256–1258.

116. Dumolard, "Comment l'abbé Grégoire," pp. 265–267.

117. Albert Gallatin to William H. Crawford, 17 July 1817, AG Papers, Reel 29. Albert Gallatin to John Forsyth, 5 May 1819, AG Papers, Reel 32.

118. Goyet to Benjamin Constant, 17 and 20 May 1819, in *Correspondance*, pp. 93, 97.

119. Lafayette to Goyet, 14 May 1819, Galpin.

120. Lafayette had earlier tried to recruit Durrieu as military commander of Le Mans.

121. Lafayette to Durrieu, 5 Aug. 1819, Special Collections, University of Chicago, and same to same, 12 Sept. 1819, catalogue entry in LG Papers (trans.). See chapter 6, note 21, for another letter to Durrieu discussing conspiracy.

122. It is possible as well that the "misunderstanding" was a

derailed conspiracy of some sort. Broglie mentions that he knew of one. Broglie, *Souvenirs*, II, 87. See below, chapter 5.

123. Paul Leuilliot, *L'Alsace au début du XIXe siècle; essai d'histoire politique, économique et religieuse, 1815–1830* (3 vols.; Paris: S.E.V.P.E.N., 1959–1960), I, 259–264. In the first issue of 5 January 1820, Marchand is identified as previously attached to the *Censeur européen*. The *Patriote alsacien* was printed in double columns, one in French, the other in German. It announced that it would maintain contact with Germany and report uncensored news from there. Bibliothèque Nationale et Universitaire de Strasbourg, M.39.061.

124. Lafayette to Voyer d'Argenson, 22 Sept. 1816, Université de Poitiers, no. 2 (trans.).

125. Lafayette to Voyer d'Argenson, "dimanche au soir" [12 Jan. 1817?], Université de Poitiers, no. 34 (trans.).

126. Lafayette to Voyer d'Argenson, 12 July 1817, Université de Poitiers, no. 47 (trans.).

127. It would be useful to check the correspondence of other revolutionaries during the Empire and the Restoration to see if examples of similar usage can be found. Maurice Agulhon, *Marianne into Battle: Republican Imagery and Symbolism in France, 1789–1880* (Cambridge, G.B.: Cambridge Univ. Press; and Paris: Editions de la Maison des Sciences de l'Homme, 1981), p. 9, argued that the name began as a derisive connotation by enemies of the republic and that only during the Second Republic was it adopted by supporters. Christian Laux, "D'Où Vient Donc Marianne?" *Annales Historiques de la Révolution Française*, 55 (1983), 628–633, demonstrated that the name had been used in the south of France early in the French Revolution by republicans, but assumes that the usage was abandoned until the Second Republic. Lafayette's use of the term shows that it was more widespread than previously believed and that A. Debidour's article on "Marianne" in the *Grande Encyclopédie* which dated the origin of the term to the secret societies of the Restoration, probably has more merit than Agulhon was willing to give it. The term *angélique* may be an allusion to the goddess of liberty, a frequent symbol during the Revolution.

128. Morris, "Joseph Rey," pp. 91–92. Hoefer, *Nouvelle biographie générale depuis les temps les plus reculés jusqu'à nos jours* (Paris: Firmin Didot frères, 1857–1866), vol. 29, p. 267, says Ledru des Essarts was given command in 1818 and was replaced in 1819, after which he was employed in inspections.

129. Durrieu's views and his relationship to Lafayette are mysterious. He had supported Napoleon's return from Elba. Durrieu to his father, 22 Mar. 1815, in *Revue d'histoire diplomatique* (1912), p. 153. Durrieu kept his army post throughout the Restoration despite his

friendship with Lafayette, a friendship known to the authorities since Lafayette's letter to Goyet recommending him as military commander in the Sarthe was seized in 1820. the authorities released portions of this correspondence (with some changes) on the occasion of Goyet's trial and these portions have been reporduced by Harpaz in *Correspondance*, p. 60. The correct date of the letter shown there is 12 March 1819. General "L" was General Loverdo (not Lauriston, as Harpaz hypothesized), and General "R" was General Rousseau. The last paragraph is from a letter dated 28 March 1819. The originals of the letters to Goyet are in Galpin. If Durrieu was involved in a plot with Ledru des Essarts and informed his superiors about it, that might explain Ledru des Essarts's transfer. In which case, Lafayette's trust in him had been misplaced. But this is really no more than speculation. In 1828 when Durrieu was named to the French expedition to Greece, Lafayette wrote recommending his friends Fabvier and Pisa, who were already fighting there. Durrieu knew Fabvier, and Lafayette was hoping that Fabvier would be named a *maréchal de camp* in the French service. This would, he said, be an act of justice, but at the same time "an act of politics here as well as in Greece. I know in advance your views on this question." Lafayette to Durrieu, 30 July 1828, Special Collections, University of Chicago (trans.).

130. The dates also need to be confirmed. Rey says the general was removed in July, but in early August, Goyet referred to an inhabitant of Le Mans, the abbé Ledru, brother of the general, whom he described as a commander at Grenoble. Goyet to Benjamin Constant, 9 Aug. 1819, in *Correspondance*, p. 132.

131. Lafayette to Voyer d'Argenson, 6 Aug. 1819, Université de Poitiers.

5. The Fight for the Election Law

1. Lafayette to Goyet, 29 Sept. 1819, Galpin.

2. Lafayette to Voyer d'Argenson, 24 Oct. 1819, Université de Poitiers, no. 14 (trans.).

3. Broglie, *Souvenirs*, II, 91 (trans.).

4. See, for example, Goyet to Benjamin Constant, 27 Sept. 1819, in *Correspondance*, p. 149.

5. Lafayette to Monsieur Mouchet, 12 Jan. 1820, Dean. His response later in the year to a request from an old associate was, "You will have become more and more aware from reading the newspapers that I will have very little influence in the ministries, even that of war, despite my personal ties with the current minister. I have nonetheless entrusted your note to his brother, my son-in-law, and I certainly hope your cousin

obtains advancement." Lafayette to Morizot, 20 July 1820, in Jean Fromageot, *Jacques Philippe Grattepain, dit Morizot: Procureur des biens du marquis de La Fayette originaire d'Arthonnay en Tonnerrois* (Tonnerre: Société d'archéologie et d'histoire du Tonnerrois, 1982), p. 46 (trans.). Benjamin Constant described Victor Latour-Maubourg as "an ultra fanatic, and without any personal capacities. La Fayette no longer sees him." Constant to Goyet, 30 Dec. 1819, in *Correspondance*, p. 222 (trans.).

6. Benjamin Constant to Goyet, 8 Oct. 1819, in *Correspondance*, pp. 152–153.

7. Benjamin Constant to Goyet, [10 Oct. 1819], in *Correspondance*, p. 156.

8. Goyet to Benjamin Constant, 8 Nov. 1819, and Benjamin Constant to Goyet, 9 Nov. 1819, in *Correspondance*, pp. 186, 190.

9. *Censeur*, 30 Oct. 1819.

10. Auguste de Staël, for example, begged him to resign on 2 October. Jean Tild, *L'Abbé Grégoire* (Paris: Nouvelles Editions latines, 1946), p. 98. For these maneuvers, see Broglie, *Souvenirs*, II, 89–107.

11. Goyet to Benjamin Constant, 27 Oct. 1819, which includes a copy of his letter to Grégoire of the same date, in *Correspondance*, pp. 173–175.

12. Broglie, *Souvenirs*, II, 103.

13. He made this comment at Mme de Broglie's during one of his few short trips to Paris. Mme de Broglie's journal entry, 9 Oct. 1819, in Broglie, *Souvenirs*, II, 98.

14. Rémusat, *Mémoires*, II, 169–170; Charles de Rémusat to his mother, 26 Oct. 1819, in Rémusat, *Correspondance*, VI, 169. Necheles includes Lafayette among those asking him to resign, but the sources on which she based this conclusion are not clear. Necheles, *The Abbé Grégoire*, p. 218.

15. Lafayette remarked that he seemed "as he has been for the last twenty years, as unfamiliar with everything in the past that was said or printed by him or under his name, as I was myself who knew only half of it and who knew that badly." Lafayette to Voyer d'Argenson, 24 Oct. 1819, Université de Poitiers, no. 14 (trans.). Lafayette's meeting with Grégoire probably took place around 9 October.

16. Grégoire to Goyet, 5 Nov. 1819, Galpin. D'Argenson's letter to Grégoire, dated 7 October 1819 is reproduced in Tild, *L'Abbé Grégoire*, p. 99. Albertine de Broglie believed that Grégoire had almost been persuaded to resign when d'Argenson's letter arrived and changed his mind. Journal entry, 22 Oct. 1819, in Broglie, *Souvenirs*, II, 101.

17. Lafayette to Voyer d'Argenson, 24 Oct. 1819, Université de Poitiers, no. 14 (trans.).

18. Lafayette to Voyer d'Argenson, 24 Oct. 1819, Université de Poitiers, no. 14; Lafayette to [unknown], 10 Dec. 1819, *Mémoires*, VI, 54–55.

19. Lafayette to [unknown], 10 Dec. 1819, in *Mémoires*, VI, 57.

20. The law required at least half a department's delegation to be political residents of the department. Out of the four deputies of the Isère, two were said to be foreigners (though one of them disputed this classification). Grégoire, the last chosen, would therefore be ineligible.

21. Benjamin Constant to Goyet, 6 Dec. 1819, in *Correspondance*, p. 204.

22. AP, vol. 25, pp. 738–739.

23. Lafayette to Goyet, 30 Nov. 1819, Galpin. Goyet insisted to Benjamin Constant that "the immense majority wants neither a republic nor a change of dynasty, nor even the improvement of the Charter. In short, it wants the current system with an independent Chamber. To speak of improving the Charter even in a liberal direction would make you unpopular." Goyet to Benjamin Constant, 11 Dec. 1819, in *Correspondance*, p. 212. Goyet was presumably sending the same message to Lafayette.

24. Lafayette to Goyet, 13 Dec. 1819, Galpin.

25. GWL to Bonne Chevant, 6 Dec. 1819, Dean (trans.).

26. GWL to Bonne Chevant, 6 Dec. 1819, Dean. Lafayette to Goyet, 13 Dec. 1819, Galpin. Goyet to Benjamin Constant, 8 Dec. 1819, in *Correspondance*, p. 207.

27. Description of Gévaudan's friendship with Béranger in Béranger, *Lettres inédites de Béranger à Dupont de l'Eure* (Paris: Maison Pierre Douville, [1908]), pp. 9, 18.

28. *Procès de la Société dite les Amis de la liberté de la Presse*, pp. xxv-xxvi (trans.).

29. *Censeur européen*, 12 Dec. and 19 Dec. 1819.

30. Benjamin Constant to Goyet, 19 Dec. 1819, in *Correspondance*, p. 216.

31. Lafayette to Goyet, 9 Jan. 1820, Galpin.

32. Lafayette to Goyet, 22 Dec. 1819, Galpin.

33. A partial list of petitions (with the reference for each in parenthesis): Champeix in the Auvergne (Lafayette to [unknown], 9 Jan. 1820, Dean), Briançon in Hautes-Alpes, Soudeval in Manche, Lorial in Drôme (*Censeur européen*, 31 Jan. 1820), Saint-André-le Désert near Rouen, Saint-Léger-sur-d'Heune in Saône-et-Loire, three towns in Ariège, from a man named Jean Cahusac from Fleurance (Jean Cahusac to Lafayette, 25 Jan. 1820, Special Collections, University of Chicago, MS798), Meaux and Coulommiers in Seine-et-Marne (*Censeur européen*, 4 Feb. 1820), Thiers in Puy-de-Dôme, Pierrelatte in Drôme, and d'Aubusson in Creuse (*Censeur européen*, 15 Feb. 1820).

34. Lafayette to Jay, 7 Jan. 1820, catalogue entry, James Lowe Autographs, 1986, item no. 89.

35. *Censeur européen*, 16 Jan. 1820 (trans.). For more on the debate between Constant and Pasquier, especially its effect in the Sarthe, see *Correspondance*, pp. 229–239.

36. The Chambers could not initiate legislation, that was the prerogative of the king. They could, however, petition the king to propose legislation, and this was the form these speeches took.

37. Examples of abusive regulations had been appearing frequently in the *Censeur européen*. For the history of the institution, see Girard, *La Garde nationale*.

38. See Jean Vidalenc, *Les Demi-Soldes: Etude d'un catégorie sociale* (Paris: Librairie Marcel Rivière, 1955).

39. Douglas Porch, *Army and Revolution: France 1815–1848* (London: Routledge & Kegan Paul, 1974), 1–8.

40. He presented his petition to the Chamber in the closed session of 29 January 1820. The speech in support of the petition was delivered in the closed session of 10 February. Lafayette to Chambre des Députés, 29 Jan. 1820, Princeton University Library, photocopy at LPP. *Censeur*, 31 Jan. and 11 Feb. 1820. Lafayette to Goyet, 5 Feb. 1820, Galpin. *Mémoires*, VI, 60–65.

41. Lafayette to Goyet, 5 Feb. 1820, Galpin. A portion of this letter is in *Correspondance*, p. 254, with the incorrect date of 15 February assigned to it by the police who seized it. The difference of dates is, of course, significant in how one interprets the sentiments. This letter is another instance of Lafayette's praise of not acting in one's own self-interest. See Lafayette to [unknown], 13 Dec. 1819, in *Mémoires*, VI, 58, on compromises liberals were making to save the electoral law.

42. Goyet to Lafayette, 8 Feb. 1820, in *Correspondance*, pp. 247–248.

43. Constant's good friend J. J. Coulmann, who recounted the anecdote, does not indicate the tone of the remarks, but it seems likely that they were reflecting ruefully on the widely held view that Lafayette was the inveterate enemy of the Bourbons and on the injustice they felt was being done to him. J. J. Coulmann, *Réminiscences* (3 vols.; Paris: Michel Lévy, 1862–1869), I, 285–289 (trans.). Bellart, *procureur-général à la cour royale de Paris*, had supported Napoleon, then become a staunch royalist. He was the prosecutor at General Ney's trial. See above, chapter 4, for another exchange between Bellart and Lafayette.

44. Lafayette to Goyet, 17 Feb. 1820, Galpin.

45. See Benjamin Constant to Goyet, [4 Mar. 1820], in *Correspondance*, pp. 271–272.

46. Lafayette to Goyet, 19 Feb. 1820, Galpin.

47. Lafayette to Goyet, 22 Feb. 1820, Galpin. He is quoting from his letter of 20 May 1802 to Bonaparte explaining his reasons for voting against the life consulate.

48. AP, vol. 26, pp. 299–307.

49. Lafayette to Goyet, 3 Mar. 1820, Galpin.

50. Constant to Goyet, [4 Mar. 1820], in *Correspondance*, p. 271.

51. *Mémoires*, VI, 65–67.

52. Lafayette to Goyet, 10 Mar. 1820, Galpin.

53. Speech of 8 Mar. 1820, in *Mémoires*, VI, 67–70.

54. Speech of 23 Mar. 1820, *Mémoires*, VI, 70–74.

55. Lafayette to Goyet, 31 Mar. 1820, Galpin.

56. Lafayette to Goyet, 31 Mar. 1820, Galpin. A spy reported to Baron Mounier, the director of police, that Gallatin, who gave the left advice, had disapproved of the plan to walk out of the Chamber. JED to Baron Mounier, 29 Mar. 1820, AN 234 AP.

57. Lafayette to Goyet, 31 Mar. 1820, Galpin. A fragment of this letter is reproduced in *Correspondance*, p. 290.

58. See Comte d'Hérisson, *Un Pair de France policier*, vol. 1 of *Les Girouettes politiques* (3 vols.; Paris: P. Ollendorff, 1892–1894), I, beginning p. 138.

59. On the workings of the censorship system, see Albert Crémieux, *La Censure en 1820 et 1821: Etude sur la presse politique et la résistance libérale* (Paris: Edouard Cronély, 1912).

60. Lafayette told Goyet that he had "the honor of presiding" over the committee and that Mérilhou was the secretary. Lafayette to Goyet, 26 Apr. 1820, Galpin. Though I have not seen him so identified elsewhere, Lafayette's name does appear first among signatories of letters by the committee. For lists of other members, see *Censeur*, 30 Mar. and 1 Apr. 1820.

61. A copy of this letter in Lafayette's hand is in Dean. The signers were: Lafayette, Chauvelin, Manuel, Dupont de l'Eure, Laffitte, d'Argenson, Kératry, Casimir Perier, and Benjamin Constant. The members on trial were: Gévaudan, General Pajol, Etienne, Odilon Barrot, and Mérilhou. *Censeur*, 14 Apr. 1820.

62. Lafayette to Goyet, 26 Apr. 1820, Galpin. See also Benjamin Constant to Goyet, 26 Apr. 1820, in *Correspondance*, p. 310.

63. *Moniteur*, 1 July and 2 July 1820 (trans.). GWL to Bonne Chevant, 6 July 1820, Dean.

64. See Daniel P. Resnick, *The White Terror and the Political Reaction after Waterloo* (Cambridge: Harvard Univ. Press, 1966). See above, chapter 2, for Voyer d'Argenson's speech on the subject.

65. AP, vol. 27, pp. 354–355.

66. Lafayette to Goyet, 26 Apr. 1820, Galpin.

67. Benjamin Constant to Goyet, 28 Apr. 1820, in *Correspondance*, p. 312.

68. Benjamin Constant to Goyet, 7 May 1820, in *Correspondance*, p. 314.

69. Lafayette to Goyet, 7 May 1820, Galpin.

70. *Censeur*, 17 Apr. 1820.

71. *Mémoires*, VI, 75–85.

72. *Mémoires*, VI, 83.

73. Vaulabelle, *Histoire des deux Restaurations*, V, 186–187.

74. Vaulabelle dates the preliminary meetings of the conspirators to April, but his discussion of the goals of the various allied groups appears to place the decision on a common goal in June. Vaulabelle, *Histoire des deux Restaurations*, V, 186–187. The letter from Lafayette to Goyet is mentioned in Benjamin Constant to Goyet, 3 June 1820, in *Correspondance*, p. 323. It is not in Galpin.

75. *Mémoires*, VI, 85n; *Moniteur*, 28 May 1820, pp. 735-736 (trans.).

76. *Moniteur*, 28 May 1820, pp. 735–736 (trans.).

77. *Moniteur*, 28 May 1820, pp. 735–736 (trans.).

78. Attacks on Lafayette were continued by Puymarin in a speech of 29 May 1820. Vaulabelle, *Histoire des deux Restaurations*, V, 134n. *Moniteur*, 1 June and 3 June 1820.

79. Vaulabelle, *Histoire des deux Restaurations*, V, 141–144. *Moniteur*, 1 June and 3 June 1820.

80. *Moniteur*, 6 June 1820 (trans.).

81. Lafayette to Goyet, 8 June 1820, Galpin; GWL to Bonne Chevant, 13 June 1820, Dean.

82. *Moniteur*, 8 June 1820, pp. 797–798.

83. Lafayette to "mon cher collègue representant," "vendredi 9 juin" [1820], facsimile in Hippolyte Castille, *Lafayette* ("Portraits historiques, dix-neuvième siècle") (Paris: Sartorius, 1858), notes in LG Papers. Benjamin Constant told Goyet that though he had only missed one day of speaking "because my chest is ailing," the newspapers commented on it. Benjamin Constant to Goyet [10 June 1820], in *Correspondance*, p. 326.

84. Vaulabelle, *Histoire des deux Restaurations*, V, 169. For an analysis of the debate, see Alan B. Spitzer, "Restoration Political Theory and the Debate over the Law of the Double Vote," *Journal of Modern History*, 55 (Mar. 1983), 54–70. He stresses the common ground between the right and the left. But it is important to remember that those leading the debate for the left were trying to keep moderate support by emphasizing their similarities rather than their differences. Lafayette's speech did not make that attempt, but Spitzer does not mention his contribution. One of the deputies Spitzer points to as breaking with the boundaries that contained the debate was Martin de Gray, a close friend of Lafayette's.

85. Vaulabelle, *Histoire des deux Restaurations*, VI, 77–79. Broglie, *Souvenirs*, II, 87, says he could foresee already by late 1819 the direction into which Voyer d'Argenson and Lafayette were going to lead the left and mentions "machinations with pretenders such as the Prince of Orange or Prince Eugene" (trans.).But Broglie does not say when these occurred. He mentions as well an enterprise which was disclosed to him after its failure, presumably before the fall of 1819. Perhaps this is the plot described by Rey. See above, chapter 4.

86. He commented that though they were a minority in the Chamber, there was "no question" that they were a majority "in the nation . . . since a selection of a hundred thousand electors, the richest, and of course the most likely to oppose popular principles, has not been thought fit to be trusted." Lafayette to Gen. Samuel Smith, 24 Aug. 1820, Lilly.

6. The Call to Revolution

1. Lafayette to Goyet, 14 June 1820, Galpin. This is his last letter to Goyet until October, another sign of either his lack of attention to politics or of his avoiding the mail because of the government's surveillance of Goyet's correspondence.

2. Benjamin Constant complained that the liberals were not participating in the debates on the budget and were thus missing their chance to defend their interests, and yet their actions did not have the impact of a formal boycott. Benjamin Constant to Goyet, 16 June 1820, in *Correspondance*, p. 329. Lafayette to [his family at La Grange], 26 June 1820, in *Mémoires*, VI, 87. George stayed by his father's side in Paris instead of taking a scheduled trip to Chavaniac, probably to help him in his plans. GWL to Bonne Chevant, 19 Feb. and 24 June 1820, Dean.

3. Goyet to Benjamin Constant, 23 June and 2 July 1820, in *Correspondance*, pp. 331, 341–343. A letter from Lafayette to Goyet, mentioned on page 342, is not preserved in Galpin. Constant lodged a protest about this seizure in the Chamber and published a pamphlet on the question. Goyet alledged that their seizure was illegal when he had not been accused of any crime. *Correspondance*, p. 339.

4. Hérisson, *Un Pair de France policier*, p. 189: Report of 10 Apr. 1820; Lafayette to [unknown], 26 June 1820, in *Mémoires*, VI, 88; Arthur Birembaut, "Sauquaire-Souligné," *Stendhal Club*, vol. 25 (1983), 549–550. In the Spring of 1819, Sauquaire-Souligné had tried to get the support of Lafayette and Voyer d'Argenson for a newspaper he was planning. See Lafayette to Voyer d'Argenson, "jeudi matin" [Spring 1819], Université de Poitiers, no. 69.

5. GWL to Bonne Chevant, 6 July 1820, Dean.

6. Leuilliot, *L'Alsace*, I, 241–264. The authorities were pleased to see the newspaper shut down because it "was doing a lot of harm in the countryside because of its German translation" (trans.). A jury acquitted Marchand in June, but the paper never resumed publication. See correspondence between officials in Strasbourg and Decazes in Archives Départementales du Bas-Rhin, 3M19.

7. *Moniteur*, 22 July and 12 Aug. 1820. Benjamin Constant to Goyet, 23 July 1820 in *Correspondance*, p. 349.

8. GWL to Bonne Chevant, 11 Aug. 1820, Dean (trans.).

9. Lafayette to [unknown, probably Mme Soehnée], 27 July 1820, LG notes of catalog entry: Victor Degrange, *Autographes* (1951), Catalog no. 53 (trans.).

10. Lafayette's punctuation in this part of the letter seems to have been misread. Chinard has it: "there is also Sympathy Between the German and french Nations, Nay, among Us and the liberal part of the British Empire. However averse they Generally are to Mingle with an extensive Common interest, in this European Contest Between Right and privilege, france Holds the Honor." It would make more sense for the portion beginning "However averse" to refer back to the British Empire, rather than to the French, and I have so interpreted it.

11. Lafayette to Jefferson, 20 July 1820, in Chinard, pp. 398–399.

12. Spitzer, *Old Hatreds*, p. 93.

13. GWL to Bonne Chevant, 24 June and 30 July 1820, Dean (trans.).

14. GWL to Bonne Chevant, 13 June 1820, Dean.

15. Lafayette to "Messieurs les Jeunes Gens du Mans, signataires de l'Adresse aux députés," 26 Apr. 1820, Galpin.

16. Goyet to Benjamin Constant, 3 June 1820, in *Correspondance*, p. 323.

17. *Moniteur*, 20 Aug. 1820.

18. Spitzer, *Old Hatreds*, p. 45.

19. Spitzer, *Old Hatreds*, p. 42.

20. Morris, "Joseph Rey," pp. 100–101. On all of these questions, Spitzer is indispensable. A close examination of Lafayette's activities reveals that Bertier de Sauvigny's description of the plot is misleading. He writes that Richelieu prevented the coup and that "the leaders, taking fright, canceled the movement and ran for cover in the country, La Fayette in the lead." Bertier de Sauvigny, *La Restauration*, pp. 171–172 (trans.). Lafayette had spent the whole summer at La Grange, not Paris. I have no evidence that he went to Paris in August, though he could have done so for a day or two. Still, returning to La Grange is not exactly running for cover. For a possible reference to this plot, see GWL to Bonne Chevant, 11 Aug.

1820, Dean, discussed above. Conspiratorial activity was not limited to Paris, of course. Frequent travel by suspicious individuals was reported in Alsace, and on the night of 19 August, a banquet was held at Mulhouse in honor of Voyer d'Argenson. Leuilliot, *L'Alsace*, I, 270–272.

21. The Chambrun card file on Lafayette materials at La Grange lists at Côte 1568, "Liste des Secours après l'échec" of the 19 August conspiracy. One intriguing letter survives from Lafayette to a fellow conspirator in which (if I have interpreted the veiled language correctly) Lafayette tried to ascertain the fate of his friend and of other conspirators and inquire about their plans for the future. Lafayette noted that the replacement of the commander of the Légion de la Meurthe (one of the regiments most deeply implicated in the affair), "will perhaps diminish the opportunities." This mysterious letter is to the same general Durrieu with whom Lafayette had corresponded the previous year. Though Durrieu's name was mentioned by at least one confessing military man, he was never publicly implicated and his military career continued undisturbed. Lafayette to Antoine-Simon Durrieu, 3 Sept. 1820, Special Collections, University of Chicago (trans.). See Bérard's confession to General Montélégier, as reported by Marshall Marmont, 21 Sept. 1820, in Charles Nauroy, *Le Curieux*, II (Feb. 1888), 368. Bibliothèque Nationale Rés. p.Z.586.

22. GWL to Monsieur Parker, 22 Sept. 1820, Special Collections, University of Chicago. Lafayette ADS [receipt], 20 Oct. 1820, LG notes of catalogue entry: Vente Hôtel Drouot, 8 Dec. 1971, item 93.

23. See Waquet, *Les Fêtes royales*.

24. See, for example, dossiers on Martin de Gray and Beauséjour in AN F⁷ 6718, tracing their travels during 1820 and describing the banquets and serenades held in their honor.

25. AN F⁷ 6719, Lieutenant de Police to Mounier, 5 Aug., 10 Aug., 22 Aug. and 27 Sept. 1820. Prefect of Rhône to Mounier, 5 Sept. 1820 (trans.).

26. For more on the Goyet and Sauquaire-Souligné case, see AN BB³⁰ 192, dossier 5. The government took the case very seriously. The decision to bring Goyet before the authorities in Paris had the personal approval of the king.

27. Goyet to Constant, 25 Aug. 1820, in *Correspondance*, p. 372.

28. Goyet to Benjamin Constant, 3 Sept. and 15 Sept. 1820, in *Correspondance*, pp. 375, 382.

29. P. Thoré-Cohendet to Benjamin Constant, 9 and 16 Sept. 1820, in *Correspondance*, pp. 378, 383. Goyet might have gone to Paris to convince them to come. See footnote 2, *Correspondance*, p. 389. George accompanied his father to the Sarthe. My description of the visit is based on government reports and Goyet's notes on the trip, reproduced in

Correspondance, pp. 385–388. See also Gustave Rudler, "Benjamin Constant, député de la Sarthe (1819–1822)," *La Révolution dans la Sarthe*, VIII (Apr.–June 1913), 65–128.

30. Goyet, "Lettre à Mr. P . . . de la Ferté-Bernard," dated 14 Sept. 1820, enclosed in Prefect of the Sarthe to Mounier, 21 Sept. 1820, AN F^7 6718.

31. Prefect of Sarthe to Mounier, 8, 12, and 15 Sept. 1820. AN F^7 6718. The new perfect was Achille-Charles-Stanislas-Emile Le Tonnelier de Breteuil.

32. Broadside dated 23 Sept. 1820, AN F^7 6718. The same orders were given in La Ferté-Bernard and Conerré. Goyet typically attributed the prefect's change of direction to the influence of the Pasquier brothers. In his correspondance with Mounier, Breteuil mentions no conference with Goyet or with Jules Pasquier.

33. *Correspondence*, p. 387. Perfect of the Sarthe to Mounier, 25 and 27 Sept. 1820, AN F^7 6718.

34. Procureur général at Angers, 30 Sept. 1820, AN F^7 6718 (trans.). Reports on their trip can also be found in AN BB^{30}, 237, dossier 4.

35. A. Debidour, *Le Général Fabvier; sa vie militaire et politique* (Paris: Plon-Nourrit, 1904), pp. 153, 156–158, 164–169. He had recently begun a wine business to provide a cover for his frequent trips around the country.

36. Procureur général at Orléans to Portalis, 28 Apr. 1820, AN BB^{30} 192, dossier 5. In September Goyet printed a pamphlet detailing proper preparations for the elections, written in the form of a letter to a correspondent in Angers, the *chef-lieu* of the department. Goyet, "Lettre à Mr B . . . à Angers," dated 1 Sept. 1820, enclosed in Prefect of the Sarthe to Mounier, 10 Sept. 1820, AN F^7 6718.

37. They spent the night at the nearby estate of General Lauberdière. See *Correspondance*, pp. 388–406.

38. Benjamin Constant to Louise d'Estournelles, 15 Oct. 1820, and Benjamin Constant to Goyet, [25 Oct. 1820], in *Correspondance*, pp. 407, 417. While he was at La Grange, a former sub-perfect of Coulommiers, M. Frestel, came for a visit, according to the current sub-prefect. Archives Départementales de Seine-et-Marne, M10207. The pamphlet, *Lettre à M. le marquis de Latour-Maubourg, ministre de la guerre, sur ce qui s'est passé à Saumur les 7 et 8 octobre 1820* (Paris: Béchet ainé, 1820), bears the inaccurate dateline: "Blois, 10 octobre 1820." In the third printing, Constant responded to the *Moniteur's* comments on the pamphlet.

39. See Neely, "Rural Politics," p. 333.

40. [Unknown] to Lafayette, 20 Sept. 1820, LG notes of letter in the Le Puy Archives, 2E:684, no. 4.

41. Lafayette to James Madison, 22 July 1820, Dreer Collection, The Historical Society of Pennsylvania, photo at Lilly.

42. GWL to Bonne Chevant, 20 Sept. 1820, Dean.

43. Dupont de l'Eure to Lafayette, 28 Sept. 1820, Dean (trans.).

44. Lafayette to Ternaux, 28 Oct. 1820, text in LG of letter in Collection Landresse, Bibliothèque Municipale de Mantes (trans.).

45. Report of Sub-prefect of Meaux to Prefect, 7 Sept. 1820, Archives Départementales de Seine-et-Marne, M10207 (trans.). In the aftermath of the conspiracy, Mounier had asked prefects for regular reports on their departments, and they had, in turn, requested them from sub-prefects and mayors. This period is therefore rich in government reports.

46. GWL to Bonne Chevant, 20 Sept. 1820, Dean. Marchand had begun promoting George's candidacy in Alsace, and George asked Voyer d'Argenson to persuade Marchand that it was a bad idea. GWL to Voyer d'Argenson, 17 Oct. 1820, Université de Poitiers, no. 117. At the last moment, the liberals settled on Bignon, and he was elected along with Jacques Koechlin, the recently dismissed mayor of Mulhouse. Leuilliot, *L'Alsace*, I, 287–290.

47. Lafayette to Ary Scheffer, 26 Nov. 1820, in Psichari, "Lettres," pp. 541–542.

48. Duvergier de Hauranne, *Histoire*, VI, 63–64.

49. Vaulabelle, *Histoire des deux Restaurations*, VI, 238, says that seventy-six of those elected in the new departmental colleges had been in the *Chambre Introuvable*. However, this figure does not coincide with Beck's numbers. See Beck, *French Legislators*, pp. 74, 175. According to Beck, of all the seats up for election in 1820, 39 were won by the left, 187 by the right.

50. Le Comte Rolland d'Erceville was a member of the *conseil général* of the department; Huerne de Pommeuse had been in the *Chambre Introuvable*. AN C1303, Seine-et-Marne.

51. Dupont de l'Eure to Lafayette, 20 Nov. 1820, Dean (trans.).

52. Report of 23 July 1820, AN BB³⁰ 192; Goyet to Benjamin Constant, 4 Nov. 1820, in *Correspondance*, pp. 434–435.

53. Goyet to Benjamin Constant, 12 Nov. 1820, in *Correspondance*, pp. 452–453.

54. Goyet to Constant, 29 Dec. 1820, [25 Jan. 1821], and 1 Feb. 1821, in *Correspondance*, pp. 467, 484, 495.

55. Goyet to Benjamin Constant, 4 Feb. 1821, in *Correspondance*, p. 497.

56. Lafayette, Constant, and Picot Desormeaux to Bertin d'Aubigny, président des assises de la Seine, 10 Feb. 1821, in *Correspondance*, p. 504.

57. *Correspondance*, p. 503. Hérisson, *Un Pair de France policier*, pp. 357–367 has text of the petition.

58. Goyet to Lafayette, 17 Feb. and 25 Feb. 1821, in *Correspondance*, pp. 507, 509.

59. Goyet to Constant, 1 Mar. 1821, in *Correspondance*, p. 510.

60. See Hérisson, *Un Pair de France policier*, p. 138.

61. *Mémoires*, VI, pp. 99–102.

62. GWL to Tailhand, 20 Jan. 1821, Lilly (trans.).

63. Both speeches are in *Mémoires*, VI, 94–98, 106–124.

64. See AP, vol. 29, 22 Dec. 1820, beginning p. 471, and 26 Dec. 1820, beginning p. 499.

65. Broglie, *Souvenirs*, II, 197, 204–205 (trans.).

66. Debidour, *Le Général Fabvier*, pp. 169–175. Lafayette missed the party of celebration at Fabvier's release given by Madame de Tracy, but sent his congratulations. Lafayette to Fabvier, "mercredi," [14? Feb. 1821], Benjamin Franklin Papers, Yale University.

67. Debidour, *Le Général Fabvier*, pp. 180–181.

68. Lafayette to Odilon Barrot, 23 May 1821, AN 271 AP2-Ba6. The lawyers were Odilon Barrot and Saint-Albin Berville.

69. Lafayette to Odilon Barrot, 21 Feb. and 15 July 1821, AN 271 AP2-Ba6; Lafayette to Fabvier, [July 1821], Benjamin Franklin Papers, Yale University. Lafayette to Goyet, 14 July 1821, Galpin. Duvergier de Hauranne, *Histoire*, VI, 474–475. The verdict in Maziau's case was not handed down until December 1821, but the peers showed themselves once again to be quite lenient. He was found guilty of having made a proposal to conspire. Though the punishment for that crime was banishment, his sentence was reduced to five years' imprisonment. The leniency of the sentence prompted fifty-two peers to sign a protest, which appeared in the *Moniteur* and to refuse to sign the final judgment.

70. Quoted in Roy Bridge, "Allied Diplomacy in Peacetime: the Failure of the Congress 'System,' 1815–23," in Alan Sked, ed., *Europe's Balance of Power: 1815–1848* (New York: Barnes & Noble, 1979), p. 43. See Henry Contamine, "La Grande Tentative d'expansion de la Charte et l'Italie, 1820–1821," in *Atti del XXXVII Congresso di storia del risorgimento italiano* (Roma: Istituto per la Storia del Risorgimento Italiano, 1961), pp. 60–68.

71. Lafayette explained to Thomas Clarkson that "the Rules of the House are so awkward in every, proprio motu, case, that to introduce an immediate debate upon the intervention of the Congress at Layback into the interior concerns of Naples, has been a matter of some difficulty. The ice however has been broken and our complaints and declarations shall be renewed." Lafayette to Clarkson, 15 Feb. 1821, Benjamin Franklin Papers, Yale University. Colonel Jules Alix petitioned the Chamber of

Deputies to respect the Charter. Discussion of his petition led to debate over the government's respect for constitutions, including that of Naples, and Chauvelin asked the government to explain its participation in putting down the revolt. When the Chamber next met, the left continued the discussion by questioning the accuracy of the minutes. AP, vol. 29, p. 758.

72. Lafayette's remarks, 12 Feb. 1821, in *Mémoires*, VI, 94–98. The editors of the *Mémoires* omitted a portion of the second paragraph on p. 94, perhaps because it was considered too sympathetic to the Napoleonic Empire: "A famous opponent of our Revolution, M. Burke, had said that under the influence of that Revolution, France would no longer be anything but *a large void* in the European system. That prediction, greeted at the time with raptures by the spirit of party, has been overabundantly refuted by more than twenty years of glory and power; but we have at least the right to ask, to insist that . . . " AP, vol. 30, p. 2 (trans.).

73. Lafayette to [unknown correspondent in England], 15 Feb. 18[21], photocopy at LPP of letter at James Monroe Memorial Library (trans.).

74. Lafayette to Goyet, 4 Apr. 1821, Galpin.

75. Lafayette to Goyet, 12 May 1821, Galpin.

76. For details of founding, see Spitzer, *Old Hatreds*, pp. 230–233. *Mémoires*, VI, 135, dates the conspiracies to the "first months of 1821."

77. Spitzer, *Old Hatreds*, p. 235.

78. See P. F. Dubois, "Augustin Thierry," *Revue Bleue*, 5th series, X (no. 23, 5 Dec. 1908), 741–742, on use of these secret symbols.

79. Lafayette to Henry Clay, 9 June 1821, Papers of Henry Clay, Library of Congress.

80. Spitzer, *Old Hatreds*, p. 240.

81. Rémusat, *Mémoires*, II, 242 (trans.).

82. *Mémoires*, VI, 135–143.

83. *Mémoires*, VI, 137.

84. *Mémoires*, VI, 138.

85. For an analysis of the conflicting testimony on the leadership of the organization, see Spitzer, *Old Hatreds*, pp. 236–241. Duvergier de Hauranne, *Histoire*, VI, 574–575, comments on the independence of the Breton Carbonarist cells because of their long tradition of conflicts in the area. Dubois, "Augustin Thierry," p. 743, says the Breton Carbonarists constituted "the most disciplined, the most numerous and the most formidable group, if it had been called upon to act, but at the same time also the most prudent, the most independent, the most unamenable to the intrigues and the internal struggles of the Parisian *Charbonnerie*, to the bold and insane attempts which compromised several generous

souls, some entire provinces" (trans.). Lafayette, who was Breton on his mother's side, always attended the *Banquet breton* where veterans of the conspiracies met annually in later years.

86. Spitzer, *Old Hatreds*, p. 243, discusses the regions with Carbonarist cells.

87. *Mémoires*, VI, 139–140.

88. See Spitzer, *Old Hatreds*, pp. 237–241, on this vexing issue. *Mémoires*, VI, 140–142.

89. Lafayette to [unknown general], 16 May 1821, Lilly (trans.). The name of the correspondent is crossed out, but it looks like Begaret. Lafayette mentions a colonel George who apparently did not live in Paris and whom Lafayette did not know.

90. Louis Gootschalk's notes of an unsigned letter dated 20 Sept. 1820, in the Le Puy Archives, 2E:684, no. 4, LG Papers (trans.).

91. See Spitzer, *Old Hatreds*, pp. 253–254, for an analysis of this idea.

92. Lafayette to Goyet, 31 May and 5 June 1821, Galpin.

93. Lafayette to [his family?], 12 June 1821, in *Mémoires*, VI, 125.

94. *Mémoires*, VI, 106–124.

95. Indeed, the speech is so much better then his ordinary effort that one suspects substantial help from his literary friends.

96. Lafayette to Goyet, 5 June 1821, Galpin.

97. Constant to Goyet, 19 June 1821, in *Correspondance*, p. 561. Duvergier de Hauranne, *Histoire*, VI, 334–335.

98. Lafayette to [his family?], 12 June 1821, in *Mémoires*, VI, 125–126.

99. *The speech of General La Fayette, delivered in the Chamber of Deputies, in the sitting of the 4th of June, 1821, on the question of granting the public supplies* (London, Printed for James Ridgway, 1821). Copy at Benjamin Franklin Papers, Yale University, Franklin 895/1821 Lg. A copy of the speech sent by Lafayette to Sir Robert Wilson might have been the text for the translation. Lafayette to Sir Robert Wilson, 18 June 1821, British Museum, Additional 30, 116, f.49. Lafayette also sent it to James Perry who promised to mention it in the *Morning Chronicle*. James Perry to Lafayette, 5 July 1821, Dean. See *Morning Chronicle* of 2 July, 7 July, and 12 July 1821.

100. Lafayette to Monroe, 8 Aug. 1821, LG Photo of Monroe Papers, New York Public Library.

101. Lafayette to Monroe, 8 July 1821, LG Photo of Monroe Papers, New York Public Library. Lafayette to [his family], 5 July 1821, in *Mémoires*, VI, 127; Lafayette to Goyet, 14 July 1821, Galpin.

102. Quoted in Bridge, "Allied Diplomacy in Peacetime," in Sked, *Europe's Balance of Power*, p. 45.

103. Quoted in Matthew Anderson, "Russia and the Eastern Question, 1821–41," in Sked, *Europe's Balance of Power*, p. 81.

104. See Spitzer, *Old Hatreds*, pp. 202–209.

105. Lafayette to [unknown, probably Mme Soehnée], 27 July 1820, LG notes of catalogue entry: Victor Degrange, *Autographes* (1951), catalogue no. 53. Lafayette wrote: "I expect any day the mail coach from *Milan*" (trans.). See rest of quote above, this chapter. Confalonieri, a Piedmontese revolutionary, visited La Grange in 1818. See above, chapter 3. See Spitzer, *Old Hatreds*, pp. 266–272, for an analysis of the evidence on the ties between French Carbonari and other European secret societies. The connections among these groups appear to have been more extensive than Spitzer says.

106. The contacts among revolutionaries increased after the failures of some of the efforts sent people into exile where they met others in exile. They appear to have acted independently at first, then helped each other in defeat. Lafayette then became a link among the various national groups.

7. The Conspirator

1. Lafayette to Jefferson, 10 Dec. 1817, in Chinard, pp. 391–392.

2. Lafayette to Goyet, 7 Nov. 1820, Galpin. See the *Censeur* for examples of anti-British sentiment among this faction of the French left. For example, in their review of Mme de Staël's *Considérations sur la Révolution Française*, the authors criticize her for being too admiring of England. *Censeur*, XI (1819), 259. For Lafayette's views on the differences between the countries, see "Quelques Idées sur les institutions de la France, des Etats-Unis, et de l'Angleterre," Appendix III of *Mémoires*, VI, 795–805.

3. Lafayette to Sir Charles Morgan, 30 Nov. 1823, Lilly.

4. See Destutt de Tracy selection in Walter Simon, ed., *French Liberalism, 1789–1848* (New York: John Wiley & Sons, 1972), p. 47. On Tracy's analysis of Montesquieu, see Kennedy, *Destutt de Tracy*, pp. 167–183, 245.

5. Quoted in René Rémond, *Les Etats-Unis devant l'opinion française, 1815–1852* (2 vols.; Paris: Librairie Armand Colin, 1962), II, 663–664, footnote 20.

6. Cited in Simon, *French Liberalism*, pp. 113–114.

7. Pouthas, *Guizot pendant la Restauration*, p. 326.

8. Lafayette to Jefferson, 20 Dec. 1823, in Chinard, p. 417.

9. Lafayette to Alderman Wood, 15 Feb. 1821, in John A. Sainsbury, *The Napoleon Museum; the history of France illustrated from Louis XIV to the end of the reign and death of the emperor* (London,

1845), p. 580. He also wrote to Clarkson on Laroche's behalf, 15 Feb. 1821, Benjamin Franklin Papers, Yale University. Mellon, *The Political Uses of History*, p. 25. Lafayette also provided a letter of introduction to Wood for Guyet, a journalist associated with the *Renommée*. Lafayette to Alderman Wood, 14 Sept. 1820, Catalogue entry for Maggs catalogue #965, Spring 1975, item #78, in LG Papers. Sir John Bowring remembered that the abbé Grégoire promoted the marriage of Laroche with the exiled daughter of the former king of Haiti. Sir John Bowring, *Autobiographical Recollections*. (London: Henry S. King, 1877), p. 393.

10. Michael Glover, *A Very Slippery Fellow: The Life of Sir Robert Wilson, 1777–1849* (Oxford: Oxford Univ. Press, 1977), p. 77.

11. Glover, *Slippery Fellow*, pp. 152–160.

12. Lafayette to Sir Robert Wilson, 26 June 1821, British Museum, Additional, 30,116, f.45. This M. Baud appears to be the same man whom Rey identifies as "Baude, de Valence," an early member of the Union Rey founded at Grenoble, who was named prefect of police at the end of 1830. Joseph Rey, "Mémoires Politiques," p. 92, Bibliothèque de Grenoble, T3939. Jean-Jacques Baude is identified by Spitzer, p. 266, as a Carbonarist who "installed himself in the name of the Revolution at the Hotel de Ville" in 1830. Baude served as prefect of the Manche, as prefect of police and as deputy of the Loire under the July Monarchy. Bargeton, et al., *Les Préfets*, p. 43.

13. Frances Wright to Lafayette, 16 July 1821, Special Collections, University of Chicago.

14. Carlo Giuseppe Guglielmo Botta, *Storia della guerra dell'independenza degli Stati Uniti d'America* (4 vols.; Parigi: D. Colas, c. 1809), appeared in French translation in 1812–13, published by J. G. Dentu. This version must have been the one she read, as the English translation was published only in 1820. Lafayette frequently recommended Botta's book as the best available on the subject.

15. A. J. G. Perkins and Theresa Wolfson, *Frances Wright, Free Enquirer. The Study of a Temperament* (New York: Harper & Brothers, 1939), pp. 12–13.

16. Their friend, Mrs. Craig Millar (widow of Mrs. Milne's brother), had lived in the United States for two years with her husband when he fled Britain because of his sympathy with the French Revolution.

17. Celia Morris Eckhardt, *Fanny Wright: Rebel in America* (Cambridge: Harvard University Press, 1984), p. 49.

18. Cited in Lafayette to Jefferson, 1 June 1822, Chinard, p. 413.

19. John Bowring, ed., *The Works of Jeremy Bentham*, (11 vols.; Edinburgh: W. Tait, 1838–43), X, 474–476, 514. Frances Wright to Lafayette, 16 July 1821, Special Collections, University of Chicago. Edward Blaquière (1779–1832), a lieutenant in the British navy, intro-

duced himself to Bentham in 1813 after reading some of his works. Edward Blaquière to Jeremy Bentham, 7 July 1813, Jeremy Bentham, *The Correspondence of Jeremy Bentham*, ed. by Timothy L. S. Sprigge, Ian R. Christie, A. T. Milne, J. R. Dinwiddy, and Stephen Conway (9 vols. to date; London: various, 1968–1989), viii, 330. Blaquière wrote works on the Greek and Spanish revolutions as well as on Latin America and the Caribbean.

20. Frances Wright to Jeremy Bentham, in Bowring, *Works of Bentham*, X, 526.

21. Perkins and Wolfson, *Frances Wright*, pp. 64–65.

22. Perkins and Wolfson, *Frances Wright*, p. 25.

23. Stendhal, *Souvenirs d'egotisme*, pp. 51–54 (trans.). Stendhal lists Lafayette among the "*hommes d'un vrai mérite*" whom he has known. Cited in Jean Touchard, *La Gloire de Béranger* (2 vols.; Paris: Librairie Armand Colin, 1968), I, 339. Stendhal does not mention Frances Wright.

24. Frances Wright to Lafayette, 29 Dec. 1821, Special Collections, University of Chicago.

25. Lafayette to Frances Wright, 25 Apr. 1824, Catherwood. In his letters to Emilie, George's wife, Lafayette used similar terms, generally referring to her as "*ma bien aimée Emilie.*" See letters in AN 252 AP3.

26. Lafayette to Lady Morgan, 8 Mar. 1823, LG Photo of Lilly.

27. Lafayette's grandson-in-law, Charles de Rémusat, met Fanny Wright in 1827 and described her as "disproportionately tall; but she possessed youth, a rather pretty face and hair in ringlets which cascaded on her neck." She showed toward Lafayette "a great deal of admiration and even tenderness; she flattered him and tried to convert him to her ideas. He did not contradict her, answered her questions on the French Revolution, accepted her compliments, calmly allowed himself to be admired, and almost believed that she felt for him a more tender sentiment. I have always believed that she would have given proof of it, if he had asked her for it." Rémusat, *Mémoires*, II, 223 (trans.).

28. For Lafayette's use of the term *colony*, see Lafayette to Gallatin, 1 Sept. 1816, AG Papers, Reel 28; Lafayette to Alderman Wood, 1 Dec, 1821, Lilly; Lafayette to Gallatin, 9 Aug. 1821, New-York Historical Society, AG Papers, Reel 34.

29. Cited in Eckhardt, *Fanny Wright*, pp. 57–58.

30. Lafayette to Albert Gallatin, 9 Aug. 1821, New-York Historical Society, AG Papers, Reel 34; Baud to Frances Wright, 10 Aug. 1821, Special Collections, University of Chicago.

31. Lafayette had especially sought to make corrections in Wright's description of the attempt to free Lafayette from the prison at Olmütz, a story she had learned from a member of the Huger family. Frances Wright

to Lafayette, 16 July 1821, Special Collections, University of Chicago. Gallatin was unhappy with an improbable anecdote describing Jefferson's rudeness to the Spanish ambassador. Fanny replaced the story with another (probably supplied by Gallatin) before the second edition. Frances Wright, *Views of Society and Manners in America*, ed. by Paul R. Baker (Cambridge: Harvard Univ. Press, 1963; reprint of the first London edition of 1821), pp. 67–68. Frances Wright to Albert Gallatin, 7 Oct. 1821 and "Wednesday morning" [Oct. 1821], New-York Historical Society, AG Papers, Reel 34. In recommending the second edition to Jefferson, Lafayette remarked that she had replaced the suspect anecdote with "A very pretty story which she Had Reasons to Believe perfectly Correct." Lafayette to Jefferson, 1 June 1822, in Chinard, pp. 412–413.

32. Lafayette to Jacques-Théodore Parisot, "lundi au soir" [ca. 1822], Missouri Historical Society, photo at LPP; Lafayette to Jullien de Paris, 6 Mar. 1822, Lilly.

33. Lafayette to Dumont, 11 May 1821, LG Photo of Bibliothèque publique et universitaire à Genève—Mss. Dumont, 75, 179 verso. By June 1822 there had been German, French, and Greek translations. Lafayette to Jefferson, 1 June 1822, in Chinard, p. 413.

34. Helen Heineman, *Restless Angels: The Friendship of Six Victorian Women* (Athens, Ohio Univ. Press, 1983), pp. 9, 11, 40. There are some inaccuracies in Heineman's chronology. Fanny describes the Garnetts in *Views of Society*, pp. 71–72.

35. J. H. Burns, "Bentham and the French Revolution," *Transactions of the Royal Historical Society*, 5th. Series, vol. 16 (1966), 99–100. It is possible that Lafayette saw Bentham in October 1802 when Bentham visited Paris (Bowring, *Works of Bentham*, X, 399). Although some biographies of Lafayette state that Bentham visited La Grange in 1816 or 1818, I have seen no evidence for this visit. Bentham does not appear to have gone abroad then. See Bentham, *Correspondence*, vols. 8 and 9. He did visit La Grange in 1825. It is possible that Jeremy Bentham's brother visited La Grange, for Sir Samuel Bentham and his wife lived in France at that time. *John Mill's Boyhood Visit to France Being a Journal and Notebook Written by John Stuart Mill in France, 1820–1821*, edited by Anna Jean Mill ([Toronto]: Univ. of Toronto Press, 1960), p. xi. The source of the story of Bentham's visit is apparently Broglie, *Souvenirs*, I, 386, but there are some other inaccuracies in this section as well. For example, Broglie recalls that his visit to La Grange in September 1817 was his second visit, that he had taken Ticknor there the year before. Ticknor actually visited La Grange with Broglie in September 1817, and Ary Scheffer (whom Broglie remembers meeting at La Grange in 1817) apparently made his first trip there in 1818. Ticknor, *Life, Letters, and Journals*, I, 151–152.

36. Jeremy Bentham to the duc de la Rochefoucauld [?], early May 1789[?], "Advice to Fayette"; André Morellet to Jeremy Bentham, 8 May 1789; and Jeremy Bentham to Brissot, [mid-Aug. 1789], in Bentham, *Correspondence*, IV, 51, 55, 84. The only work on Bentham's relations with France is the rather unsatisfactory thesis by Janko Zagar, *Bentham et la France* (1958), available at Bibliothèque Nationale 4-Z.5433.

37. For the argument on Bentham's conversion to democracy, see J. R. Dinwiddy, "Bentham's Transition to Political Radicalism," *Journal of the History of Ideas*, 36 (1975), 683–700. Bentham's views on natural rights are analysed in Nancy L. Rosenblum, *Bentham's Theory of the Modern State* (Cambridge: Harvard Univ. Press, 1978), pp. 62–65. See also, Mary P. Mack, *Jeremy Bentham: An Odyssey of Ideas* (New York: Columbia Univ. Press; and London: Heinemann, 1963).

38. John Bowring, who became Bentham's friend, biographer, and literary executor, first met Bentham because Blaquière suggested that Bowring's knowledge of Spain would be of interest to him. Bowring, *Works of Bentham*, X, 516. On Bentham's interest in Spanish America, see Miriam Williford, *Jeremy Bentham on Spanish America: An Account of His Letters and Proposals to the New World* (Baton Rouge: Louisiana State Univ. Press, 1980). Bowring first went to Spain in 1813 as a commercial agent. Bowring, *Autobiographical Recollections*, p. 99.

39. Elie Halevy, *The Growth of Philosophic Radicalism* (Boston: Beacon Press, 1955), pp. 269–273, 285–289.

40. Lafayette to Clarkson, 16 Sept. 1821, Benjamin Franklin Papers, Yale University. Lafayette to Bentham, 14 Sept. 1821, LG notes of Bentham Mss., portfolio 10, folder 20, X, 105 (trans.).

41. J. Lucas-Dubreton, *Le Culte de Napoléon, 1815–1848* (Paris: Albin Michel, 1960), p. 172, gives that date.

42. Ernest d'Hauterive, "Conversations de L'Empereur avec le Grand-Maréchal, [Gen. Bertrand], 22–26 avril 1821," *Revue des deux mondes*, 7th ser., vol. 48 (Paris, 1928), pp. 863–864.

43. Bourienne, for example, recorded Napoleon's comments in 1802: "Monsieur Lafayette is a political monomaniac, a mule. He doesn't understand. I'm sorry about this, because he's a decent fellow. I wanted to make him a senator, and he refused. Well, so much the worse for him. I can manage without his vote." Cited in J. Christopher Herold, *The Mind of Napoleon: A Selection from His Written and Spoken Words* (New York: Columbia University Press, 1955), p. 70. Lafayette mentioned the letter to Bonaparte in a letter to Jefferson dated 8 Oct. 1804, in Chinard, p. 233. In 1801, Mme de Staël had commented that Lafayette conserved "his noble and pure character, accepting nothing, desiring still less, and always regretting that perfect liberty, the idol of his life." Mme de Staël to P.-S. DuPont de Nemours 30 Germinal Yr. IX [20 April 1801], in Madame

de Staël, *Correspondance Générale*, vol. IV, part 2 (Paris: Jean-Jacques Pauvert, 1978), p. 370 (trans.).

44. Recorded by Montholon on 17 Apr. 1821, cited in Herold, *The Mind of Napoleon*, p. 251.

45. Lafayette to Fabvier, "lundi," [July 1821], Benjamin Franklin Papers, Yale University. Debidour, *Le Général Fabvier*, p. 182, gives this date. I cannot find any reference to this petition in the AP. See Comte de Grote to King of England, 26 July 1821, cited in Hérisson, *Le Cabinet noir: Louis XVIII—Napoléon—Marie Louise* (9th. ed.; Paris: Paul Ollendorff, 1887), p. 260. He is pleased that the early departure of the deputies will make it impossible for the Chamber to take up this petition. See Georges Lote, "La mort de Napoléon et l'opinion bonapartiste en 1821," *Revue des études napoléoniennes*, vol. 31 (July 1930), p. 49. He gives the names of the signers as Gourgaud, Fabvier, le comte de Bréqueville, F. Cassin and H. Hartmann. Lote's conclusion does not take sufficiently into account the divisions within the liberal ranks. He writes that liberals and Bonapartists were now more or less indistinguishable and that Lafayette, among others, had converted to Bonapartism. "The death of the Emperor brought together liberals and Bonapartists in the same grief, because both thought that the great cause of political and social emancipation of peoples . . . had just lost its most resolute defender" (pp. 30–31, trans.). Lafayette certainly did not feel this way about Napoleon. His alliance with Bonapartists was a strategy to unite opponents of the government and did not stem from either an endorsement of Napoleonic principles or admiration for the emperor.

46. Paul Thureau-Dangin, *Le parti libéral sous la Restauration*, (Paris: E. Plon, 1876), p. 177. Thureau-Dangin goes on to say that Lafayette "no longer exhibits opposition to all the Bonapartes" (trans.) and repeats the questionable story from Louis Blanc, *Histoire de dix ans, 1830–1840* (5 vols.; 6th ed.; Paris: Pagnerre, 1846), I, 89–90, that Lafayette considered an offer of five million francs to support a revolution in favor of Prince Eugene.

47. Benjamin Constant to Goyet, [24 July 1821], in *Correspondance*, p. 584.

48. Goyet to Benjamin Constant, 19 Sept. 1821, in *Correspondance*, pp. 603–604.

49. After the expected electoral defeat, Goyet continued this theme: "Thus we are now clearly and completely into a false representative government, the most convenient of all for a king. The ministers can oppress individuals, the nation, overload them with taxes, in the very name of the nation." And the opposition could do nothing about it. Indeed, he continued, an opposition was necessary for "modern despotic governments" to give the impression that laws had been debated and

arrived at openly. Goyet to Benjamin Constant, 19 Oct. 1821, in *Correspondance*, p. 614.

50. Lafayette to Sir Charles and Lady Morgan, 21 Oct. 1821, Lilly.

51. Lafayette to Goyet, 29 Oct. 1821, Galpin. Constant also lost interest in the Chamber. Mme de Broglie noted in her diary, (30 Oct.): "he is sick of politics and is starting again to work on his book on religions. He seeks refuge in skepticism, as others do in faith." Broglie, *Souvenirs*, II, 218 (trans.).

52. Goyet mentions receipt of a letter from Lafayette in Goyet to Benjamin Constant, 9 Feb. 1822, in *Correspondance*, p. 642, but the letter is not in Galpin. At one point, Goyet reminded Constant that he was not writing directly to Lafayette and asked him to present his regards to the general. Goyet to Benjamin Constant, 22 Apr. 1822, in *Correspondance*, p. 674.

53. Even Benjamin Constant supported this policy, an indication of how much the left mistrusted the ministry. Benjamin Constant to Goyet, [6 Oct. 1821] and 17 Nov. [1821], in *Correspondance*, pp. 609, 623.

54. On Koechlin, see A. Brandt, "Une famille de fabricants Mulhousiens au début du XIXe siècle: Jean Koechlin et ses fils," *Annales*, VI (1951), 319–330. See also F. Zickel-Koechlin, "Souvenirs d'un contemporain sur les événements de 1820 à 1823 en Alsace," *Revue d'Alsace*, I (1850), 543–556, and II (1851), 76–96.

55. Leuilliot, *L'Alsace*, I, 322.

56. Spitzer, *Old Hatreds*, pp. 84–85. See Vaulabelle, *Histoire des deux Restaurations*, VI, 8–20.

57. Two anecdotes about Bastien's involvement exist. One recounts that Bastien was ordered to stay at La Grange, but when they started out, Bastien "climbed up to the box beside the coachman." When Lafayette remonstrated with him, warning him that they were risking their lives, he supposedly answered that he well knew what was going on and that he wanted to join them on his own account. Whitlock, *La Fayette*, II, 201. Charavay, *Le Général La Fayette*, p. 423n, gives as the source for this story Bardoux, *Les Dernières Années*, pp. 285–286. The other anecdote, recorded by [Ulysse] Trélat, "La Charbonnerie," in *Paris Révolutionnaire*, II, 298–299, states that Bastien had not known the purpose of the trip to Belfort but that, when they were forced to make a detour at the last moment, George said to him, "All this must seem quite extraordinary to you, my dear Bastien." The servant replied "Oh, messieurs, when we left, I suspected that it was for something serious, and, no matter what might have happened, you can be sure that I was not out of place here" (trans.). Both anecdotes seem improbable. Lafayette and George were not likely to have kept secrets from such a trusted servant,

nor is it likely that at the time of their departure they had not yet settled on who would accompany them.

58. Spitzer, *Old Hatreds*, pp. 248–250. The story is frequently repeated that Lafayette was delayed at La Grange because he insisted on commemmorating the anniversary of his wife's death. See for example, R.-G. Nobécourt, *La Vie d'Armand Carrel* (Paris: Librairie Gallimard, 1930), p. 28. But since the anniversary was Christmas Eve, it would not have interfered with his arrival in Belfort by 29 December.

59. Trélat, "La Charbonnerie," pp. 295–300.

60. Spitzer, *Old Hatreds*, p. 250. Debidour, *Le Général Fabvier*, p. 185, reports that Fabvier, Dupont de l'Eure, and Manuel, all on their way to Alsace, were also warned away. Zickel-Koechlin, "Souvenirs," I, p. 549, says that the other deputies involved were Dupont de l'Eure and Corcelle (not Manuel), but that they were both unable to come for reasons beyond their control.

61. F. Zickel-Koechlin, "Souvenirs," II (1851), 78. His reminiscences seem more credible than Odilon Barrot's story that the carriage was seized by the authorities, but that Lafayette's associates were able to sneak into the shed and dispose of it piece by piece. Barrot, after all, states that he did not join the conspiracies, so his testimony is hearsay. Odilon Barrot, *Mémoires Posthumes* (4 vols.; Paris: Charpentier, 1875), I, 78–79.

62. D'Argenson's step-son, Broglie, wrote that the impetus for the revolt came from d'Argenson and Koechlin, though he acknowledged that he learned about these events only after the fact. Broglie, *Souvenirs*, II, 227. There are many indications that these men were conspiring. They were borrowing money, and it was well known that d'Argenson, despite his great wealth, was having financial difficulties. Leuilliot, *L'Alsace*, I, 312.

63. Spitzer, *Old Hatreds*, p. 248.

64. Vaulabelle, *Histoire des deux Restaurations*, VI, 9 (trans.).

65. Duvergier de Hauranne, *Histoire*, VII, 67, states that Demarçay did not conspire. For this question, see Spitzer, *Old Hatreds*, pp. 237–240. In one letter, which may refer to a meeting of Carbonarist deputies, Lafayette mentions Manuel, d'Argenson, Dupont, Caumartin, Beauséjour, and "les Saint-Aïgnan." Lafayette to Voyer d'Argenson, "dimanche à huit heures" [1823?], Université de Poitiers, no. 78. For more on this letter, see below, chapter 8. Louis-Marie Rousseau de Saint-Aignan was elected a deputy in Loire-Inférieure in 1819. Nicolas-Auguste-Marie Rousseau de Saint-Aignan pursued a military career under Napoleon and was elected a deputy from Côtes-du-Nord in 1820. Both were born in Nantes. Robert and Cougny, *Dictionnaire*, vol. 5, p. 234.

66. Frances Wright to Lafayette, 29 Dec. 1821, Special Collections, University of Chicago.

67. Perkins and Wolfson, *Frances Wright*, p. 73.

68. Cited in Vaulabelle, *Histoire des deux Restaurations*, VI, 125n (trans.).

69. Laffitte's contributions to liberal causes were frequently exaggerated. Béranger complained that Laffitte did not make a contribution to a subscription raised for him in 1829. "When I think that he is the man to whom the public insists on giving credit for Manuel's electoral eligibility, and for what Thiers earns at the *Constitutionnel*, and for the slender revenue which nourishes me and mine, I sometimes get out of humor. I do not owe him the slightest obligation." Béranger to Dupont de l'Eure, 30 Sept. 1829, in Béranger, *Lettres*, p. 128 (trans.). The police suspected Laffitte of financing a ship to Spain in March 1823. Prefect of Seine-Inférieure to Min. of the Interior, 19 Mar 1823, AN F⁷ 6720, dossier 10.

70. Cited in Duvergier de Hauranne, *Histoire*, VII, 3 (trans.).

71. On the trials, see Spitzer, *Old Hatreds*, pp. 143–188.

72. Morris, "Joseph Rey," pp. 120, 130–140.

73. By December 1822, the French police had discovered this correspondence; Coutard, General Commanding First Military Division, to Min. of the Interior, 7 Dec. 1822, and Report of 12 Dec. 1822, in AN F⁷ 6720, dossier 11. It is possible that they knew of it earlier, since Neapolitan officials did. Castelcicala to Circello, 25 May 1822, in Ruggero Moscati, ed., *Guglielmo Pepe*, vol. 1 (only vol. published) (Rome: Vittoriano, 1938), p. 259. Fanny Trollope would become famous as the author of *Domestic Manners of the Americans* (1832) and many other travel books and novels, and even more famous currently as the mother of the novelist Anthony Trollope. Frédéric Degeorge, "Les Proscrits de la Restauration," *Paris révolutionnaire*, (4 vols.; Paris: Guillaumin, 1833–1834), IV, p. 123, mentions that Thomas Trollope was among those helping the exiles in London.

74. See George T. Romani, *The Neapolitan Revolution of 1820–1821* (Evanston: Northwestern Univ. Press, 1950).

75. Romani, *Neapolitan Revolution*, pp. 171–172, argues that "Impractical though Pepe may have been at times, the only solution of the Neapolitan problem may well have been that which he advocated, that is, an active Muratist leadership which would admit the more reliable of the Carbonari to a share in the Government and guide the rest into a willingness to support the regime as something representative of their own interests. The division which persisted, instead, between Muratists and Carbonari was second only to Austrian opposition as a cause of failure."

76. Lafayette to Pepe, 3 May 1822, in Guglielmo Pepe, *Memoirs of General Pepe Comprising the Principal Military and Political Events of Modern Italy* (3 vols.; London: Richard Bentley, 1846), III, 236, 210–211.

77. Lafayette to Sir Charles Morgan, 2 May 1822, Lilly.

78. Perkins and Wolfson, *Frances Wright*, pp. 76–77. Pepe's biographer, Francesco Carrano, confirms this assessment, saying Pepe acted more from "impulse of heart than by way of subtle speculation." He tended to act impulsively from a sense of fervent patriotism, rather than from calculation. Quoted in Romani, *Neapolitan Revolution*, pp. 25–26.

79. This letter was written in early March and in French (trans.). The originals of these letters are lost. Before they were misplaced, A. J. G. Perkins took extensive notes of them. Her notes are now at the Catherwood Library at Cornell University. I consulted photocopies of the collection kindly prepared by Martha Hodges. References to letters at the Catherwood Library are to these notes. For the sake of readability, I have converted the abbreviations used in the notes to complete words.

80. Perkins and Wolfson, *Frances Wright*, pp. 78–79.

81. Wright to Lafayette, [March 1822], Catherwood. The identity of this noble being who inspired Fanny Wright's love has remained a mystery because she referred to him in her letters by the code name of "Eugene." The most important clue to his identity was Fanny's frequent reference to Colonel Pisa as her friend's Pylades, the friend of Orestes, whose name is proverbial for devoted friendship. The key to the puzzle can be found in Pepe's memoirs. In commenting on an 1824 letter from Lafayette, Pepe noted that "To understand it properly, it is necessary to know that he termed Colonel Pisa, . . . my Pylades." Pepe's *Memoirs*, III, 271. For a summary of the evidence on the identity of this person, see Perkins and Wolfson, *Frances Wright*, pp. 77–83. The notes taken by Miss Perkins from the 1853 diary of Sylva d'Arusmont (Fanny's daughter) show that in going through her mother's papers Sylva found letters from Pepe. Sylva noted: "Among which we found 2 letters written in an insolent manner and a bad tone which prove to us also that Mam. F. must have acted viciously to separate them" (trans.). This is possibly a reference to Mrs. Trollope whom she describes elsewhere in the diary as "*intrigante*." Fanny Trollope and Pepe continued to be good friends for some time.

82. Frances Wright to Lafayette, 15 Mar. 1822, Catherwood, reproduced in Perkins and Wolfson, *Frances Wright*, p. 78.

83. Frances Wright to Lafayette, 7 Apr. [1822], Catherwood.

84. Fanny met him at Dover in May 1822 (see below) and saw him again in London in the spring of 1824. Lafayette to Pepe, 14 May 1824, in Aldo Romano, "Lafayette, Guglielmo Pepe e l'Italia," *Rassegna storica del Risorgimento*, XX (1933), 594.

85. Lafayette to Pepe, 13 Mar. 1823, in Pepe's, *Memoirs*, III, 261 (trans.).

86. Pepe, *Memoirs*, II, 143–145. But later, in 1850, Pepe did marry Maria Anna Gilchrist-Cowendry, the widow of the orientalist, Dr.

John Borthwick Gilchrist (1759–1841). Pepe's friendship with her appears to have begun before the spring of 1823. See Moscati, *Guglielmo Pepe*, p. 297.

87. Pepe to Vincenzo Pisa, 19 Apr. [1822], in Moscati, *Guglielmo Pepe*, p. 248.

88. Lafayette to Mme de Lasteyrie, 3 Mar. 1820 in Hérisson, *Un Pair de France policier*, pp. 169–170; Raymond Carr, *Spain: 1808–1939* (Oxford: Clarendon, 1966), pp. 125–127. A leader of the guerilla war against Napoleon, Mina had turned to liberalism and revolt because of the way he was treated by the restored King Ferdinand. In exile in Paris, Mina received financial assistance from Wellington. Miguel Artole Gallego, ed., *Biblioteca de autores españoles: Memorias del General Don Francisco Espoz y Mina* (2 vols.; Madrid: Ediciones Atlas, 1962), I, 229. Lafayette's informant was a brother-in-law of General Juan Porlier, who had led an unsuccessful revolt against Ferdinand in 1815.

89. Lafayette to Monroe, 8 July 1821, LG photo of letter in Monroe Papers, New York Public Library.

90. Lafayette to Jefferson, 1 July 1821, in Chinard, p. 405.

91. Jean Sarrailh, *Un Homme d'état espagnol: Martínez de la Rosa (1787–1862)* (Bordeaux: Feret & Fils; Paris: E. de Boccard, 1930), p. 103.

92. Alberto Gil Novales, *Las sociedades patrioticas (1820–1823)* (2 vols.; Madrid: Editorial Tecnos, 1975) provides a wealth of valuable detail on the membership and history of these groups.

93. Constant to Goyet, 1 May 1823, in *Correspondance*, p. 538. Gil Novales is less charitable about Toreno, calling him "one of the most immoral individuals of this whole era." Gil Novales, *Sociedades*, I, 131 (trans.). His analysis of Toreno's support for illiberal measures against the popular societies is on pages 537–539.

94. Lafayette to [his family at La Grange], 17 July 1821, in *Mémoires*, VI, 129. Don José Maria Queipo de Llano y Ruiz de Saravia, count of Toreno (1786–1843) espoused liberal ideas and fought against the Napoleonic presence in Spain. Forced into exile upon the return of Ferdinand VII, he returned at the outbreak of revolution. He spent the years from 1823 to 1833 in exile in France, where he worked on a history of the Spanish revolutions. *Enciclopedia Italiana*, vol. 34.

95. In July 1821, he asked Louis XVIII for help, warning that otherwise events in Spain would disrupt France. William Spence Robertson, *France and Latin-American Independence* (New York: Octagon Books, 1967, reprint of 1939 edition), p. 200.

96. Gil Novales, *Sociedades*, I, 604. Their name, *comuneros*, was a reminder of the revolt of sixteenth-century Spaniards against the foreign government of Charles V and reflected their patriotic and democratic attitudes.

97. Lafayette first mentioned the possibility of a war in a letter to Sir Charles and Lady Morgan, [22 or 21] Oct. 1821, Lilly. Lafayette to Pepe, 15 Apr. 1822, in Moscati, *Guglielmo Pepe*, p. 246.

98. See police reports in Appendix I. B of Margaret Campbell Walker Wicks, *The Italian Exiles in London, 1816–1848* ([Manchester]: Manchester Univ. Press, 1937), pp. 212–215, and diplomatic correspondence in Moscati, *Guglielmo Pepe*, pp. 240–273.

99. Frances Wright's trip to England at the end of January might have been in response to plans that Wilson communicated while in France. By the end of January, the Neapolitan minister in England was already informed of Pepe's plans: Ludolf to Circello, 29 Jan. 1822, in Moscati, *Guglielmo Pepe*, p. 140. Lafayette knew that Wilson was planning a trip to Paris: Lafayette to Alderman Wood, 1 Dec. 1821, Lilly.

100. Frances Wright to Lafayette, 21 Mar. 1821, Catherwood.

101. David Bushnell, *The Santander Regime in Gran Colombia* (Newark: University of Delaware Press, 1954), pp. 112–114. Bushnell's description of Zea's mission does not mention his proposal to the liberals.

102. Pepe, *Memoirs*, III, 248–250.

103. Paul W. Schroeder, *Metternich's Diplomacy at Its Zenith, 1820–1823* (Austin: Univ. of Texas Press, 1962), pp. 179–191.

104. Pepe to Pisa, 27 May [1822], in Moscati, *Guglielmo Pepe*, pp. 260–261.

105. William Spence Robertson, "The Policy of Spain Toward its Revolted Colonies, 1820–1823," *Hispanic American Historical Review* (1926), 21–46.

106. José Moreno Guerra, *Compte Rendu de ce qui s'est passé dans les sessions des Cortes d'Espagne, pendant les années 1821 et 1822, qui annonce l'avenir* (Paris: Imprimerie de Moreau, 1822). The piece was dated 16 Feb. 1822. The original Spanish is reproduced in Iris M. Zavala, *Masones, comuneros y carbonarios* (Madrid: Siglo XXI de España Editores, 1971), pp. 250–279.

107. Moreno Guerra, *Compte rendu*, p. 30 (trans.).

108. Moreno Guerra, *Compte rendu*, p. 60 (trans.).

109. See, for example, Pepe to Pisa, 14 May [1822], in *Guglielmo Pepe*, p. 255.

110. Lafayette to Richard Rush, 25 May 1822, LG photo of letter at Princeton University Library. Lafayette to Gallatin, 21 May 1822, New-York Historical Society, AG Papers, Reel 34. The French authorities suspected that Gallatin's secretary was providing a means of communication between the French and Spanish liberals and that money was also being transferred through the American consulates. Rafael Sánchez Mantero, *Las conspiraciones liberales en Francia 1815–1823)* (Sevilla: Publicaciones de la Universidad de Sevilla, 1972), p. 212.

111. Lafayette to Monroe, 13 July 1822, LG photo of New York Public Library. Forsyth, the American minister in Spain, commented that, although the Spanish were acknowledging that they were sending commissioners to initiate negotiations with those in power in Spanish America and knew that they could not force a reunion, "there exists a perverse determination not to adopt the only measure which promises to be advantageous to Spain." Forsyth to Adams, 23 June 1822, in Robertson, "The Policy of Spain," p. 36. Forsyth seems to be referring to Zea's offer of money in exchange for a forthright recognition. The *Gazette de France* of 27 April complained that US ambassadors offered "toasts in public to the success of rebellions." Cited in Robertson, *France and Latin-American Independence*, p. 217.

112. Lafayette to Jefferson, 1 June 1822, in Chinard, p. 408. Also mentioned in Lafayette to Dumont, 11 May 1822, LG photo of Bibliothéque publique et universitaire à Genève, Manuscrits Dumont, 75, 179 verso.

113. Robertson, *France and Latin-American Independence*, p. 212. An excerpt from Zea's note is in Sir Charles Stuart to the Marquis of Londonderry, 11 Apr. 1822, in *Britain and the Independence of Latin America, 1812–1830*, edited by C. K. Webster (2 vols.; New York: Octagon Books, 1970; reprint of 1938 edition), II, 108–109.

114. The news that something was brewing reached the liberals in Alsace by early April. The prefect reported that the liberals were expressing hopes, apparently based on expectations of war between Russia and Turkey, a fall in the value of government bonds, and belief that the Holy Alliance was falling apart. They were counting on "this disunion to put their guilty schemes into execution finally." Prefect of Haut-Rhin to Minister of Interior, Colmar, 5 Apr. 1822, AN F^7 6771, dossier 10 (trans.).

115. Castelcicala to Circello, 25 May 1822, in Moscati, *Guglielmo Pepe*, p. 259. General Laffitte had been sent to the region to prepare the revolt, and Zea had apparently forwarded some money for this purpose. Castelcicala to Circello, 1 June 1822, in Moscati, *Guglielmo Pepe*, p. 263.

116. Pepe to Pisa, 10 May [1822], written from Dover, in Moscati, *Guglielmo Pepe*, p. 253.

117. Pepe to Pisa, 14 May [1822], in Moscati, *Guglielmo Pepe*, pp. 255–256.

118. Broglie, *Souvenirs*, II, 248–250.

119. Chateaubriand to Madame Récamier, 30 April 1822, 7 May 1822; Chateaubriand to Montmorency, 17 May 1822, in Chateaubriand, *Correspondance*, pp. 55, 72, 80. From this and other evidence, it is clear that Broglie and d'Argenson were in England at the same time. However, Broglie's reminiscences are written so as to give the impression that

d'Argenson went to England after he had completed his own trip there, another example of his later desire to distance himself from his more radical friends. See Victor de Pange, "Le Séjour de Victor de Broglie et d'Auguste de Staël à Londres en mai 1822," *Cahiers staëliens*, n.s., no. 17 (Dec. 1973), 1–58 and n.s., no. 18 (June 1974), 11–42, for a description of the other people whom Staël and Broglie saw in England. Pange makes no mention of Voyer d'Argenson. D'Argenson profited from his visit to study British techniques of metal founding to apply in his establishment in Alsace. Naturally, he met with French refugees and their English friends, among them Jeremy Bentham. Leuilliot, *L'Alsace*, I, 380–381; II, 334. D'Argenson to Bentham, 24 Aug. 1822, British Museum, Additional 33,545, f.594.

120. Lafayette to Jefferson, 1 June 1822, in Chinard, pp. 410–411.

121. G. Cobianchi to V. Pisa, 7 July 1822, in Moscati, *Guglielmo Pepe*, p. 270, 270n. The file on Cobianchi in the archives of the French police includes a report that Cobianchi was in hiding at La Grange in September 1822. This information appears to be in error because he was sending reports to Pisa from Switzerland. Delavau to Minister of the Interior, 27 Sept. 1822, AN F⁷ 6653.

122. Pirro de Capitani to Pisa, 5 Aug. 1822, in Moscati, *Guglielmo Pepe*, pp. 272–273.

8. Reverses

1. Gallatin informed John Quincy Adams that this government represented a complete change in the administration of France. Albert Gallatin to John Quincy Adams, 27 Dec. 1821, AG Papers.

2. Lafayette to Sir Robert Wilson, 30 Jan. 1822, British Museum, Additional 30,110. Gérard replaced Etienne Pasquier, who was made a peer. *Correspondance*, p. 665n.

3. Duvergier de Hauranne, *Histoire*, VI, 395; Blanche-Joséphine de Corcelle, Comtesse Roederer, *Notice et Souvenirs de famille* (Brussels: Lyon-Claesen, 1899), p. 160.

4. *Correspondance*, p. 172n; GWL to Bonne Chevant, 20 Feb. 1822, Dean.

5. Duvergier de Hauranne, *Histoire*, VII, pp. 7–10. He gives the totals as 30 royalists and 23 liberals in the arrondissement colleges, 24 royalists and 9 liberals in the departmental colleges. Leuilliot, *L'Alsace*, I, 353, 358–359.

6. Lafayette to Colomb, 15 Aug. 1822, Lilly.

7. Duvergier de Hauranne, *Histoire*, VII, 31, asserts that Wolfel

came to the area with Lafayette's recommendation. Spitzer, *Old Hatreds*, p. 257, agrees. His source is Vaulabelle. *Histoire des deux Restaurations*.

8. Spitzer, *Old Hatreds*, pp. 132–133; Duvergier de Hauranne, *Histoire*, VII, 32.

9. Spitzer, *Old Hatreds*, pp. 136–138.

10. *Mémoires*, VI, 147–148; Duvergier de Hauranne, *Histoire*, VII, 48.

11. Spitzer, *Old Hatreds*, pp. 161–163. Salveton and Grenier, two young students from Auvergne who were friends of the Lafayettes, were freed. See GWL to Bonne Chevant, 20 Feb., 9 Mar., and 14 Apr. 1822, Dean, for the family's interest in their case.

12. Cited in Duvergier de Hauranne, *Histoire*, VII, 73 (trans.).

13. Benjamin Constant and Laffitte called it a lie, Foy demanded an investigation. Duvergier de Hauranne, *Histoire*, VII, 74–76.

14. Duvergier de Hauranne, *Histoire*, VII, 79 (trans.).

15. *Mémoires*, VI, 142–143.

16. His statement that he would be willing to challenge anybody "in whatever rank" has led some to conclude that Lafayette was referring to Louis XVIII and that his immunity from prosecution during the Restoration was a result of his knowing something devastating about the king which the king did not want to have revealed. De La Fuye and Babeau, *The Apostle*, pp. 241–242, 260. This explanation does not ring true to me. Lafayette, after all, was not the only deputy involved, and no others were arrested either. An analysis of the evidence against Lafayette's having blackmailed Louis XVIII over the Favras case is in Gottschalk and Maddox, *Through the Federation*, pp. 558–560.

17. Grandmesnil's true role in the Saumur plot was not proven until 1841, when he sued those who continued to call him an agent provocateur. Spitzer, *Old Hatreds*, p. 258.

18. Spitzer, *Old Hatreds*, p. 135.

19. Cited in Spitzer, *Old Hatreds*, p. 180. Baudrillet was merely a witness at this trial. He was put on trial in early 1823 at Orléans and, after being condemned to death, admitted that he had given a false description of the person Grandmesnil took him to see. A. Calmette, "Les Carbonari en France sous la Restauration, 1821–1830," *La Révolution de 1848*, vol. 9 (1912–1913), pp. 401–417, and vol. 10 (1913–1914), pp. 117–137, 214–230.

20. *Correspondance*, p. 707n.

21. Spitzer, *Old Hatreds*, p. 183.

22. Duvergier de Hauranne, *Histoire*, VII, 118–119 (trans.).

23. Spitzer, *Old Hatreds*, pp. 125–128.

24. Spitzer, *Old Hatreds*, pp. 3–6.

25. Lafayette to Sir Robert Wilson, 8 Apr. 1822, British Museum, Additional 30,116, f.47 (trans.).

26. Cited in Spitzer, *Old Hatreds*, pp. 259–260.

27. Chauvet to Wilson, 14 May 1822, British Museum, Additional 30,110, f.46. In September Chauvet was condemned to death in absentia. On his involvement in the Saumur plot, see Alfred Hachette, "Un Conspirateur Universitaire—François Chauvet," *Revue Bleue*, 5th Series, 9 (6 & 13 June 1908), 726–30, 753–758.

28. Confidential bulletin dated 5 Oct. 1822, in AN F⁷ 6655, folder on Santarosa.

29. Debidour, *Le Général Fabvier*, pp. 194–196. Bowring, *Works of Bentham*, X, 534. Spitzer, *Old Hatreds*, pp. 174, 192, 260n. AN F⁷ 6659, dossier 152. Bowring, *Autobiographical Recollections* pp. 132–137. Bowring was barred from France and visited there again only after the Revolution of 1830.

30. Spitzer, *Old Hatreds*, pp. 240, 268, 305. For more on Cousin, see Spitzer, *The French Generation of 1820*, pp. 71–96. Lafayette kept tabs on other exiled revolutionaries, too, as is indicated by a request for information from the Morgans about an Italian friend who they heard was being persecuted by the Austrians. Lafayette to Sir Charles and Lady Morgan, 21 and 29 Oct. 1821, Lilly.

31. Michaud, *Biographie*, vol. 37, pp. 674–681. Georges Bourgin, "Santa Rosa et la France, 1821–1822," *Revue historique*, vol. 104 (May–June 1910), 68. See also Salvo Mastellone, "Un Aristocratico in esilio: Santorre di Santarosa," *Rivista storica italiana*, vol. 65 (1953), 56–75; 553–576.

32. Santorre di Santarosa, *Lettere dall'esilio 1821–1825*, ed. by Antonio Olmo (Rome: Istituto per la storia del Risorgimento italiano, 1969), p. 172, footnote 1 and p. 174, footnote 1: (extract from Santarosa's unedited "Autobiography") "Thus M. Delavau [Prefect of Police] became aware, without the slightest difficulty, of my relations with La Fayette and some other liberals (M. Manuel, M. Cousin); but when he tried to clarify some points about those circumstances, about which he was interested, he obtained only vague responses, which I gave with feigned nonchalance and frankness, being persuaded that my hesitant behavior would have appeared damaging in the predicament of those sad days" (trans.).

33. Bourgin, "Santa Rosa," pp. 72–73. The two friends were Pietro Muschietti and Giuseppe Calvetti.

34. Cousin had asked Santarosa whether their plight should be brought up in the Chamber, but Santarosa refused to give an opinion. Santarosa to Cousin, 16 June 1822, in Santarosa, *Lettere*, pp. 212–213. His later actions show that he did favor publicity as a tactic.

35. Lafayette to [Victor Cousin], 8 Aug. [1822], LG notes of letter at Bibliothèque Victor Cousin, ms. 235, Tome XXII, pièce 2892.

36. Girardin wrote the Minister of the Interior on 22 July 1822 asking for copies of printed government circulars regarding passport policy. The government responded that such communications were private and could not be released. AN F⁷ 6720, dossier 2. Santarosa's lawyer, Isambert, protested that his detention was illegal, that they could not punish someone who had not been convicted of a crime. If a foreigner were denied asylum, he should be asked to leave the country. Isambert to Min. of the Interior, 23 Sept. 1822, AN F⁷ 6655, folder on Santarosa.

37. Bourgin, "Santa Rosa," pp. 75–83. In spite of the French government's fears, Santarosa was remarkably moderate. He and his fellow noblemen and revolutionaries Lisio, San Marzano, and Dal Pozzo della Cisterna had favored for Piedmont a constitution on the model of the French Charter, but lacking the cooperation of the king, had reluctantly settled on the model of the Spanish Constitution of 1812. Santarosa refused to aid the radical Spanish revolutionaries in 1822, though he did eventually fight in Greece where he was killed. See Stuart Woolf, *A History of Italy 1700–1860: the Social Constraints of Political Change* (London: Methuen, 1979), pp. 260–262.

38. Lafayette's *Mémoires*, p. 135, assert that the society "ceased to exist in the course of the year 1823." Ten Carbonarists had been executed and one had committed suicide.

39. Reports to police by Prefect of Côte d'Or, 12 July 1822; Bellune, 28 July 1822; Prefect of the Meurthe, 6 August 1822; letter from Minister of Police to Prefect of the Gironde, 12 Sept. 1822; AN F⁷ 6659. Schonen, too was reported to have been at Bordeaux, where his passport was visaed on 19 September. AN F⁷ 6720, dossier 25.

40. Trélat, "La Charbonnerie," pp. 330–331. *Mémoires*, VI, 137n, 139n.

41. Cited in Duvergier de Hauranne, *Histoire*, VII, 112 (trans.).

42. This conclusion about the roles is Spitzer's, pp. 236–241.

43. See Trélat, "La Charbonnerie," p. 295.

44. Spitzer, *Old Hatreds*, pp. 253–254.

45. Cited in Duvergier de Hauranne, *Histoire*, VI, 653–654 (trans.).

46. See Schroeder, *Metternich's Diplomacy*, pp. 195–246, and Roger Bullen, "The Great Powers and the Iberian Peninsula, 1815–1848," in Sked, *Europe's Balance of Power*, pp. 54–65.

47. Duvergier de Hauranne, *Histoire*, VII, 189, mentions the ministry's fears over their candidates' losing, the fall of the *rentes*, and so on, but finds the eventual success of the ministry inexplicable.

48. Pasquier, *Mémoires*, V, 467 (trans.). The minister was Jacques-Joseph-Guillaume Corbière.

49. Goyet to Constant, 22 Apr., 8 June, 28 July 1822, in *Correspondance*, pp. 673, 681, 695.

50. Goyet to Constant, 10 June 1822, in *Correspondance*, p. 683.

51. Constant to Goyet, 15 June [1822], in *Correspondance*, p. 690. Goyet responded that like Christ they must be willing to endure persecution. 21 June 1822, in *Correspondance*, p. 693.

52. Jacques Laffitte, *Mémoires de Laffitte*, ed. by Paul Duchon (Paris: Firmin-Didot, n.d.), pp. 134–135 (trans.). The literal translation is: "he would not give six farthings." Although Lafitte undoubtedly embroidered his stories to make them better, this one has a ring of truth to it. Royer-Collard's speech is discussed in Duvergier de Hauranne, *Histoire*, VII, 83–85.

53. Goyet to Constant, 28 July 1822, in *Correspondance*, p. 694.

54. Goyet to Constant, 18 Aug. 1822, in *Correspondance*, p. 701.

55. Benjamin Constant, *Lettres à sa famille*, intro. by Jean H. Menos (Paris: Librairie Stock, 1932), pp. 35–36.

56. Letter to *Courrier Français*, 15 Sept. 1822, in *Correspondance*, pp. 706–707. See *Correspondance*, p. 719. Also Bastid, *Benjamin Constant*, I, 357–381. On appeal the imprisonment was annulled, but the fines were maintained.

57. GWL to Audry de Puyraveau, 15 Oct. 1822, Lilly (trans.).

58. Lafayette to Monsieur Duclos à Melun, 22 Sept. 1822, Benjamin Franklin Papers, Yale University. Lafayette to Directeur des Contributions Directes de Seine-et-Marne, 9 Oct. 1822, LG photo of letter at Marquis de Lafayette Manuscript Collection, David Bishop Skillman Library, Lafayette College.

59. See copy of Adrienne's will in AN C1303, Seine-et-Marne.

60. See Lafayette [draft] to Prefect of Seine-et-Marne, 19 Oct. 1822, Dean, forwarding the documents on which his demand to be reinstated was based.

61. Prefect of Seine-et-Marne to Minister of the Interior, 22 Oct. 1822, Archives Départementales de Seine-et-Marne, 3M24.

62. Lafayette to Prefect, 28 Nov. 1822; Prefect [draft] to Lafayette, 11 Dec. 1822; Archives Départementales de Seine-et-Marne, 3M24. This struggle led to government harassment of a Melun man who had helped Lafayette regain his voting rights. Lafayette to [Gresy], 4 Nov. 1822, photo at LPP of letter at Harvard Autograph File.

63. Lafayette to Goyet, 18 Oct. 1822, Galpin.

64. This issue is raised in a document in George's hand submitted to the Chamber of Deputies along with the documents proving Lafayette's eligibility. AN C1303, Seine-et-Marne. In addition to his half of the La Grange estate, Lafayette owned property in the commune of Vilbert, also in Seine-et-Marne. He paid personal taxes on the furniture at

La Grange and on the house he rented in Paris. The other major portion of his taxes came from property in Brittany owned in eight different communes: Plaintel, Plésidy, St. Laurent, St. Jullien, Bourbriac, Louargat, Lohuec, Loguivyplougas, all in the department of Côtes-du-Nord.

65. Lafayette rented a house in Paris only after his election to the Chamber in 1818, there were no taxes reported for Paris in 1818. AN C1303, Seine-et-Marne; C1290, Sarthe.

66. Lafayette to Goyet, 18 Oct. 1822, Galpin. The only record of previous correspondence is a letter of 6 February 1822, which has been lost. However, there were probably others. Goyet was in Paris in May and probably saw Lafayette then. Still the correspondence had been interrupted for several months. Lafayette also sent a pamphlet to the voters in the Sarthe.

67. Archives Départementales de la Sarthe M61/6.

68. Conseiller de préfecture to Min. of the Interior, 29 Jan. 1823, AN F^{1C} III, Sarthe 3 (trans.).

69. Sub-prefect of Meaux to Prefect of Seine-et-Marne, 20 July 1820, Archives Départementales de Seine-et-Marne, M10207 (trans.). In the summer of 1820, the government requested a series of detailed reports from all arrondissements focusing especially on political opinions. Unfortunately, these immensely helpful reports were continued for only about a year. The sub-prefect reported few poor people and plentiful opportunities for work available at textile factories and on construction of the Canal d'Ourcq.

70. Note the similarity here to the situation in the Sarthe, where liberal elections were also due to agricultural interests. This challenges the accepted explanation that liberal strength was concentrated in cities. See Sylvia Neely, "Rural Politics."

71. Note the liberalism of the Protestant voters in Alsace and the left's identification with the interests of Protestants, for example, Voyer d'Argenson's speech against the White Terror in 1815. Daniel Robert, *Les Eglises réformées en France (1800–1830)* (Paris: Presses universitaires de France, 1961), p. 2, writes that at the time of the Revolution the major groups of Protestants were in the extreme south and in part of the west. The rest of Protestants were isolated in small communities, one being the "*région de Meaux et de Château-Thierry.*"

72. Reports from Sub-prefects, 1820–1821; Report from Sub-prefect of Meaux, 3 Feb. 1822; Archives Départementales de Seine-et-Marne, M10207 (trans.).

73. Lafayette to Goyet, 1 Nov. 1822, Galpin. See above, chapter 3.

74. AN C1303, Seine-et-Marne (trans.). Out of 349 members of the electoral college, 312 voted. Lafayette received 54 percent of the votes cast.

75. In a report from the prefecture, he was described as a "*proprié-taire et cultivateur à Messy, arrondissement de Meaux*," and as one of those who participated actively in the "deplorable choice" at Meaux (i.e., Lafayette). 19 Mar. 1823, AN F^7 6741, dossier 35.

76. See Lafayette to Casimir Périer [1822] and Lafayette to [un-known, 1822], Benjamin Franklin Papers, Yale University, which mention Baillot.

77. Prefect of Seine-et-Marne to Min. of the Interior, 22 Nov. 1822, Archives Départementales de Seine-et-Marne, 3M24 (trans.); AN C1303, Seine-et-Marne.

78. Constant to Goyet, 22 Sept. and 1 Nov. 1822, in *Correspondance*, pp. 709, 727.

79. Duvergier de Hauranne, *Histoire*, VII, 189–190.

80. He won decisively: 101 to 46 for the nearest competitor. AN C1317, Vendée 1822. See Maguelonne, "L'Election de Manuel en Vendée en 1818," *Révolution de 1848*, IX (1912), 199–211, which despite its misleading title is actually about Manuel's election in 1822 and reproduces a revealing letter from a voter, Lubin Impost, describing the election. In the Vendée, this voter suggests, the ultras had the support of the peasantry. Because of its geographical position, he believed Manuel should opt for Sables d'Olonne rather than Fontenay, which was better able to protect itself from ultra violence (p. 210). Manuel won handily in Fontenay as well, 193 to 83. He opted for Sables d'Olonne. In the election of April 1823 in Fontenay to replace him, a government supporter defeated Perreau, one of the liberals who had won in 1818, but by a close margin, 192 to 160. AN C1317, Vendée 1823.

81. Lafayette to Sir Charles Morgan, 2 Dec. 1822, Lilly (trans.).

82. Lafayette to Sir Charles Morgan, 2 Dec. 1822, Lilly (trans.).

83. Bertier de Sauvigny, *La Restauration*, pp. 185–189; Roger Bullen, "The Great Powers and the Iberian Peninsula, 1815–48," in Sked, *Europe's Balance of Power*, pp. 54–66.

84. See chapter 7 of Schroeder, *Metternich's Diplomacy*, pp. 195–236.

85. Rémusat, *Mémoires*, II, 55 (trans.).

86. Part of this apparent coolness may be a consequence of the correspondence that has survived. There are surprisingly few of Manuel's letters extant. The biography by Bonnal (de Ganges), *Manuel et son temps*, is based almost exclusively on speeches and government reports.

87. Béranger to Dupont de l'Eure, 12 Oct. 1838, in *Lettres*, p. 219 (trans.).

88. Touchard, *Béranger*, I, 291; Béranger, *Lettres*, pp. 219–220 (trans.). Béranger commented that the items in the *Mémoires* "almost always lacked the charm which one found in the general's conversations."

89. The Napoleonic myth owed much of its vigor to the popular poems of Béranger. Guizot recalled that in 1822 Manuel had suggested to him that Napoleon II might be the best choice after the Bourbon's were deposed. François Guizot, *Mémoires pour servir à l'histoire de mon temps* (8 vols.; Paris: Michel Lévy frères, 1858–1867), I, 310.

90. Fabvier reminded Lafayette on 18 Jan. 1823 that "at the time of Belfort, despite my opinion which turned out to be well founded, I did not hesitate to follow you." Cited in Debidour, *Le Général Fabvier*, p. 184n (trans.).

91. Manuel's biographer, Bonnal (de Ganges), plays down his participation in the conspiracies, assuming that the reluctant deputy mentioned in a letter in Lafayette's *Mémoires* is indeed Manuel. This man delayed joining the conspiracy for two years, and in 1822 he refused to commit himself to anything more than sharing information and cooperating to encourage opposition. It seems more likely that this mysterious deputy was someone else, perhaps Benjamin Constant or Laffitte. Lafayette to "M***," [n.d., 1822?], in *Mémoires*, VI, 140–141. Bonnal (de Ganges), *Manuel et son Temps*, pp. 193–196, 200.

92. Lafayette to Fabvier, 13 Aug. 1822, Benjamin Franklin Papers, Yale University, reproduced in Debidour, *Le Général Fabvier*, p. 192n (trans.).

93. Fabvier to Lafayette, 18 Jan. 1823, in Debidour, *Le Général Fabvier*, pp. 205–206 (trans.).

94. Lafayette to Voyer d'Argenson, "dimanche à huit heures" [1823?], Université of Poitiers, no. 78 (trans.). George became a deputy in May 1822, therefore the letter must be after that date. D'Argenson was in England from May to September and was in Paris after 13 December (Leuilliot, *L'Alsace*, I, 380). But it is most likely that this meeting was held in late January or early February 1823, after the beginning of the new session of the Chambers, when all the deputies would have been in town. Lafayette turned sixty-six in September 1823, so his statement was only a slight exaggeration of his age. He was born in 1757 and entered public life in 1777. Manuel, who was born in 1775 and who entered political life at the time of the First Restoration of 1814, fits the description at the end.

95. Gil Novales, *Sociedades*, pp. 682–683, 702n. When Pepe arrived in Spain in late summer, he tried to get the *comuneros* to endorse his and Lafayette's project, but when he presented the plans at a meeting held at Riego's home in July, attended by the duque del Parque, Riego, Ballesteros, Quiroga, Istúriz, Alcalá Galiano, Flórez Estrada, Ramón Salvato, Bertrán de Lis, Romero Alpuente, and Palarea, he reported that Alcalá Galiano vetoed the project. Still they were more likely to entertain these ideas than were the members of San Miguel's government.

96. Sánchez Mantero, *Las conspiraciones liberales en Francia*, p. 213 (trans.). Among the papers at the Catherwood are notes of a copy in Frances Wright's handwriting of a 10 January 1823 letter from Lafayette to a secret Spanish organization, apparently the society established by Pepe on his first trip to Spain.

97. Gil Novales, *Sociedades*, pp. 697–698.

98. Count Pecchio, *Anecdotes of the Spanish and Portuguese Revolutions*, intro. and notes by Edward Blaquière, Esq. (London: G. and W. B. Whittaker, 1823), pp. 31–33, 35, 147, 151.

99. Debidour, *Le Général Fabvier*, p. 204n. Fabvier's complaints that Lafayette had revealed to untrustworthy people the name of the general working to subvert the French troops on the border seems less serious in hindsight, since the authorities appear to have been well informed about the activities in the area anyway. The prefect of Basses-Pyrénées reported that tricolor flags had been found in streets of Bayonne and that General Lamothe was making dangerous remarks at the posts of the *cordon sanitaire*. Prefect to Min. of the Interior, Pau, 8 Mar. 1822, AN F⁷ 6771, dossier 6. Fabvier calls him "General L . . ." (see Debidour, *Le Général Fabvier*, p. 222). Spies reported that the general sent to subvert the troops on the Pyrenees in the spring and summer of 1822 was General Laffitte. Castelcicala to Circello, 1 June 1822, Moscati, *Guglielmo Pepe*, p. 263. It is possible that someone else was sent in the winter of 1822–23.

100. Spitzer, *Old Hatreds*, pp. 98, 200, 264. There are others whom Fabvier might also have had in mind. Cobianchi, Pepe's contact in Paris who had close ties to Lafayette, seems rather suspicious. The government knew a great deal about his activities. He seemed to be well connected with highly placed people in the British ministry. See file "Cobianchi" in AN F⁷ 6653. Another Frenchman in Spain, Cugnet de Montarlot, was arrested by the Spanish authorities in 1821 on suspicion of antigovernment plots. It is not clear, however, what his ties were to Lafayette. He surely knew him and many other liberals in Paris since Cugnet had been associated with Cauchois-Lemaire and Brissot-Thivars in the publication of the *Nouvel Homme gris* in 1818 and had served as editor of the *Indépendant* in 1819. It is possible that the persecution of Cugnet de Montarlot was motivated by a desire to discredit Riego. Gil Novales, *Sociedades*, pp. 220–225. Hatin, *Bibliographie historique*, p. 335.

101. Lafayette to Riego, 18 Mar. 1822, quoted in its entirety in Pepe to Pisa, 19 Apr. [1822], in Moscati, *Guglielmo Pepe*, pp. 248–249.

102. Debidour, *le Général Fabvier*, p. 224.

103. Bonnal (de Ganges), *Manuel et son temps*, pp. 377–381. Vaulabelle, *Histoire des deux Restaurations*, VIII, 53–60 (trans.).

104. *Mémoires*, VI, 153.

105. Broglie, *Souvenirs*, II, 326 (trans.). She said that, after the sergeant's refusal to obey, "I have rarely felt a stronger emotion."

106. Lafayette to Sir Charles and Lady Morgan, 8 Mar. 1823, Lilly (trans.).

107. Subscriptions were raised for them. AN F[7] 6720. F[7] 6718 contains twenty folders on subscriptions in various departments.

108. *Mémoires*, VI, 155–156.

109. Lafayette to Sir Charles and Lady Morgan, 8 Mar. 1823, Lilly.

110. "Aux électeurs du collége électoral de Meaux," in *Mémoires*, VI, 156–158. The first part of this address has been ommitted from the *Mémoires*. A draft of the complete address in Lafayette's handwriting is at Dean (trans.).

111. All four of the deputies of Haut-Rhin (including George) boycotted the Chamber. A lithographed copy of their joint explanation to their electors is in the William Harris Crawford Collection, Duke University. George said three deputies resumed their seats. GWL to Bonne Chevant, 18 Mar. 1823, Dean.

112. Procureur général at Colmar to Min. of Justice, 22 July 1823, and other correspondence in AN BB[30] 204, dossier 2.

113. Debidour, *Le Général Fabvier*, pp. 222–230. For more on this general, see above.

114. Vincent Nolte, *Fifty Years in Both Hemispheres* (New York: Redfield, 1854), p. 323. This anecdote contradicts the report of a police spy that Laffitte directed all the liberal activities toward Spain. "He pulls the wires of the intrigue, and *Manuel* the little Mirabeau of our era is his prime minister, his council, and exercises the greatest influence over him." Spy's report forwarded by Coutard, General commanding the First Military Division to Minister of the Interior, 7 Dec. 1822, AN F[7] 6720, dossier 11 (trans.).

115. Prefect of Seine-Inférieur to Minister of the Interior, 19 Mar. 1823, F[7] 6720, describes the contents of the ship that the authorities believed was on the way to Spain.

116. Touchard, *Béranger*, I, 220 (trans.). The poem is entitled *The New Order of the Day*.

117. See Rafael Sánchez Mantero, *Los Cien Mil Hijos de San Luis y las relaciones franco-españolas* (Sevilla: Anales de la Universidad Hispalense, 1981) for a recent book on the invasion.

118. Lafayette to Albert Gallatin, 9 Aug. 1821; N. Piccolo & C. Polychroniades to Gallatin, 16 Aug. 1821; Gallatin [draft] to Piccolo & Polychroniades, 17 Aug. 1821, AG Papers, Reel 34 (trans.). Lafayette to Gallatin, 5 July 1822, New-York Historical Society, AG Papers, Reel 34, introducing Vogorides, who had replaced Piccolo as the Greek agent in France.

119. Lafayette to Monroe, 22 Jan. 1822, LG photo of letter at New York Public Library.

120. Lafayette to Monroe, 13 July 1822, LG photo of letter at New York Public Library. Lafayette reported rumors in Europe that the United States had concluded a treaty with Greece. Lafayette to Monroe, 27 Sept. 1822, LG photo of letter in New York Public Library.

121. Lafayette to Jefferson, 1 June 1822, in Chinard, pp. 411–412.

122. Lafayette [copy] to [Boyer], 26 Mar. 1822, Dean (trans.).

123. Lafayette to Sir Charles and Lady Morgan, 8 Mar. 1823, Lilly (trans.).

124. William Lee to Lafayette, 20 Apr. 1823, Lilly.

125. Gen. Simon Bernard to Lafayette, 9 Apr. 1823, Dean (trans.).

9. An Asylum of Liberty

1. Lafayette to [unknown], 4 Aug. 1823, photo at LPP of letter at St. Paul's School, Concord, N. H. In July, Lafayette attended the funeral in Paris of Savoie-Rollin, a liberal deputy.

2. Trollope's description differs from Cloquet's emphasis on simplicity: "Lafayette had banished from his table silver covers, and rare and expensive dishes and wines; his habits of temperance forbidding him to waste his time and destroy his health in protracted and sumptuous dinners." Cloquet, *Recollections*, pp. 224–225.

3. Frances Trollope's Journal, Trollope Family Papers, University of Illinois.

4. Chef de la 1ere Légion to Prefect of Police, 30 Sept. 1823, AN F⁷ 6720, dossier 11.

5. They believed his name might be Gry or Gray or Grant, and they believed he was related to Frances Wright. The person they wanted to discover was perhaps Major Frye. But by searching recent arrivals of Englishmen into the country, they concluded that it must be William Keir Grant. The police reported that he visited La Grange on 21 September, returning to Paris on 24 September. Though Mrs. Trollope mentioned no new visitor on 21 September, she did record that Lafayette returned to Paris on 24 September and so could have returned with such a guest. There is no evidence, though, that Lafayette knew Major Grant or that Grant was involved with the events on the peninsula. Eight police reports dated from 3 Sept. to 12 Nov. 1823, AN F⁷ 6720, dossier 11. William Keir Grant was a British officer who had most recently been posted to India and had helped put down piracy in the Persian Gulf. *Dictionary of National Biography*, vol. 8, 407–408. Delavau to Min. of the Interior, 12 Nov. 1823, reports that Grant arrived in Paris on 20 September, stayed at

Boulevard des Invalides, no. 5, left next day for La Grange, returned on 24 September, and left next day to return to England.

6. Chef de la 1ere Légion to Director of Police, 22 Sept. 1823, AN F7 6720, dossier 11.

7. See also *Le Livre Noir de Messieurs Delavau et Franchet, ou Répertoire alphabétique de la police politique sous le ministère déplorable* (4 vols.; Paris: Moutardier, 1829), III, beginning p. 64, on surveillance of La Grange in June 1823. Many people of several nationalities were reportedly there.

8. Lafayette to James Hillhouse, 16 May 1823, photo at LPP of letter at Connecticut Historical Society, MS. 68395. Lafayette to [unknown], 6 July 1823, LG photo of Lilly. Lafayette to David Bailey Warden, 15 Aug. [1823], photo at LPP of letter at Maryland Historical Society.

9. Lafayette to Renouard, 15 Aug. 1823, LG typescript of letter at Benjamin Franklin Papers, Yale University. Lafayette to Renouard, [1823? probably before 15 Aug., perhaps as early as late June 1823], LG photo of letter at Lafayette College (trans.). Joseph-François Michaud, editor of the *Biographie universelle*, was founder of the royalist paper, the *Quotidienne*.

10. Lafayette notes of 21 Aug. and 5 Sept. 1823, Dean.

11. Lafayette to Monroe, 26 Oct. 1823, LG photo of Monroe Papers, New York Public Library.

12. Lafayette to Sir Matthew Wood, 10 Aug. [1823], LG photo of letter in Pierpont Morgan Library. On Degeorge, see André Fortin, *Frédéric Degeorge (1797–1854)* (Lille: Université de Lille Faculté des lettres et sciences humaines, 1964). Lafayette to Say, 26 Oct. 1823, Franklin Papers, Yale, forwarding letters to England; J. B. Say to Bentham, 13 Oct. 1823, LG notes of Bentham Mss., portfolio 10, folder 19.

13. Lafayette to Fanny Wright, "mercredi" [ca. 1823] and "jeudi" [ca. 1823], Special Collections, University of Chicago. These letters are catalogued at [ca. 1824], but I think 1823 is more likely. The first letter reads: "I found on my list of visitors the secretary and confidant of the duc d'Orleans, which gave me the idea that perhaps one could employ his prince. But all of this is very vague in my head" (trans.).

14. Cloquet, *Recollections*, p. 192. Lafayette [extract] to Monroe, 25 Nov. 1823, Dean. Lafayette to Sir Charles Morgan, 30 Nov. 1823, Lilly. The relics can still be seen at La Grange.

15. Lafayette to William Lee, 20 Dec. 1823, Lilly.

16. Lafayette [extract] to Monroe, 25 Nov. 1823, Dean. See also Lafayette to Monroe, 26 Oct. 1823, LG Photo of letter at Monroe Papers, New York Public Library.

17. Lafayette [extract] to Monroe, 25 Nov. 1823, Dean. See also Lafayette to M. Dupuy d'Alençon, 27 Nov. 1823, in Victor Glachant,

"Quelques lettres inédites du général marquis de La Fayette (1822–1830)," *Les Annales Romantiques*, vol. 5 (1908), 350–351, for the duties which kept him in France.

18. Lafayette to William Lee, 20 Dec. 1823, Lilly.

19. He sent this information to Fanny Wright in Paris by way of the Scheffer brothers, who had been visiting at La Grange. Notes of Lafayette to Frances Wright, 17 Nov. 1823, Catherwood.

20. He told General Miollis, a veteran of the American Revolution, that "The dissolution of the Chamber . . . will send me back to my *Département* for the period of the elections." Lafayette to Miollis, Nov. 1823, cited in De La Fuye and Babeau, *The Apostle*, p. 264.

21. Lafayette to Peyre, 15 Jan. 1824, Department of Rare Books, Cornell University Library, letter bound in Rare/E/207/L2D81.

22. On Lafayette's help to Chauvet in 1822, see chapter 8.

23. Hachette, "Un Conspirateur Universitaire," pp. 729–730.

24. Morris, "Joseph Rey," p. 122. Rey also sent a letter for Mérilhou. Frédéric Degeorge, "Les Proscrits," pp. 108–109, mentions Rey and Chauvet as members of a group of exiles who met regularly in London in the winter of 1824. Another letter carried by Mme Chauvet, written by Sauquaire-Souligné, the man brought to trial with Goyet in 1820, urged Chauvet to join him in Lisbon.

25. Lafayette to Lady Morgan, 12 Feb. 1824, Lilly (trans.).

26. Hachette, "Un Conspirateur Universitaire," pp. 753–754.

27. *Mémoires*, VI, 150–152. Sauquaire-Souligné was a codefendant and was condemned to death in absentia.

28. GWL to Bonne Chevant, 15 and 25 Jan. 1824, Dean (trans.).

29. Lafayette to Bonne Chevant, 12 Feb. 1824, Dean.

30. This arrangement was apparently the price to be paid for the withdrawal of another candidate at Meaux, M. Béjot. Lafayette to Voyer d'Argenson, 26 Feb. 1824, Univ. de Poitiers, no. 53. Simon of Provins had been a member of the *conseil général* of the department, according to the voting list of 1818. Boby de la Chapelle was an adjoint. Mesnager lived in Meaux. Archives Départementales de Seine-et-Marne, 3M24, List of electors of Meaux 1822.

31. Lafayette to Frances Wright, 25 Feb. 1824, Special Collections, University of Chicago; AN C1303, Seine-et-Marne. The winner was Huerne de la Pommeuse by a vote of 216 to 109.

32. 348 people voted. These are the figures Lafayette reported to Voyer d'Argenson. The official statistics are somewhat different, 184 to 152, but Lafayette apparently included in his total the nine nullified ballots. Ballots were routinely nullified for various reasons, the most common being that the exact identity of the candidate was not known. Thus, if a voter had written merely "Lafayette" without indicating wheth-

er he meant the son or the father, the ballot would most likely be nullified. Lafayette to Voyer d'Argenson, 26 Feb. 1824, Université de Poitiers, no. 53; AN C1303, Seine-et-Marne.

33. In 1827, Lafayette told his American friend Charles Wilkes that "it has been discovered and even acknowledged, that when in 1824, I was not returned, there had been an unfair reading of the tickets, a happy circumstance to me, as it removed the only difficulty in the way of my blessed American voyage." Lafayette to Charles Wilkes, 28 Nov. 1827, Lafayette College.

34. Sub-Prefect of Meaux to Prefect, 20 July 1820, Archives Départementales de Seine-et-Marne, M10207, who reported that among the influential *ultra-libéraux* were "MM Petit one of whom operates the horse-relay station" (trans.). Note that Charles Petit had recently lent money to Lafayette; see above. The royalist voters were obviously suspicious of Clement Petit's conversion to the government side. Normally, the voters endorsed or rejected the provisional bureau as a block; party considerations were the only ones at issue. But this time, they singled out Clement Petit and denied him election to the permanent bureau, the only member of the provisional bureau who was not chosen.

35. Lafayette to Charles Petit, [12 Mar. 1824], photo at Library of Congress of letter at Lafayette College. Though this letter is dated 12 Feb. 1824, internal evidence shows it to be March, after the elections at Melun which began on 3 March. The connection between the discouragement of liberal voters and the defeat of their candidates is indicated by Beck, *French Legislators*, p. 87, who notes that in 1824, "The Left again fared best when turnout was the largest, 49 percent of its deputies were elected when the turnout was over 90 percent while the Right, on the other hand, had only 15 percent of its deputies elected in this type of district."

36. Beck, *French Legislators*, pp. 173, 175.

37. GWL to Bonne Chevant, 5 Mar. 1824, Dean (trans.). Manuel suspected that Constant was happy to be rid of him, and Laffitte, Manuel's friend, might have opposed Constant's election because of that.

38. Lafayette to Dupuy d'Alençon, 27 Feb. 1824, in Glachant, "Quelques lettres," pp. 351–352 (trans.).

39. Lafayette to Charles Petit, [12 Mar. 1824, misdated 12 Feb.], photo at Library of Congress of letter at Lafayette College (trans.).

40. Lafayette to Dupuy d'Alençon, 9 Apr. 1824, in Glachant, "Quelques lettres," p. 352.

41. Lafayette to Jefferson, 20 Dec. 1823, in Chinard, p. 417.

42. Lafayette to Jefferson, 20 Dec. 1823, in Chinard, p. 417.

43. Thomas Jefferson to James Monroe, 11 June 1823, microfilm of Monroe Papers, Reel 8.

44. Harry Ammon, *James Monroe: The Quest for National Identi-*

ty, (New York: McGraw-Hill, 1971), pp. 484–485. Ernest R. May, *The Making of the Monroe Doctrine* (Cambridge: Harvard Univ. Press, 1975), pp. 214–217.

45. Albert Gallatin to James Monroe, 1 Mar. 1823, AG Papers, Reel 35.

46. Lafayette to Albert Gallatin, 3 Oct. 1823, AG Papers, Reel 35.

47. Lafayette to Albert Gallatin, 13 Oct. 1823, AG Papers, Reel 35.

48. For the domestic political considerations involved in the formulation of the Monroe Doctrine, see May, *The Making of the Monroe Doctrine*.

49. Lafayette to William Lee, 20 Dec. 1823, Lilly.

50. Webster's speech in defense of his resolution was on 19 January 1824. *Annals of Congress*, 18th Congress, 1st Session, I, 1084–1110, 1174. The resolution regarding Lafayette was introduced on 12 January 1824, and was passed on 20 January, *Annals of Congress*, 18th Congress, 1st Session, I, 988, 1004, 1104.

51. *Annals of Congress*, 18th Congress, 1st Session, I, 1103; Lafayette, *Mémoires*, VI, 160; Lafayette [extract] to Monroe, 25 Nov. 1823, Dean. This letter is cited earlier in this chapter.

52. See Edward Mead Earle, "American Interest in the Greek Cause, 1821–1827," *American Historical Review*, 33 (Oct. 1927), 44–63.

53. May, *The Making of the Monroe Doctrine*, pp. 231–232.

54. May, *The Making of the Monroe Doctrine*, p. 220.

55. For more on American politics and the invitation, see Sylvia Neely, "The Politics of Liberty in the Old World and the New: Lafayette's Return to America in 1824," *Journal of the Early Republic*, 6 (Summer 1986), 151–171.

56. The Honorable J. Lloyd of Boston to Monroe, 3 Feb. 1824, microfilm of Monroe Papers, Reel 8.

57. Lafayette to Charles Petit La Mothe, 12 Feb. 1824, photo at Library of Congress of letter at Lafayette College. Brown also brought letters from Lafayette's American friends, including Monroe; James Brown to Monroe, 23 Jan. 1824, microfilm of Monroe Papers, Reel 8.

58. James Brown to Monroe, 15 Apr. 1824, microfilm of Monroe Papers, Reel 8.

59. Conspiracies, whether successful or not, were costly. Another Carbonarist leader, Voyer d'Argenson, also experienced serious financial difficulties in 1824. Mayor of St. Louis to Minister of the Interior, 26 Mar. 1824, AN F⁷ 6720, dossier 28.

60. James Brown to Monroe, 12 July 1824, microfilm of Monroe Papers, Reel 8.

61. One loan for ten thousand francs for two years at 6 percent

interest was negotiated with a Louisiana resident, Jean François Girod. Lafayette to Girod, 18 June 1824, Photo at Lilly of letter at Pierpont Morgan Library. Receipt to Jacob Gerhard Koch for thirty thousand francs, 18 June 1824, Dean. I. Cox Barnet to William H. Crawford, 10 July 1824, William Harris Crawford Collection, Duke University. Lafayette to Marcilly, 12 May 1824, Benjamin Franklin Papers, Yale University. Lafayette to Marcilly, 3 June 1824, Dean. Thomas Jefferson to James Monroe, 5 Feb. 1824, James Monroe Papers, Library of Congress. See also Nolte, *Fifty Years*, pp. 306–309.

62. James Brown to Monroe, 12 July 1824, microfilm of Monroe Papers, Reel 8. Fred Somkin, *Unquiet Eagle: Memory and Desire in the Idea of American Freedom, 1815–1860* (Ithaca: Cornell Univ. Press, 1967), pp. 137–142. Anne C. Loveland, *Emblem of Liberty: The Image of Lafayette in the American Mind* (Baton Rouge: Louisiana State Univ. Press, 1971), pp. 53–56.

63. Lafayette to Dupuy d'Alençon, 9 Apr. 1824, in Glachant, "Quelques lettres," p. 353. Clogenson to Torrijos, 16 Apr. 1824, AN F[7] 6653, file on Joseph Capell. Capell, who was arrested at Calais, was carrying the letters written by Clogenson. Other letters mentioned the bookseller Renouard, who was taking money to exiles in England, and recommended Salvandy, who was on his way to England.

64. Lafayette to Crawford, 14 May 1824, American Philosophical Society; Lafayette to Pepe, 14 May 1824, in Romano, "Lafayette, Guglielmo Pepe e l'Italia," p. 594. He also tried to help Pisa, who was in prison in Spain, by asking the American minister to intercede on his behalf.

65. Lafayette to Victor Toré, 25 April 1824, Dean (trans.).

66. Hoefer, *Nouvelle biographie*, vol. 39, pp. 44–45. Robert and Cougny, *Dictionnaire*, IV, 530–531. Constant, *Recueil d'Articles: Le Mercure, La Minerve et La Renommée*, I, xi. Lafayette to Pagès, 22 Nov. 1824, microfilm of private collection, LG Papers. Jefferson promised a subscription for the University of Virginia.

67. Lafayette [copy] to Regnault-Warin, 22 Feb. 1824, Dean.

68. Jean-Joseph Regnault-Warin, *Mémoires pour servir à la vie du Général LaFayette, et à l'histoire de l'assemblée constituante* (2 vols.; Paris: Hesse, 1824). A copy can be found at Cornell: Rare DC 146/ L16/R33. Volume 1 was a biography of Lafayette and volume 2 was a history of the Constituant Assembly followed by "*Pièces justificatives*" on the life of Lafayette.

69. Lafayette [copy] to Regnault-Warin, 25 Mar. 1824, Dean.

70. Lafayette to Pagès, "mardi matin," microfilm of private collection, LG Papers (trans.).

71. The issue is examined in detail in *Mémoires*, III, 502–515, Appendix IV. See also pp. 344–349, for Lafayette's description of what

happened during the summer of 1792. The letter has received wide currency because Adolphe Thiers included it in his history of the French Revolution.

72. Lafayette to Pagès, "mercredi" [7 Apr. 1824?] and "A Bord du Cadmus," 12 Aug. 1824, microfilm of private collection, LG Papers. Lafayette wrote to Regnault-Warin in 1818 arranging to meet him. Lafayette to Regnault de Warin, 25 Mar. [1818], Lilly.

73. Lafayette to his family, 11 Aug. 1824, Dean (trans.). Spitzer, *Old Hatreds*, p. 247; Lafayette to Audry de Puyraveau, 26 July 1824, Lilly. GWL to Bonne Chevant, 4 July 1824, Dean. The earliest mention of Levasseur in the Lafayette correspondence is in Lafayette [copy] to Regnault-Warin, 25 Mar. 1824, Dean.

74. Lafayette to his family, 21 Apr. 1825, Dean; Levasseur to Pagès, 9 and 24 Oct. 1824, microfilm of private collection, LG Papers.

75. Fanny reported that Madame Charles de Lasteyrie made this remark. Frances Wright to Camilla Wright, 23 May 1824, Catherwood.

76. Lafayette to Frances Wright, 25 Apr. 1824, copy in Catherwood.

77. Frances Wright to Camilla and Mrs. Millar, 22–23 May 1824, copy in Catherwood. His attack occurred around the first of May. Lafayette to Baron Denon, 8 May [1824], Special Collections, University of Chicago, forwarding Ary Scheffer's lithograph, mentions that he has been sick. Other letters at this time also mention the lithograph, so the Denon letter can be dated to 1824.

78. In his long letter to César de La Tour-Maubourg describing Adrienne's last illness, Lafayette does not mention such a promise. However, such a promise does seem consistent with Lafayette's veneration of Adrienne's memory. See Maurois, *Adrienne*, pp. 443–461.

79. Frances Wright to Camilla and Mrs. Millar, 23 May 1824, Catherwood.

80. Frances Wright to Camilla, 2 June [1824], Catherwood.

81. Vaulabelle, *Histoire des deux Restaurations*, VI, 13–14n (trans.).

82. Frances Wright to Camilla, 10 June [1824], Catherwood. Fanny reproduced long segments of her letter to Lafayette in this letter to Camilla.

83. Frances Wright to Pagès, 11 June 1824, microfilm of private collection, LG Papers (trans.).

84. Lafayette offered to pay him, but Allyn declined the offer: "We are all sensible of the honor conferred upon us by your taking passage in the Cadmus, and should Congress never remunerate us, General Lafayette will owe us nothing." Francis Allyn to Lafayette, 1 Sept. 1824, in 30th Congress 2d Session, House of Representatives, Report No. 12,

"Francis Allyn—Lafayette's passage to America," 3 Jan. 1849, a report of the committee investigating Allyn's claim for compensation.

85. Frances Wright to Pagès, 18 June 1824, and Lafayette to Pagès, "jeudi" [25 June 1824?], microfilm of private collection, LG Papers (trans.). Letter begins, *"Mde Charles Lasteyrie m'a chargé de vous dire,"* and was probably written on the Thursday following Fanny's letter to Pagès, dated 18 June, a Friday.

86. Lafayette to Madame Charles de Lasteyrie, 13 July 1824, microfilm of private collection, LG Papers.

87. Camilla Wright to James Mylne, 20 July 1824, Catherwood.

88. Sub-prefect of Le Havre to Directeur Général, 13 July 1824, in AN[7] 6720, dossier 11. He reported that the people on horseback numbered around thirty-six. Camilla, on the other hand, said around sixty. Camilla Wright to James Mylne, 20 July 1824, Catherwood. Another report from the Procureur du Roi du Havre to Vatismenil, 18 July 1824, AN BB[30] 235, dossier 3, mentions sixty men on horseback and "several hundred young fools on foot, whose agreed upon costume was a black jacket and white trousers, and who went out on the Honfleur road, to provide an escort for Lafayette" (trans.).

89. The way the crowds were handled became a matter of dispute. The *procureur du roi* believed that the sub-prefect had been negligent in not keeping the demonstrators out of the town entirely and reported that the few royalists in town were unhappy with the administration of the town. He called Lafayette "one of the first executioners of the unfortunate Louis 16," and "one of the authors of the assassination of Louis 16" (trans.). AN BB[30] 235, dossier 3.

Afterword

1. See for example, Alan Sked, "Metternich's Enemies or the Threat from Below," in Sked, *Europe's Balance of Power,* p. 181. In discussing constitutional models available to revolutionaries in the 1820s, the author does not mention the American constitution.

2. Rémond, *Etats-Unis,* p. 650. Rémond provides an excellent analysis of Lafayette's role as a mediator between the United States and France during this period.

Works Cited

Documents

The following repositories contain material cited which I consulted directly, either in person or by correspondence. In addition, some repositories contain copies of items from other collections. Those are indicated in the notes. Especially important sources for such copies were the Louis Gottschalk Papers at the University of Chicago and the Lafayette Papers Project at Cornell University.

United States

Albert Gallatin Papers, Microfilm edition
Benjamin Franklin Papers, Yale University
Brown University Library
Dean Collection, Cornell University Library
Houghton Library, Harvard University
James Monroe Papers, Library of Congress
James Monroe Papers, Microfilm
Lafayette Manuscripts, Lilly Library, Indiana University
Marquis de Lafayette Manuscripts Collection, David Bishop
      Skillman Library, Lafayette College
Martin P. Catherwood Library, Cornell University
Papers of Henry Clay, Library of Congress
Special Collections, University of Chicago
Thomas Jefferson Papers, Library of Congress
Trollope Family Papers, University of Illinois
University of Virginia Library
William Harris Crawford Collection, Duke University Library

Europe

Archives Nationales, Paris (AN)

    138 AP213
    234 AP
    252 AP3

271 AP2-Ba6
BB ^{30} 192
BB ^{30} 204
BB ^{30} 235
BB ^{30} 237
C1290, Sarthe
C1294A, Seine
C1303, Seine-et-Marne
C1317, Vendée
F^{1C} III, Sarthe 3
F^{1C} III Seine-et-Marne 4
F^7 4352^A, Sarthe
F^7 6653
F^7 6655
F^7 6659
F^7 6718
F^7 6719
F^7 6720
F^7 6741
F^7 6771
F^{17} 11775—Enseignement Mutuel

Archives de la Famille Galpin
Archives Départementales du Bas-Rhin, 2M13, and 3M19
Archives Départementales de la Sarthe M61/6
Archives Départementales de Seine-et-Marne, 3M23, 3M24, 132F2, and M10207
Bibliothèque de Grenoble, Joseph Rey, "Mémoires Politiques" T3939 and T3958
Bibliothèque Nationale, N. A. Fr. 20280
Université de Poitiers, Lafayette letters to Voyer d'Argenson
British Museum, Additional 30,110
British Museum, Additional 30,116
British Museum, Additional 33,545

Newspapers

Censeur européen
Conservateur
Constitutionnel
Journal des débats
Minerve
Moniteur

Patriote alsacien, Bibliothèque Nationale et Universitaire de
    Strasbourg, M.39.061.
Propagateur
Revue encyclopédique

Books

Adams, Henry, ed. *Writings of Albert Gallatin*. 3 vols. New York:
    Antiquarian Press, 1960.
Agulhon, Maurice. *Marianne into Battle: Republican Imagery and
    Symbolism in France, 1789–1880*. Cambridge, G. B.:
    Cambridge Univ. Press; Paris: Editions de la Maison des Sciences
    de l'Homme, 1981.
Alison, Sir Archibald. *Lives of Lord Castlereagh and Sir Charles
    Stewart*. Vol. 3. Edinburgh & London: Blackwood, 1861.
Ammon, Harry. *James Monroe: The Quest for National Identity*. New
    York: McGraw-Hill, 1971.
Annals of Congress. 18th Congress, 1st Session, I.
Archives parlementaires de 1787 à 1860.
Barante, Amable-Guillaume-Prosper-Bruguière. *Souvenirs du baron de
    Barante, 1782-1866*. 6 vols. Paris: Calmann-Lévy, 1890–1901.
Bardoux, A. *Les Dernières Années de La Fayette*. Paris: C. Lévy, 1893.
Bargeton, René, Pierre Bougard, Bernard Le Clère, and Pierre-François
    Pinaud, *Les Préfets du 11 Ventôse an VIII au 4 septembre 1870*.
    Paris: Archives Nationales, 1981.
Barrot, Odilon. *Mémoires posthumes*. 4 vols. Paris: Charpentier, 1875.
Bastid, Paul. *Benjamin Constant et sa doctrine*. 2 vols. [Paris]:
    Librairie Armand Colin, 1966.
———— . *Les Institutions politiques de la monarchie parlementaire
    française (1814–1848)*. Paris: Editions du Recueil Sirey, 1954.
Beck, Thomas D. *French Legislators, 1800–1834: A Study in
    Quantitative History*. Berkeley: Univ. of California Press, 1974.
Bentham, Jeremy. *The Correspondence of Jeremy Bentham*. Ed. by
    Timothy L. S. Sprigge, Ian R. Christie, A. T. Milne, J. R.
    Dinwiddy, and Stephen Conway. 9 vols. to date. London: various,
    1968–1989.
Béranger. *Lettres inédites de Béranger à Dupont de l'Eure*. Paris:
    Maison Pierre Douville, [1908].
Bergeron, Louis. *Banquiers, négociants et manufacturiers parisiens
    du Directoire à l'Empire*. Paris: Ecole des hautes études en
    sciences sociales, 1978.
Bernier, Olivier. *Lafayette: Hero of Two Worlds*. New York: E. P. Dutton,
    1983.

Bertier de Sauvigny, Guillaume de. *La Restauration*. 3d ed. rev. Paris: Flammarion, 1974.

———. *Le Comte Ferdinand de Bertier (1782–1864) et l'énigme de la Congrégation*. Paris: Presses continentales, 1948.

Biaudet, Jean-Charles, and Françoise Nicod, eds. *Correspondance de Frédéric-César de La Harpe et Alexandre Ier*. 3 vols. Neuchâtel: Baconnière, 1978–1980.

Billington, James H. *Fire in the Minds of Men: Origins of the Revolutionary Faith*. New York: Basic Books, 1980.

Biographie des hommes vivants. 5 vols. Paris: L. G. Michaud, 1816–1819.

Bonnal (de Ganges), ed. *Manuel et son temps, étude sur l'opposition parlementaire sous la Restauration*. Paris: E. Dentu, 1877.

Bottin, Sebastien. *Almanach du commerce de Paris, des départemens de la France, et des principales villes du monde*. Paris: Au Bureau del'Almanach du commerce, [1819].

Bowring, John. *Autobiographical Recollections*. London: Henry S. King, 1877.

———, ed. *The Works of Jeremy Bentham*. 11 vols. Edinburgh: W. Tait, 1838–1843.

Broglie, Achille-Charles-Léonce-Victor, duc de. *Souvenirs du feu duc de Broglie, (1785–1870)*. 4 vols. Paris: Calmann Lévy, 1886.

Buckman, Peter. *Lafayette: A Biography*. New York: Paddington Press, 1977.

Bushnell, David. *The Santander Regime in Gran Colombia*. Newark: Univ. of Delaware Press, 1954.

Carr, Raymond. *Spain: 1808–1939*. Oxford: Clarendon, 1966.

Chaffanjon, Arnaud. *La Fayette et sa descendance*. [Paris?]: Berger-Levrault, 1976.

Chandler, David G. *Dictionary of the Napoleonic Wars*. New York: Macmillan, 1979.

Charavay, Etienne. *Le Général La Fayette (1757–1834)*. Paris: Société de l'histoire de la Révolution française, 1898.

Chateaubriand. *Correspondance générale de Chateaubriand*. Vol 3. Ed. by Louis Thomas. Paris: Honoré et Edouard Champion, 1913.

Chinard, Gilbert, ed. *Jefferson et les Idéologues*. Baltimore: Johns Hopkins Press, 1925; Paris: Presses Universitaires de France, 1925.

———. *The Letters of Lafayette and Jefferson*. Baltimore: Johns Hopkins Press, 1929; Paris: "Les Belles Lettres," 1929.

Cloquet, Jules. *Recollections of the Private Life of General Lafayette*. London: Baldwin and Cradock, 1835.

Constant, Benjamin, *Journaux intimes*. [Paris]: Gallimard, 1952.

———. *Lettre à M. le marquis de Latour-Maubourg, ministre de la guerre, sur ce qui s'est passé à Saumur les 7 et 8 octobre 1820*. Paris: Béchet ainé, 1820.

———. *Lettres à sa famille*. Intro. by Jean H. Menos. Paris: Librairie Stock, 1932.

———. *Mémoires sur les Cent Jours*. [Paris]: Jean-Jacques Pauvert, 1956.

———. *Oeuvres*. Paris: Gallimard, 1957.

———. *Recueil d'articles: Le Mercure, La Minerve et La Renommée*. Ed. by Ephraïm Harpaz. 2 vols. Geneva: Droz, 1972.

———. *Recueil d'articles 1795-1817*. Ed. by Ephraïm Harpaz. Geneva: Droz, 1978.

———, and Goyet de la Sarthe. *Correspondance, 1818–1822*. Ed. by Ephraïm Harpaz. Geneva: Droz, 1973.

Coppolani, Jean-Yves. *Les Elections en France à l'époque napoléonienne*. Paris: Editions Albatros, 1980.

Corcelle, Blanche-Joséphine de, Comtesse Roederer. *Notice et souvenirs de famille*. Brussells: Lyon-Claesen, 1899.

Coulmann, J. J. *Réminiscences*. 3 vols. Paris: Michel Lévy, 1862–1869.

Crémieux, Albert. *La Censure en 1820 et 1821: Etude sur la presse politique et la résistance libérale*. Paris: Edouard Cronély, 1912.

Cunliffe, Marcus. *George Washington: Man and Monument*. Boston: Little Brown, 1958.

Daudet, Ernest. *La Police politique: Cronique des temps de la Restauration d'après les rapports des agents secrets et les papiers du cabinet noir, 1815–1820*. Paris: Plon, 1912.

Debidour, A. *Le Général Fabvier; sa vie militaire et politique*. Paris: Plon-Nourrit, 1904.

De La Fuye, Maurice, and Emile Babeau. *The Apostle of Liberty: A Life of La Fayette*. Trans. by Edward Hyams. New York: Thomas Yoseloff, 1956.

Didier, Franklin J. *Letters from Paris and Other Cities of France, Holland, &c. Written During a Tour and Residence in These Countries in the Years, 1816, 17, 18, 19, and 20*. New York: James V. Seaman, 1821.

Dupin, André-Marie-Jean-Jacques. *Mémoires de M. Dupin*. 2 vols. Paris: Henri Plon, 1855.

Duvergier, J. B. *Collection complète des lois, decrets, ordonnances, règlemens, avis du Conseil-d'état*. Paris: various, 1834–1918.

Duvergier de Hauranne, Prosper. *Histoire du gouvernement parlementaire en France, 1814–1848*. 10 vols. Paris: Michel Lévy frères, 1857–1871.

Eckhardt, Celia Morris. *Fanny Wright: Rebel in America.* Cambridge: Harvard Univ. Press, 1984.

Esquisse historique sur les Cent Jours, et fragments inédits relatifs aux séances secrètes des chambres, à la marche du gouvernement provisoire, et aux négociations d'Haguenau. Paris: Baudouin Frères, 1819.

Ford, Franklin L. *Political Murder: From Tyrannicide to Terrorism.* Cambridge: Harvard Univ. Press, 1985.

Fortin, André. *Frédéric Degeorge (1797–1854).* Lille: Université de Lille Faculté des lettres et sciences humaines, 1964.

Fouché, Joseph. *Mémoires.* 2 vols. Paris: Le Rouge, 1824.

———. *Mémoires.* New York: Merrill & Baker, n.d.

Fromageot, Jean. *Jacques Philippe Grattepain, dit Morizot: Procureur des biens du marquis de La Fayette originaire d'Arthonnay en Tonnerrois.* Tonnerre: Société d'archéologie et d'histoire du Tonnerrois, 1982.

Furet, François, and Mona Ozouf, eds. *A Critical Dictionary of the French Revolution.* Trans. by Arthur Goldhammer. Cambridge: Belknap Press of Harvard Univ. Press, 1989.

Gallego, Miguel Artole, ed. *Biblioteca de autores españoles: Memorias del General Don Francisco Espoz y Mina.* 2 vols. Madrid: Ediciones Atlas, 1962.

Gil Novales, Alberto. *Las sociedades patrioticas (1820–1823).* 2 vols. Madrid: Editorial Tecnos, 1975.

Girard, Louis. *La Garde nationale, 1814–1871.* Paris: Librairie Plon, 1964.

Glover, Michael. *A Very Slippery Fellow: The Life of Sir Robert Wilson, 1777–1849.* Oxford: Oxford Univ. Press, 1977.

Goetz, Helmut. *Marc-Antoine Jullien de Paris (1755–1848): L'Evolution spirituelle d'un révolutionnarie.* Paris: Institut Pédagogique National, 1962.

Gontard, M. *L'Enseignement primaire en France de la Révolution à la loi Guizot.* Paris: Belles Lettres, [1959].

Gottschalk, Louis. *Lafayette Comes to America.* Chicago: Univ. of Chicago Press, 1935.

———. *Lafayette Joins the American Army.* Chicago: Univ. of Chicago Press, 1937.

———. *Lafayette and the Close of the American Revolution.* Chicago: Univ. of Chicago Press, 1942.

———. *Lafayette Between the American and the French Revolution (1783–1789).* Chicago: Univ. of Chicago Press, 1950.

———, and Margaret Maddox. *Lafayette in the French Revolution through the October Days.* Chicago: Univ. of Chicago Press, 1969.

———— , and Margaret Maddox. *Lafayette in the French Revolution from the October Days through the Federation*. Chicago: Univ. of Chicago Press, 1973.

———— , Phyllis S. Pestieau, and Linda J. Pike. *Lafayette: A Guide to the Letters, Documents, and Manuscripts in the United States*. Ithaca: Cornell Univ. Press, 1975.

Grégoire, Abbé Henri. *Mémoires de Grégoire*. Ed. by H. Carnot. 2 vols. Paris: J. Yonet, 1840.

Guizot, François. *Mémoires pour servir à l'histoire de mon temps*. 8 vols. Paris: Michel Lévy frères, 1858–1867.

Halevy, Elie. *The Growth of Philosophic Radicalism*. Boston: Beacon Press, 1955.

Harpaz, Ephraïm. *L'Ecole libérale sous la Restauration, le "Mercure" et la "Minerve," 1817–1820*. Geneva: Droz, 1968.

Harvey, W. W. *Sketches of Hayti from the Expulsion of the French to the Death of Christophe*. London: F. Cass, [1971], reprint of 1827 edition.

Hatin, E. *Bibliographie historique et critique de la presse périodique en France*. Paris: Firmin-Didot, 1866.

Heineman, Helen. *Restless Angels: The Friendship of Six Victorian Women*. Athens: Ohio Univ. Press, 1983.

Hérisson, Comte d'. *Le Cabinet noir: Louis XVIII—Napoléon—Marie Louise*. 9th. ed. Paris: Paul Ollendorff, 1887.

———— . *Un Pair de France policier*. Vol. 1 of *Les Girouettes politiques*. 3 vols. Paris: P. Ollendorff, 1892–1894.

Herold, J. Christopher. *The Mind of Napoleon: A Selection from His Written and Spoken Words*. New York: Columbia Univ. Press, 1955.

———— . *Mistress to an Age*. Indianapolis: Bobbs-Merrill, 1958.

Hoefer. *Nouvelle biographie générale depuis les temps les plus reculés jusqu'à nos jours*. Paris: Firmin Didot frères, 1857–1866.

Hofstadter, Richard. *The Idea of a Party System*. Berkeley: Univ. of California Press, 1969.

Hopkins, James F., ed. *The Papers of Henry Clay*. Lexington: Univ. of Kentucky Press, 1959.

Houssaye, Henri. *1815*. 32d. ed. 3 vols. Paris: Parrin, 1900.

Hugues, Adolphe. *Le département de Seine-et-Marne de 1800 à 1895*. Melun: E. Drosne, 1895.

Hunt, Gaillard. *Fragments of Revolutionary History*. Brooklyn, N. Y.: The Historical Printing Club, 1892; reprinted by Arno Press, 1971.

Idzerda, Stanley J., ed. *Lafayette in the Age of the American Revolution*. 5 vols. Ithaca: Cornell Univ.Press, 1977–1983.

Jackson, Stuart W. *La Fayette: A Bibliography*. New York: Burt Franklin, 1968; reprint of 1930 edition.

Jardin, André. *Histoire du libéralisme politique*. [Paris]: Hachette, 1985.

Kennedy, Emmet. *Destutt de Tracy and the Origins of "Ideology."* Philadelphia: American Philosophical Society, 1978.

Kennedy, Melvin D. *Lafayette and Slavery from His Letters to Thomas Clarkson and Granville Sharp*. Easton, Pa.: American Friends of Lafayette, 1950.

Kieswetter, James K. *Etienne-Denis Pasquier: The Last Chancellor of France*. Philadelphia: American Philosophical Society, 1977.

Kolb, Marthe. *Ary Scheffer et son temps, 1795–1858*. Paris: Boivin, 1937.

Lafayette, Gilbert du Motier de. *Mémoires, correspondance et manuscrits du général La Fayette, publiés par sa famille*. 6 vols. Paris: H. Fournier aîné, 1837–1838.

————— . *The speech of General La Fayette, delivered in the Chamber of Deputies, in the sitting of the 4th of June, 1821, on the question of granting the public supplies*. London: Printed for James Ridgway, 1821.

Laffitte, Jacques. *Mémoires de Laffitte*. Ed. by Paul Duchon. Paris: Firmin-Didot, [1932].

Langeron, Roger. *Decazes: Ministre du roi*. [Paris]: Hachette, 1960.

Lee, William. *A Yankee Jeffersonian: Selections from the Diary and Letters of William Lee of Massachusetts*. Ed. by Mary Lee Mann. Cambridge: The Belknap Press of Harvard Univ. Press, 1958.

Le Gallo, Emile. *Les Cents-Jours*. Paris: Librairie Félix Alcan, 1924.

Le Livre noir de Messieurs Delavau et Franchet, ou Répertoire alphabétique de la police politique sous le ministère déplorable. 4 vols. Paris: Moutardier, 1829.

Lettres autographes composant la collection de Madame G. Whitney Hoff. Paris: P. Cornuau [etc.], 1934. University of Chicago Rare Books, Z42f.H7.

Leuilliot, Paul. *L'Alsace au début du XIXe siècle; essai d'histoire politique, économique et religieuse, 1815–1830*. 3 vols. Paris: S.E.V.P.E.N., 1959–1960.

Longford, Elizabeth. *Wellington, The Years of the Sword*. London: Weidenfeld & Nicolson, 1969.

Loveland, Anne C. *Emblem of Liberty: The Image of Lafayette in the American Mind*. Baton Rouge: Louisiana State Univ. Press, 1971.

Lucas-Dubreton, J. *Le Culte de Napoléon, 1815–1848*. Paris: Albin Michel, 1960.

Mack, Mary P. *Jeremy Bentham: An Odyssey of Ideas*. New York: Columbia Univ. Press; London: Heinemann, 1963.

Madelin, Louis. *Fouché, 1759–1820*. Paris: Librairie Plon, 1923.

Maës, Pierre. *Un Ami de Stendhal. Victor Jacquemont*. Paris: Desclée de Brower, [1934].

Mansel, Philip. *The Court of France, 1789–1830*. Cambridge, G. B.: Cambridge Univ. Press, 1988.

———. *Louis XVIII*. London: Blond & Briggs, 1981.

Manuel, Frank E. *The New World of Henri Saint-Simon*. Cambridge: Harvard Univ. Press, 1956.

Marshall, J. F., ed. *Victor Jacquemont, Letters to Achille Chaper: Intimate Sketches of Life among Stendhal's Coterie*. Philadelphia: The American Philosophical Society, 1960.

Maurois, André. *Adrienne: The Life of the Marquise de La Fayette*. Trans. by Gerard Hopkins. New York: McGraw-Hill, 1961.

May, Ernest R. *The Making of the Monroe Doctrine*. Cambridge: Harvard Univ. Press, 1975.

McConnell, Allen. *Tsar Alexander I: Paternalistic Reformer*. New York: Thomas Y. Crowell, 1970.

Mellon, Stanley. *The Political Uses of History: A Study of Historians in the French Restoration*. Stanford:Stanford Univ. Press, 1958.

Michaud. *Biographie universelle ancienne et moderne*. Reprint of 2d edition of 1854.

Mill, Anna Jean, ed. *John Mill's Boyhood Visit to France Being a Journal and Notebook Written by John Stuart Mill in France, 1820–1821*. [Toronto]: Univ. of Toronto Press, 1960.

Mongan, Agnes. *Harvard Honors Lafayette*. Cambridge: Fogg Art Museum, 1976.

Monroe, James. *Writings of James Monroe*. Ed. by Stanislaus Murray Hamilton. 7 vols. New York: Putnam's, 1898–1903.

Montcalm-Gozon, Armande Marie Antoinette, marquise de. *Mon journal, 1815–1818, pendant le premier ministère de mon frère*. Paris: Editions Bernard Grasset, [c. 1936].

Moreno Guerra, José. *Compte rendu de ce qui s'est passé dans les sessions des Cortes d'Espagne, pendant les années 1821 et 1822, qui annonce l'avenir*. Paris: Imprimeriede Moreau, 1822.

Morgan, Lady Sydney. *Passages from My Autobiography*. New York: Appleton, 1859.

Morris, Richard. "Joseph Rey of Grenoble, 1779–1855: Reformer, Educator, Humanitarian." Ph.D. Diss. University of Iowa.

Moscati, Ruggero, ed. *Guglielmo Pepe*. Vol. 1 (only vol. published). Rome: Vittoriano, 1938.

Mouchot, Marion. "'Le Constitutionnel,' Contribution à l'histoire de la presse sous la Restauration." Thèse. Ecole des Chartes.

Necheles, Ruth F. *The Abbé Grégoire, 1787–1831: The Odyssey of an Egalitarian*. Westport, Conn.: Greenwood, 1971.

Neely, Sylvia. "Lafayette and Liberal Politics in the Early Restoration."
Ph.D. Diss. University of Notre Dame, 1981.

Nesselrode, Comte A. de, ed. *Lettres et papiers du chancelier comte de Nesselrode.* 11 vols. Paris: A. Lahure, [1904–1912?].

Newman, Edgar Leon. *Historical Dictionary of France from the 1815 Restoration to the Second Empire.* 2 vols. Westport, Conn.: Greenwood, 1987.

Nicholls, David. *From Dessalines to Duvalier: Race, Colour and National Independence in Haiti.* Cambridge, G. B.: Cambridge Univ. Press, 1979.

Nobécourt, R.-G. *La Vie d'Armand Carrel.* Paris: Librairie Gallimard, 1930.

Nolte, Vincent. *Fifty Years in Both Hemispheres.* New York: Redfield, 1854.

Nouvelle biographie générale. Paris: Didot, 1858.

Papers of James A. Bayard, 1796–1815. Vol. 2 of *Annual Report of the American Historical Association for 1913.*

Pasquier, Etienne-Denis. *Mémoires du Chancelier Pasquier.* 6 vols. Paris: Plon, Nourrit, 1893–1895.

Pecchio, Count. *Anecdotes of the Spanish and Portuguese Revolutions.* Intro. and notes by Edward Blaquière. London: G. and W. B. Whittaker, 1823.

Penman, John Simpson. *Lafayette and Three Revolutions.* Boston: Stratford, 1929.

Pepe, Guglielmo. *Memoirs of General Pepe Comprising the Principal Military and Political Events of Modern Italy.* 3 vols. London: Richard Bentley, 1846.

Perceval, Emile de. *Un Adversaire de Napoleon: Le Vte Lainé et la vie parlementaire au temps de la Restauration.* 2 vols. Paris: Librairie Ancienne Honoré Champion, 1926.

Perkins, A. J. G., and Theresa Wolfson. *Frances Wright, Free Enquirer. The Study of a Temperament.* New York: Harper & Brothers, 1939.

Piccirilli, Ricardo. *Rivadavia y su tiempo.* 3 vols. Buenos Aires: Ediciones Peuser, 1960.

Ponteil, Félix. *Histoire de l'enseignement, 1789–1964.* [Paris]: Sirey, 1966.

Porch, Douglas. *Army and Revolution: France 1815–1848.* London: Routledge & Kegan Paul, 1974.

Pouthas, Charles H. *Guizot pendant la Restauration: préparation de l'homme d'état.* Paris: Plon-Nourrit, 1923.

Pozzo di Borgo, Charles, ed. *Correspondance diplomatique du comte Pozzo di Borgo, ambassadeur de Russie en France, et du comte de Nesselrode depuis la Restauration des Bourbons jusqu'au congrès d'Aix-la-Chapelle (1814–1818).* 2 vols. Paris: Calmann Lévy, 1890–1897.

Procès de la Société dite les Amis de la liberté de la Presse. Paris: Librairie constitutionnelle de Brissot-Thivars, 1820.

Regnault-Warin, Jean-Baptiste-Joseph-Innocent-Philadelphe. *Mémoires pour servir à la vie du Général LaFayette, et à l'histoire de l'Assemblée constituante.* 2 vols. Paris: Hesse, 1824.

Reinhard, Marcel. *Le Grand Carnot.* Vol. 2: *L'Organisateur de la victoire.* Paris: Hachette, 1952.

Rémond, René. *Les Etats-Unis devant l'opinion française, 1815–1852.* 2 vols. Paris: Librairie Armand Colin, 1962.

Rémusat, Charles de. *Correspondance de M. de Rémusat pendant les premières années de la Restauration.* 6 vols. Paris: C. Lévy, 1884–1886.

———. *Mémoires de ma vie.* 3 vols. Paris: Plon, [1958–1960].

Resnick, Daniel P. *The White Terror and the Political Reaction after Waterloo.* Cambridge: Harvard Univ. Press, 1966.

Ribe, Georges. *L'Opinion publique et la vie politique à Lyon lors des premières années de la Seconde Restauration.* Paris: Sirey, 1957.

Robert, Adolphe, and Gaston Cougny. *Dictionnaire des parlementaires français.* 5 vols. Paris: Bourloton, 1890.

Robert, Daniel. *Les Eglises réformées en France (1800–1830).* Paris: Presses universitaires de France, 1961.

Robertson, William Spence. *France and Latin-American Independence.* New York: Octagon, 1967; reprint of 1939 edition.

Robinson, Henry Crabb. *Diary, Reminiscences and Correspondence.* Ed. by Thomas Sadler. 2 vols. London: Macmillan, 1872.

Romani, George T. *The Neapolitan Revolution of 1820–1821.* Evanston: Northwestern Univ. Press, 1950.

Romberg, Edouard, and Albert Malet, eds. *Louis XVIII et les Cent-Jours à Gand: Recueil de documents inédits publiés pour La Société d'histoire contemporaire.* 2 vols. Paris: Alphonse Picard et fils, 1898.

Rosenblum, Nancy L. *Bentham's Theory of the Modern State.* Cambridge: Harvard Univ. Press, 1978.

Sainsbury, John A. *The Napoleon Museum; The History of France Illustrated from Louis XIV to the End of the Reign and Death of the Emperor.* London, 1845.

Sánchez Mantero, Rafael. *Las conspiraciones liberales en Francia*

(1815–1823). Sevilla: Publicaciones de la Universidad de Sevilla, 1972.

——— . *Los Cien Mil Hijos de San Luis y las relaciones franco-españolas*. Sevilla: Anales de la Universidad Hispalense, 1981.

Santarosa, Santorre di. *Lettere dall'esilio 1821–1825*. Ed. by Antonio Olmo. Rome: Istituto per la storia del Risorgimento italiano, 1969.

Sarrailh, Jean. *Un Homme d'état espagnol: Martínez de la Rosa (1787–1862)*. Bordeaux: Feret & Fils; Paris: E. de Boccard, 1930.

Say, J. B. *Oeuvres diverses de J. B. Say* . . . . Ed. by Charles Comte, E. Daire, and Horace Say. Osnabrück: Otto Zeller, 1966; reprint of 1848 edition.

Scheffer, C. A. *De l'état de la liberté en France*. Brussels: Demat, 1818.

Schroeder, Paul W. *Metternich's Diplomacy at Its Zenith, 1820–1823*. Austin: Univ. of Texas Press, 1962.

Seybert, Adam. *Statistiques des États-Unis*. Trans. by C. A. Scheffer. Paris: Librairie constitutionnelle de Brissot-Thivars, 1820.

Simon, Walter, ed. *French Liberalism, 1789–1848*. New York: John Wiley & Sons, 1972.

Sked, Alan, ed. *Europe's Balance of Power: 1815–1848*. New York: Barnes & Noble, 1979.

Somkin, Fred. *Unquiet Eagle: Memory and Desire in the Idea of American Freedom, 1815–1860*. Ithaca: Cornell Univ. Press, 1967.

Spitzer, Alan B. *The French Generation of 1820*. Princeton: Princeton Univ. Press, 1987.

——— . *Old Hatreds and Young Hopes: The French Carbonari against the Bourbon Restoration*. Cambridge: Harvard Univ. Press, 1971.

Staël, Madame de. *Correspondance générale*. Vol. IV, Part 2. Paris: Jean-Jacques Pauvert, 1978.

Stendhal. *Correspondance*. Vol. 1. [Paris]: Gallimard, 1962.

——— . *Souvenirs d'égotisme*. Paris: Le Divan, 1927.

Suddaby, Elizabeth, and P. J. Yarrow, eds. *Lady Morgan in France*. Newcastle upon Tyne: Oriel Press, 1971.

Taillemite, Etienne. *La Fayette*. [Paris]: Fayard, 1989.

Thureau-Dangin, Paul. *Le Parti libéral sous la Restauration*. Paris: E. Plon, 1876.

Ticknor, George. *Life, Letters, and Journals of George Ticknor*. 2 vols. Boston: Osgood, 1876.

Tild, Jean. *L'Abbé Grégoire*. Paris: Nouvelles Editions latines, 1946.

Touchard, Jean. *La Gloire de Béranger*. 2 vols. Paris: Librairie Armand Colin, 1968.

Tourtier-Bonazzi, Chantal de. *Lafayette: Documents conservés en France*. Paris: Archives Nationales, 1976.

Troyat, Henri. *Alexander of Russia: Napoleon's Conqueror*. New York: E. P. Dutton, 1982.

U. S. Congress, House of Representatives. *Francis Allyn—Lafayette's passage to America*. Report of the committee investigating Allyn's claim for compensation. 30th Congress, 2d Session., 3 Jan. 1849.

Vaulabelle, Achille de. *Histoire des deux Restaurations jusqu'à la chute de Charles X*. 10 vols. 2d ed. Paris: Garnier Frères, [1874?].

Vidalenc, Jean. *Les Demi-Soldes: Etude d'une catégorie sociale*. Paris: Librairie Marcel Rivière, 1955.

Voyer d'Argenson, Marc-René-Marie de. *Discours et opinions de Voyer d'Argenson . . . précédés d'une notice biographique et publiés par son fils*. 2 vols. Paris: Bureau de la "Revue générale biographique," 1845–1846.

Waquet, Françoise. *Les Fêtes royales sous la restauration, ou L'Ancien régime retrouvé*. Geneva: Droz, 1981.

Webster, C. K., ed. *Britain and the Independence of Latin America, 1812–1830*. 2 vols. New York: Octagon, 1970; reprint of 1938 edition.

Whitlock, Brand. *La Fayette*. 2 vols. New York: D. Appleton, [c. 1929].

Wicks, Margaret Campbell Walker. *The Italian Exiles in London, 1816-1848*. [Manchester]: Manchester Univ. Press, 1937.

Williford, Miriam. *Jeremy Bentham on Spanish America: An Account of His Letters and Proposals to the New World*. Baton Rouge: Louisiana State Univ. Press, 1980.

Wood, Gordon. *The Creation of the American Republic, 1776–1787*. Chapel Hill: Univ. of North Carolina Press, 1969.

Woolf, Stuart. *A History of Italy 1700–1860: The Social Constraints of Political Change*. London: Methuen, 1979.

Wright, Frances. *Views of Society and Manners in America*. Ed. by Paul R. Baker. Cambridge: Harvard Univ. Press, 1963; reprint of the first London edition of 1821.

Zagar, Janko. *Bentham et la France*. Thesis, 1958.

Zavala, Iris M. *Masones, comuneros y carbonarios*. Madrid: Siglo XXI de España Editores, 1971.

Articles

Abbey, Katherine T. "The Land Ventures of General LaFayette in the Territory of Orleans and State of Louisiana." *The Louisiana Historical Quarterly* 16 (July 1933): 359–373.

Augustin-Thierry, A. "Augustin Thierry d'après sa correspondance."
    Revue des deux mondes 6 (1 Nov. 1921): 146–178, 836–866.

Birembaut, Arthur. "Sauquaire-Souligné." *Stendhal Club* 25 (1983):
    549–550.

Bizardel, Yvon. "Un acquéreur de biens nationaux: Richard Codman de
    Boston." *Bulletin de la Société de l'histoire de Paris et de l'Ile
    de France* 92 (1965): 67–73.

Bourgin, Georges. "Santa Rosa et la France, 1821–1822." *Revue
    historique* 103 (Mar.–Apr. 1910): 306–316, and 104 (May–June
    1910): 67–89.

Brandt, A. "Une famille de fabricants Mulhousiens au début du XIXe
    siècle: Jean Koechlin et ses fils." *Annales* 6 (1951): 319–330.

Burns, J. H. "Bentham and the French Revolution." *Transactions of
    the Royal Historical Society* 5th series, 16 (1966): 96–114.

Calmette, A. "Les Carbonari en France sous la Restauration, 1821–
    1830." *La Révolution de 1848* 9 (1912–1913): 401–417, and 10
    (1913–1914): 117–137, 214–230.

Cappadocia, Ezio. "The Liberals and Madame de Staël in 1818." In
    Ideas in History, ed. by Richard Herr and Harold T.Parker, 182–
    198. Durham, N. C.: Duke Univ. Press, 1965.

Contamine, Henry. "La Grande Tentative d'expansion de la Charte et
    l'Italie, 1820–1821." In *Atti del XXXVII Congresso di storia del
    Risorgimento italiano*, 60–68. Rome: Istituto per la storia del
    Risorgimento italiano, 1961.

Daline, V. "Marc-Antoine Jullien après le 9 Thermidor." *Annales
    historiques de la Révolution française* 36 (1964): 159–173; 37
    (1965): 187–203; 38 (1966): 390–412.

Degeorge, Frédéric. "Les Proscrits de la Restauration." In *Paris
    révolutionnaire*, vol. 4, pp. 103–127. Paris: Guillaumin, 1833–
    1834.

Dinwiddy, J. R. "Bentham's Transition to Political Radicalism."
    Journal of the History of Ideas 36 (1975): 683–700.

Dubois, P. F. "Augustin Thierry." *Revue Bleue* 5th series, 10 (5 Dec.
    1908): 741–744.

Dumolard, Henry. "Comment l'abbé Grégoire fut élu dans l'Isère."
    Annales de l'Université de Grenoble 5 (1928): 231–277.

———. "Joseph Rey de Grenoble (1779–1855) et ses mémoires
    politiques." *Annales de l'Université de Grenoble* 4 (1927): 71–111.

Earle, Edward Mead. "American Interest in the Greek Cause, 1821–
    1827." *American Historical Review* 33 (Oct. 1927): 44–63.

Glachant, Victor. "Quelques lettres inédites du général marquis de La
    Fayette (1822–1830)." *Les Annales romantiques* 5 (1908): 347–
    366.

Grignon, Max. "Le Parti libéral dans la Sarthe de 1815 à 1830." *La Révolution dans la Sarthe* 22 (Jan.–Dec., 1927).

Hachette, Alfred. "Un Conspirateur Universitaire—François Chauvet." *Revue Bleue* 5th series, 9 (6 and 13 June 1908): 726–730, 753–758.

Harpaz, Ephraïm. "'Le censeur européen'; histoire d'un journal industrialiste." *Revue d'histoire économique et sociale* 37 (1959): 185–218, 328–357.

——— . "Sur un écrit de jeunesse d'Augustin Thierry." *Revue d'histoire littéraire de la France*, no. 3 (July–Sept. 1959): 342–364.

——— . "Une lettre inconnue de Benjamin Constant à Napoleon (30 avril 1815)." *Revue de la Bibliothèque Nationale* 1 (Mar. 1982): 27–34.

Hauterive, Ernest d'. "Conversations de L'Empereur avec le Grand-Maréchal [Gen. Bertrand], 22–26 avril 1821." *Revue des deux mondes* 7th series, 48 (15 Dec. 1928): 847–873.

Kramer, Lloyd S. "America's Lafayette and Lafayette's America: A European and the American Revolution." *William and Mary Quarterly*, 38 (Apr. 1981), 228–241.

Laux, Christian. "D'Où Vient Donc Marianne?" *Annales historiques de la Révolution française* 55 (1983): 628–633.

Liggio, Leonard P. "Charles Dunoyer (1786–1862) and French Classical Liberalism." *The Journal of Libertarian Studies* 1 (1977): 153–178.

Lote, Georges. "La Mort de Napoléon et l'opinion bonapartiste en 1821." *Revue des études napoléoniennes* 31 (July 1930): 19–58.

Maguelonne. "L'Election de Manuel en Vendée en 1818." *Révolution de 1848* 9 (1912): 199–211 [actually about election of 1822].

Manigat, Leslie F. "Le Délicat Problème de la critique historique." *Revue de la Société haitienne d'histoire, de géographie et de géologie* (Oct. 1954): 29–59.

Mastellone, Salvo. "Un aristocratico in esilio: Santorre di Santarosa." *Rivista storica italiana* 65 (1953): 56–75, 553–576.

Miller, Marc. "Lafayette's Farewell Tour and American Art." In *Lafayette, Hero of Two Worlds*, 91–194. Hanover: Univ. Press of New England, 1989.

Nauroy, Charles. "La conspiration d'août 1820." *Le Curieux* 2 (Feb. 1888): 366–368.

Neely, Sylvia. "The Politics of Liberty in the Old World and the New: Lafayette's Return to America in 1824." *Journal of the Early Republic* 6 (Summer 1986): 151–171.

———— . "Rural Politics in the Early Restoration: Charles Goyet and the Liberals of the Sarthe." *European History Quarterly* 16 (July 1986): 313–342.

Pange, Victor de. "Le Séjour de Victor de Broglie et d'Auguste de Staël à Londres en Mai 1822." *Cahiers staëliens,* new series, no. 17 (Dec. 1973): 1–58; no. 18 (June 1974): 11–42.

Psichari, Jean. "Lettres inédites du général La Fayette." *La Revue, ancienne Revue des revues* 43 (1 and 15 Dec. 1902): 529–544, 662–671.

Reeves, Jesse S. "The Napoleonic Exiles in America: A Study in American Diplomatic History, 1815–1819." In *Johns Hopkins University Studies in Historical and Political Science,* series XXIII, no. 9–10 (Sept.–Oct. 1905), pp. 526–656.

Robertson, William Spence. "The Policy of Spain Toward Its Revolted Colonies, 1820–1823." *Hispanic American Historical Review* (1926): 21–46.

Robiquet, Paul. "La Disgrace de Fouché." *La Révolution française* 73 (July–Sept. 1920): 193–224; 73 (Oct.–Dec. 1920): 315–335.

Romano, Aldo. "Lafayette, Guglielmo Pepe e l'Italia." *Rassegna storica del Risorgimento* 20 (1933): 585–614.

Rudler, Gustave. "Benjamin Constant, député de la Sarthe (1819–1822)." *La Révolution dans la Sarthe* 8 (Apr.–June 1913): 65–128.

Spitzer, Alan B. "Restoration Political Theory and the Debate over the Law of the Double Vote." *Journal of Modern History* 55 (Mar. 1983): 54–70.

Trélat, [Ulysse]. "La Charbonnerie." In *Paris révolutionnaire,* vol. 2, pp. 275–341. Paris: Guillaumin, 1833–1834.

Weill, Georges. "D'Argenson et la question sociale." *International Review for Social History,* 4 (1939): 1611–69.

———— . "Les Mémoires de Joseph Rey." *Revue historique* 158 (Jan.–Apr., 1928): 291–307.

Welvert, Eugène. "La Princesse d'Hénin." *Revue de l'histoire de Versailles et de Seine-et-Oise* 25 (1922): 123–138, 232–243; 26 (1923): 93–104.

Zickel-Koechlin, F. "Souvenirs d'un contemporain sur les événements de 1820 à 1823 en Alsace." *Revue d'Alsace* 1 (1850): 543–556; 2 (1851): 76–96.

Index

Sylvia Neely is associate professor of history at Indiana University–Purdue University at Fort Wayne. In addition to work on Lafayette, she has published an article on the sixteenth-century French statesman Michel de l'Hospital. Her future research on Lafayette will focus on his role in the French Revolution and the Revolution of 1830.